WITHDRAWN

A Psychology of Human Strengths

A Psychology of Human Strengths

Fundamental Questions and Future Directions for a Positive Psychology

EDITED BY LISA G. ASPINWALL
AND URSULA M. STAUDINGER

AMERICAN PSYCHOLOGICAL ASSOCIATION
WASHINGTON, DC

First Printing September 2002
Second Printing July 2003

Published by
American Psychological Association
750 First Street, NE
Washington, DC 20002
www.apa.org

To order   Tel: (800) 374-2721; Direct: (202) 336-5510
APA Order Department   Fax: (202) 336-5502; TDD/TTY: (202) 336-6123
P.O. Box 92984   Online: www.apa.org/books/
Washington, DC 20090-2984   Email: order@apa.org

In the U.K., Europe, Africa, and the Middle East, copies may be ordered from
American Psychological Association
3 Henrietta Street
Covent Garden, London
WC2E 8LU England

Typeset in Goudy by EPS Group Inc., Easton, MD

Printer: Sheridan Books, Ann Arbor, MI
Cover Designer: Anne Masters, Washington, DC
Technical/Production Editor: Casey Ann Reever

The opinions and statements published are the responsibility of the authors, and such opinions and statements do not necessarily represent the policies of the American Psychological Association.

Library of Congress Cataloging-in-Publication Data
A psychology of human strengths : fundamental questions and future
directions for a positive psychology / Lisa G. Aspinwall and Ursula M.
Staudinger, editors.
    p. cm.
  Includes bibliographical references and indexes.
  ISBN 1-55798-931-1 (alk. paper)
   1. Psychology. I. Aspinwall, Lisa G. II. Staudinger, Ursula M.
  BF121 .P763 2002
  150.19'8—dc21

                               2002008033

British Library Cataloguing-in-Publication Data
A CIP record is available from the British Library.

Printed in the United States of America

To my mother and her sisters
Lisa G. Aspinwall

To my brother
Ursula M. Staudinger

CONTENTS

CONTRIBUTORS

Lisa G. Aspinwall, PhD, Department of Psychology, University of Utah, Salt Lake City

Paul B. Baltes, PhD, Max Planck Institute for Human Development, Berlin, Germany

Ellen Berscheid, PhD, Department of Psychology, University of Minnesota, Minneapolis

John T. Cacioppo, PhD, Department of Psychology, University of Chicago, Chicago, IL

Nancy Cantor, PhD, Chancellor, University of Illinois at Urbana-Champaign

Gian Vittorio Caprara, PhD, Department of Psychology, University of Rome "La Sapienza"

Laura L. Carstensen, PhD, Department of Psychology, Stanford University, Stanford, CA

Charles S. Carver, PhD, Department of Psychology, University of Miami, Miami, FL

Daniel Cervone, PhD, Department of Psychology, University of Illinois at Chicago

Susan T. Charles, PhD, Department of Psychology and Social Behavior, University of California, Irvine

Mihaly Csikszentmihalyi, PhD, Drucker School of Management, Claremont Graduate University, Claremont, CA

Amanda B. Diekman, PhD, Department of Psychological Sciences, Purdue University, West Lafayette, IN

Alice H. Eagly, PhD, Department of Psychology, Northwestern University, Evanston, IL

Nancy Eisenberg, PhD, Department of Psychology, Arizona State University, Tempe

Hans-Peter Erb, PhD, Psychiatric University Clinic, University of Halle-Wittenberg, Halle, Germany

Rocío Fernández-Ballesteros, PhD, Faculty of Psychology, Autonoma University of Madrid, Madrid, Spain

Alexandra M. Freund, PhD, Max Planck Institute for Human Development, Berlin, Germany

Dieter Frey, PhD, Institute of Psychology, Social Psychology Unit, Ludwig-Maximilians-University, Munich, Germany

Tobias Greitemeyer, PhD, Institute of Psychology, General and Biological Psychology Unit, Chemnitz University, Chemnitz, Germany

Dale Griffin, PhD, Professor of Marketing and Consumer Behavior, Faculty of Commerce, University of British Columbia, Vancouver

Scott H. Hemenover, PhD, Department of Psychology, Kansas State University, Manhattan

Alice M. Isen, PhD, Johnson Graduate School of Management, and Department of Psychology, Cornell University, Ithaca, NY

Eva Jonas, PhD, Institute of Psychology, Social Psychology Unit, Ludwig-Maximilians-University, City, Country

Daniel Kahneman, PhD, Professor of Psychology and Public Affairs, Princeton University, Princeton, NJ

Arie W. Kruglanski, PhD, Department of Psychology, University of Maryland, College Park

Jeff T. Larsen, PhD, Department of Psychology, Princeton University, Princeton, NJ

David Magnusson, PhD, Department of Psychology, Stockholm University, Stockholm, Sweden

Joseph L. Mahoney, PhD, Department of Psychology, Yale University, New Haven, CT

Rodolpho Mendoza-Denton, PhD, Department of Psychology, Columbia University, New York City

Walter Mischel, PhD, Department of Psychology, Columbia University, New York City

Jeanne Nakamura, PhD, Quality of Life Research Center, Claremont Graduate University, Claremont, CA

Catherine J. Norris, PhD, Department of Psychology, University of Chicago, IL

Vivian Ota Wang, PhD, Division of Psychology in Education, Arizona State University, Tempe

Christopher Peterson, PhD, Department of Psychology, University of Michigan, Ann Arbor

Antonio Pierro, PhD, Department of Psychology, University of Rome "La Sapienza"

Carol D. Ryff, PhD, Department of Psychology, University of
Wisconsin–Madison

David O. Sears, PhD, Director of Institute for Social Science Research,
University of California–Los Angeles

Michael F. Scheier, PhD, Department of Psychology, Carnegie Mellon
University, Pittsburgh, PA

Martin E. P. Seligman, PhD, Department of Psychology, University of
Pennsylvania, Philadelphia

Burton Singer, PhD, Woodrow Wilson School of Public and
International Affairs, Princeton University, Princeton, NJ

Scott Spiegel, PhD, Psychology Department, Columbia University,
New York

Ursula M. Staudinger, PhD, Department of Psychology IV, Dresden
University of Technology, Dresden, Germany

Robert J. Sternberg, PhD, Center for the Psychology of Abilities,
Competencies, and Expertise, Yale University, New Haven, CT

Daniel Stokols, PhD, School of Social Ecology, University of California,
Irvine

PREFACE

In January 1999, we attended a positive psychology meeting in Akumal, Mexico, where we had the opportunity to meet and interact with other scholars interested in human strengths. The diversity of perspective, intellectual reach, and applied importance of the topic inspired us to take a closer look at how scientific psychology has treated human strengths, how this focus has influenced psychology's knowledge base, and how the study of human strengths may influence the future of psychology.

We became excited about the idea of collecting essays from some of the great minds in contemporary psychology on how they viewed a psychology of human strengths. We were interested in the ideas not only of scholars who have been concerned with human strengths in their own work but also of other leading contributors to major topic areas in psychology. Our aim was to bring together a wide range of expert views on the potentials and pitfalls of a psychology of human strengths. By doing so, we hoped to contribute to the long-term success of a human strengths perspective in psychology.

We believe the resulting collection of essays, brought together in this volume, will be useful to students, faculty, and researchers at all levels of academic and applied psychology. At one level, the chapters examine fundamental assumptions about human beings and how such assumptions have shaped what we know in psychology. At another level, the chapters offer reviews of progress in vital topics such as development and aging, emotion, personality, organizational change, gender roles, intelligence, and health. At still another level, regardless of specific topic areas and level of analysis, the chapters illustrate the different ways of systematically and programmatically studying the complex systems of development and self-regulation that underlie human strengths in many life domains. We learned a great deal from our contributors and hope that others, too, will enjoy reading the collected wisdom presented in this book.

We thank Marty Seligman and Mike Csikszentmihalyi for organizing the initial positive psychology meeting and for inviting us to attend. Given that we work in different fields and live in different countries, the Akumal meeting had a synergistic effect that otherwise would not most likely have occurred. We also thank our mentors, Shelley E. Taylor and Paul B. Baltes, who nominated us to be invited and taught us an appreciation of and respect for human strengths, as well as the skills to study and communicate them scientifically. We thank also the contributing authors who were so generous with their ideas and so open to working with the novel format of the volume.

We are grateful to Patty Curran, Samantha Leaf, and especially Angela Newman for their assistance in the preparation of this book and to the Templeton Foundation for its support of Lisa G. Aspinwall with a Templeton Positive Psychology Prize. Last, but not least, we would like to thank APA Books, and particularly Susan Reynolds, Kristine Enderle, and Casey Reever for their support throughout the process.

A Psychology of Human Strengths

INTRODUCTION

LISA G. ASPINWALL AND URSULA M. STAUDINGER

This volume provides a forum for many of the great minds of contemporary psychology to discuss the promise, pitfalls, and future of a psychology of human strengths and of positive psychology more generally. Instead of commissioning typical chapters that review the empirical research, we asked our authors to provide conceptual and forward-looking chapters on the topic of understanding and cultivating human strengths.

To this end, we asked our contributors to respond to several questions we thought important to an understanding of both the history and the potential of scientific efforts to study human strengths and positive aspects of human functioning:

- Historically, how has psychology treated human strengths and other approaches to positive functioning?
- Has psychology been predominantly deficit and repair oriented, or otherwise limited, in its view of human nature and capabilities? If so, why, and with what effect?
- Does (or would) a positive approach illuminate important findings or gaps in your field?
- Is a new field of the psychology of human strengths or positive psychology necessary? What unique contributions might it make to psychology? What mistakes should be avoided?
- What recommendations would you make for the scientific study of human strengths in terms of theoretical develop-

ment, research paradigms, measurement strategies, or particular strengths to study?

- What potential for theoretical advancement and practical application might there be?

Thus, we asked contributors to comment on how what is known in their respective fields may have been influenced by a negative view of human motives and capabilities and what might be learned by taking a different, more balanced view. We asked them to outline a research agenda that would illuminate gaps in the current understanding of positive aspects of human functioning. Finally, we asked them to comment on the emerging field of positive psychology and to offer suggestions for how it might best develop to increase scientific knowledge about human strengths.

Many contributors are scholars who have examined one or more aspects of human strengths and positive functioning as a central aspect of their careers. In many cases, their findings concerning human strengths turned established wisdom on its head, leading to new ways of thinking about such topics as intelligence, judgment, self-regulation, social behavior, close relationships, development, aging, and health. The selection of authors, however, was not confined to scholars with a history of investigating human strengths. Other contributors are leading scholars who apply their broad knowledge and scientific experience in commenting on the prospects and pitfalls of a psychology of human strengths for their specific fields of study and, more generally, for psychology as a field. Our aim was to bring together both supportive and challenging voices in this volume to stimulate discourse.

FUNDAMENTAL THEMES OF A PSYCHOLOGY OF HUMAN STRENGTHS

Collectively, the 23 resulting chapters touch on several critical themes that we believe will be useful in stimulating discussion and future research. The chapters examine multiple aspects of human strengths and scientific approaches to studying them. Questions such as "Who (or what) defines what is positive?" "Are human strengths characteristics or processes?" and "How are positive and negative phenomena related?" are in our view essential starting points for any consideration of a psychology of human strengths. Answers to such fundamental questions have far-reaching implications for theory and research, as well as for interventions in such areas as psychotherapy, education, and the workplace, and many of our authors address these issues in detail.

Further, understanding how human strengths are embedded in social, environmental, and developmental contexts provides a window into new ways to study and apply what is known about human strengths. Finally, many of our authors include a detailed consideration of how more macro-level factors, such as changes in demographics (e.g., increased life span), aspects of the social and physical environment, globalization, and cultural and political life, influence how psychologists think about human strengths in various domains and which kinds of strengths will help people adapt to and capitalize on changing conditions. Chapter 1 provides an overview of these and other issues represented in the book, so we recommend starting there.

ORGANIZATION OF THE VOLUME

As noted earlier, the rationale underlying our selection of authors was not topical. As a consequence, the chapters cut across traditional fields of psychological study, and grouping them by topic did not seem appropriate. The chapters are therefore featured in alphabetical order by author, and their main content areas are listed in Table 1. Table 1 may be useful to instructors wishing to add a consideration of human strengths to courses in personality, emotion, development and aging, social behavior, and other areas.

To place our selection of authors and topics in context, it is important to note that the issues we have identified here, as important as they are for efforts to understand human strengths, are surely only the tip of the iceberg. As we reflect on the topics covered in the volume, we see that there are some important areas that are not addressed in depth—for example, the more microanalytic level of psychological research as represented by the growing fields of neuroscience and biopsychology, or evolutionary approaches to human strengths. Another obvious candidate for a human strengths analysis is the study of infancy and early childhood. Finally, cross-cultural and historical analyses of human strengths would also be illuminating. Nevertheless, we hope that the chapters included in this volume offer at least a starting point for an ongoing discussion of scientific approaches to the psychology of human strengths.

IDENTIFYING AND BUILDING ON PROGRESS IN A PSYCHOLOGY OF HUMAN STRENGTHS

Finally, although there is some disagreement among authors about the best way to proceed in developing a psychology of human strengths, it is clear to us that the contributors as a group see the same collective promise of such an approach—to complement the traditional focus on understanding, preventing, and curing negative psychological states by gaining a better

TABLE 1
Major Content Areas Addressed by Chapters

Chapter	Cognition, Judgment, Intelligence	Creativity, Excellence, Wisdom	Development, Aging	Emotion	Health, Well-Being	Institutions, Culture	Self, Personality	Social Relations
1. Aspinwall & Staudinger		X	X	X		X	X	X
2. Baltes & Freund		X	X			X	X	X
3. Berscheid			X	X				X
4. Cantor			X		X			X
5. Caprara & Cervone	X		X			X	X	X
6. Carstensen & Charles			X	X		X	X	
7. Carver & Scheier			X				X	
8. Eagly & Diekman						X		X
9. Eisenberg & Ota Wang			X	X		X	X	X
10. Fernández-Ballesteros			X		X	X		
11. Frey, Jonas, & Greitemeyer		X		X		X		X
12. Griffin & Kahneman	X							
13. Isen	X	X		X				
14. Kruglanski, Erb, Spiegel, & Pierro	X							X
15. Larsen, Hemenover, Norris, & Cacioppo				X	X			
16. Magnusson & Mahoney			X					
17. Mischel & Mendoza-Denton			X	X			X	
18. Nakamura & Csikszentmihalyi		X						
19. Ryff & Singer			X	X	X			
20. Sears						X		X
21. Seligman & Peterson		X			X		X	X
22. Sternberg	X	X		X	X	X	X	
23. Stokols			X	X	X	X		X

understanding of human strengths and how to facilitate them. Thus, although an important goal of this volume is to provide a critical analysis of what strengths are and how they may be studied, we sought at the same time to highlight the progress of diverse approaches to human strengths in intelligence, creativity, lifespan development, emotion, health, personality, self-regulation, close relationships, collective action, and other vital areas (see Table 1). We hope that the reader will in the end share our analysis of the potential of the study of human strengths and that this volume will both contribute to the accumulation and integration of available psychological evidence and stimulate new research and discussion about a psychology of human strengths.

1

A PSYCHOLOGY OF HUMAN STRENGTHS: SOME CENTRAL ISSUES OF AN EMERGING FIELD

LISA G. ASPINWALL AND URSULA M. STAUDINGER

A growing number of scholars in psychology are interested in investigating positive aspects of well-being and health, rather than negative aspects such as distress and disease (for reviews, see Ickovics & Park, 1998; Ryff & Singer, 1998; Seligman & Czikszentmihalyi, 2000). Arguing that scientific psychology has focused disproportionately on pathology and repair, Seligman and Czikszentmihalyi recently issued a broader call for the study of strengths and prevention, as well as the individual, community, and societal factors that "make life worth living." In the history of psychological science, this interest in salutogenesis (Antonovsky, 1987), mental health rather than mental illness (Jahoda, 1958), and maturity and growth (e.g., Erikson, 1959) is certainly not new. The current revival, however, may be of a larger scale (and possibly greater impact) than ever before. Thus, the field may be at a critical juncture for revisiting and redefining some central issues in the understanding of human strengths.

Our goal in this volume is to generate critical discourse on different ways the study of human strengths might progress. In this chapter, we highlight several questions and issues that we believe will be important to the development of a field of human strengths. In doing so, we draw on lessons learned from our respective research programs on optimism and coping with adversity (LGA) and wisdom, resilience, and lifespan development (UMS), as well as some more general observations about this emerging field. This list of questions and issues we address in this chapter is not intended to be comprehensive, but rather to stimulate discussion and provide some guiding perspectives when reading the other chapters included in this volume.

THE DIFFICULTY OF DEFINING HUMAN STRENGTHS

One of the reasons that the repair and healing approach in psychology historically has been predominant seems to be a value issue. It is much easier to define the desired or adaptive direction of change if the goal of such change is to restore an earlier or a "normal" state. It is much more difficult to define a human strength if one considers psychological changes other than return to prior levels of functioning. Relatively speaking, different areas of psychological functioning may involve more or less difficulty making such determinations (e.g., Staudinger, Marsiske, & Baltes, 1995). For instance, with regard to cognitive functioning, it seems rather obvious that solving a problem quickly is better than solving it slowly, but how would this logic be applied to such concepts as personality growth or successful aging?

If psychologists are interested in assessing more than return to prior functioning, we are faced with several difficult sets of questions. For example, do we determine which characteristics represent a human strength vis-à-vis their adaptiveness or functionality? And if so, how then do we operationalize adaptiveness or functionality? Do we use subjective (e.g., subjective well-being) or objective (e.g., longevity) indicators? Should we consult ethical or value systems, such as the seven primary virtues of Christian ethics or the Aristotelian ethos composed of selection and sagacity? If so, why these, and not others? And whose standpoint should be used to decide what is good or optimal? For example, should we assess perceptions of improvement or change from the perspective of the person, or of those with whom he or she interacts, or of experts or of lay people?

These normative issues need to be discussed and settled when studying human strengths. As research on resilience has demonstrated (e.g., Rutter & Rutter, 1993; Staudinger et al., 1995), objective and subjective criteria often result in very different ideas about what is functional or adaptive; therefore, it seems that both kinds of criteria may need to be considered and would ideally be balanced when drawing conclusions about what is a human strength. The approach taken in the study of wisdom—a prototypical human strength with a long cultural history—may provide some guidance. Defining *functionality* as balancing one's own good and the good of others—one of the core definitional features of wisdom (e.g., see Baltes & Staudinger, 2000; Sternberg, 1998)—may solve some of the value problems involved when studying human strengths. This definition of wisdom combines objective ("the good of others") and subjective ("one's own good") criteria and at the same time does not prescribe what that "good" is. Rather, the definition is placed on a meta-level.

The decision about when this balance between one's own good and the good of others is reached does not follow an absolute truth criterion but rather, as is the case with any complex and ill-defined decision, follows a consensus criterion of truth. Research on wisdom has reliably demonstrated that there is high consensus about whether or not a certain judgment satisfies the wisdom definition and to what degree (e.g., Baltes & Staudinger, 2000; Staudinger, in press). Further, it is important that the definition of balancing one's own good with the good of others does not link human strengths too closely to given circumstances, as is often the case with definitions of adaptivity (e.g., when adaptivity is defined as increasing subjective well-being or increasing objective rewards, such as income or prestige). Rather, it is crucial for a definition of human strengths to include the possibility of transcending and improving given personal and societal circumstances. Thus, searching for the definition of "human strengths" or "the good life" on a meta-level rather than a concrete level and adopting a consensus rather than an absolute criterion of truth seem to be worthwhile suggestions to discuss.

The chapters in this book address multiple aspects of these fundamental definitional questions and their implications for understanding mental and physical health, as well as processes and outcomes in such domains as social development, aging, intelligence, and judgment. It is important to emphasize that these definitional questions are not purely academic. Many societal decisions rest on how human strengths and capabilities are defined, measured, and used—for example, to open the doors of educational and professional opportunity (or to close them; see Sternberg, chapter 22, this volume), to evaluate the outcomes of different medical and psychological treatments (see Ryff & Singer, chapter 19, this volume; Seligman & Peterson, chapter 21, this volume), or to develop interventions in such areas as peace education (Eisenberg & Ota Wang, chapter 9, this volume) and corporate cultures of excellence (Frey, Jonas, & Greitemeyer, chapter 11, this volume).

HUMAN STRENGTHS: CHARACTERISTICS OR PROCESSES?

One of the first associations with the term "human strength" is probably a personality characteristic. Many efforts to understand and identify human strengths have focused on the individual-level traits—intelligence, optimism, self-efficacy, ego resilience—associated with good life outcomes (e.g., Staudinger & Pasupathi, 2000). The trait approach, while often fostering important developments in measurement and allowing the study of mean-level changes of traits over the life span or in response to interventions such as psychotherapy, may represent only one type of human strength. Dispositional approaches typically do not consider the underlying processes or dynamics, nor do they focus on the interplay between dispositions and particular situations (see Mischel & Shoda, 1999).

Several important processes may be involved in any given trait or strength, and understanding such processes is essential to understanding how people will encode and respond to different situations and to developing interventions that promote the development of human strengths (see, e.g., Mischel & Mendoza-Denton, chapter 17, this volume). In the following sections, we will explore some of the potential advantages of complementing a trait approach with a process-oriented approach to human strengths, using dispositional optimism as an example.

Optimism, conceptualized in terms of generalized positive expectancies (Scheier & Carver, 1985) or in terms of explanatory style (Peterson & Seligman, 1984), has been linked to good outcomes over the life course, but how are such outcomes realized? In some frameworks, the benefits of optimism are seen to reside primarily in its link to persistence in goal pursuit (Carver & Scheier, 1990). Optimists are those who see their prospects favorably and thus will continue efforts to meet their goals. Such an approach would likely yield good outcomes much of the time, but it might also carry certain liabilities if the tendency to assess one's prospects favorably predisposed one to ignoring objective information about risks in the environment or to devoting continued effort to goals that cannot realistically be met.

One approach to understanding how optimists navigate these risks has been to examine the prospective relation of optimism to the processing of negative information and to problem-solving efforts for both solvable and unsolvable problems (see Aspinwall, Richter, & Hoffman, 2001, for a review). These examinations have found that optimism is associated with greater, not lesser, attention to self-relevant negative information and that optimists, when presented with unsolvable problems, are quicker, rather than slower, to disengage from them when some alternative task is available. These findings suggest two important properties of optimism that would not be apparent from a trait-level analysis alone: (a) Optimism is not maintained by ignoring negative information—optimists attend closely to relevant risk information—and (b) optimism seems to be flexible—optimists vary their behavior depending on the objective properties of the problems they face.

These and other findings give a different view of what constitutes a human strength. It seems that it is not so much one or the other personality characteristic—for example, an optimistic outlook or internal control beliefs—that should be called a human strength. Rather, it seems that human strengths may primarily lie in the ability to flexibly apply as many different resources and skills as necessary to solve a problem or work toward a goal (e.g., Staudinger et al., 1995; Staudinger & Pasupathi, 2000). Such strengths may draw on discriminative facilities (see Cantor, chapter 4, this volume; Mischel & Mendoza-Denton, chapter 17, this volume) and self-regulatory skills or algorithms that help people draw on the optimal characteristic or regulatory mechanism at the right time to the right degree (e.g., Frederick & Loewenstein, 1999; Staudinger, 2000; see also Baltes & Freund, chapter 2, this volume).

For instance, returning to the optimism example, there is evidence that people seem to deploy optimism strategically, using favorable beliefs to motivate action toward implementing plans, but suspending such beliefs at the point at which specific plans are made (Taylor & Gollwitzer, 1995; see also Armor & Taylor, 1998). These findings, in turn, give rise to an interest in understanding the cognitive, behavioral, and social processes that support such flexible self-regulatory efforts, among them the ability to change one's perspective on a problem and to elicit and use information from one's own or others' experiences with particular problems in planning one's own course of action (Ashby, Isen, & Turken, 1999; Aspinwall, 1998, 2001; Aspinwall, Hill, & Leaf, 2002). Identifying such processes provides a way of understanding flexible problem solving and suggests ways of teaching specific skills to increase human strengths rather than just yielding a general injunction to be more optimistic.

ARE ALL HUMAN STRENGTHS CONSCIOUS AND INTENTIONAL?

A related issue that arises from this consideration of characteristics and regulatory processes is the question of whether all human strengths are necessarily conscious and intentional. Even though reflexivity is one of the major discriminating features of the human species, it may not necessarily be the case that human strengths are always conscious and linked to intentional action or reaction. Rather, it is possible that human evolution, as well as ontogenesis, has produced "strength patterns" of perception, action, and reaction on an automatic and unintentional level.

For instance, subjective well-being in heterogeneous samples of adults on a scale from 0 to 10 is always located slightly above 6, rather than 5, which would be the theoretical mean of the scale. Well-being researchers have argued that the ability to retain or regain slightly positive feelings of well-being may have had a survival advantage (Diener, 1994). The development of expertise provides another example of the "unintentional" facets of human strengths. With increasing levels of knowledge and skill in a given domain, actions and reactions become increasingly automatized and intuitive (e.g., Ericsson & Smith, 1991). Thus, limiting the study of human strengths to the conscious and intentional realm would exclude many important phenomena (see also Berridge, 1999).

HUMAN STRENGTHS IN DEVELOPMENTAL, SOCIAL, AND MATERIAL CONTEXT

In trying to define and study human strengths, it is crucial to acknowledge contextual dependencies. It seems useful to emphasize that even if observed or measured in the individual, the microgenesis and ontogenesis of many (if not all) human strengths involve interactions with certain material or person contexts or some combination of these. The identification of particular developmental, material, and social contexts that promote or debilitate human strengths thus should be an important focus in a psychology of human strengths. In research on lifespan development that addresses contextual dependencies and the plasticity of human development, this has always been a topic of pivotal interest (see Baltes & Freund, chapter 2, this volume; Carstensen & Charles, chapter 6, this volume; Fernández-Ballesteros, chapter 10, this volume; Magnusson & Mahoney, chapter 16, this volume). Another research area emphasizing the importance of considering context when studying human strength is human social ecology (see Stokols, chapter 23, this volume).

Understanding the situations and experiences—both everyday and extraordinary—that promote the microgenesis and ontogenesis of strengths will be an important goal in the study of human strengths. What is known so far, for instance, is that experiencing and mastering very difficult and threatening situations in the long run often support the development of personal growth. Research on lifespan development (e.g., Elder, 1998), as well as investigations in the area of post-traumatic stress syndrome (e.g., Maercker, Schützwohl, & Solomon, 1999) speak to the ontogenetic importance of context. However, it is not only over time that people need contexts to develop human strengths; in addition, within a given situation certain contextual features promote and others debilitate the expression of human strengths.

Research on wisdom again serves as an example; it has been demonstrated that wisdom-related knowledge and judgment concerning difficult life problems were increased by one standard deviation if participants were offered the possibility to discuss the difficult life problem with a person whom they knew well before they gave their individual response (Staudinger & Baltes, 1996). Thus, the opportunity to talk with a familiar person about the problem at hand, exchange thoughts, and create new ideas and perspectives supported the strength of good insight into difficult life matters. Research in organizational psychology on the conditions of corporate culture that foster and sustain effective group decision making and organizational innovation provides additional examples (Frey et al., chapter 11, this volume). Thus, a contextual and social perspective on human strengths may be especially important to researchers interested in creating interventions to promote human strengths.

There is another important sense in which human strengths may be wedded to the social context: Many human strengths are themselves relational or collective. Based on a wide range of evidence linking close relationships to health and happiness, the ability of human beings to form loving bonds with one another is possibly one of their greatest strengths (Berscheid, chapter 3, this volume). Given the importance of forming and maintaining social bonds, we suspect that many human strengths may be found (and developed) in each person's relationships with other people. Such interpersonal and relational strengths as patience, empathy, compassion, cooperation, tolerance, appreciation of diversity, understanding, and forgiveness, though they remain understudied in comparison to "individual" strengths, seem ripe for continued investigation from evolutionary, developmental, and social perspectives (see, e.g., Eisenberg & Ota Wang, chapter 9, this volume). Still other kinds of strength may be found at the collective or group level (see, e.g., Caprara & Cervone, chapter 5, this volume; Frey et al., chapter 11, this volume).

THE POSITIVE AND THE NEGATIVE: INTERDEPENDENT OR INDEPENDENT PROCESSES?

Another central task for a psychology of human strengths is to understand whether and how positive and negative experiences depend on each other and work together. Thus, a call for the scientific study of such positive states as joy, play, hope, and love—of what is positive, successful, and adaptive in human experience—should not be misunderstood as a call to ignore negative aspects of human experience. That is, a psychology of human strengths should not be the study of how negative experience may be avoided or ignored, but rather how positive and negative experience may be interrelated (see, e.g., Baltes & Freund, chapter 2, this volume; Carstensen & Charles, chapter 6, this volume; Larsen, Hemenover, Norris, & Cacioppo, chapter 15, this volume; Ryff & Singer, chapter 19, this volume).

Indeed, some philosophical perspectives suggest that the positive and negative are by definition dependent on each other; that is, human existence seems to be constituted by basic dialectics, such as gains and losses, happiness and sorrow, autonomy and dependency, or positive and negative (e.g., Riegel, 1976). It is part of the very nature of such pairs that one component cannot exist without the other. Thus, from this perspective, the goal of a psychology of human strengths should not be to cultivate exclusively positive outcomes, but to intervene such that the balance between the two components of any such pairs is optimized with regard to the respective circumstances. Examining the positive aspects of negative states and the negative aspects of positive states would thus be an essential part of a psychology of human strengths.

The study of stress, coping, and adaptation provides many rich examples of the interrelation of positive and negative phenomena. First, the importance of positive beliefs, such as optimism, in adapting to negative experience has been demonstrated in many different contexts, including life-threatening illness (see, e.g., Carver et al., 1993; Taylor et al., 1992). Second, in many cases, positive beliefs seem to develop because of people's experience in dealing with adversity. For example, Taylor's pioneering (1983) work on adjustment to life-threatening illnesses identified several cognitive strategies people used when trying to find meaning in their illness and to restore a sense of self-esteem and mastery in their new situations. Many patients reported learning that they were stronger than they would have believed prior to their illness, saw advantages in their situation that they had not previously appreciated, and accentuated positive aspects of their lives in creative ways (see also Affleck & Tennen, 1996; Carver & Scheier, chapter 7, this volume; Updegraff & Taylor, 2000).

That people deliberately accentuate the positives in life to better deal with the negatives is surely a human strength. That people can draw on these strengths without ignoring or diminishing the negative realities of their situations is also important. Indeed, later studies showed that people who experienced such positive changes as a result of having a serious illness also reported many negative ones (see, e.g., Collins, Taylor, & Skokan, 1990) and that the relative balance of positive and negative changes depended on important features of the life domain, such as whether improvements were likely to be amenable to the patient's control.

Similarly, the study of lifespan development has promoted a systematic investigation of the relation between gains and losses (e.g., Uttal & Perlmutter, 1989). Evidence can be found for independence; that is, growth and decline may happen independently of each other. But it has also been demonstrated that often the advent of losses promotes growth or that some growth may be possible only because of losses (e.g., Baltes, Lindenberger, & Staudinger, 1998). Two examples may illustrate these two points. Consider, for instance, the losses in physical functioning that come with age. It is exactly those losses that have promoted the development of many technical means to compensate. Or take language development. With increasing language ability in their mother tongue (gain), infants lose their ability to discriminate sounds from other languages (loss). In this case growth actually depends on loss.

Despite these illustrations of fundamental dependencies between positive and negative phenomena, it would be a serious mistake to assume that all or even most positive experiences and characteristics must derive (or derive their meaning from) negative experiences and characteristics, or that positive experiences and characteristics have no functional benefit or importance in their own right. Such assumptions have hindered the development of research on positive phenomena in many ways. For example, negative motivations are frequently ascribed to positive characteristics (for example, creative accomplishment may be interpreted as the narcissistic pursuit of fame; see Nakamura & Csikszentmihalyi, chapter 18, this volume). As another example, it is often assumed that positive states are simply the inverse in form and effect of related negative states—that is, that negative and positive states are symmetrical in form and effect (see Isen, chapter 13, this volume). However, such assumptions may lead to misleading conclusions about positive states or to research designs that mask distinct effects of positive states. For example, in research on mood, many experiments have compared the effects of positive and negative mood inductions; however, without a neutral condition, it is impossible to tell whether any observed differences are due to the effects of positive mood, negative mood, or both. Experiments that include a neutral condition clearly show that the effects of positive and negative mood on decision making and on social behaviors such as helping are not symmetrical (see Isen, 1993; chapter 13, this volume).

Further, emerging evidence in affective neuroscience suggests that the relations between positive and negative experiences are likely to be much more complex than a simple opposite or reciprocal relation and that these different affective phenomena may be supported by different neurotransmitters and brain structures (see Berridge, 1999; Davidson & Sutton, 1995; Isen, 2002, for reviews). Finally, abandoning the assumed symmetry of positive and negative states may open up new areas of research by allowing the study of other configurations and blends of positive and negative experience, such as the coactivation of positive and negative states (see Larsen et al., chapter 15, this volume). As these examples suggest, discarding the assumptions that positive phenomena either derive from or are simple opposites of negative phenomena may change the profession's understanding of human strengths and may open the door to new research questions.

TEMPTATIONS TO BE RESISTED IN DEVELOPING A PSYCHOLOGY OF HUMAN STRENGTHS

As excited as we are about potential developments in the understanding of human strengths, we see several areas in which caution must be exercised if a psychology of human strengths is to advance scientific understanding. The first, and perhaps most important, is to avoid using findings in this area to prescribe what people should do and how they should live. Linked to the value problem discussed at the outset is the danger of prescribing universal ideals. There is only a small step from investigating human strengths in order to improve the well-being and welfare of people to adopting a given value system and preaching this value system. This behavior carries many dangers for psychology as a scientific discipline.

A second caution involves the possibility that there are situations and contexts where attributes or processes that work as strengths in one setting may be liabilities in another, and vice versa. Many findings suggest that for some characteristics that have been identified as "strengths," counterexamples can be found. For instance, there is research that shows that internal control beliefs and problem-focused coping may become highly dysfunctional under conditions of high constraints, such as poor health (Staudinger, Freund, Linden, & Maas, 1999), and situations that cannot be controlled (Filipp, 1999). Among certain people (e.g., defensive pessimists; see Cantor, chapter 4, this volume; Frese, 1992; Norem, 2001) and in some non-Western cultures (e.g., Asian cultures; see Chang, 2001), pessimism has been found to be adaptive rather than dysfunctional, because it promotes active problem solving. In these cases, focusing on the underlying processes (how people discriminate controllable from uncontrollable situations, how worry may promote problem solving and preparation) may provide more information about strengths that appear to take different forms in different situations.

Our third caution comes from the observation that not everything that shines is gold. It would be a major mistake to assume that all that is positive is good—that is, that all positive beliefs, characteristics, and experiences have beneficial effects on well-being and health, both for people and for their social networks. Instead, efforts to understand when positive beliefs are linked to good outcomes, when they may not be, and why will yield a more realistic and balanced view.

REFERENCES

Affleck, G., & Tennen, H. (1996). Construing benefits from adversity: Adaptational significance and dispositional underpinnings. *Journal of Personality, 64,* 899–922.

Antonovsky, A. (1987). *Unraveling the mystery of health: How people manage stress and stay well.* San Francisco: Jossey-Bass.

Armor, D. A., & Taylor, S. E. (1998). Situated optimism: Specific outcome expectancies and self-regulation. In M. P. Zanna (Ed.), *Advances in experimental social psychology: Vol. 30* (pp. 309–379). New York: Academic Press.

Ashby, F. G., Isen, A. M., & Turken, A. U. (1999). A neurological theory of positive affect and its influence on cognition. *Psychological Review, 106,* 529–550.

Aspinwall, L. G. (1998). Rethinking the role of positive affect in self-regulation. *Motivation and Emotion, 22,* 1–32.

Aspinwall, L. G. (2001). Dealing with adversity: Self-regulation, coping, adaptation, and health. In A. Tesser & N. Schwarz (Eds.), *Blackwell handbook of social psychology: Intraindividual processes* (pp. 591–614). Malden, MA: Blackwell Publishers.

Aspinwall, L. G., Hill, D. L., & Leaf, S. L. (2002). Prospects, pitfalls, and plans: A proactive perspective on social comparison activity. In W. Stroebe & M. Hewstone (Eds.), *European review of social psychology* (Vol. 12, pp. 267–298). New York: John Wiley & Sons.

Aspinwall, L. G., Richter, L., & Hoffman, R. R. (2001). Understanding how optimism "works": An examination of optimists' adaptive moderation of belief and behavior. In E. C. Chang (Ed.), *Optimism and pessimism: Theory, research, and practice* (pp. 217–238). Washington, DC: American Psychological Association.

Baltes, P. B., Lindenberger, U., & Staudinger, U. M. (1998). Life-span theory in developmental psychology. In R. M. Lerner (Ed.), *Handbook of child psychology: Vol. 1. Theoretical models of human development* (5th ed., pp. 1029–1143). New York: Wiley.

Baltes, P. B., & Staudinger, U. M. (2000). Wisdom: A metaheuristic (pragmatic) to orchestrate mind and virtue towards excellence. *American Psychologist, 55,* 122–136.

Berridge, K. C. (1999). Pleasure, pain, desire, and dread: Hidden core processes of emotion. In D. Kahneman, E. Diener, & N. Schwarz (Eds.), *Well-being: The foundations of hedonic psychology* (pp. 525–557). New York: Russell Sage Foundation.

Carver, C. S., Pozo, C., Harris, S. D., Noriega, V., Scheier, M. F., Robinson, D. S., Ketcham, A. S., Moffat, F. L., Jr., & Clark, K. C. (1993). How coping mediates the effect of optimism on distress: A study of women with early stage breast cancer. *Journal of Personality and Social Psychology, 65,* 375–390.

Carver, C. S., & Scheier, M. F. (1990). Principles of self-regulation: Action and emotion. In E. T. Higgins & R. M. Sorrentino (Eds.), *Handbook of motivation and cognition: Vol. 2* (pp. 3–52). New York: Guilford Press.

Chang, E. C. (2001). Cultural influences on optimism and pessimism: Differences in Western and Eastern conceptualizations of the self. In E. C. Chang (Ed.), *Optimism and pessimism: Theory, research, and practice* (pp. 257–280). Washington, DC: American Psychological Association.

Collins, R. L., Taylor, S. E., & Skokan, L. A. (1990). A better world or a shattered vision? Changes in perspective following victimization. *Social Cognition, 8,* 263–285.

Davidson, R. J., & Sutton, S. K. (1995). Affective neuroscience: The emergence of a discipline. *Current Opinions in Neurobiology, 5,* 217–224.

Diener, E. (1994). Assessing subjective well-being: Progress and opportunities. *Social Indicators Research, 31,* 103–157.

Elder, G. H., Jr. (1998). The life course and human development. In R. M. Lerner (Ed.), *Handbook of child psychology: Vol. 1. Theoretical models of human development* (5th ed., pp. 939–992). New York: Wiley.

Ericsson, K. A., & Smith, J. (Eds.). (1991). *Towards a general theory of expertise: Prospects and limits.* New York: Cambridge University Press.

Erikson, E. H. (1959). *Identity and the life cycle.* New York: International University Press.

Filipp, S. H. (1999). A three-stage model of coping with loss and trauma: Lessons from patients suffering from severe and chronic disease. In A. Maercker, M. Schützwohl, & Z. Solomon (Eds.), *Posttraumatic stress disorder: A lifespan developmental perspective* (pp. 43–80). Seattle: Hogrefe & Huber.

Frederick, S., & Loewenstein, G. (1999). Hedonic adaptation. In D. Kahneman, E. Diener, & N. Schwarz (Eds.), *Well-being: The foundation of hedonic psychology* (pp. 302–329). New York: Russell Sage Foundation.

Frese, M. (1992). A plea for realistic pessimism: On objective reality, coping with stress, and psychological dysfunction. In L. Montada, S. Filipp, & M. J. Lerner (Eds.), *Life crises and experiences of loss in adulthood* (pp. 81–94). Hillsdale, NJ: Erlbaum.

Ickovics, J. R., & Park, C. L. (1998). Paradigm shift: Why a focus on health is important. *Journal of Social Issues, 54*(2), 237–244.

Isen, A. M. (1993). Positive affect and decision making. In M. Lewis & J. M. Haviland (Eds.), *Handbook of emotions* (pp. 261–277). New York: Guilford Press.

Isen, A. M. (2002). A role for neuropsychology in understanding the facilitating influence of positive affect on social behavior and cognitive processes. In C. R. Snyder & S. J. Lopez (Eds.), *Handbook of positive psychology* (pp. 528–540). New York: Oxford University Press.

Jahoda, M. (1958). *Current concepts of positive mental health.* New York: Basic Books.

Maercker, A., Schützwohl, M., & Solomon, Z. (Eds.). (1999). *Posttraumatic stress disorder: A lifespan developmental perspective.* Seattle, WA: Hogrefe & Huber.

Mischel, W., & Shoda, Y. (1999). Integrating dispositions and processing dynamics within a unified theory of personality: The cognitive-affective personality system. In L. A. Pervin & O. P. John (Ed.), *Handbook of personality: Theory and research* (pp. 197–218). New York: Guilford Press.

Norem, J. K. (2001). Defensive pessimism, optimism, and pessimism. In E. C. Chang (Ed.), *Optimism and pessimism: Theory, research, and practice* (pp. 77–100). Washington, DC: American Psychological Association.

Peterson, C., & Seligman, M. E. P. (1984). Causal explanations as a risk factor for depression: Theory and evidence. *Psychological Review, 91,* 347–374.

Riegel, K. F. (1976). The dialectics of human development. *American Psychologist, 31,* 689–700.

Rutter, M., & Rutter, M. (1993). *Developing minds: Challenge and continuity across the life span.* New York: Basic Books.

Ryff, C. D., & Singer, B. (1998). The contours of positive human health. *Psychological Inquiry, 9,* 1–28.

Scheier, M. F., & Carver, C. S. (1985). Optimism, coping and health: Assessment and implications of generalized outcome expectancies. *Health Psychology, 4,* 219–247.

Seligman, M. E. P., & Csikszentmihalyi, M. (2000). Positive psychology: An introduction. *American Psychologist, 55,* 5–14.

Staudinger, U. M. (2000). Social cognition and a psychological approach to an art of life. In F. Blanchard-Fields & T. Hess (Eds.), *Social cognition, adult development and aging* (pp. 343–375). New York: Academic Press.

Staudinger, U. M. (in press). Wisdom, assessment of. In R. Fernández-Ballesteros (Ed.), *Encyclopedia of psychological assessment.* London: Sage.

Staudinger, U. M., & Baltes, P. B. (1996). Interactive minds: A facilitative setting for wisdom-related performance? *Journal of Personality and Social Psychology, 71,* 746–762.

Staudinger, U. M., Freund, A., Linden, M., & Maas, I. (1999). Self, personality, and life regulation: Facets of psychological resilience in old age. In P. B. Baltes & K. U. Mayer (Eds.), *The Berlin Aging Study: Aging from 70 to 100* (pp. 302–328). New York: Cambridge University Press.

Staudinger, U. M., Marsiske, M., & Baltes, P. B. (1995). Resilience and reserve capacity in later adulthood: Potentials and limits of development across the life span. In D. Cicchetti & D. Cohen (Eds.), *Developmental psychopathology: Vol. 2. Risk, disorder, and adaptation* (pp. 801–847). New York: Wiley.

Staudinger, U. M., & Pasupathi, M. (2000). Lifespan perspectives on self, personality and social cognition. In T. Salthouse & F. Craik (Eds.), *Handbook of cognition and aging* (pp. 633–688). Hillsdale, NJ: Erlbaum.

Sternberg, R. J. (1998). A balance theory of wisdom. *Review of General Psychology, 2,* 347–365.

Taylor, S. E. (1983). Adjustment to threatening events: A theory of cognitive adaptation. *American Psychologist, 38,* 1163–1173.

Taylor, S. E., & Gollwitzer, P. M. (1995). The effects of mindset on positive illusions. *Journal of Personality and Social Psychology, 69,* 213–226.

Taylor, S. E., Kemeny, M. E., Aspinwall, L. G., Schneider, S. G., Rodriguez, R., & Herbert, M. (1992). Optimism, coping, psychological distress, and high-risk sexual behavior among men at risk for acquired immunodeficiency syndrome (AIDS). *Journal of Personality and Social Psychology, 63,* 460–473.

Updegraff, J. A., & Taylor, S. E. (2000). From vulnerability to growth: Positive and negative effects of stressful life events. In J. H. Harvey & E. Miller (Eds.), *Loss and trauma: General and close relationship perspectives* (pp. 3–28). Philadelphia: Brunner-Routledge.

Uttal, D. H., & Perlmutter, M. (1989). Toward a broader conceptualization of development: The role of gains and losses across the life span. *Developmental Review, 9,* 101–132.

2

HUMAN STRENGTHS AS THE ORCHESTRATION OF WISDOM AND SELECTIVE OPTIMIZATION WITH COMPENSATION

PAUL B. BALTES AND ALEXANDRA M. FREUND

One approach to the concept of human strengths is to define human strengths not as a set of specific properties but as *wisdom*, or knowledge about fundamental pragmatics of life and implementation of that knowledge through the life management strategies of selection, optimization, and compensation (P. B. Baltes & Baltes, 1990; P. B. Baltes & Staudinger, 2000; Freund & Baltes, 2000). We conceive of this end state as being universal and bound by general principles associated with wisdom and the theory of selective optimization with compensation. In addition, because of variations in individual, social, and cultural contexts, the conceptual frame we propose in this chapter permits variations in phenotypic expressions of the end state.

The concept of human strengths is inherently multidisciplinary, contextually dynamic, and norm dependent. It is multidisciplinary because human strengths entail properties that reach from the physical over the social-economic and psychological to the spiritual (Baltes & Baltes, 1990;

Staudinger, 1999). These properties exist somewhat independently, but also suggest some form of transdisciplinary linkage if not integration. Sayings such as "a healthy mind in a healthy body" make this point. The concept of human strengths is contextually dynamic, because the function of a given human behavior depends on its context and its outcomes. Age, gender, social group, ethnicity, geographic migration, and the like signify different contexts. Moreover, these contexts are dynamic; contexts not only differ among people but also change during their lifetimes. Finally, the concept of human strengths is norm dependent, because it is a fundamental property of human society that it contains normative—that is, prescriptive—information about what is desirable and undesirable human behavior.

The ensemble of multidisciplinary, contextual, and normative factors and perspectives that need consideration when delineating the concept of human strengths may be reason for despair. Universal statements seem unattainable. Whatever criterion one considers, others will highlight the flaws of the approach chosen. What seems possible, however, is to use a particular theoretical orientation—such as life span psychology (P. B. Baltes, 1997; P. B. Baltes, Lindenberger, & Staudinger, 1998)—and to specify its implications for the concept of human strengths. In this line of inquiry and recognizing the boundedness, or constraints, implied in a given theoretical orientation, it may also be possible to advance some propositions about human strengths that within the frame chosen purport to generalize across individuals, time, and space.

This chapter addresses how human strengths can be understood from the perspective of lifespan psychology. One of the emphases of the field of lifespan psychology has been the search for the optimal human mind or the optimal or ideal person. One exemplar of the notion of the optimal human mind is the idea of wisdom (P. B. Baltes & Smith, 1990; P. B. Baltes & Staudinger, 2000; Kekes, 1995; Sternberg, 1998). Another emphasis is the search for optimal strategies of life management, one exemplar of which is the strategy of selective optimization with compensation, referred to as the SOC model (P. B. Baltes & Baltes, 1990; Freund & Baltes, 2000; Marsiske, Lang, Baltes, & Baltes, 1995). Using work on these two concepts as the guiding theoretical framework, we propose to view the orchestration of wisdom and selective optimization with compensation—the theoretical knowledge about the good and right life (wisdom) and its practical implementation (SOC)—as an expression and target of human strengths.

END STATES: FROM A DOMAIN-SPECIFIC TO A SYSTEMIC AND DYNAMIC PERSPECTIVE

Our selection of the joining of wisdom and SOC as an ideal "meta-end state" of the mind and the person requires further justification, because some authors consider end states an abandoned concept in developmental psychology. The central question of traditional developmental psychology had been how people achieve predefined end states in various domains of functioning.

For instance, developmental stage theories such as Piaget's (1970) model of cognitive development and Erikson's (1968) model of psychosocial stages have great theoretical merits and have stimulated many empirical studies. However, the goals and contexts of human development are more complex, dynamic, and variable than these traditional views of domain-specific definitions of end states suggest. Moreover, there is a high degree of cohort and historical variation (e.g., Elder, 1998). For instance, in previous historical times, people's life courses were more clearly scripted and had higher stability than they do nowadays (e.g., Settersten, 1997). In fact, it is arguable that the modern world accentuates a condition where the central point is not the definition of a particular end state, but the delineation of a behavioral system that promotes as a "whole" the continued adaptation to and mastery of new life circumstances. In this vein, the search for a concept of human strengths requires an integrative and systemic perspective, such as the concept of "the art of life" (Staudinger, 1999) or a version of holistic theory (P. B. Baltes & Smith, 1999; Magnusson & Stattin, 1998).

THE 21ST CENTURY: THE CENTURY OF THE PERMANENTLY INCOMPLETE MIND

The argument for a new, more domain-general, and more dynamic conception of human strengths is strengthened by certain fundamental changes in modern life. Whereas in the past the world presented a set of conditions where adulthood was akin to maturity, where becoming an adult was a relatively fixed goal, and where "being" (i.e., achieving and staying in a relatively stable state) was a possibility, adulthood in the modern world is not the final stage of life. In the modern world, adulthood remains a state of continued "becoming," of permanent transitions to subsequent events and phases. Several reasons make this so. Among the most important are increased longevity, rapid technological changes, and globalization.

The average length of life has dramatically increased during the past century (Kannisto, Lauritsen, Thatcher, & Vaupel, 1994), but development of a culture of old age has lagged behind (P. B. Baltes, 1997; Riley & Riley, 1992). Such a culture is most needed in old age because humans are genetically not well equipped for old age. At the same time, older people are expected to continue to actively participate in social life and to optimize their level of functioning.

Because of the need to keep abreast of rapidly changing technological knowledge and the ease of accessibility of knowledge through modern communication, the half-life of knowledge and professional skills has declined at a faster pace than was true in the past. For those who want to participate efficiently in modern society, selective unlearning of past skills and learning of new skills is necessary.

Technological changes are closely associated with the globalization of human lives. Globalization (i.e., the interconnection of the world as a market of ideas, technology, and labor) is bringing about a new level of selection pressure regarding adaptive fitness and human strengths. For instance, globalization places one in professional competition with experts around the world.

Together, these changes have generated what could be called a state of "permanent incompleteness" (P. B. Baltes, 1999; see also Brandtstädter, 2000). On the one hand, this new scenario offers more chances for personal growth throughout the life span. On the other hand, it puts pressure on people to ceaselessly acquire new information and skills in order to adapt flexibly to the ongoing changes. In our view, "lifelong learning nonstop" is an appropriate metaphor for modern life, because it hints at both the gains and losses that result from these historical changes. Increasingly, developmental acquisitions and outcomes are never final; they are under continuous pressure to demonstrate their adaptive fitness.

TOWARD A NEW AND DYNAMIC CONCEPTION
OF END STATES

It seems, then, that the idea of a fixed and domain-specific end state as conceptualized by Piaget or Erikson has come under additional challenge not only by the articulation of new conceptions of human development; but also by the way the world as a whole is developing. Specific expressions of high-level expertise, such as formal-logical intelligence, are not sufficient. The longer life span and technological and global changes require a new target: The new target of human strengths is an ensemble of properties or competencies that make the individual an effective navigator in a world of change.

In this vein, the concept of human strengths needs to be transformed to a more dynamic conception of adaptive fitness. It needs to be seen as a genuine developmental and open-systems construct. More specifically, we argue that the concept of human strengths

- is a dynamic and context-general property in the sense of adaptive fitness or a general-purpose mechanism;
- represents a condition for lifelong learning and flexibility in mastery;

- regulates the direction of goals of individual development, as well as of the means of goal-attainment; and
- contributes not only to help individuals develop, but also to make them effective participants in the creation of the common good.

To return to the question of the meaningfulness of the concept of an end state, in this change in what constitutes a good life and good development, our view is that the search for ideal end states associated with the idea of human strengths continues to be a central concern. However, instead of conceptualizing good development as a fixed, domain-specific end state of "being," it seems more appropriate to think of it as "becoming," highlighting the overall adaptive fitness of the behavioral systems involved. In this spirit, we argue that the integration of wisdom and SOC represents one important facet of human strengths that can be viewed as an ideal outcome of development.

WISDOM: A DESIRABLE END STATE OF DEVELOPMENT

What is wisdom? In the traditions of philosophy and cultural anthropology, and at a high level of abstraction, one of the most general definitions of wisdom is that it characterizes the convergence of means and ends for the highest personal and common good (P. B. Baltes & Staudinger, 2000; Kekes, 1995). In this sense, and when approached with the methods of psychology, in our own work we conceptualize wisdom as an expert knowledge system about the fundamental pragmatics of life, including knowledge and judgment about the conduct, purpose, and meaning of life (P. B. Baltes & Smith, 1990; Smith & Baltes, 1990; Staudinger & Baltes, 1996). The following seven general criteria of the Berlin wisdom model are based on cultural-historical and philosophical accounts of wisdom:

1. Wisdom addresses important and difficult questions and strategies about the conduct and meaning of life.
2. Wisdom includes knowledge about the limits of knowledge and the uncertainties of the world.
3. Wisdom represents a truly superior level of knowledge, judgment, and advice.
4. Wisdom constitutes knowledge with extraordinary scope, depth, measure, and balance.
5. Wisdom involves a perfect synergy of mind and character, that is, an orchestration of knowledge and virtues.
6. Wisdom represents knowledge used for the good or well-being of oneself and that of others.

7. Wisdom, though difficult to achieve and to specify, is easily recognized when manifested.

The notion of fundamental pragmatics was chosen to mark the specific subject matter (domain) of wisdom. It includes knowledge and judgment about the most essential aspects of the human condition and the ways and means of planning, managing, and understanding a good life, that of ourselves and that of others. Concrete examples are knowledge about the social, cultural, biological, individual, and historical conditions of life, about between-person and between-context variability, about ontogenetic changes of development, about the limitations of one's own knowledge, about the tolerance and reciprocity that are essential to implementing fundamental human rights in a multicultural world, and about ways to bring intelligence, emotion, and motivation into convergence to promote the individual and common good (P. B. Baltes, Glück, & Kunzmann, 2002).

In the Berlin wisdom model (P. B. Baltes & Smith, 1990; P. B. Baltes & Staudinger, 2000), a model that was advanced to assess with empirical observations the degree and quality of wisdom, the concept of wisdom is operationalized as wisdom-related knowledge. An ensemble of five criteria defines this expert body of knowledge. These five criteria are meant to be approximations to the "utopian" ideal of wisdom—which incidentally is not only located in individual minds but as a matter of principle is a collective construct.

The first two criteria, (a) *rich factual* (*declarative*) and (b) *procedural knowledge* about the fundamental pragmatics of life, stem from the expertise literature (e.g., Ericsson & Smith, 1991). Based on lifespan theory, three additional metacriteria are considered to be specific for wisdom: (c) *Lifespan contextualism* identifies knowledge about the many themes and contexts of life (e.g., family, work, leisure, the public good of society), including their interrelations and cultural variations, and incorporates a lifetime temporal perspective. (d) *Relativism* of values and life priorities concerns the acknowledgment of and tolerance for variability in individuals, cultures, and societies. This does not at all imply full-blown relativity of values but rather an explicit concern with the essence of wisdom: that is, the bringing into convergence of the goals and means of the individual and the common good. (e) *Recognition and management of uncertainty* evolves from the awareness that human information processing is necessarily constrained, that individuals have access only to select parts of reality, and that there is always uncertainty about what happened in the past and what will happen in the future.

Wisdom is considered to be the rare case when excellence in all five criteria are integrated into one coordinated whole body of knowledge about the fundamental pragmatics of life. Furthermore, it is important to recognize that the Berlin model of wisdom does not limit the substance of wisdom to the cognitive. Rather, "wisdom identifies a state of mind and behavior that includes the coordinated and balanced interplay of intellectual, affective, and motivational aspects of human functioning" (P. B. Baltes & Staudinger, 2000, p. 123).

What is the implication of this concern with wisdom for a conceptualization of human strengths? Proposing to consider wisdom as the most general good of human development and the most general indicator of optimality spans a general frame for defining the goal territory of the end state of human development. Wisdom can be considered the most general end state of human development for two reasons: First, it represents the highest level of knowledge about the goals and means of life that, according to philosophical and cultural anthropological analysis, human evolution has generated. Second, it is general because it is conceived of at a high level of abstraction, permitting therefore variations in phenotypic expressions. In this sense, it combines universalism with cultural, regional, or personal particularism.

Wisdom, then, forms the most general cognitive, emotional, and motivational space of goals and means within which specific realizations of living a good life can proceed. In this sense, wisdom gives direction to the nature of adaptive fitness that people are expected to move toward. At the same time, wisdom is dynamic and open to individual, social, and cultural variations in life circumstances. It is important to recognize, however, that these variations are bound by the criterion of convergence between means and ends of life and the joint attention to the individual and common good that the concept of wisdom requires.

SOC: A WAY TO HUMAN STRENGTHS

As indicated by many areas of research, the correlation between knowledge and behavior is far from perfect. For this reason, there is an important difference between wisdom as knowledge and wisdom as wise behavior. A key question, therefore, is how wisdom-related knowledge is acquired and especially translated into development-enhancing behavior directed at oneself as well as others.

How expressions of wisdom are possibly acquired and how wisdom as a theoretical frame may be translated into practical behavior is a key concern of SOC, a model that describes a specific strategy of effective life management (M. M. Baltes & Carstensen, 1996; P. B. Baltes, 1997; P. B. Baltes & Baltes, 1990; Freund & Baltes, 2000; Marsiske et al., 1995). As is true for practically all domains of life beyond wisdom, we argue that selection, optimization, and compensation are central processes for the acquisition and behavioral expression of wisdom-related knowledge as well (Freund & Baltes, 2002). The SOC-related processes do not specify what goals and means might be ethically and morally appropriate. Criminals and Mafia bosses, for instance, can be masters of SOC. In other words, the specification of the norm-based valence or desirability of goals and means is the topic of wisdom, not of SOC.

In a nutshell, the SOC model posits that there are three fundamental processes of developmental regulation across the life span: selection, optimization, and compensation. The processes can be active or passive, external or internal, and conscious or subconscious. Selection, optimization, and compensation can occur at various levels of analysis or integration ranging from the macro-level (e.g., societies) to the micro-level (e.g., biological cells). Knowing how to orchestrate selection, optimization, and compensation is a very powerful "general-purpose mechanism" by which individuals, groups, and societies move ahead in reaching higher levels of functioning and in mastering future challenges.

Selection

Selection (developing, elaborating, and committing to goals) gives direction to development by directing and focusing resources on certain domains of functioning (specialization) and guiding behavior across situations and time. Selection can occur either electively ("elective selection") or as a response to losses (e.g., focusing on the most important goals, a mechanism we call "loss-based selection"). The importance of the selection of goals is also empirically supported. For instance, on a more micro-level of analysis, goals guide attention toward the kind of information that is goal relevant (for an overview, see Gollwitzer & Moskowitz, 1996). On a more macro-level of analysis, goals contribute to a sense of purpose and meaning in life (e.g., Freund & Baltes, 2000; Staudinger, 1999).

Optimization

Optimization denotes the process of acquiring, refining, coordinating, and applying the relevant means or resources to attain goals in the selected goal domains. The importance of optimization in achieving higher levels of functioning has been demonstrated in different areas of psychology. On the one hand, there are means—such as reading, writing, and arithmetic —that have a high degree of generalization. On the other hand, there are means that are domain specific, such as the cognitive skills required to play chess. The literature on expertise has demonstrated the central role of deliberate practice of skills, encompassing the acquisition of new skills, the refinement of existing skills, and the integration and automatization of skills, for achieving peak performance (Ericsson & Smith, 1991).

Compensation

In our definition, *compensation* concerns the use of alternative means when existing means are lost in order to maintain a given level of functioning. Management of transient or permanent losses is a central aspect of human strengths (cf. the notion of resilience, e.g., Rutter, 1987; Staudinger, Marsiske, & Baltes, 1995). Key processes related to compensation involve the substitution of means either by acquiring new ones (e.g., a wheelchair to compensate for loss in mobility) or by activating unused internal resources (e.g., training muscles that support balance) or external resources (e.g., asking friends for help when walking).

Returning to the functional coordination of SOC and wisdom, the concept of wisdom can be considered a selector mechanism for means, whether these are part of optimization or compensation. On the one hand, wisdom encompasses general knowledge about means-ends relationships, or which means best serve to achieve a given goal in a specific person-context constellation. On the other hand, wisdom also specifies which means are in accordance with and maximize both the personal and the common good. Clearly, when wisdom is involved, means that serve personal ends at the cost of others' well-being would not appear acceptable.

WISDOM AND SOC: AN INTEGRATION FOSTERING HUMAN STRENGTHS

Our central position, then, is that wisdom and SOC constitute an ensemble of knowledge and behavioral strategies that if operative in a conjoint manner constitute a major component of human strengths. Wisdom provides a selector concerning which goals and means are of fundamental significance in the life course and, in addition, are ethically and morally desirable. SOC specifies how goals are reached, irrespective of the nature of the goals and means involved (see Figure 2.1). Because we argue that the general cognitive, emotional, and motivational space of wisdom, as well as the principles of SOC, evince a high degree of universality (Baltes & Freund, in press; Baltes & Staudinger, 2000), we suggest that the use of coordinated wisdom-related knowledge as a selector of SOC-related strategies carries high generalizability.

What about the more direct reciprocal relationship between SOC and the acquisition of wisdom itself? SOC-related behaviors should also be important for acquiring and refining wisdom-related knowledge. Learning to select and optimize goals and to compensate for losses in a way that fosters successful development should provide insights into what goals are best suited for a person of a specific age living in a given sociohistorical context. Moreover, acquiring and refining optimization and compensation

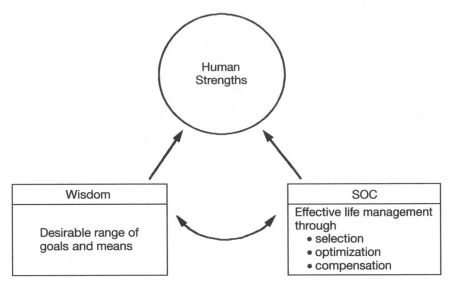

Figure 2.1. The concept of human strengths as the integration of wisdom, for example, the knowledge about the fundamental pragmatics of life, and the life management strategies of selection, optimization, and compensation.

bring knowledge about means–ends relationships that is also part of the pragmatic knowledge about how to live a good life. In this sense, it is likely that with the acquisition and refinement of SOC, the kind of knowledge evolves that we have characterized as the core of wisdom—that is, an expertise in the fundamental pragmatics of life. Similarly, as wisdom-related knowledge evolves, for instance during late adolescence (Pasupathi, Staudinger, & Baltes, 2001), we expect a corresponding advance in SOC.

CONCLUSION

As developmental psychology extended its reach to the entire life span, considered gains and losses as functional parts of any developmental process, attended to the systemic whole of functions, and included the varied cultural contexts in which individuals live, the traditional notion of fixed end states of development lost status. The level of dissatisfaction grew even further when noncognitive aspects were considered, such as the role of values and multiculturation. Thus, there was a tendency to avoid the search for end state-oriented conceptions of human strengths.

These reservations about ideal end states of human development cannot be taken to imply that developmental psychologists should completely abstain from efforts to give substance to the concept of human strengths. Guidance is necessary because, aside from the notion of developmental advances toward a state of "maturity," rapid technological changes, globalization, and increased longevity stress the necessity for lifelong learning. On the one hand, this lack of a predefined end state can be seen as opening up possibilities for continued growth and encouraging people to explore personal strengths even in unconventional ways. It gives a large share of freedom to the course of individual development. On the other hand, this freedom can turn into a ruthless pressure to fulfill the ideal of permanent growth and achievement of higher and higher levels of functioning at the expense of others, both individuals and societies.

We see the contribution of this chapter as being its outline of an alternative "general-purpose" and "universal" constellation of properties of human strengths. In this line of argument, we kept the search for an end state. This end state, however, we propose to define not as a specific property such as logical thinking, but as a system of means and goals that are integrative and consider the person as a whole and in the context of society and citizenship.

In this integration, we propose that wisdom, the knowledge about fundamental pragmatics of life, be viewed as a desirable end state of human development that can be lived and implemented through selective optimization with compensation. In this view, the end state is relativistic and dynamic in that its expression depends on the specific (social, historical, life span) context and the characteristics of a person. On an abstract level, however, this conception of an end state is universal and bound by the general principles of wisdom and of the fundamental life-management processes of SOC that conjointly allow the pursuit of the individual and common good. We consider this integration of wisdom and SOC to be the most general version of a psychology of human strengths. As an ensemble, we expect the orchestration of wisdom and SOC to be a powerful regulator as people navigate their lives in a changing society.

REFERENCES

Baltes, M. M., & Carstensen, L. L. (1996). The process of successful ageing. *Ageing and Society, 16,* 397–422.

Baltes, P. B. (1997). On the incomplete architecture of human ontogeny: Selection, optimization, and compensation as foundation of developmental theory. *American Psychologist, 52,* 366–380.

Baltes, P. B. (1999). *Lebenslanges Lernen: Das Zeitalter des Unfertigen Menschen* (Akademische Causerie) [Lifelong learning: The incompleteness of humankind]. Berlin: Berlin-Brandenburgische Akademie der Wissenschaften.

Baltes, P. B., & Baltes, M. M. (1990). Psychological perspectives on successful aging: The model of selective optimization with compensation. In P. B. Baltes & M. M. Baltes (Eds.), *Successful aging: Perspectives from the behavioral sciences* (pp. 1–34). New York: Cambridge University Press.

Baltes, P. B., & Freund, A. M. (in press). The intermarriage of wisdom and selective optimization with compensation (SOC): Two meta-heuristics guiding the conduct of life. In C. L. M. Keyes (Ed.), *Flourishing: The positive person and the good life*. Washington, DC: American Psychological Association.

Baltes, P. B., Glück, J., & Kunzmann, U. (2002). Wisdom: Its structure and function in regulating successful lifespan development. In C. R. Snyder & S. J. Lopez (Eds.), *The handbook of positive psychology* (pp. 327–347). New York: Oxford University Press.

Baltes, P. B., Lindenberger, U., & Staudinger, U. M. (1998). Life-span theory in developmental psychology. In R. M. Lerner (Ed.), *Handbook of child psychology: Vol. 1. Theoretical models of human development* (5th ed., pp. 1029–1143). New York: Wiley.

Baltes, P. B., & Smith, J. (1990). The psychology of wisdom and its ontogenesis. In R. J. Sternberg (Ed.), *Wisdom: Its nature, origins, and development* (pp. 87–120). New York: Cambridge University Press.

Baltes, P. B., & Smith, J. (1999). Multilevel and systemic analyses of old age: Theoretical and empirical evidence for a fourth age. In V. L. Bengtson & K. W. Schaie (Eds.), *Handbook of theories of aging* (pp. 153–173). New York: Springer.

Baltes, P. B., & Staudinger, U. M. (2000). Wisdom: A metaheuristic (pragmatic) to orchestrate mind and virtue toward excellence. *American Psychologist, 55,* 122–136.

Brandtstädter, J. (2000). *Agency in developmental settings of modernity: The dialects of commitment and disengagement.* Unpublished manuscript, University of Trier, Germany.

Elder, G. H., Jr. (1998). The life course and human development. In R. M. Lerner (Ed.), *Handbook of child psychology: Vol. 1. Theoretical models of human development* (5th ed., pp. 939–992). New York: Wiley.

Ericsson, K. A., & Smith, J. (Eds.). (1991). *Towards a general theory of expertise: Prospects and limits.* New York: Cambridge University Press.

Erikson, E. H. (1968). Life cycle. In D. L. Sills (Ed.), *International encyclopedia of the social sciences* (Vol. 6, pp. 286–292). New York: Macmillan & Free Press.

Freund, A. M., & Baltes, P. B. (2000). The orchestration of selection, optimization, and compensation: An action-theoretical conceptualization of a theory of developmental regulation. In W. J. Perrig & A. Grob (Eds.), *Control of human behavior, mental processes and consciousness* (pp. 35–58). Mahwah, NJ: Erlbaum.

Freund, A. M., & Baltes, P. B. (2002). Life-management strategies of selection, optimization, and compensation. Measurement by self-report and construct validity. *Journal of Personality and Social Psychology, 82,* 642–662.

Gollwitzer, P. M., & Moskowitz, G. B. (1996). Goal effects on action and cognition. In E. T. Higgins & A. W. Kruglanski (Eds.), *Social psychology: Handbook of basic principles* (pp. 361–399). New York: Guilford Press.

Kannisto, V., Lauritsen, J., Thatcher, A. R., & Vaupel, J. W. (1994). Reductions in mortality at advanced ages: Several decades of evidence from 27 countries. *Population and Development, 20,* 793–810.

Kekes, J. (1995). *Moral wisdom and good lives.* Ithaca, NY: Cornell University Press.

Magnusson, D., & Stattin, H. (1998). Person-context interaction theories. In R. M. Lerner (Ed.), *Handbook of child psychology: Vol. 1. Theoretical models of human development* (pp. 685–760). New York: Wiley.

Marsiske, M., Lang, F. R., Baltes, M. M., & Baltes, P. B. (1995). Selective optimization with compensation: Life-span perspectives on successful human development. In R. A. Dixon & L. Bäckman (Eds.), *Compensation for psychological defects and declines: Managing losses and promoting gains* (pp. 35–79). Hillsdale, NJ: Erlbaum.

Pasupathi, M., Staudinger, U. M., & Baltes, P. B. (2001). Seeds of Wisdom: Adolescents' knoweldge and judgment about difficult life problems. *Developmental Psychology, 37,* 359–367.

Piaget, J. (1970). Piaget's theory. In P. H. Mussen (Ed.), *Carmichael's manual of child psychology* (Vol. 1, pp. 703–732). New York: Wiley.

Riley, M. W., & Riley, J. W. (1992). *The hidden age revolution: Emergent integration at all ages* (Distinguished lectures in aging series). Syracuse, NY: Syracuse University.

Rutter, M. (1987). Resilience in the face of adversity: Protective factors and resistance to psychiatric disorder. *British Journal of Psychiatry, 147,* 598–611.

Settersten, R. A. J. (1997). The salience of age in the life course. *Human Development, 40,* 257–281.

Smith, J., & Baltes, P. B. (1990). A study of wisdom-related knowledge: Age/cohort differences in responses to life planning problems. *Developmental Psychology, 26,* 494–505.

Staudinger, U. M. (1999). Social cognition and a psychological approach to an art of life. In F. Blanchard-Fields & T. Hess (Eds.), *Social cognition, adult development and aging* (pp. 343–375). New York: Academic Press.

Staudinger, U. M., & Baltes, P. B. (1996). Interactive minds: A facilitative setting for wisdom-related performance? *Journal of Personality and Social Psychology, 71,* 746–762.

Staudinger, U. M., Marsiske, M., & Baltes, P. B. (1995). Resilience and reserve capacity in later adulthood: Potentials and limits of development across the life span. In D. Cicchetti & D. Cohen (Eds.), *Developmental psychopathology: Vol. 2. Risk, disorder, and adaptation* (pp. 801–847). New York: Wiley.

Sternberg, R. J. (1998). A balance theory of wisdom. *Review of General Psychology, 2,* 347–365.

3

THE HUMAN'S GREATEST STRENGTH: OTHER HUMANS

ELLEN BERSCHEID

Almost half a century ago, Maslow sharply criticized psychologists for neglecting to study the antecedents and consequences of one human's love for another human:

> It is amazing how little the empirical sciences have to offer on the subject of love. Particularly strange is the silence of the psychologists, for one might think this to be their particular obligation. Probably this is just another example of the besetting sin of the academicians, that they prefer to do what they are easily able rather than what they ought, like the not-so-bright kitchen helper I knew who opened every can in the hotel one day because he was so *very* good at opening cans. (Maslow, 1954, p. 235)

At the time Maslow wrote those words, psychologists had tried many times to open the can labeled "human emotion," whose many fascinating contents include love. Discouraged each time, they chucked that unyielding can back into the dusty depths of the cupboard of human behavioral phenomena. There it remained relatively undisturbed until Schachter (e.g., 1964) performed his seminal emotion experiments in the early 1960s and stimulated a renaissance of theory and research on human emotion that continues to the present day. That psychologists got a late start on human emotional phenomena, and that as a consequence human emotion continues to be poorly understood, is reflected in the fact that even the most fundamental questions about emotion—including just what an emotion is—remain controversial (see Ekman & Davidson, 1994).

The troubled history of emotion in psychology is partially a consequence of psychologists' neglect of the fact that each human's behavior is embedded in his or her relationships with other humans. Neglect of this fundamental truth in the study of emotion is surprising, because Darwin (1899), who lifted human emotion from the realm of philosophy and firmly placed it in the scientific arena, emphasized from the very beginning the social nature of emotion and its role in the survival of the species. Nevertheless, the implications of Darwin's insight were neglected for many years. Today, however, most emotion theorists at least formally recognize the close association between relationships and the experience of emotion. Zajonc (1998) succinctly described the association:

> Emotions, even though their hallmark is the internal state of the individual—the viscera, the gut—are above all social phenomena. They are the basis of social interaction, they are the products of social interaction, their origins, and their currency. (pp. 619–620)

But beyond cursory recognition of the fact that people usually experience emotion most frequently and intensely in the context of their close relationships with other people (Berscheid & Ammazzalorso, 2001), its many implications for human emotional experience mostly remain unexplored.

An understanding of many other behavioral phenomena has suffered from neglect of the fact that humans are embedded in a web of relationships with other humans from their conception to their death and, thus, that most human behavior takes place in the context of interpersonal relationships. The omnipresent relationship context both influences an individual's behavior and is influenced by it (Berscheid & Reis, 1998; Reis, Collins, & Berscheid, 2000). For this reason, no science that aspires to understand human behavior can afford to continue to overlook the human's social nature and the effects an individual's relationships with others have on that person's behavior.

It seems particularly obvious that recognition of the fact that humans are embedded in a web of relationships with others throughout their lives is vital to the development of a psychology of human strengths. Paramount among these strengths is surely the human's inclination and capacity to form and maintain relationships with other humans. It is within relationships with others that most people find meaning and purpose in their lives (e.g., Klinger, 1977); that they typically experience the positive emotions of love, joy, happiness, and contentment; and that they successfully overcome the physical and psychological challenges to well-being and survival all humans encounter.

THE EVOLUTIONARY PERSPECTIVE

There is growing agreement among evolutionary psychologists that relationships constitute the single most important factor responsible for the survival of *Homo sapiens*. For example, Buss and Kenrick (1998) stated,

> evolutionary psychology places social interaction and social relationships squarely within the center of the action. In particular, social interactions and relationships surrounding mating, kinship, reciprocal alliances, coalitions, and hierarchies are especially critical, because all appear to have strong consequences for successful survival and reproduction. (p. 994)

Many now argue, for example, that the small, cooperative group has constituted the primary survival strategy of humans from the beginning of evolutionary time. As Brewer and Caporael (1990) put the thesis, social relationships "provided a buffer between early hominids and the natural physical environment, including protection from predators, access to food supplies, and insulation from the elements" (p. 240).

Many evolutionary psychologists thus reason that if the capacity to form and maintain cooperative relationships with other humans was critical to human survival, then biological characteristics of humans selected for at the individual level should have been features that facilitated those relationships. They hypothesize, therefore, that over evolutionary time humans were biologically wired with properties that promote the formation and maintenance of relationships with conspecifics. Evidence in support of their thesis is accumulating in many areas of psychology. For example, psychoneuroscientists have proposed that because relationships with other humans undoubtedly were necessary to human survival, one of the most important tasks of our ancestors' perceptual systems was recognition of the faces of other humans. They have reasoned that if face perception was of special importance, then humans may have evolved a special neurological processing system for face perception different from the system used in other forms of object perception. Evidence in support of their thesis has been obtained in findings that face perception and object perception depend on different regions of the brain, that the two systems are functionally independent, and that the systems process information differently (Kanwisher, McDermott, & Chun, 1997; see also Gazzaniga, Ivry, & Mangun, 1998).

Yet another apparently innate system that facilitates the formation and maintenance of relationships is the "attachment" system, first identified by Harlow (e.g., 1958) in his experimental studies with infant primates and by Bowlby (e.g., 1969/1982) in his observations of human infants. Both viewed attachment behavior as an evolved tendency for the individual to maintain proximity to another stronger, wiser, caring member of the species. The defining feature of attachment over the human life span is that the attachment figure serves as a source of reassurance and aid in the face of perceived threat. There is evidence that an attachment bond between a human infant and his or her caregiver emerges universally in the second half of the first year of human life (Reis et al., 2000). Evidence also is mounting that the close relationships adults later form with romantic partners, friends, and others often function in ways similar to the attachments formed between a child and a caregiver (e.g., Shaver & Hazan, 1993). As appears to be true of other species (Latane & Hothersall, 1972), the human is especially likely to turn to attachment figures in times of stress; indeed, the mere presence of an attachment figure may reduce the intensity of the individual's physiological reactions to the stressful event (e.g., Lynch, 1977).

Although the importance of the human attachment system for infant survival has been widely acknowledged, its role in the development of the human brain only recently has been recognized. Neuroscientific evidence suggests that because the human brain is not completely differentiated at birth, the infant's experiences with the social environment interact with gene expression to shape neurological circuits within the major structures of the brain (e.g., Blakemore, 1998). Reviewing much of this evidence, Siegel (1999) argued that the infant's early social relationships "have a direct effect on the development of the domains of mental functioning that serve as our conceptual anchor points: memory, narrative, emotion, representations, and states of mind" (p. 68). In support of this proposition, evidence from nonhuman species suggests that even minor deprivation of early contact from responsive conspecifics results in abnormal neuroanatomical structures and impaired endocrinological sensitivity associated with stress. Studies of human infants who have had few opportunities to interact and form relationships with other humans also reveal neurohormonal abnormalities (e.g., Gunnar, 2000).

Finally, at the psychological level of analysis, there is an impressive array of evidence that humans possess what Baumeister and Leary (1995) termed a fundamental "need to belong." This evidence suggests that the individual's need to belong to the human community is fulfilled by frequent and affectively pleasant interactions with at least a few other people so long as those interactions take place in the context of a stable and enduring framework of the partners' mutual concern for each other's welfare. Satisfaction of this need (e.g., as in the formation of a new friendship or romantic relationship or acceptance by a larger group) is usually manifested in the experience of positive emotions and feelings, whereas its frustration (e.g., rejection by others) typically results in the experience of negative emotions and feelings.

MORBIDITY, MORTALITY, AND INTERPERSONAL RELATIONSHIPS

Evidence supporting the supposition that relationships with others were critical to the survival of *Homo sapiens* now is supplemented by evidence that relationships with other humans continue to play a critical role in human physical and mental health. Durkheim (1897/1963) long ago systematically documented the association between the likelihood of the individual's committing suicide and his or her degree of "social integration," or his or her maintenance of relationship ties with others. Nevertheless, only within the past few decades have psychologists begun to investigate the role that relationships play in human physical well-being and survival.

Evidence documenting the association between human physical health and relationships with others is strong and robust. House, Landis, and Umberson's (1988) review of five large-sample, long-term prospective epidemiological studies concluded that low social integration is a major risk factor for premature death. The strength of the association is illustrated by the fact that this review and others (e.g., Atkins, Kaplan, & Toshima, 1991) concluded that the age-adjusted relative risk ratio between low social integration and mortality exceeds that of the highly publicized risks associated with smoking and obesity.

Psychologists' attempts to identify the causal pathways between social relationships and morbidity and mortality have centered on the construct of social support. The central hypothesis has been that relationships with others promote physical well-being through the health-promoting actions of those with whom the individual is in relationship. Unfortunately, and similar to the current state of affairs in the study of human emotion, the immaturity of social support theory and research is revealed by the fact that few social support researchers agree on the proper definition of their central construct (see Berscheid & Reis, 1998; Vaux, 1988). Nevertheless, as Reis et al. (2000) observed, "nearly all existing [social support] research incorporates some of the basic themes involved in positive-quality relationships, such as affection, caring, reassurance of worth, advice and guidance, proximity to caregivers, coping assistance, opportunities to nurture, reliable alliances, and tangible assistance" (p. 853). As this overflowing basket of positive relationship qualities reflects, discovery of the precise causal connections between social relationships and physical well-being is likely to occupy psychological researchers for some time, and further advances will require closer attention to the nature and qualities of the individual's interpersonal relationships.

RELATIONSHIPS: THE SOURCE OF HUMAN HAPPINESS

Most people are surprised to learn of the close association between the status of their social relationships and their risk of premature death. Few, however, are surprised to learn of the association between their mental health and happiness and the state of their interpersonal relationships. Not even Americans, who have one of the world's most individualistic cultures and thus who are most likely to deny and minimize their dependence on other people (Fiske, Kitayama, Markus, & Nisbett, 1998), are surprised by this finding. A wealth of research documents that when Americans are asked what makes them happy, most cite their close personal relationships with other people (see Berscheid & Reis, 1998). Indeed, people who have formed and maintain satisfying relationships with others do in fact appear to be happier than those who have not succeeded in doing so. Diener, Suh, Lucas, and Smith (1999) concluded from their review of the data that married people, for example, tend to be happier than unmarried people, whether always single, divorced, or widowed, and this is true for both men and women of all ages. On the other side of the coin, the significant associations between loneliness and unhappiness, as well as between loneliness and a multitude of mental and physical ills, have been well documented (see Berscheid & Reis, 1998). Additionally, meta-analyses of a wealth of studies reveal the deleterious impact that discordant and disruptive family relationships have on children's physical and psychological well-being, both during childhood and in later life (Amato & Keith, 1991a, 1991b).

Because psychologists have only begun to systematically investigate the role that relationships with others plays in human life, the causal pathways between relationships and psychological well-being have yet to be mapped. Like those investigating many other psychological phenomena integral to the human's omnipresent relationship context, the efforts of these investigators will be dependent on the further development of a science of relationships.

A MULTIDISCIPLINARY SCIENCE OF RELATIONSHIPS

Many psychologists now are in the process of remedying psychology's neglect of the human's social nature. They are doing so with astonishing speed and determination. Developmental, clinical, and social psychologists currently are among the major contributors to the rapidly developing science of relationships, an endeavor that is engaging scholars in almost all of the behavioral and social sciences and in several of the biological and health sciences as well (Berscheid, 1998). If it is true that the human's greatest strength is the inclination and capacity to form and sustain relationships with others of the species, then the further development of relationship science and the development of a psychology based on human strengths will prove to be symbiotic enterprises.

The maturity of these two scientific endeavors is likely to result in a different portrait of the human than that currently painted by psychological theory and evidence. The present unflattering picture of *Homo sapiens* is reflected by the fact that if one were to place in one pile all the psychological theories and research directed toward an understanding of human aggression and competition, including the many theories that assume humans are innately aggressive, and put in another pile all theory and evidence focused on human altruism and other prosocial behaviors, the first pile surely would tower over the second. Similarly, if one were to stack all psychological theory and research pertaining to the experience of negative emotion, such as anger and fear, alongside that directed toward love and the other positive emotions, one would see a similar disparity. Strangely, this is true despite the fact that the word "love" has one of the highest frequencies of usage of any in the English language and, as Harlow (e.g., 1958) noted in his reports of infant attachment, it also has the highest frequency of any word cited in Bartlett's *Familiar Quotations* (1957). Nevertheless, as many emotion theorists have observed (e.g., Berscheid, 1983), psychological theories of emotion historically have had great difficulty accounting for the positive emotions. The problem arises from the fact that most theorists have taken their principal task to be an accounting of the negative emotions.

HUMAN "NATURE"

Psychology's traditional focus on the negative both reflects and contributes to popular assumptions about the nature of humankind. In his book *Human Nature Explored*, Mandler (1997) noted that when people are asked to list the characteristics of human nature, "Usually the result looks something like this: Greed, Competition, Ambition, Jealousy, Violence, Intelligence, Joy, Aggression" (p. 4). Discounting intelligence (presumably affectively neutral), the only positive trait popularly believed to be characteristic of humans is the capacity to be joyful. Mandler continued, "It is only after some probing that the positive side of human nature emerges in everyday discourse. It is often referred to as one's 'essential humanity,' which refers to the caring, empathic nature of beast" (p. 5). Commenting on Gould's (1993) observation that, in comparison with other animals, "*Homo sapiens* is a remarkably genial species" (p. 281), Mandler speculated that because most human interactions are positive or neutral, truly destructive acts, such as aggression and violence, stand out against this background of general human harmony and appear to be more prevalent than they actually are.

Psychology's failure to "accentuate the positive"—its emphasis on the dark side of human behavior—at least partially has been the result of the noble motivation to "eliminate the negative." Many have believed that only by subjecting the human's liabilities to close scrutiny can understanding—and, ultimately, prevention and remedy—of human flaws and weaknesses be achieved. Nevertheless, psychology's failure to appreciate human strengths and assets may be retarding effective prevention and control of undesirable human behaviors. For example, if it is true that humans are above all else social creatures whose evolved biological properties promote harmonious bonds with other humans, then a different light is thrown on the destructive acts humans sometimes perpetrate on other humans.

To illustrate the difference in perspective, one need only consider Shelley's (1831/1992) classic tale of Frankenstein's monster, who confessed at the end of his life, "I have murdered the lovely and the helpless; I have strangled the innocent as they slept, and grasped to death his throat who never injured me or any other living thing" (p. 184). Reviewing his wretched life, in which his ugly appearance prompted horror, revulsion, and cruelty by others, the monster also sadly recalled,

> Once I falsely hoped to meet with beings, who, pardoning my outward form, would love me for the excellent qualities which I was capable of unfolding. . . . When I run over the frightful catalogue of my sins, I cannot believe that I am the same creature whose thoughts were once filled with sublime and transcendent visions of the beauty and the majesty of goodness. But it is even so; the fallen angel becomes a malignant devil. . . . I am alone. (p. 183)

A portrait that depicts the human as teeming with innate malignancies toward other humans—malignancies that require containment, at minimum, and exorcism, if possible—has different implications for the treatment and control of undesirable human behaviors than does a portrait that depicts the human as eager to love other humans and to be loved by them. One wonders how many human monsters were born ready and eager to love and to be loved but were denied the expression of what appears to be a fundamental human quality.

In sum, *Homo sapiens* is an extraordinarily tough animal to have survived on planet Earth for as long as it has. It seems likely that our ancestors survived, and that we survive today, only with the aid of other humans. The development of a positive psychology, one that focuses on human strengths rather than weaknesses, would do well to lay its foundation on this fundamental fact of human existence. Whether it does so or not, no psychology—whether positive or negative—can advance its understanding of human nature by ignoring the fact that, far from being born predisposed to be hostile toward other humans, it appears that we are innately inclined to form strong, enduring, and harmonious attachments with others of the species—or, as Harlow (1958) simply put it, to "love" them.

REFERENCES

Amato, P. R., & Keith, B. (1991a). Parental divorce and adult well-being: A meta-analysis. *Journal of Marriage and the Family, 53,* 43–58.

Amato, P. R., & Keith, B. (1991b). Parental divorce and the well-being of children: A meta-analysis. *Psychological Bulletin, 110,* 26–46.

Atkins, C. J., Kaplan, R. M., & Toshima, M. T. (1991). Close relationships in the epidemiology of cardiovascular disease. In W. H. Jones & D. Perlman (Eds.), *Advances in personal relationships* (Vol. 3, pp. 207–231). London: Jessica Kingsley.

Bartlett, J. (1957). *Familiar quotations: A collection of passages, phrases, and proverbs traced to their sources in ancient and modern literature.* London: Little Brown.

Baumeister, R. F., & Leary, M. R. (1995). The need to belong: Desire for interpersonal attachments as a fundamental human motivation. *Psychological Bulletin, 117,* 497–529.

Berscheid, E. (1983). Emotion. In H. H. Kelley, E. Berscheid, A. Christensen, J. H. Harvey, T. L. Huston, G. Levinger, E. McClintock, L. A. Peplau, & D. R. Peterson (Eds.), *Close relationships* (pp. 110–168). New York: Freeman.

Berscheid, E. (1998). The greening of relationship science. *American Psychologist, 54,* 260–266.

Berscheid, E., & Ammazzalorso, H. (2001). Emotional experience in close relationships. In M. Hewstone & M. Brewer (Eds.), *Blackwell handbook of social psychology: Vol. 2. Interpersonal processes* (pp. 308–330). Oxford, UK: Blackwell.

Berscheid, E., & Reis, H. T. (1998). Attraction and close relationships. In D. T. Gilbert, S. T. Fiske, & G. Lindzey (Eds.), *The handbook of social psychology* (4th ed., Vol. 2, pp. 193–281). New York: McGraw-Hill.

Blakemore, C. (1998). How the environment helps to build the brain. In B. Cartledge (Ed.), *Mind, brain, and the environment: The Linacre lectures 1995–6* (pp. 28–56). New York: Oxford University Press.

Bowlby, J. (1982). *Attachment and loss: Vol. 1. Attachment* (2nd ed.) New York: Basic Books. (Original work published 1969)

Brewer, M. B., & Caporael, L. R. (1990). Selfish genes vs. selfish people: Sociobiology as origin myth. *Motivation and Emotion, 14,* 237–243.

Buss, D. M., & Kenrick, D. T. (1998). Evolutionary social psychology. In D. T.

Gilbert, S. T. Fiske, & G. Lindzey (Eds.), *The handbook of social psychology* (4th ed., pp. 982–1026). New York: McGraw-Hill.

Darwin, C. (1899). *The expression of the emotions in man and animals.* New York: D. Appleton.

Diener, E., Suh, E. M., Lucas, R. E., & Smith, H. L. (1999). Subjective well-being: Three decades of progress. *Psychological Bulletin, 125,* 276–302.

Durkheim, E. (1963). *Suicide.* New York: Free Press. (Original work published 1897)

Ekman, P., & Davidson, R. J. (Eds.). (1994). *The nature of emotion: Fundamental questions.* New York: Oxford University Press.

Fiske, A. P., Kitayama, S., Markus, H. R., & Nisbett, R. E. (1998). The cultural matrix of social psychology. In D. T. Gilbert, S. T. Fiske, & G. Lindzey (Eds.), *The handbook of social psychology* (4th ed., Vol. 2, pp. 915–981). New York: McGraw-Hill.

Gazzaniga, M. S., Ivry, R. B., & Mangun, G. R. (1998). *Cognitive neuroscience: The biology of the mind.* New York: Norton.

Gould, S. J. (1993). *Eight little piggies.* New York: Norton.

Gunnar, M. R. (2000). Early adversity and the development of stress reactivity and regulation. In C. A. Nelson (Ed.), *The effects of adversity on neurobehavioral development: Minnesota Symposia on Child Psychology: Vol. 31* (pp. 163–200). Mahwah, NJ: Erlbaum.

Harlow, H. F. (1958). The nature of love. *American Psychologist, 13,* 673–685.

House, J. S., Landis, K. R., & Umberson, D. (1988). Social relationships and health. *Science, 241,* 540–545.

Kanwisher, N., McDermott, J., & Chun, M. M. (1997). The fusiform face area: A module in human extrastriate cortex specialized for face perception. *Journal of Neuroscience, 17,* 4302–4311.

Klinger, E. (1977). *Meaning and void: Inner experience and the incentives in people's lives.* Minneapolis: University of Minnesota Press.

Latane, B., & Hothersall, D. (1972). Social attraction in animals. In P. C. Dodwell (Ed.), *New horizons in psychology 2* (pp. 259–275). New York: Penguin Books.

Lynch, J. J. (1977). *The broken heart: The medical consequences of loneliness.* New York: Basic Books.

Mandler, G. (1997). *Human nature explored.* New York: Oxford University Press.

Maslow, A. H. (1954). *Motivation and personality.* New York: Harper.

Reis, H. T., Collins, W. A., Berscheid, E. (2000). The relationship context of human behavior and development. *Psychological Bulletin, 126,* 844–872.

Schachter, S. (1964). The interaction of cognitive and physiological determinants of emotional state. In L. Berkowitz (Ed.), *Advances in experimental social psychology* (Vol. 1, pp. 49–80). New York: Academic Press.

Shaver, P. R., & Hazan, C. (1993). Adult romantic attachment: Theory and evidence. In W. H. Jones & D. Perlman (Eds.), *Advances in personal relationships* (Vol. 4, pp. 29–70). London: Jessica Kingsley.

Shelley, M. (1992). *Frankenstein*. New York: St. Martin's Press. (Original work published 1831)

Siegel, D. J. (1999). *The developing mind: Toward a neurobiology of interpersonal experience*. New York: Guilford Press.

Vaux, A. (1988). *Social support: Theory, research, and intervention*. New York: Praeger.

Zajonc, R. B. (1998). Emotions. In D. T. Gilbert, S. T. Fiske, & G. Lindzey (Eds.), *The handbook of social psychology* (4th ed., Vol. 2, pp. 591–632). New York: McGraw-Hill.

4

CONSTRUCTIVE COGNITION, PERSONAL GOALS, AND THE SOCIAL EMBEDDING OF PERSONALITY

NANCY CANTOR

In considering a psychology of human strengths, I begin with the view that personality psychology has more often than not emphasized the shortcomings of individuals as compared with their potentials. In this regard, one can point to four dimensions of what I call a "normative analysis" (admittedly an overgeneralization) in personality psychology that encourage this emphasis on shortcomings. Now, I should say from the outset that I plead as guilty as the next in following this approach. Fortunately, there are also emerging trends in the field that may serve as an antidote to our traditional ways, and, after briefly noting some features of the normative approach, in this chapter I will comment on where to search for alternatives. In particular, I will argue that we should be looking for evidence of the opportunistic proclivities of individuals embedded in what they are trying to do, often as these goals change over time and place, and in the ways in which people garner social supports in their meaningful life activities.

LIMITATIONS OF THE NORMATIVE APPROACH

First, however, let me consider some of the facets of our traditions that may serve to hide these human strengths.

Emphasis on Outcomes

First, individual differences have traditionally been characterized in terms of the *outcomes* that a person has achieved (i.e., what he or she has), as contrasted with the *processes* in which the individual is engaged (i.e., what he or she is doing or trying to do). This emphasis, which I have previously portrayed as a "having" versus "doing" approach to personality (Cantor, 1990), tends to focus attention on failures of attainment rather than possibilities for the future. This emphasis is particularly ironic in the analysis of personal goals, when the focus shifts from the motivational process—for example, from how a person's goals have mobilized energy and behavior—to the distance between a current state and the desired outcomes.

Search for Simplicity

A second feature of the normative approaches is a desire to find parsimony or simplicity in the characterization of fundamental individual differences (e.g., five-factor model, basic goals) with a parallel eschewing of complexity in the portrait of personality. Whereas it is certainly an appropriate and important task to find a fundamental scheme for personality, unfortunately it is difficult to do so without moving to a level of abstraction that turns quickly into a contrast between "good and bad" or functional and dysfunctional attributes (e.g., optimistic vs. pessimistic, approach vs. avoidance goals). In placing a person on these fundamental dimensions, it is very hard not to use the positive reference point as a benchmark against which many fall short. Moreover, the desired level of generality in such descriptions typically encompasses quite a range of behaviors and life situations, thereby moving a person closer, on average, to the good or bad pole than he or she might be if we attended closely to the specificity of day-to-day actions and motivations.

Focus on Consistency and Stability

In a related vein, a third feature of many approaches is the search for broad-based patterning instead of the specificity of behavior and goals. Whereas cross-situational consistency in behavior may have its virtues, from the perspective of a "positive psychology," there is much to be claimed for individuals' discriminative facilities (Mischel, 1973) as they adapt to the exigencies of different situations with different behaviors (e.g., Mischel, 1999; Shoda, 1999). Similarly, we may miss a great deal about adaptive human behavior by looking for temporal stability in behavior aggregated over periods in a person's life. That is, by focusing on stable aspects of personality rather than malleable ones, perhaps the individual's novel responses to opportunities are overlooked (Cantor, Zirkel, & Norem, 1993; Helson, Mitchell, & Moane, 1984).

Isolation of the Individual

Another, often defining feature of most characterizations of personality is the attempt to separate the individual from the social context (cf., Stewart & Healy, 1989). This feature has many aspects to it, some of which are captured by the emphasis on cross-situational consistency and temporal stability. However, an important part of this normative approach also involves isolating the individual as an independent actor, attributing only to the individual those things that are not somehow dependent on others. So, for example, we rarely characterize people in terms of their characteristic interdependencies, such as the ways in which they work with others who complement their skills or get help from others in constructive ways.

A COGNITIVE–MOTIVATIONAL–SOCIAL BASIS FOR PERSONALITY AND SOCIAL BEHAVIOR

For the most part, therefore, personality psychologists typically characterize individuals in terms of attributes that are simple, general, consistent, stable, and independent of social relationships. This normative approach might profitably be contrasted with an approach that emphasizes what individuals are trying to do, often differently in each new setting and over time, and with the help of others, therein capturing perhaps more of people's opportunistic proclivities.

So the question then becomes, what units of analysis or perspective on personality will be most likely to reveal these opportunistic proclivities? No doubt, there are many such approaches. Personally, I have gravitated to the study of the cognitive bases of personality and social behavior in large part because I believe that the creativity and ingenuity and resilience of individuals often reside in the mind and frequently are imperfectly translated into action (Cantor, 1990; Cantor & Kihlstrom, 1987). As Kelly (1955) so insightfully argued, *constructive alternativism* permits people to construe events, and other people, and even themselves, in a new light, as well as to see things differently than others do.

Of course, the literature also is replete with examples of the ways in which the mind can be doggedly rigid and self-defeating (e.g., Fiske &

Taylor, 1984). Nevertheless, there are important aspects of everyday cognition that do not always get enough emphasis in the literature and that show instead people's ability to imagine and contemplate a different world than the one in which they are currently operating (Bruner, 1986). People's willingness to engage in counterfactual thinking and to construct possibilities for themselves and for others, supplemented by the occasional openness to changing their minds, provides reason to believe that thinking can constructively inform behavior (Cantor, 1990; Fiske, 1992; Markus & Nurius, 1986).

Constructive cognition is especially important because it connects to the motivational bases of social behavior—that is, to what people are trying to do in their daily lives (Snyder & Cantor, 1998). The proclivity to imagine worlds other than those that currently exist, and to take the cognitive perspective of others in ways that open up new possibilities for the self, can energize new strivings, projects, goals, and tasks. This then becomes a basis for individuals' heightened sensitivity to social affordances, so that they look for opportunities to take part in activities and to join groups that foster goal pursuit (Cantor, 1994). The tendency to select and to shape environments to fit personal needs is, for the most part, a human strength that should always be recognized and emphasized (Buss, 1987; Snyder, 1981).

Most social situations afford different specific tasks ideally suited to serve different motivations, as Snyder and his colleagues (e.g., Snyder & Omoto, 1992) have detailed in their analyses of the alternative goals— some more self-interested and some more purely prosocial—at stake in volunteerism. Therefore, there is a great deal of room for opportunism in goal pursuit. And, at its best, constructive cognition mobilizes motivation and guides social behavior toward and within environments that afford personal fulfillment and renewal. What observers of human behavior often lose sight of are the alternative routes that different individuals take toward personally fulfilling ends. By focusing on the process of working on goals —how individuals see their tasks, what they are trying to do, what kinds of social supports they mobilize in the process—it is often possible to see meaning and positive purpose in what may appear to an observer to be at best unnecessary or at worst self-defeating behavior.

As noted previously, the sometimes disparaging view of people in personality psychology may also derive from a perceived mandate to isolate what is characteristic about the person, separating person and context as if in a signal detection analysis of signal and noise. This may be problematic because people are fundamentally social beings (Cantor, 1990; Caporael & Brewer, 1991), interdependent with and even dependent on the talents and supports and behaviors of others (in dyads, in groups, in organizations and collectives), and so much of what people accomplish doesn't stand well on its own. This inherently social and embedded feature of personality and of people implies that a substantial side of human strengths resides in the proclivity and ability to find fulfilling social niches (Cantor, 1994; Snyder & Cantor, 1998)—that is, in individuals' intelligence for seeing how to embed the self in "helpful environments" that facilitate goal pursuit (Cantor & Sanderson, 1999) and how to mix and match individual talent with the skills and attributes of others. Personality psychology may underplay the strengths of individuals by inadequately recognizing their constructive interdependencies with others.

REVEALING HUMAN STRENGTHS

In the service of concretizing this alternative approach, I will briefly describe some examples of ways in which human strengths can be revealed by looking at how people think, what they are trying to do, and how they enlist social and contextual supports in goal pursuit.

Constructive Cognition

One of the signature features of individuals' proclivity for constructive cognition is its creativity, as contrasted with two attributes—accuracy and straightforwardness—that one might instead expect to characterize the strengths of social cognition. In fact, a great deal of what people think about themselves and others is adaptive precisely to the extent that it plays creatively with "reality." For example, there are a host of widely recognized nonconscious cognitive biases that bolster the self and motivation in the face of threats to self-esteem (Kernis, 1995). In this regard, people are decidedly nonaccurate in evaluating their own individual performance (e.g., self-serving attributions) and contributions to group performance (e.g., contribution biases), at least as compared to evaluations from observers or partners. Similarly, people enhance their own positions with downward social comparisons and with other selective interpretations, even when they are in quite trying life circumstances or belong to stigmatized groups (Baumeister, 1998; Crocker & Major, 1989).

Importantly, the creativity of these examples of constructive everyday cognition is not restricted to ostensibly self-enhancing strategies, as Norem and I (e.g., Cantor & Norem, 1989; Norem & Cantor, 1986; Norem & Illingworth, 1993) demonstrated in our work on the strategy of defensive pessimism. Defensive pessimists readily acknowledge their past successes, even as they fully embrace their likelihood of failing at the upcoming task, extensively simulate this worst-case scenario in their minds, and at the same time work hard to avoid a disappointing outcome—thereby ensuring, once again, their success. Their strategy is anything but apparently optimistic or straightforward, but it is quite adaptive and mobilizes motivation for risky tasks. Unlike either self-handicapping or real pessimism, this form of constructive cognition is a positive force, though it certainly doesn't appear as such at first glance. In other words, in considering the effectiveness of cognitive strategies, it is critical not to be taken in by appearances, nor should one expect to straightforwardly equate positivity of outlook with success and negativity with failures.

What is adaptive about constructive cognition is not that it is optimistic in some decontextualized and deindividualized sense, but rather that it serves to mobilize a person's energy to try to do what they want to do in that circumstance. Most of the time, an optimistic outlook does the trick (see Baumeister, 1998), but this is not the case for all individuals and in all contexts. In fact, sometimes the most constructive response is to construe one's current goals as unfeasible to attain and to relinquish them with grace (Brandtstädter & Renner, 1990).

Mobilizing Goals and Seeing Opportunities

Just as a real virtue of everyday social cognition is the proclivity for "creative" construal, it is also critical that individuals be ready to mobilize energy for goal pursuit to meet the particular opportunities that arise in different situations and at different points in the life course (Cantor & Kihlstrom, 1987). This discriminative facility (Mischel, 1973)—that is, sensitively picking up on social affordances across contexts—is a signal human strength that psychologists sometimes underplayed in portrayals of (consistency in) personality. For example, everyday life situations vary a great deal in the profile of behavior commonly observed in them (e.g., libraries are less accepting of loud socializing than are parties), and one signature of dysfunctional behavior is to fail to pick up on these diagnostic affordances, thus perhaps rigidly displaying preferred dispositions under less-than-ideal circumstances (Mischel & Shoda, 1995).

There is also a systematic affordance structure to the tasks that are typically encouraged in different life periods. For example, midlife is frequently seen as a time for career and family, whereas older adulthood sometimes affords more time for community engagement and social and leisure time (Havighurst, 1953). As such, there is often a "right time" to pursue particular goals or tasks, and individuals do better if they can pick up the cues of the "social clock" (Helson et al., 1984). Again, this aspect of individuals' discriminative facility may be missed in analyses of cross-temporal stability in relatively broad dispositions (Costa & McCrae, 1980). This is not to say that dispositional stability is unimportant—in fact, Caspi and Moffitt (1993) argued that individuals' dispositional signatures emerge clearly during periods of life transition—but instead, researchers should also notice individuals' facility for trying new tasks or pursuing familiar goals in new ways across the life course (Cantor et al., 1993).

This latter ability to be opportunistic and discriminative in goal pursuit can contribute substantially to increases in well-being (Cantor & Sanderson, 1999). Harlow and Cantor (1996) observed two forms of well-timed discriminative goal pursuit in a longitudinal analysis of life satisfaction among older adults. In that study, participation in social and community service pursuits contributed significantly to increased life satisfaction among retired (as compared with nonretired) adults. Among the retirees in the sample, there were two patterns of changing participation across time. For some, these social pursuits represented a shift in participation patterns (from a self-directed career focus), producing a new source of life satisfaction in line with the normative affordances of this life stage. Others had always been socially motivated, but in earlier stages they had pursued their motivation through relationships at work and now had shifted to a more explicitly social arena in retirement, also with a resulting boost in life satisfaction. In this latter instance, we saw how discriminative goal pursuit can go hand in hand with continuity in personality and motivation (Sanderson & Cantor, 1999).

Socially Embedded Goals and Behavior

As much as we like to think of personality as residing within the individual, and to think of motivation and goal pursuit as attributes of the person, a great human strength is the propensity for enlisting others in one's projects and the ability to embed oneself in supportive environments with others whose talents complement one's own. The literature on social support amply documents the benefits for well-being of both receiving (e.g., Cutrona, 1986) and giving (e.g., Brickman & Coates, 1987) support, and it also shows individuals' sensitivity and intelligence in their choices of supporters, supportees, and partners. What is in some sense most remarkable about this aspect of social intelligence is its routineness in daily life; that is, people turn to the right people at the right time for support, for example, amidst the normal fluctuations of daily hassles and uplifts (e.g., Folkman & Lazarus, 1985; Langston, 1994).

As an example of this social sensitivity and intelligence, Harlow and Cantor (1995) used daily experience sampling of emotions, social interactions, and goal pursuits to show that when participants' social pursuits went poorly, they differed systematically in terms of the types of people to whom they turned for support and social contact. Not only were these differentiated patterns of support seeking systematic, they were also sensible in light of the particular goals of the individuals. Specifically, participants who were focused on the outcomes of their social pursuits looked for emotional support when things went poorly, whereas participants who were eager for improvement in their social lives turned to others who personified their ideals and who therefore could provide informational support at times of distress. Most importantly, these differentiated and sensitive patterns of reassurance seeking occurred in a very "natural" way, without prompting or intervention, in the course of busy daily life pursuits.

Similar instances of "social intelligence" can be observed in the more consequential choices that individuals make to help others and to "partner" with others in their sustained life task pursuits. For example, Snyder and his colleagues (e.g., Omoto & Snyder, 1990; Snyder, 1993) have shown a close link between the nature of individuals' motives for volunteerism and the type of volunteer role they pursue. If someone does volunteer work to meet prosocial motives, then a role that involves providing direct help and support to others will be most attractive, whereas someone who strives for self-recognition may prefer to take on a supervisory role in a volunteer organization to meet their needs and still help others. Sanderson and Cantor (e.g., 1995, 1997) observed a related form of complementarity between college students' personal goals and their preferences for dating. Students with relatively strong needs for interpersonal intimacy gravitated toward and derived more satisfaction from steady dating relationships, whereas more self- and identity-focused students preferred exploring multiple dating partners. Thus, people sustain both volunteering and dating engagements better and longer when they have chosen goal-congruent roles and partners.

Of course, sometimes there is little room for such fine-tuned preference seeking, and/or one may purposely choose to try something a bit outside one's comfort zone. Under those circumstances, it is a sign of intelligence to willingly take the lead of others and to rely more assertively on the affordances in the situation. For example, Sanderson and Cantor (1997) found that once in steady dating relationships, individuals who themselves did not possess strong intimacy goals were especially dependent on social affordances, such as time alone with the partner or support giving from the partner, to derive relationship satisfaction and in the maintenance of their relationships. That is, individuals who were relatively less inclined themselves to focus on and elicit intimacy prospered much more in their close relationships when they could be in situations in which opportunities for intimacy were available to them. As Miller (1990) suggested, for example, partners in relationships can go a long way to set up the context for intimacy so as to elicit relationship-strengthening actions (e.g., self-disclosure) from their mate. Hence, another important side of social intelligence and a distinct human strength rests in how individuals embed themselves within personally fulfilling and supportive social relationships, be it in dyads or groups or in institutions (Snyder & Cantor, 1998).

THE PERSONALITY GLASS: HALF FULL AND HALF EMPTY

In summary, I see human strengths in people's capacities for constructive cognition, for trying to reach goals and seizing opportunities to do so, and for interacting in a social world in ways that can support and complement the self. Of course, it is also important to take note of the ways in which such capacities can mislead and deter people from reaching their goals. Again, the capacity for constructive cognition can be very adaptive when individuals use their personal constructs (Kelly, 1955) to take control and to navigate in their world. Conversely, it can mislead them about the complexity of the world, constraining their vision of what is necessary to do to reach a goal and perhaps leading them to fail to be alert to novel opportunities for goal fulfillment. Cantor and Kihlstrom (1987) referred to this as the "double-edged sword of social intelligence." By building up expertise about the social world and about the self, people free themselves from the strain of deliberation at every turn. On the other hand, they also often narrow their vision to the familiar, seeing more of what they expect to see than might be good for them. And to the extent that, optimally, constructive cognition can mobilize motivation and heighten sensitivity to opportunities in the social environment, then narrowing one's horizons is not altogether good.

Whereas responding effortlessly (and thus mindlessly) in familiar arenas of expertise can free cognitive capacity for attunement to opportunities in the social environment, it is not always the case that people take advantage of this freedom to explore. Sometimes they are cognitively—and motivationally—lulled by the ease of continuing to see, to strive for, and to do the familiar, and their engagements with the same people and groups reinforce these routines. As such, it is possible to have too much expertise and security, to be too insulated and thus not sufficiently opportunistic. At other times, people get too opportunistic, setting goals and taking risks that are, by any standard, out of reach and failing to see when they should relinquish them in favor of more feasible pursuits.

In these regards, however, I would say that if psychologists pay more attention to human strengths—for example, to constructive cognition, to what people are trying to do, and to how they embed themselves in situations and with others—we will also see some of these human frailties, and the glass will be both half full and half empty. By contrast, as I suggested at the outset, our more typical analyses of personality have tended, instead, to a more one-dimensional (albeit quite coherent) portrayal of individuals' central tendencies as functional or dysfunctional, intelligent or not, good or bad. This happens, I believe, because we focus narrowly on the outcomes of people's efforts (rather than their strivings), on their general tendencies aggregated over time and place (rather than on their discriminative facilities), and on people by themselves (rather than on the network of social affordances on which they intelligently rely).

A fuller, more differentiated portrait of people would most likely reveal instead both the strengths and the frailties, the good and the bad, as they vary from person to person and across the contexts within which these pluses and minuses emerge, thus pointing the way to arenas worthy of personal effort and intervention for the better. Researchers already know a great deal about how to uncover these more differentiated personal portraits; we just need to start looking for them more regularly. A focus on human strengths may well induce us to do just that.

REFERENCES

Baumeister, R. F. (1998). The self. In D. T. Gilbert, S. T. Fiske, & G. Lindzey (Eds.), *The handbook of social psychology* (4th ed., Vol. 1, pp. 680–740). New York: McGraw-Hill.

Brandtstädter, J., & Renner, G. (1990). Tenacious goal pursuit and flexible goal adjustment: Explication and age-related analysis of assimilative and accommodative strategies of coping. *Psychology and Aging, 5,* 58–67.

Brickman, P., & Coates, D. (1987). Commitment and mental health. In P. Brickman (Ed.), *Commitment, conflict, and caring* (pp. 222–309). Englewood Cliffs, NJ: Prentice Hall.

Bruner, J. S. (1986). *Actual minds, possible worlds.* Cambridge, MA: Harvard University Press.

Buss, D. (1987). Selection, evocation, and manipulation. *Journal of Personality and Social Psychology, 53,* 1214–1221.

Cantor, N. (1990). From thought to behavior: "Having" and "doing" in the study of personality and cognition. *American Psychologist, 45,* 735–750.

Cantor, N. (1994). Life task problem-solving: Situational affordances and personal needs. *Personality and Social Psychology Bulletin, 20,* 235–243.

Cantor, N., & Kihlstrom, J. F. (1987). *Personality and social intelligence.* Englewood Cliffs, NJ: Prentice Hall.

Cantor, N., & Norem, J. K. (1989). Defensive pessimism and stress and coping. *Social Cognition, 7,* 92–112.

Cantor, N., & Sanderson, C. A. (1999). Life task participation and well-being: The importance of taking part in daily life. In D. Kahneman, E. Diener, & N. Schwarz (Eds.), *Well-being: The foundations of hedonic psychology* (pp. 230–243). New York: Russell Sage.

Cantor, N., Zirkel, S., & Norem, J. K. (1993). Human personality: Asocial and reflexive? *Psychological Inquiry, 4,* 273–277.

Caporael, L. R., & Brewer, M. B. (1991). Reviving evolutionary psychology: Biology meets society. *Journal of Social Issues, 47*(3), 187–195.

Caspi, A., & Moffitt, T. E. (1993). When do individual differences matter? A paradoxical theory of personality coherence. *Psychological Inquiry, 4,* 247–271.

Costa, P. T., & McCrae, R. R. (1980). Still stable after all these years: Personality as a key to some issues in adulthood and old age. In P. B. Baltes & O. G. Brim, Jr. (Eds.), *Life span development and behavior* (Vol. 3, pp. 65–102). New York: Academic Press.

Crocker, J., & Major, B. (1989). Social stigma and self-esteem: The self-protective properties of stigma. *Psychological Review, 96,* 608–630.

Cutrona, C. E. (1986). Behavioral manifestations of social support: A microanalytic investigation. *Journal of Personality and Social Psychology, 51,* 201–208.

Fiske, S. T. (1992). Thinking is for doing: Portraits of social cognition from daguerreotype to laserphoto. *Journal of Personality and Social Psychology, 63,* 877–889.

Fiske, S. T., & Taylor, S. E. (1984). *Social cognition.* New York: McGraw-Hill.

Folkman, S., & Lazarus, R. S. (1985). If it changes it must be a process: Study of emotion and coping during three stages of a college examination. *Journal of Personality and Social Psychology, 48,* 150–170.

Harlow, R. E., & Cantor, N. (1995). To whom do people turn when things go poorly? Task orientation and functional social contacts. *Journal of Personality and Social Psychology, 69,* 329–340.

Harlow, R. E., & Cantor, N. (1996). Still participating after all these years: A study of life task participation in later life. *Journal of Personality and Social Psychology, 71,* 1235–1249.

Havighurst, R. J. (1953). *Human development and education.* New York: Longmans, Green, & Co.

Helson, R., Mitchell, V., & Moane, G. (1984). Personality and patterns of adherence and nonadherence to the social clock. *Journal of Personality and Social Psychology, 46,* 1079–1096.

Kelly, G. A. (1955). *The psychology of personal constructs.* New York: Norton.

Kernis, M. H. (1995). *Efficacy, agency, and self-esteem.* New York: Plenum.

Langston, C. A. (1994). Capitalizing upon and coping with daily-life events: Expressive responses to positive events. *Journal of Personality and Social Psychology, 67,* 1112–1125.

Markus, H. R., & Nurius, P. S. (1986). Possible selves. *American Psychologist, 41,* 954–961.

Miller, L. C. (1990). Intimacy and liking: Mutual influence and the role of unique relationships. *Journal of Personality and Social Psychology, 59,* 50–60.

Mischel, W. (1973). Toward a cognitive social learning reconceptualization of personality. *Psychological Review, 80,* 253–283.

Mischel, W. (1999). Personality coherence and dispositions in a cognitive-affective personality (CAPS) approach. In D. Cervone & Y. Shoda (Eds.), *The coherence of personality: Social-cognitive bases of consistency, variability, and organization* (pp. 37–60). New York: Guilford.

Mischel, W., & Shoda, Y. (1995). A cognitive-affective system theory of personality: Reconceptualizing situations, dispositions, dynamics, and invariance in personality structure. *Psychological Review, 102,* 246–268.

Norem, J. K., & Cantor, N. (1986). Defensive pessimism: "Harnessing" anxiety as motivation. *Journal of Personality and Social Psychology, 51,* 1208–1217.

Norem, J. K., & Illingworth, K. S. (1993). Strategy-dependent effects of reflecting on self and tasks: Some implications of optimism and defensive pessimism. *Journal of Personality and Social Psychology, 65,* 822–835.

Omoto, A. M., & Snyder, M. (1990). Basic research in action: Volunteerism and society's response to AIDS. *Personality and Social Psychology Bulletin, 16,* 152–165.

Sanderson, C. A., & Cantor, N. (1995). Social dating goals in late adolescence: Implications for safer sexual activity. *Journal of Personality and Social Psychology, 68,* 1121–1134.

Sanderson, C. A., & Cantor, N. (1997). Creating satisfaction in steady dating relationships: The role of personal goals and situational affordances. *Journal of Personality and Social Psychology, 73,* 1424–1433.

Sanderson, C. A., & Cantor, N. (1999). A life task perspective on personality coherence: Stability versus change in tasks, goals, strategies, and outcomes. In D. Cervone & Y. Shoda (Eds.), *The coherence of personality: Social-cognitive bases of consistency, variability, and organization* (pp. 372–394). New York: Guilford Press.

Shoda, Y. (1999). Behavioral expressions of a personality system: Generation and perception of behavioral signatures. In D. Cervone & Y. Shoda (Eds.), *The coherence of personality: Social-cognitive bases of consistency, variability, and organization* (pp. 155–184). New York: Guilford Press.

Snyder, M. (1981). On the influence of individuals on situations. In N. Cantor & J. F. Kihlstrom (Eds.), *Personality, cognition, and social interaction* (pp. 309–329). Hillsdale, NJ: Erlbaum.

Snyder, M. (1993). Basic research and practical problems: The promise of a "functional" personality and social psychology. *Personality and Social Psychology Bulletin, 19,* 251–264.

Snyder, M., & Cantor, N. (1998). Understanding personality and social behavior: A functionalist strategy. In D. T. Gilbert, S. T. Fiske, & G. Lindzey (Eds.), *The handbook of social psychology* (4th ed., Vol. 1, 635–679). New York: McGraw-Hill.

Snyder, M., & Omoto, A. M. (1992). Volunteerism and society's response to the HIV epidemic. *Current Directions in Psychological Science, 1*(6), 113–116.

Stewart, A. J., & Healy, J. M., Jr. (1989). Linking individual development and social change. *American Psychologist, 44,* 30–42.

5

A CONCEPTION OF PERSONALITY FOR A PSYCHOLOGY OF HUMAN STRENGTHS: PERSONALITY AS AN AGENTIC, SELF-REGULATING SYSTEM

GIAN VITTORIO CAPRARA AND DANIEL CERVONE

Appeals for a psychology of human strengths commonly are introduced with a lament. The discipline of psychology, writers complain, has overemphasized human vulnerability, frailty, and vice. It thus has deflected attention from human resilience, hardiness, and virtue.

This argument has much validity, despite the many lines of theory and research that have explored human strengths over the years. A key question, however, is not just the degree to which vulnerabilities have been overemphasized in the past; a broader question is why research programs might overrepresent a select subset of the human experience. Why do research trends so rarely capture a broad representation of human proclivities and potentials?

One answer to this question is that research programs commonly are not embedded within a comprehensive portrait of human nature. Investigators frequently study isolated variables without locating these constructs in a broad network of determinants of psychological functioning (cf. Magnusson, 1999). A challenge for a psychology of human strengths is to avoid this narrow focus. Although investigators of the past quarter century may have overestimated human vulnerabilities, the solution to this problem is not for investigators of the next quarter century to overestimate human strengths. The "swinging pendulum" approach can be avoided by centering research on human strengths within an integrated, comprehensive model of the person.

PERSONALITY PSYCHOLOGY'S MODELS OF THE PERSON

The subdiscipline of psychology that is most directly charged with providing a model of the person is personality psychology. A basic claim of this chapter is that recent advances in personality psychology (Caprara & Cervone, 2000) do, indeed, yield a comprehensive portrait of the individual that can inform, and profitably guide, a psychology of human strengths.

This claim may at first seem unwarranted. Personality psychology currently contains popular theoretical frameworks that seem to say more about human limitations than potentials. In some views, personality consists of inherited dispositional tendencies that exhibit little change across the life course (Costa & McCrae, 1994). In others, the mind is composed of evolved, domain-specific mechanisms whose basic structure and functioning similarly are fixed across the course of life, even if environmental inputs may alter the threshold of activation of a given mechanism (Buss, 1999). In such views, personality is determined primarily by genetic endowment. People appear to have little potential to develop their capacities in a self-directed manner.

Despite their popularity, however, these particular theoretical views are only a narrow segment of the overall trends in personality psychology in recent years. Much work provides a more uplifting perspective on the human capacity for positive self-direction. This work is grounded in an analysis of the nature of the causal processes that underlie the development of the individual.

Person–Situation Reciprocity

People do not develop according to fixed paths that are determined by a genetic blueprint. Personality develops through more complex causal processes that feature dynamic transactions between people and the socio-cultural environment (e.g., Baltes, Lindenberger, & Staudinger, 1998; Caspi, 1998). Internal personality factors, overt behavior, and the social environment reciprocally determine one another (Bandura, 1986, 1999). This claim is supported by numerous longitudinal studies of personality development. Findings reveal that a complex—yet understandable—matrix of personal, interpersonal, and sociocultural factors determines the psychological qualities of the individual.

To take but one example (Magnusson, 1992; see also Magnusson & Mahoney, chapter 16, this volume), adolescent girls who experience relatively early biological maturation are more likely to experience problem behavior (e.g., truancy, drunkenness). The effects of biology, however, are neither direct, nor inevitable, nor enduring. Early maturing girls develop different peer relations, and these interpersonal relations are found to be more direct determinants of self-image and behavior in adolescence. Later in life, as interpersonal relations change, few differences between early and late maturers are found (Magnusson, 1992). The study of such interactions among biology, interpersonal relations, and behavior helps one to understand why individuals are highly resilient to long-term effects of even severe negative experiences that may occur at a particular age of development (see also Kagan, 1998). Human strengths, then, reside partly in the interpersonal nets that nurture the resilient qualities of the individual.

At this point in the history of personality psychology, person–situation reciprocity is so well documented and widely recognized that reciprocal interactionism functions as a metatheoretical principle that organizes much of the theoretical and empirical work in the field (Caprara & Cervone, 2000). This viewpoint is bolstered by numerous findings outside of personality psychology per se. Neural systems are found to display extraordinary plasticity in the face of new behavioral experiences (Garraghty, Churchill, & Banks, 1998; Kolb & Whishaw, 1998). Gene expression is influenced by environmental factors that affect hormone levels and the cytoplasm of cells (Gottlieb, 1998). Humans evolved through a "coevolutionary" process in which biological and cultural factors shaped one another (Durham, 1991). Lewontin (2000) compellingly argued that reciprocal transactions between organisms and the environment are a basic feature of biological life. All organisms, he stressed, partly construct their environments.

The Self-System and Personal Agency

In the case of human development, the general biological capacity to construct one's environment is combined with the unique human capacities to anticipate future contingencies and to reflect on one's capability to cope with them. These capacities for forethought and self-reflection underpin a most central aspect of personality functioning—namely, people's ability to exert intentional influence over, or to "self-regulate," their experiences and actions.

The capacity for self-regulation rests on a number of distinct component processes. These include the abilities to evaluate one's action in relation to internalized standards of performance, to plan and to set goals for the future, to assess one's personal efficacy for upcoming challenges, and to motivate one's actions through affective self-evaluation, especially feelings of pride versus dissatisfaction with current and prospective attainments. These distinct self-regulatory mechanisms are functionally interrelated. They thus do not operate as independent influences on behavior, but as parts of a coherent psychological system through which people regulate their emotions and actions (Caprara & Cervone, 2000). Extensive bodies of theory and research have explored the development and functioning of the self-system (Bandura, 1986; Boekaerts, Pintrich, & Zeidner, 2000; Carver & Scheier, 1998; Deci & Ryan, 1985; Harter, 1999; Higgins, 1999; Mischel, Cantor, & Feldman, 1996; Schunk & Zimmerman, 1998).

The analysis of self-regulatory processes has a major implication for an overall view of the nature of personality: Personality need not be viewed as a collection of biologically determined tendencies or evolved modules. Such views underestimate human strengths by implicitly depicting persons as passive carriers of a predetermined personality structure. Instead, the study of self-regulatory processes, and of reciprocal relations between the self-regulating individual and the social environment, indicates that people contribute agentically to the development of their personalities. People are not passive. They are proactive. By selecting, interpreting, and influencing the environments they encounter, people contribute to the development of their own capacities and tendencies. Personality itself, then, can be conceptualized as an agentic, self-regulatory system (Bandura, 1999, 2001; Caprara & Cervone, 2000). In this view, people are proactive agents who are capable of planfully making things happen by their own actions.

In an agentic view, a basic goal of personality psychology is to shed light on the self-regulatory processes through which people contribute to their experiences and personal development. This goal cannot be achieved by studying individuals in isolation. Instead, one must study people in context (e.g., Cervone, Shadel, & Jencius, 2001), including an analysis of environmental settings and interpersonal relations that promote the development of the self-system. Such an agenda obviously speaks directly to a psychology of human strengths. Interestingly, it does not do so by asking whether one or another isolated individual-difference variable is related to effective functioning. Instead, it takes up the question of how a dynamic, interactive system of personal qualities contributes to human self-direction and resilience. By providing a coherent, system-level view of the individual, personality psychology may help the psychology of human strengths to avoid a narrow focus that illuminates only isolated aspects of human experience.

It is of note that viewing personality as an agentic, self-regulating system speaks not only to a psychology of human strengths, but also to the traditional agenda of personality psychology. The psychological structures that form the self-regulatory system are enduring personality factors that contribute to the coherence of personality functioning and to stable differences among individuals (see Cervone & Shoda, 1999b; Mischel & Shoda, 1998).

The nature of personality and its agentic functions must be considered in light of recent evidence from cultural psychology. Conceptions of personal agency vary across cultures (Kitayama & Markus, 1999; Markus, Kitayama, & Heiman, 1996). People in European and American societies appear more oriented toward self-enhancement, personal achievement, and personal control than people in Asian cultures, for whom social obligations and group-level accomplishments are more salient. This, however, does not imply that people in Eastern cultures have little capacity for self-regulation and personal agency, but merely that the aims of their actions and the role of specific self-referent beliefs in motivation may vary from one culture to another. People with communal goals may exert much self-control in an effort to reach these aims.

Potentials

An agentic view of personality highlights the fact that personality psychology must include the study of not only habitual dispositions, but also individual potentials (Caprara, 1999; Caprara & Cervone, 2000). Personality psychologists have the responsibility to address the personal and social processes that can contribute to the full expression of human capacities.

The inclusion of potentials in the discipline of personality psychology goes beyond the focus on static dispositions or traits that have dominated the recent history of the discipline (Cervone & Shoda, 1999a). It surely is important to assess what people typically "are like," that is, their typical dispositions. However, it is of equal importance to explore what they can become. Society demands that personality psychology contribute not only to the assessment of individual differences but also to the development of individual potentials. Boykin (1994) compellingly advanced this point in discussing the educational attainments of African American youths: "We must shift from a preoccupation with talent assessment . . . [to] a commitment to talent development. . . . [This] will require a fundamental change in . . . how we conceptualize the individual" (p. 119). His point applies not only to the study of intellectual capacities, but to the study of the whole person.

A potentialist view goes hand in hand with the focus on reciprocal interactionism noted earlier. People may possess potentials that can be realized only as they act within particular environments. Kagan (1998) provided an apt analogy: A rock lying at the bottom of a lake belongs to the category "potentially dangerous object." Its "dangerousness" is not an inherent, isolated property of the rock itself (as is its mass or hardness). Instead, dangerousness is a relational quality. It describes the relation between the rock and particular settings (e.g., being thrown indoors). Similarly, many psychological qualities are not inherent properties of isolated minds or brains. Instead, they are relational, in that the expression of the quality requires a social setting that elicits, supports, or requires the quality in question. One cannot be "sociable" by oneself. Many readers of this text are "potentially great parents," although that quality may not yet have expressed itself.

A focus on potentials erodes the traditional distinction between nature and nurture. As many investigators now realize, "nature" and "nurture" are not distinct opposing forces. Biology and experience influence one another. The nature of this influence must be given particular attention in a modern world that features rapid changes brought by technological innovation. The traditional dimensions of human life associated with the categories of time and space have dramatically changed due to the prolonged length of life, the speed of social movement, and the multiplicity of interpersonal encounters people experience. As new opportunities are made available, new problems arise and new decisions are required for which established capacities are outmoded. Thus, nature has to be nurtured to meet the challenges of modernity. People's immense potential to manage new environments must be fostered by novel methods of promoting personal growth. The rapidly changing world requires that people develop new visions and capacities to deal with the outer world and themselves.

The control people may exert over the environment and themselves becomes particularly critical in an age in which people are able to extend their control over evolutionary processes through biotechnologies. The ability to exert control over one's own biology and that of one's offspring heightens the impact of personal psychological qualities on one's biological being. Self-directedness and personal choice come to govern domains that, throughout all prior stages of human history, were products of chance and necessity.

SELF-REFLECTIVE CAPABILITIES AS THE CORE OF HUMAN STRENGTHS

A psychology that can promote the realization of potentials and the development of human strengths must focus heavily on self-reflective capacities. Consciousness is at the heart of prediction, control, and people's ability to plan in a generative manner for the future. Consciousness enables people to contemplate and predict the behavior of others and themselves (Humphrey, 1984). It allows people to plan courses of action and gauge their capacity to act. People often face novel challenges that might, in principle, be solved if one could optimally orchestrate one's skills. The organism "may have resources in it that would be very valuable in the circumstances *if only it could find them and put them to use in time!*" (Dennett, 1991, p. 222). Conscious reasoning about a problem enables people to anticipate challenges and to maximize their personal resources and chances for success. As Bandura (2001) put it, "consciousness is the very substance of mental life that not only makes life personally manageable but worth living" (p. 3). What ultimately matters is the quality of consciousness, especially whether one's conscious thoughts are full of fear and preoccupation or of hope and trust.

Perceived Self-Efficacy

A critical aspect of self-reflection involves people's reflection on their capabilities for action. This aspect of mental life is studied most directly in research on perceived self-efficacy (Bandura, 1997). Self-efficacy beliefs are a central feature of human strengths and potentials for a number of reasons. First, self-efficacy perceptions directly contribute to decisions, actions, and experiences. People who doubt their efficacy for performance tend to avoid challenges, to abandon activities when faced with setbacks, and to experience debilitating anxiety (Bandura, 1997). Second, self-efficacy beliefs influence other cognitive and emotional factors that, in turn, contribute to performance. People with higher efficacy beliefs tend to commit themselves to more challenging goals (Locke & Latham, 1990), to attribute positive outcomes to stable and controllable factors (McAuley, Duncan, & McElroy, 1989), and to develop superior strategies for coping with highly complex tasks (Cervone, Jiwani, & Wood, 1991). A third consideration is that self-efficacy perceptions may moderate the impact of other variables that have the potential to enhance achievement. The acquisition of skills and knowledge enhances achievement, but not if people so doubt their capabilities that they fail to put their knowledge into practice.

Though often studied in achievement contexts, self-efficacy perceptions also are crucial to interpersonal behavior and experience. Findings reveal that beliefs in one's efficacy to regulate emotional experiences directly influence rates of depression and prosocial behavior. Further, people's perceptions of self-efficacy for regulating emotions influence their appraisals of their capabilities for effective interpersonal functioning, which, in turn, contribute to rates of prosocial behavior, antisocial behavior, and depression (Caprara, Scabini, et al., 1999).

The social-cognitive analysis of self-efficacy processes also facilitates the psychology of human strengths by providing concrete tools for boosting self-efficacy beliefs and achievement. A wealth of research documents that the most reliable way of instilling self-confidence is through firsthand success experiences (Bandura, 1997). The personal experience of mastery is difficult to deny, even among individuals who typically doubt their performance capabilities. Novel experiences of mastery in domains of personal significance have the potential to generalize to diverse life domains and thus to have a broad-based impact on people's lives (Weitlauf, Cervone, & Smith, 2001; Weitlauf, Smith, & Cervone, 2000).

The Role of Collective Efficacy

Psychological strengths cannot be understood by viewing individuals in isolation. A great many of the capacities that we call human strengths derive from the strengths of the communities in which people live. This raises the question of the psychological mechanisms that mediate the influence of community factors on individual actions. Recent work has highlighted the mediating influence of collective efficacy—that is, people's beliefs in the ability of their surrounding social group to function in a cohesive and effective manner in accomplishing group goals. Sampson and colleagues' analysis of neighborhood characteristics, collective efficacy, and violent crime is exemplary (Sampson, Raudenbush, & Earls, 1997). The effects of neighborhood characteristics (involving poverty, immigration, and residential stability) on violent crime were found to be mediated heavily by people's beliefs that their community was a socially cohesive setting in which community members would intervene to maintain social order when necessary.

More recent work has explored how appraisals of personal efficacy can influence perceptions of collective efficacy (Fernández-Ballesteros, Diez-Nicolás, Caprara, Barbaranelli, & Bandura, 2002). In this work, participants rated Personal Efficacy beliefs—that is, their capability to manage common, daily demands involving family, work, finances, and health. They also judged their Individual Social Efficacy, or their efficacy in contributing to improvements in social problems such as terrorism, unemployment, corruption, crime, and economic crises. Finally, they also indicated their Collective Efficacy beliefs—that is, their perceptions of the capability of society as a whole to effect desired improvement in major societal conditions. Results suggested that Personal and Individual Social efficacy beliefs influenced their Collective Efficacy beliefs. It is likely that perceived self-efficacy for managing daily demands contributes most to personal efficacy in being able to contribute to society, whereas personal efficacy in improving social conditions affects collective efficacy beliefs.

In organizational settings, both personal and collective efficacy beliefs are critical to indicators of motivation such as commitment, job involvement, and satisfaction. It is likely that self-efficacy beliefs influence individuals' construals of an organization, including its main figures, roles, operations, and relationships. Individuals with higher perceptions of personal efficacy may select more effective organizations, contribute more actively to their functioning, and perceive organizational operations and relationships more positively. In a study involving more than 600 junior high school teachers from Rome and Milan, efficacy beliefs were found to influence directly climate perception, collective efficacy, work commitment, and job involvement and satisfaction (Caprara, Borgogni, Barbaranelli, & Rubinacci, 1999). Although commitment has often been highlighted as a main determinant of job involvement and satisfaction, people have no reason to feel committed to an organization if they do not relate to its goals. Collective efficacy, specifically the firm and shared belief in the ability to master collective goals through concerted knowledge and action, proved to be a critical determinant of organizational commitment and a mediator of the influence of personal self-efficacy beliefs on commitment, and through commitment on job involvement and satisfaction.

A PSYCHOLOGY OF HUMAN STRENGTHS IN A NEW MILLENNIUM

The challenge of personality psychology is to address the complex interplay among multiple biological and sociostructural constituents of human functioning and to do so while promoting people's capacities for intentional and responsible actions. As we have stressed, this requires a psychology of personality that illuminates the personal determinants of action that enable people to take control of their lives and adapt to a rapidly changing world.

In the new millennium, technological innovation, market globalization, and multiculturalism are not merely terms in vogue. They are very real components of modern life. Technological innovations are changing the lives of people at an unprecedented rate. New information and communication technologies are tools through which people may act to maximize their individual choice and opportunities for personal growth. These technologies provide broad access to knowledge and education while also creating new interpersonal bonds, new communities, and new forms of collective consciousness by spreading ideas, values, and styles that often supplant traditional ones.

Global market forces are restructuring national economies with a tremendous impact on social policies, work organization, and governmental leadership, as well as on relations among generations. Massive migrations are changing the ethnic compositions of populations, with societies becoming less distinctive and cultures no longer insular. Such changes open tremendous opportunities for the extension of personal freedom and growth. Simultaneously, they place greater burden on individuals for their own success, as life paths are less strongly determined by social class and rank and are less predictable than in the past. The more people are able to master the challenges of their own lives in selecting and construing the environments conducive to the maximization of their potentialities, the higher their probability of success will be. Technological changes require self-directed lifelong learning that, if pursued, can enable people to cope with change and to capitalize on occupational opportunities.

In a highly interconnected world, social pursuits related to the protection of human rights and the promotion of communal well-being require shared commitments and concerted efforts. The more people can mobilize and coordinate their efforts and resources in the service of shared goals, the more they will experience latitude of freedom and opportunity and, in this sense, justice (Rawls, 1971). To these aims, the contribution of psychology in general, and personality psychology in particular, may be critical in that this field can supply knowledge that can contribute to the creation of new psychosocial technologies that, in turn, can help people to acquire the skills, beliefs, goals, and conduct that enable them to exert greater control over their lives. Thanks to the spread of the Internet, these technologies increasingly involve the creation of communication networks through which people can mobilize to promote educational, interpersonal, occupational, or political goals. The creation of these networks and pursuit of these goals often require not only a robust sense of personal efficacy, but also confidence that the collective group of which one is a part can achieve its purposes.

To make this contribution, personality psychology, and psychology as a whole, need to follow a somewhat different path than ones that have often prevailed in the past. Psychologists have commonly embraced models of human nature in which internal mental structures and overt actions are determined by preformed essential qualities that unfold in a fixed manner in the course of development, exerting control from within to the world without. Today science increasingly recognizes that heredity does not provide a fixed blueprint for life, but rather a vast range of potentialities that are realized only through interactions with the environment. The environment—as selected, interpreted, and transformed by the individual—plays a decisive role in the development of inner strengths.

Throughout much of its history, personality psychology has been concerned with individual differences in what may be termed "surface tendencies," that is, observable variations in styles of behavior. Ultimately, one must identify the psychological mechanisms that underlie patterns of individual differences and intraindividual coherence—that is, the proximal and remote determinants of those patterns and their modes of operating. The pursuit of underlying mechanisms illuminates the causal processes and structures that subserve human capacities and that are the repository of human potentialities.

Psychologists have mostly addressed the dark side of human behavior —failure, despair, pathology, violence—by focusing on the struggle between the opposing constraints and demands of nature and culture. Today it seems reasonable to complement the traditional reparatory and compensatory views with one that aims to maximize the opportunities provided by both culture and nature. Knowledge of the determinants and mechanisms of personality functioning can enable psychology to expand the control people may exert over their own lives and thus contribute to human freedom and to individual and collective welfare. The compelling tasks for the field are to extend the horizons of human capacity and thereby grant people greater ability to adapt to the world's rapidly changing contingencies and demands.

Taking a potentialist view does not lead one to neglect the miseries of the human condition, however. One must recognize that people's inherent capacity for self-regulation may be thwarted by economic or sociopolitical conditions that fail to support individuals' efforts to realize their capacities (Cervone & Rafaeli-Mor, 1999). A potentialist view does, however, lead one to reconsider the possibilities of individual development and to explore the conditions that promote the full expression of human capabilities.

REFERENCES

Baltes, P. B., Lindenberger, U., & Staudinger, U. (1998). Life-span theory in developmental psychology. In W. Damon (Series Ed.) & R. Lerner (Vol. Ed.), *Handbook of child psychology: Vol. 1. Theoretical models of human development* (5th ed., pp. 1029–1144). New York: Wiley.

Bandura, A. (1986). *Social foundations of thought and action.* Englewood Cliffs, NJ: Prentice Hall.

Bandura, A. (1997). *Self-efficacy: The exercise of control.* New York: Freeman.

Bandura, A. (1999). Social cognitive theory of personality. In D. Cervone & Y. Shoda (Eds.), *The coherence of personality: Social-cognitive bases of consistency, variability, and organization* (pp. 185–241). New York: Guilford Press.

Bandura, A. (2001). Social cognitive theory: An agentic perspective. *Annual Review of Psychology, 52,* 1–26.

Boekaerts, M., Pintrich, P. R., & Zeidner, M. (Eds.). (2000). *Handbook of self-regulation.* San Diego, CA: Academic Press.

Boykin, A. W. (1994). Harvesting talent and culture: African-American children and educational reform. In R. Rossi (Ed.), *Schools and students at risk* (pp. 116–138). New York: Teachers College Press.

Buss, D. (1999). *Evolutionary psychology: The new science of the mind.* Boston: Allyn & Bacon.

Caprara, G. V. (1999). The notion of personality: Historical and recent perspectives. *European Review, 1,* 127–137.

Caprara, G.V., Borgogni, L., Barbaranelli, C., & Rubinacci, A. (1999). Convinzioni di efficacia e cambiamento organizzativo [Efficacy beliefs and organizational change]. *Sviluppo e Organizzazione* [Development and Organization], *174*, 19–32.

Caprara, G. V., & Cervone, D. (2000). *Personality: Determinants, dynamics, and potentials.* New York: Cambridge University Press.

Caprara, G. V., Scabini, E., Barbaranelli, C., Pastorelli, C., Regalia, C., & Bandura, A. (1999). Autoefficacia percepita emotiva e interpersonale e buon funzionamento sociale. [Perceived emotional and interpersonal self-efficacy and good social functioning.] *Giornale Italiano di Psicologia, 26,* 769–789.

Carver, C. S., & Scheier, M. F. (1998). *On the self-regulation of behavior.* New York: Cambridge University Press.

Caspi, A. (1998). Personality development across the life course. In W. Damon (Series Ed.) & N. Eisenberg (Vol. Ed.), *Handbook of child development: Vol. 3. Emotional and personality development* (5th ed., pp. 311–388). New York: Wiley.

Cervone, D., Jiwani, N., & Wood, R. (1991). Goal-setting and the differential influence of self-regulatory processes on complex decision-making performance. *Journal of Personality and Social Psychology, 61,* 257–266.

Cervone, D., & Rafaeli-Mor, N. (1999). Living in the future in the past: On the origin and expression of self-regulatory abilities. *Psychological Inquiry, 10,* 209–213.

Cervone, D., Shadel, W. G., & Jencius, S. (2001). Social-cognitive theory of personality assessment. *Personality and Social Psychology Review, 5,* 33–51.

Cervone, D., & Shoda, Y. (1999a). Beyond traits in the study of personality coherence. *Current Directions in Psychological Science, 8,* 27–32.

Cervone, D., & Shoda, Y. (Eds.). (1999b). *The coherence of personality: Social-cognitive bases of consistency, variability, and organization.* New York: Guilford Press.

Costa, P. T., & McCrae, R. R. (1994). Set like plaster? Evidence for the stability of the adult personality. In T. F. Heatheron & J. L. Weinberger (Eds.), *Can personality change?* (pp. 21–40). Washington, DC: American Psychological Association.

Deci, E., & Ryan, R. (1985). *Intrinsic motivation and self determination in human behavior.* New York: Plenum Press.

Dennett, D. C. (1991). *Consciousness explained.* Boston: Little Brown.

Durham, W. H. (1991). *Coevolution.* Stanford, CA: Stanford University Press.

Fernández-Ballesteros, R., Diez-Nicolás, J., Caprara, G. V., Barbaranelli, C., & Bandura, A. (2002). Determinants and structural relation of personal efficacy to collective efficacy. *Applied Psychology: An International Review, 51,* 107–125.

Garraghty, P. E., Churchill, J. D., & Banks, M. K. (1998). Adult neural plasticity: Similarities between two paradigms. *Current Directions in Psychological Science, 7,* 87–91.

Gottlieb, G. (1998). Normally occurring environmental and behavioral influences on gene activity: From central dogma to probabilistic epigenesis. *Psychological Review, 105,* 792–802.

Harter, S. (1999). *The construction of the self: A developmental perspective.* New York: Guilford Press.

Higgins, E. T. (1999). Persons and situations: Unique explanatory principles or variability in general principles? In D. Cervone & Y. Shoda (Eds.), *The coherence of personality: Social-cognitive bases of consistency, variability, and organization* (pp. 61–93). New York: Guilford Press.

Humphrey, N. (1984). *Consciousness regained.* Oxford: Oxford University Press.

Kagan, J. (1998). *Three seductive ideas.* Cambridge, MA: Harvard University Press.

Kitayama, S., & Markus, H. R. (1999). Yin and Yang of the Japanese self: The cultural psychology of personality coherence. In D. Cervone & Y. Shoda (Eds.), *The coherence of personality: Social-cognitive bases of consistency, variability, and organization* (pp. 242–302). New York: Guilford Press.

Kolb, B., & Whishaw, I. Q. (1998). Brain plasticity and behavior. *Annual Review of Psychology, 49,* 43–64.

Lewontin, R. (2000). *The triple helix: Gene, organism, and environment.* Cambridge, MA: Harvard University Press.

Locke, E. A., & Latham, G. P. (1990). *A theory of goal setting and task performance.* Englewood Cliffs, NJ: Prentice Hall.

Magnusson, D. (1992). Individual development: A longitudinal perspective. *European Journal of Personality, 6,* 119–138.

Magnusson, D. (1999). Holistic interactionism: A perspective for research on personality development. In L. A. Pervin & O. P. John (Eds.), *Handbook of personality: Theory and research* (2nd ed., pp. 219–247). New York: Guilford Press.

Markus, H. R., Kitayama, S., & Heiman, R. J. (1996). Culture and "basic" psychological principles. In E. T. Higgins & A. W. Kruglanski (Eds.), *Social psychology: Handbook of basic principles* (pp. 857–913). New York: Guilford Press.

McAuley, E., Duncan, T. E., & McElroy, M. (1989). Self-efficacy cognitions and causal attributions for children's motor performance: An exploratory investigation. *Journal of Genetic Psychology, 150,* 65–73.

Mischel, W., Cantor, N., & Feldman, S. (1996). Principles of self-regulation: The nature of willpower and self-control. In E. T. Higgins & A. W. Kruglanski (Eds.), *Social psychology: Handbook of basic principles* (pp. 329–360). New York: Guilford Press.

Mischel, W., & Shoda, Y. (1998). Reconciling processing dynamics and personality dispositions. *Annual Review of Psychology, 49,* 229–258.

Rawls, J. (1971). *A theory of justice.* Cambridge, MA: Harvard University Press.

Sampson, R. J., Raudenbush, S. W., & Earls, F. (1997). Neighborhoods and violent crime: A multilevel study of collective efficacy. *Science, 277,* 918–924.

Schunk, D. H., & Zimmerman, B. J. (Eds.). (1998). *Self-regulated learning: From teaching to self-reflective practice.* New York: Guilford Press.

Weitlauf, J., Cervone, D., & Smith, R. E. (2001). Assessing generalization in perceived self-efficacy: Multi-domain and global assessments of the effects of self-defense training for women. *Personality and Social Psychology Bulletin, 27,* 1683–1691.

Weitlauf, J., Smith, R. E., & Cervone, D. (2000). Generalization of coping skills training: Effects of self-defense instruction on women's task-specific and generalized self-efficacy, aggressiveness, and personality. *Journal of Applied Psychology, 85,* 625–633.

6

HUMAN AGING: WHY IS EVEN GOOD NEWS TAKEN AS BAD?

LAURA L. CARSTENSEN AND SUSAN T. CHARLES

At the close of the 20th century, news magazine programs regularly featured interviews with prominent citizens who were asked about the greatest accomplishments or inventions of the century. Respondents mentioned memorable events like "man walking on the moon" or named inventions like the Internet, the automobile, or television. Not a single person mentioned the creation of old age. Yet, in one short century, 30 years of life were added to average life expectancy.[1] For the first time in the history of the human species, the majority of those born in the Western world survive into old age.

The enormity of this advance is unprecedented. A new stage has been added to the life cycle. It came about not because of a single medical advance and certainly not by means of evolution (i.e., increasingly heartier generations). Rather, culture gets the credit for the creation of old age. Systematic efforts to accumulate and share scientific knowledge and communitywide efforts to inoculate children and improve sanitation effectively changed the natural course of life, and reductions in the number of children

---

[1] To be clear, individuals have lived into advanced age for a very long time. But most people didn't survive to old age; it was not normative.

75

born (by virtue of cultural prescription) changed the percentage of older adults in the world's population. The demographic shift in response to these adaptive advances is affecting work, health care, education, and public policies. Every aspect of life has been affected, including the nature of family, business markets, and political attitudes. No domain of life has remained untouched for old and young alike.

Despite the magnitude of these social advances, few have recognized the ramifications of these changes or celebrated the social inventions that were able to expand the quality and length of life. Rarely do debates and impassioned discussions focus on how people will use their extended years. Indeed, most people are deeply ambivalent about aging, and their ambivalence is fueled by alarming statistics that appear regularly in newspapers and on television. People have come to associate individual aging with dementia, poverty, and physical frailty and population aging with depletion of medical insurance funds and bankruptcy of government programs. On the one hand, old age is unattractive. On the other, so is the alternative.

Living longer is not inherently bad. And there is nothing inherently wrong with older, more mature societies. But few laypeople or researchers tout the benefits of old age. We argue in this chapter that social science, particularly psychology, has contributed to the negative views of old age by adopting an approach to the study of aging that has been characterized by some as "counting the wrinkles of age." There is an overwhelming tendency in the sciences to document deficiencies and to focus on problems associated with later life. Young and old are compared, and where there are differences, decrement is assumed. Aging people, and we all are, anticipate decline.

There is nothing wrong with studying problems of old age. Compelling evidence suggests that aging is related to declines in physical and sensory functioning. Hearing often becomes impaired, vision worsens, and fewer taste buds are available in savoring meals. Cognitive abilities deteriorate; one struggles increasingly to remember names and recall where one heard what one thinks one knows. Many negative aspects of aging deserve scientific attention and federal research dollars. However, by focusing only on the problems associated with aging, researchers and laypeople alike will not identify potential strengths.

Restricting empirical questions exclusively to those concerned with loss will inevitably obscure gains. Societies cannot afford to ignore the tremendous resources that older people offer. Considerable growth occurs with age, and social scientists overlook it too frequently, mainly because of this focus on loss. As scientists and as citizens in a rapidly changing society, psychologists cannot afford to limit the scope of their inquiries and the explanations for findings to aging deficits. In the following discussion we consider examples from our own research related to socioemotional functioning in later life and attempt to show that negative presumptions interfere with scientific progress.

AGE AND SOCIAL INTERACTION

One of the most reliable findings in social gerontology is that social interaction decreases with age (e.g., Harvey & Singleton, 1989; Lawton, Moss, & Fulcomer, 1987; Lee & Markides, 1990). Why? For decades all of the theoretical models offered to explain the phenomenon presumed that loss was at its core. Explanations were often based on assumptions and stereotypes instead of research findings, and many were incorrect. These explanations included such statements as

- Old people are depressed, so they withdraw.
- They have little to offer in social exchanges, so relationships weaken.
- Their friends die.
- They are too sick or cognitively impaired to maintain friendships.
- They become emotionally flattened and socially disengage in preparation for death.

Empirical findings published in the last decade, however, reveal that older people are less likely to be clinically depressed than younger and middle-aged people (although this assertion still appears in textbooks!; Lawton, Kleban, & Dean, 1993; Wittchen, Knauper, & Kessler, 1994). Cognitive declines also are not responsible. At least in nursing homes, cognitively impaired people interact lots more than people who are functioning well cognitively; it's the cognitively intact nursing home residents who are most likely to remain in their rooms (Carstensen, Fisher, & Malloy, 1995). Older people are more satisfied with their relationships than younger people and feel strong bonds to close friends (Lansford, Sherman, & Antonucci, 1998). In addition, emotional closeness with family members and close friends also increases into the later years (Carstensen, 1992). The number of close friends and confidants is very similar for centenarians and middle-aged people. Decreases in overall rates of social interaction are accounted for by decreases in casual acquaintances, not by fewer contacts with emotionally meaningful social partners (Lang & Carstensen, 1994; Lang, Staudinger, & Carstensen, 1998), and importantly, the loss of most social partners appears to be volitional, not due to deaths of friends and family (Lang, 2000).

Several years ago, we began to investigate whether older adults were taking a proactive role in their social world by "pruning" it so that only the most important people remained. In conversations with older people, we kept hearing the same comment: "I don't have time for those people." Although they never complained about the time spent with close family or friends, they said regularly that they had no interest in exploring new friendships and social partners. Eventually, we realized that when they referred to time, they meant time left in life, not time during the day. When we examined age-related change for different types of social interaction, a pattern emerged that dispelled the widely accepted assumptions of ubiquitous decrement. Although adults did report fewer interactions with casual acquaintances and strangers as they moved through young and middle adulthood, time spent with family members increased during this same period (Carstensen, 1992).

Over the years, and after many studies, we developed a conceptual model called socioemotional selectivity theory (Carstensen, Isaacowitz, & Charles, 1999; Charles & Carstensen, 1999), which argues that under time constraints, emotional aspects of life are illuminated. Goals shift from the search for novelty or information to the quest for emotional meaning. According to the theory, older people are not suffering from limited opportunities to pursue social relations with others. Rather, they are investing carefully and strategically in the people who matter most. This strategy is not used only by older adults; throughout the life span people who find themselves at life transitions perceived as endings use the same strategy (Charles & Carstensen, 1999). Life transitions that signal endings are often experienced with a mix of emotions. Graduation from high school, for example, brings the excitement of new freedom and opportunities, but also the sadness that a stage of life is coming to a close. The conditions that limit time may deepen the complexity of emotion (Carstensen, Pasupathi, Mayr, & Nesselroade, 2000). And because age is inextricably correlated with the time left in life, age is associated with changes in emotion. Our research subsequently turned more explicitly to emotion.

AGE AND EMOTIONAL FUNCTIONING

When we first began to explore emotion in older adults, we turned to the literature on emotion. As expected, we observed that the field presumed loss in the domain of emotional functioning. Although relatively little was known about emotional functioning in later life, researchers often invoked "emotional disinhibition" to explain age differences in performance on experimental tasks. In studies of source memory, researchers found that whereas younger adults were better at recalling perceptual and visuospatial information related to source, older adults recalled more thoughts, feelings, and evaluative statements when recalling perceived or imagined situations in the laboratory (Hashtroudi, Johnson, & Chrosniak, 1990). Although Hashtroudi and her colleagues interpreted these findings as age differences in what people focus on during the task (i.e., either emotional aspects or perceptual details), others have taken a different view. Researchers have often interpreted findings such as these as examples of cognitive disinhibition for emotional information and other "irrelevant information" which interferes with recollection of contextual and factual details (Zacks, Hasher, & Li, 2000).

Researchers evaluating studies of language also have used emotional disinhibition to explain age differences. There are qualitative differences between old and young in story recall, for example. Older adults engage in what researchers call "off-topic verbosity." That is, when recalling a story, older people often talk about feelings that are not explicitly part of the story and may tell personal stories or recall stories previously read in the laboratory (Gould, Trevithick, & Dixon, 1991). Off-topic verbosity is believed to be due to the inability to suppress unrelated thoughts (Arbuckle & Gold, 1993), a phenomenon that is partially mediated by psychosocial factors such as loneliness and a need to reinforce the self-concept at a time when social roles have been lost[2] (Gold, Andres, Arbuckle, & Schwartzman, 1988).

However, there are problems with the disinhibition explanation. Burke and her colleagues (e.g., James, Burke, Austin, & Hulme, 1998) found that although older storytellers did exhibit more off-topic speech, their stories were judged as more interesting and informative and of higher quality than those of younger storytellers. In this study, younger and older adults were asked to tell stories, and then these stories were judged by a different set of younger and older adults. When off-topic speech was examined apart from age, stories that were high in off-topic speech were also rated as more interesting and higher in story quality. Furthermore, the number of elaborations by older adults increased relative to the number of listeners in their audience, suggesting that older adults view elaborations as a strategy to engage listeners and therefore use more elaborations when attempting to engage a larger audience (Gould et al., 1991).

Moreover, elaboration that was evaluative or interpretative did not correlate with accuracy of recall by the storyteller, so memory for the actual story is unrelated. In short, the finding itself is highly reliable: Older adults use more elaborations (evaluations and interpretations) than younger adults. At present, evidence is not conclusive for disinhibition in working memory as an explanation of age differences in language processing, relative to other explanations such as older adults more often forming new connections in memory or language processing serving different social goals with age (Burke, 1997). Indeed, elaborations may simply serve to enhance storytelling, with older adults possibly producing more entertaining stories.

---

[2] Assuming that the self needs to be reinforced in old age is also a negative assumption that has not received empirical support. In fact, some would argue that the self is better integrated in old age (M. M. Baltes & Carstensen, 1996).

In an effort to directly assess memory for emotional versus neutral information, we used an incidental memory paradigm to assess memory in younger and older adults (Carstensen & Turk-Charles, 1994). We found that older adults recalled greater proportions of emotional material relative to nonemotional material. Importantly, there were no differences in the amount of emotional material recalled between age groups; the proportional increase was driven by reductions in nonemotional material among the older age groups. These findings suggest that instead of emotional material clouding the memories of older adults and representing poor cognitive functioning, memory for emotional material is one area which is well preserved. Very recently, we replicated this finding with memory for slides showing positively and negatively valenced emotional and nonemotional images (Charles, Mather, & Carstensen, 2002). After being presented with a series of slides, older adults show relatively superior memory for emotionally positive images than for negative or neutral images.

What about emotional experience? According to socioemotional selectivity theory, age differences in emotional salience reflect motivational changes. If, as the theory suggests, older people are more likely to pursue emotionally meaningful goals, this shift in motivation should be reflected in attention to emotional aspects of life. In several studies we hypothesized that older adults, motivated to realize emotionally gratifying experience, would perform better on interpersonal tasks drawing on the regulation of emotion and, in day-to-day life, would benefit experientially. We and other researchers in the field have supported this position. When younger and older married couples were observed discussing conflicts in their relationship, older couples expressed less negative emotion and more affection toward their partners (Carstensen, Gottman, & Levenson, 1995). Older adults have been found to solve emotionally salient problems better than younger adults and to be more likely to view interpersonal problems from multiple perspectives (Blanchard-Fields, 1986; Blanchard-Fields & Norris, 1994; Labouvie-Vief, 1997).

Older people have reported better control over their emotions and less frequent experience of negative emotions (Gross et al., 1997). Recently, in an experience sampling study, we found that older and younger people experienced positive and negative emotions at comparable levels of intensity. However, age was related to a reduction in the frequency of negative emotions (until roughly age 60 when the decrease levels), and older adults experienced positive emotions just as frequently as their younger counterparts (Carstensen et al., 2000). Older adults, relative to their younger counterparts, also have reported more differentiated emotional experience and were more likely than younger adults to experience positive and negative emotions during the same sampling occasion (Carstensen, Charles, Isaacowitz, & Kennedy, in press).

Thus, socioemotional functioning appears to be an area of continued growth well into advanced old age. Interpersonal relationships are strong, and emotional experience is, by and large, deeply satisfying. Interestingly, emotional experience in old age is best characterized not as "happy" but as richer and more complex and increasingly comes to entail episodes in which joy and sadness are intermixed in the same moment. As people approach the end of life and realize the fragility of life, simple distinctions between "positive" and "negative" blur, and emotional poignancy may dominate the horizon. An elderly couple, quoted in Ann Landers on December 13, 1995, described it well. They wrote, "When we are old, the young are kinder to us and we are kinder to each other. There is a sunset glow that radiates from our faces and is reflected on the faces of those about us. But still, it is sunset." This greater complexity may be why older adults report fewer emotions of surgency, such as excitement, yet report more contentment (Lawton et al., 1993). Greater complexity may also be why researchers have found that older adults are more adept at multiple-perspective taking in highly emotional situations (Blanchard-Fields, Chen, Schocke, & Hertzog, 1998). Cognitions may become more complex as no one emotion dominates a situation, which in turn may lead to enhanced emotion regulation.

WHAT DIFFERENCE DOES A FOCUS ON THE POSITIVE MAKE?

Traditional theories were often built on assumptions of loss, thereby framing age-related changes in negative terms and focusing on areas where these age-related changes reflect reduced functioning. Our research embedded in socioemotional selectivity theory focused on areas where age-related changes result in enhanced functioning. Indeed, the same age-related change can be seen as a loss or a gain, depending on the criteria with which it is measured.

There are many reasons to believe that recognition of positive aspects of aging would improve the science and probably the lives of older adults. In our own area of research, presumptions of loss have obscured gains. A focus on the positive will also force people to ask how the aging process might be improved. Certainly, old age, as we know it today, does not reflect *optimal* old age, so research focused on ways to enhance processes involved in optimal aging is indicated. Research on cognitive aging, for example, shows that many of the widely documented declines in cognitive performance (e.g., memory) can be improved with modest training (P. B. Baltes & Lindenberger, 1988; Schaie, 1990). Social dependency can be modified by changing environmental contingencies (M. M. Baltes, 1995). A great many of the physical health problems afflicting older adults can be postponed or reversed through diet and exercise (Whitbourne, 1985).

Moreover, across widely disparate domains, from physical health to cognitive functioning, variability in the population increases with age of cohort (Dannefer, 1987). Chronological age becomes an increasingly poor marker of functioning in successively older cohorts. To scientists, age variability is intriguing because it suggests the potential for specifying conditions that facilitate or obstruct adaptive outcomes. Variability also speaks against inevitability. In considering social and policy changes, it is in our best interest not only to find ways to limit or ration services to the elderly population, but also to find ways to facilitate the productive contributions of older citizens. Although the older population does indeed include severely demented people, it also comprises the wisest members of society. Identifying the strengths of older people will serve us all well.

Importantly, as the population rapidly grays, social scientists need to rethink the systemic relationships between individual behavior and societal structures throughout the life span (Riley, Foner, & Riley, 1999). We must recognize and consider deeply the intermingling of cultural supports and individual functioning. Cohort differences evident in this century demonstrate unequivocally that the social structures into which people are born alter the aging process: This influence does not begin in old age. Cohort differences in health care, standards of living, and educational opportunities influence people throughout the life course. Consider, for example, the fact that in 1900, 50% of infants born in the United States were dead before the age of 5, and illnesses like polio and rheumatic fever seriously compromised the lives of many survivors. In contrast, the vast majority of children born in the United States today are expected to live out their full life spans; they will be healthier and better educated than any previous cohort in human history.

WHAT'S WRONG WITH A "POSITIVE" PSYCHOLOGY MOVEMENT?

Given the argument we have made so far, readers may expect that we'd be delighted by the prospect of positive psychology. But we see as many problems as advantages. Deconstructing the scientific status quo and revealing evidence that negative presumptions have guided much of the research is one thing. Carrying a banner for a movement forcing the pendulum to swing in the other direction is quite another. Psychology is the discipline that has shown that investigators do not and cannot leave their worldviews at the doors of their laboratories. The lesson in this is not to give up the effort to objectively assess the gains and the losses associated with aging (or any other phenomenon under study) and join a movement to be more "positive." Rather, it is to generate an even-handed characterization of the problems and the strengths associated with aging. Scientific psychology should not have an objective to prove or disprove positive aspects of life. It should instead seek to understand psychological phenomena in their totality.

The positive psychology movement may benefit from lessons learned in gerontology, where a focus on "successful aging" began about 10 years ago. Recognizing the tremendous heterogeneity in aging outcomes, a number of gerontologists and life span developmental psychologists began to consider how to achieve positive outcomes in old age. The first step, of course, was to define successful aging, which in and of itself proved problematic. The initial thinking was that successful aging would entail long life, freedom from disease, good mental health, and social embeddedness.

Quickly, however, problems with this shift in focus emerged. For one, successful aging sounds a lot like not aging at all. Middle-aged standards of health were applied to old people. Should older people who become sick, or simply experience reliable cognitive changes in old age, be considered unsuccessful? If so, research on aging will focus only on an elite group of people who fit this definition, with most people culled out as soon as they show any evidence of decline. The study of older adults would be generalized only to a select few who are not representative of their age group. For example, nearly half of the population aged 65 and older report having arthritis (Helmick, Lawrence, Pollard, & Heyse, 1995), so nearly half of the older adult population would be excluded based on one chronic illness. Does it make sense to adopt a model of successful aging in which all people ultimately fail simply by surviving into old age? Certainly not. A far more satisfying approach, advocated by P. B. Baltes (1987), is to acknowledge that all stages in life have strengths and weaknesses and that all changes entail both gains and losses.

It is essential that social scientists identify inevitable deficits and exploit potential opportunities to build a society that optimizes the likelihood that all individuals will live healthy and productive lives well into old age. Given the well-documented increases in the older population, the vitality of their social and economic institutions is in jeopardy if societies do not begin serious discussions, informed by scientific findings, that will lead to the development of effective policies that allow them to maintain their economic and social vigor.

It is critical that social scientists ascertain the real gains and real losses associated with aging. We cannot do this by denying old age. We cannot do it by focusing only on problems. We cannot do it by succumbing to a polemical movement to search for the positive. We cannot do it by ignoring who people really are. Hopefully, we are all going to get old, and definitely, we are all going to die. The knowledge that our years are limited may be precisely what makes life precious.

Older people, in record numbers, are entering a stage of life that has few social scripts and even fewer supportive social structures that offer guides for roles and societal responsibilities. They do so at a point in history when less is known about the last 30 years of life than the first 5. However, considering what is known, it is inaccurate, and most certainly unwise, to characterize these 30 years as solely a time of frailty. Social scientists must study the strengths of older people, but just as surely they must understand the problems of older people if society is to harness this social resource and reap the benefits that can potentially accrue as people begin to realize their entire life spans.

REFERENCES

Arbuckle, T. Y., & Gold, D. P. (1993). Aging, inhibition, and verbosity. *Journals of Gerontology, 48*, P225–P232.

Baltes, M. M. (1995). Dependency in old age: Gains and losses. *Current Directions in Psychological Science, 4*, 14–19.

Baltes, M. M., & Carstensen, L. L. (1996). The process of successful ageing. *Ageing and Society, 16*, 397–422.

Baltes, P. B. (1987). Theoretical propositions of life-span developmental psychology: On the dynamics between growth and decline. *Developmental Psychology, 23*, 611–626.

Baltes, P. B., & Lindenberger, U. (1988). On the range of cognitive plasticity in old age as a function of experience: Fifteen years of intervention research. *Behavior Therapy, 19*, 283–300.

Blanchard-Fields, F. (1986). Reasoning on social dilemmas varying in emotional saliency: An adult developmental perspective. *Psychology and Aging, 1*, 325–333.

Blanchard-Fields, F., Chen, Y., Schocke, M., & Hertzog, C. (1998). Evidence for content-specificity of causal attributions across the adult life span. *Aging, Neuropsychology, and Cognition, 5*, 241–263.

Blanchard-Fields, F., & Norris, L. (1994). Causal attributions from adolescence through adulthood: Age differences, ego level, and generalized response style. *Aging and Cognition, 1*, 67–86.

Burke, D. (1997). Language, aging, and inhibitory deficits: Evaluation of theory. *Journals of Gerontology, 52*, 254–264.

Carstensen, L. L. (1992). Social and emotional patterns in adulthood: Support for socioemotional selectivity theory. *Psychology and Aging, 7*, 331–338.

Carstensen, L. L., Charles, S. T., Isaacowitz, D., & Kennedy, Q. (in press). Emotion and life-span personality development. In R. Davidson & K. Scherer (Eds.), *Handbook of affective science*.

Carstensen, L. L., Fisher, J. E., & Malloy, P. M. (1995). Cognitive and affective characteristics of socially withdrawn nursing home residents. *Journal of Clinical Geropsychology, 1*, 207–218.

Carstensen, L. L., Gottman, J. M., & Levenson, R. W. (1995). Emotional behavior in long-term marriage. *Psychology and Aging, 10,* 140–149.

Carstensen, L. L., Isaacowitz, D., & Charles, S. T. (1999). Taking time seriously in life span development. *American Psychologist, 54,* 165–181.

Carstensen, L. L., Pasupathi, M., Mayr, U., & Nesselroade, J. (2000). Emotional experience in everyday life across the adult life span. *Journal of Personality and Social Psychology, 79,* 644–655.

Carstensen, L. L., & Turk-Charles, S. (1994). The salience of emotion across the adult life course. *Psychology and Aging, 9,* 259–264.

Charles, S. T., & Carstensen L. L. (1999). The role of time in the setting of social goals across the life span. In T. M. Hess & F. Blanchard-Fields (Eds.), *Social cognition and aging* (pp. 319–342). San Diego, CA: Academic Press.

Charles, S. T., Mather, M., & Carstensen, L. L. (2002). *Focusing on the positive: Age differences in memory for positive, negative and neutral stimuli.* Manuscript submitted for publication.

Dannefer, D. (1987). Aging as intracohort differentiation, accentuation, the Matthew effect, and the life course. *Sociological Forum, 2,* 211–236.

Gold, D., Andres, D., Arbuckle, T., & Schwartzman, A. (1988). Measurement and correlates of verbosity in elderly people. *Journals of Gerontology, 43,* 27–33.

Gould, O. N., Trevithick, L., & Dixon, R. A. (1991). Adult age differences in elaborations produced during prose recall. *Psychology and Aging, 6,* 93–99.

Gross, J. J., Carstensen, L. L., Pasupathi, M., Tsai, J., Skorpen, K., & Hsu, A. Y. C. (1997). Emotion and aging: Experience, expression, and control. *Psychology and Aging, 12,* 590–599.

Harvey, A. S., & Singleton, J. F. (1989). Canadian activity patterns across the life span: A time budget perspective. *Canadian Journal of Aging, 8,* 268–285.

Hashtroudi, S., Johnson, M. K., & Chrosniak, L. D. (1990). Aging and qualitative characteristics of memories for perceived and imagined complex events. *Psychology and Aging, 5,* 119–126.

Helmick, C. G., Lawrence, R. A., Pollard, E., & Heyse, S. (1995). Arthritis and other rheumatic conditions: Who is affected now and who will be affected later? *Arthritis Care and Research, 8,* 203–211.

James, L. E., Burke, D. M., Austin, A., & Hulme, E. (1998). Production and perception of "verbosity" in younger and older adults. *Psychology and Aging, 13,* 355–367.

Labouvie-Vief, G. (1997). Cognitive-emotional integration in adulthood. In K. W. Schaie & M. P. Lawton (Eds.), *Annual review of gerontology and geriatrics* (Vol. 17, pp. 206–237).

Lang, F. R. (2000). Endings and continuity of social relationships: Maximizing intrinsic benefits within personal networks when feeling near to death. *Journal of Social and Personal Relationships, 17,* 155–182.

Lang, F. R., & Carstensen, L. L. (1994). Close emotional relationships in late life: Further support for proactive aging in the social domain. *Psychology and Aging, 9,* 315–324.

Lang, F., Staudinger, U. M., & Carstensen, L. L. (1998). Socioemotional selectivity in late life: How personality and social context do (and do not) make a difference. *Journal of Gerontology, 53,* 21–30.

Lansford, J. E., Sherman, A. M., & Antonucci, T. C. (1998). Satisfaction with social networks: An examination of socioemotional selectivity theory across cohorts. *Psychology and Aging, 13,* 544–552.

Lawton, M. P., Kleban, M. H., & Dean, J. (1993). Affect and age: Cross-sectional comparisons of structure and prevalence. *Psychology and Aging, 8,* 165–175.

Lawton, M. P., Moss, M., & Fulcomer, M. (1987). Objective and subjective uses of time by older people. *International Journal of Aging and Human Development, 24,* 171–188.

Lee, D. J., & Markides, K. S. (1990). Activity and mortality among aged persons over an eight-year period. *Journals of Gerontology: Social Sciences, 45,* 39–42.

Riley, M. W., Foner, A., & Riley, J. W., Jr. (1999). The aging and society paradigm. In V. Bengtson & K. W. Schaie (Eds.), *Handbook of theories of aging* (pp. 327–343). New York: Springer.

Schaie, K. W. (1990). The optimization of cognitive functioning in old age: Predictions based on cohort-sequential and longitudinal data. In P. B. Baltes & M. M. Baltes (Eds.), *Successful aging: Perspectives from the behavioral sciences* (pp. 94–117). New York: Cambridge University Press.

Whitbourne, S. K. (1985). *The aging body.* New York: Springer.

Wittchen, H., Knäuper, B., & Kessler, R. C. (1994). Lifetime risk of depression. *British Journal of Psychiatry, 165,* 16–22.

Zacks, R. T., Hasher, L., & Li, K. Z. H. (2000). Human memory. In F. I. M. Craik & T. A. Salthouse (Eds.), *The handbook of aging and cognition* (2nd ed., pp. 293–358). Mahwah, NJ: Erlbaum.

7

THREE HUMAN STRENGTHS

CHARLES S. CARVER AND MICHAEL F. SCHEIER

The concept "human strength" will probably be taken by most people as referring to ways in which humans overcome daunting obstacles, triumph over adversity, and emerge successfully from transactions that have pressed them to their limits. Strength is the solidity to stand firm against the rockslides of an uncertain world. Strength is flexibility with tensile reserve, allowing people to bend but not break when facing raging winds. Strength is the ability to maintain equilibrium and remain at the surface of a desert's shifting sands or in a maelstrom of crashing waves.

Another common view would see human strength as reflected in the ability to transform the world, to turn visions arising from one's imagination into reality. Human strength is manifested in the sustained exertions that clear fields for crops and cities, the harnessed efforts that raise buildings and aircraft thousands of feet in the air, the imagination and knowledge that channel the forces of nature into electrical power. Human strength is the mental and physical prowess that lies behind the creation of artifacts conceived by human minds.

These views share the theme that human strength involves a kind of

Preparation of this chapter was facilitated by grants CA64710, CA64711, CA78995, and P50-CA84944 from the National Cancer Institute and grants P50-HL65111 and P50-HL65112 from the National Heart, Lung, and Blood Institute.

victory over the world outside the self—either by successfully resisting outside forces or by exerting one's own force successfully on the world. Human strength is expressed in resilience against deformative pressures. Human strength is expressed in the ability to plan and to manifest that plan in a world characterized by opposition or indifference. Human strength is the capability of forcing external elements into a desired order (or a desired disorder). Human strength is about overcoming, succeeding.

These views have much to recommend them. The ability to persevere and overcome is an important—indeed critical—human strength. But that is not the entire story of human strength. Strength is not entirely about victory. It is partly about being overcome, about defeat and what follows from defeat. Strength is partly about holding on, but partly about letting go (Pyszczynski & Greenberg, 1992). Strength is also partly something else: changes that take place within the self. Strength is inherent in the processes of psychological growth. This chapter concerns these three domains of human strength.

PERSEVERANCE AS HUMAN STRENGTH

The picture of human strength as reflected in persistence and performance is a familiar one. Discussions of these aspects of experience often stress the important role in human behavior played by commitment to goals and confidence about their attainment. Commitment and confidence interact to foster persistence and perseverance, even in the face of great adversity. These ideas form the cornerstone of a good part of what is touted as "positive psychology" (e.g., Ryff & Singer, 1998; Seligman, 1999; Snyder & Lopez, 2002; Taylor, 1989). Because these ideas are so familiar to so many readers, we discuss them only briefly here.

The idea that commitment and confidence are keys to success is embedded in generations of expectancy–value models of motivation (e.g., Atkinson, 1964; Bandura, 1997; Carver & Scheier, 1998; Feather, 1982; Klinger, 1975; Kuhl, 1984; Kukla, 1972; Lewin, 1948; Scheier & Carver, 1992; Shah & Higgins, 1997; Snyder, 1994; Vroom, 1964; Wright & Brehm, 1989). In such models, engagement of effort requires both a goal that matters enough (value) and also sufficient confidence in its eventual attainment (expectancy). People do not take up goals that don't matter to them, and if they did, they wouldn't persist when things got difficult. The greater the goal's value, the greater the person's commitment to it. Still, if a goal seems unattainable (even though desirable), people won't commit themselves to it. If they do, and fail to make progress for long enough, they won't persist. If people are hopeful or confident, on the other hand, they will hold onto valued goals and remain engaged in attempts to move forward, even when the effort thus far has been futile.

Discussions of these theories usually emphasize the positive—the idea that continued effort can result in attaining desired goals. That emphasis is quite reasonable, as many of these theories have roots in analyses of achievement behavior. A person who gives up whenever encountering difficulty will never accomplish anything. To accomplish things, people must make persistent effort when confronting obstacles.

Given the importance of persistence in attaining desired ends, attempts to foster human strength from this perspective often focus on enhancing persistence. Often enough, from the expectancy–value approach, this translates directly into building people's confidence about successful outcomes to the point where effort is self-sustaining. Put simply, the attempt is to turn pessimists into optimists.

Building confidence is not as straightforward as it might seem, however. For one thing, confidence can have many focuses. People can become confident that they will encounter no adversity or confident that adversity will fall away as soon as they exert effort. Such types of confidence are unlikely to yield the desired result, however. They are too easily disconfirmed and broken. Rather, people must be confident about eventually overcoming the adversity. The longer a span of effort is reflected in the sense of "eventually," the greater should be the person's persistence under adversity. Although there are other ways to view this phenomenon (e.g., Amsel, 1967), we see it as reflecting confidence about the eventual result of extended efforts, even given the likelihood of shorter-term failures.

With confidence of eventual success, people continue to struggle toward their desires. The originators of a garage-based start-up company may endure years of hardship while their product slowly takes root. The struggling student may work for months toward the completion of a project that is very difficult. People even return to rebuild their homes in war-torn territories. The ability of people to struggle forward, to persevere against great odds even in the face of failure, represents a very important human strength.

GIVING UP AS HUMAN STRENGTH

Although perseverance is important in a great many activities of life, this is only part of the story. An equally important role is played by processes that are precisely the opposite of those just discussed. A critical role in life is also played by doubt and disengagement—by giving up (Carver & Scheier, 1998, 2000; Wrosch, Scheier, Carver, & Schulz, in press).

Giving up has a bad reputation in Western thought: "Winners never quit and quitters never win" is the credo of sports and business alike. However, everyone quits sometimes. No one goes through a lifetime without confronting an insoluble problem. Disengagement from failed efforts turns out to be a necessity—a natural and indispensable aspect of effective self-regulation (Klinger, 1975).

Giving Up in Behavioral Self-Regulation

The expectancy–value theories that place such an emphasis on perseverance also have an important role for disengagement, although one would be hard-pressed to realize it from most presentations of those theories. In general, giving up is treated within those theories as a wholly undesirable response. The emphasis has been on the failure per se. Indeed, giving up has sometimes been equated with "helplessness," in which the person subsequently fails to exert effort toward a wider variety of goals (cf. Seligman, 1975; Wortman & Brehm, 1975). Further thought makes it apparent, however, that this is too simple a picture.

To talk about the consequences of failure, one must make a distinction between giving up effort and giving up commitment to the goal. Reducing effort while staying committed has clear negative consequences in the form of distress (cf. Carver & Scheier, 1990). The person is stuck—not trying, yet unable to turn away. If commitment to the goal can be dissolved, however, failure at goal attainment does not have these consequences (Carver & Scheier, 1998). With no commitment to the unattainable goal, there's no basis for distress over the fact that the goal cannot be attained.

What determines goal commitment? It depends partly on the goal's value—its perceived importance. Real helplessness occurs when a goal cannot be reached and also cannot be abandoned, because it matters too much. What determines a goal's importance? To answer this question properly, we must address the principle of hierarchicality among the goal values of the self.

We believe that goals provide the structure that defines people's lives. The goals of the self take a variety of forms. Some are concrete (e.g., taking out the garbage); others are more abstract and ephemeral (e.g., being a good parent). What makes one goal matter more than another? Generally speaking, the higher in the hierarchy a goal is, the more important it is (the more central to the overall sense of self). Concrete action goals acquire importance from the fact that attaining them serves the attainment of broader, more abstract goals (Carver & Scheier, 1998; Powers, 1973; Vallacher & Wegner, 1985). The stronger the link between a concrete goal and the deepest values of the self, the more important is that concrete goal.

Unimportant goals are easy to disengage from. Important ones are hard to disengage from, because giving them up creates a disruption (an enlarging discrepancy) with respect to higher-level core values of the self. Thus, giving up on an important goal is difficult and painful.

The disruption at the higher order can potentially be remedied, however. How? The answer derives from the fact that people often can engage in diverse activities to satisfy a given higher order goal. For example, many actions serve as pathways to maintaining good health, including exercising, healthful eating, taking vitamins, getting regular checkups, and avoiding cigarettes and alcohol. The pathways to a given higher order goal sometimes compensate for one another (cf. Wicklund & Gollwitzer, 1982), so that if progress in one path is impeded, the person can shift efforts to a different path (see Figure 7.1, Path 1).

As an example, consider a woman who values being an environmentalist. If a chronic illness were to stop her from engaging in regular volunteer work for her local environmental group, she might compensate by increasing her charitable contributions to that organization. As one path is disrupted, another path may be taken instead, and indeed may become more important over time. By taking up an attainable alternative, the person remains engaged in forward movement.

Sometimes people don't turn to alternative paths that are already in place, but rather step outside their existing framework and develop new ones. Though there are many ways in which this can occur, we think they share a common element. We believe that the newly adopted activity will almost inevitably be one that contributes to the expression of some pre-existing core aspect of the self (see Carver & Scheier, 1999). Thus, the effect is to continue the pre-existing sense of purpose in life (Figure 7.1, Path 2).

Sometimes disengagement involves shifting from one activity to another. Sometimes, however, it involves only scaling back from a lofty goal in a given domain to a less demanding one. This is a disengagement, in the sense that the person is giving up the first goal while adopting the lesser one (Figure 7.1, Path 3). It is more limited than the cases already considered, in the sense that it does not entail leaving the domain. This limited disengagement keeps the person engaged in activity in the domain he or she had wanted to quit (cf. Sprangers & Schwartz, 1999). By scaling back the goal—giving up in a small way—the person keeps trying to move ahead, thus not giving up in a larger way. The person thereby retains the sense of purpose in activities in that domain.

It will be apparent from this discussion that many instances of goal disengagement occur in the service of maintaining continued efforts toward higher order goals. This is particularly obvious regarding concrete goals for which disengagement has little cost: People remove themselves from blind alleys and wrong streets, give up plans that have been disrupted by unexpected events, and come back later if the store is closed. The same is also true, however, with regard to certain goals that are deeply connected to the self. It serves the longer term benefit of the self to disengage and move on with life after the loss of a close relationship (e.g., Orbuch, 1992;

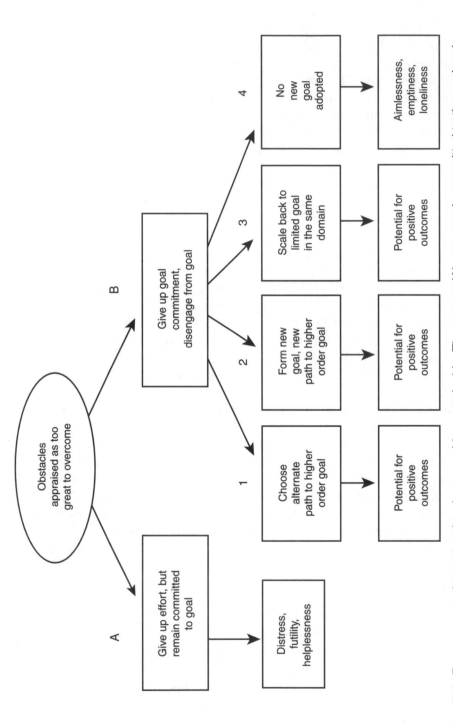

Figure 7.1. Responses to the perception that a goal is unattainable. The person (A) can remain committed to the goal and experience distress or (B) can dissolve the commitment and disengage from the goal. Disengagement has four potential patterns: (1) Choosing an alternative path to the same higher order value produces a situation in which positive outcomes and feelings are possible. (2) Choosing a new goal yields a situation in which positive outcomes and feelings are possible. (3) Scaling back aspirations while remaining in the same domain creates a situation in which positive outcomes and feelings are possible. (4) Giving up commitment without turning to another goal, however, results in feelings of emptiness.

Stroebe, Stroebe, & Hansson, 1993) or to disengage from a career path that has not worked out. People need multiple paths to the core values of the self (cf. Linville, 1987; Showers & Ryff, 1996). That way, if one path becomes barricaded, they can jump to another one.

Not every disengagement serves this adaptive function, of course. In some cases there appears to be no alternative goal to take up. In such a case, disengagement is not accompanied by a shift, because there is nothing to shift to. This is perhaps the worst situation, where there is nothing to pursue, nothing to take the place of what is seen as unattainable. If the commitment to the unattainable goal wanes, the result is simply emptiness (Figure 7.1, Path 4).

More generally, disengagement appears to be a valuable and adaptive response when it leads to—or is tied to—the taking up of other goals (cf. Aspinwall & Richter, 1999). By taking up an attainable alternative, the person remains engaged in activities that have meaning for the self, and life continues to have purpose. The willingness to make this shift, when circumstances require it, is an important human strength.

Giving Up in Lifespan Development

The foregoing discussion addressed giving up as a human strength in moment-to-moment self-regulation. The idea that disengagement plays a critically important role in life more broadly also finds support with respect to life span development (this discussion is adapted from Wrosch et al., in press). Humans have a vast potential for what they can become and accomplish in a lifetime. However, because time and resources are limited, people must make choices about which goals to pursue and which to give up (Schulz & Heckhausen, 1996; see also Carstensen, Hanson, & Freund, 1995). Such choices can be either proactive (in response to opportunities) or reactive (in response to dwindling resources or sociocultural constraints) (Baltes, 1997; Marsiske, Lang, Baltes, & Baltes, 1995). Successful self-management requires that people choose the right goals at the right time, and it requires the ability to disengage from goals that are unattainable or too costly to attain. Consistent with this, elderly persons who report being more adept at making loss-based goal choices also report less agitation and more positive well-being (Freund & Baltes, 1998).

There are several ways in which goals can be rendered unattainable (or too costly). One is the fact that the biological resources available to a person have a cycle of growth and decline over the life span (Baltes, Cornelius, & Nesselroade, 1979; Heckhausen & Schulz, 1995). At the simplest level, this cycle imposes constraints on attainable goals at a given point in the life course. Running 100 meters in 10 seconds might be a feasible goal for a 20-year-old, but not for a 5-year-old or an 80-year-old. It would be adaptive for the 5-year-old and the 80-year-old not to be committed to that goal at present (though it may become adaptive for the 5-year-old later on).

The pattern of growth through the middle years followed by a decline through old age also has another implication. Early in development a person makes choices electively as he or she actively tries to select pathways that enhance personal growth and optimize personal resources. Later on, goal selection becomes more loss based, as the person tries to replace goals that are no longer attainable because of diminishing biological resources and reserves (Baltes, 1997; Marsiske et al., 1995). Stated differently, there is a shift over the life span from an assimilative mode of coping to an accommodative mode of coping (Brandtstädter & Greve, 1994; Brandtstädter & Renner, 1990). *Assimilative coping* is the person's attempt to adjust ongoing life circumstances to match goals, needs, and desires. *Accommodative coping* is the opposite—adjusting personal preferences and goals to the situational and contextual constraints.

Biological limitations also arise from genetic variations. The potential behavioral repertoire of humans is vast, but a person's capacity to reach high levels of functioning in a given domain may be constrained genetically (e.g., Plomin, Pedersen, Lichtenstein, & McClearn, 1994; Scarr, 1993). Becoming a professional athlete is an unattainable goal for someone who does not have the needed physical attributes. Becoming a rocket scientist is an unattainable goal for someone who lacks the needed intellectual attributes. Optimal development entails providing children opportunities to test their potential in various areas. Put simply, some goals will be out of reach no matter how hard one tries, and an important task of early development is to figure out what goals are appropriate and what goals are better abandoned.

Constraints also result from the flow of behavior over time, channeling developmental processes into biographical tracks (cf. Baltes, 1993). An example is professional specialization. People acquire increasing expertise in their chosen field, but they do so at the expense of breadth across other fields. Effort directed to greater expertise in one's specialization is effort diverted from keeping up elsewhere. The strategy of specialization lets the person optimize functioning in the chosen track, but makes it correspondingly more difficult to maintain goal possibilities in other tracks.

Another very important constraint is the limited time span of the human life. Whatever is to be achieved or experienced in life has to be done in a finite period of time. Acquiring knowledge and skills of any sort takes time. This limits the extent to which people can maximize functioning in multiple domains. Because there are limits on the time available, there are limits on the ability to shift from one domain to another.

These various points can be summarized as follows: Because life is short and resources are limited, people must make decisions about where to invest those resources. Resources invested in one activity cannot be used for an alternative activity. Sometimes an activity is begun that proves not to be worth sustaining, given the many constraints on the person's life or changes in the social environment. In such cases, the activity—the goal—must be abandoned. Doing that allows the person to expend the resources more profitably in other domains of life. Thus, giving up seems to play an important role in how people negotiate development across the life span.

Choosing

We have argued that perseverance reflects human strength and that giving up reflects human strength. Those statements hold no paradox, but they hide a difficult problem (at least, they have done so thus far in this chapter). The problem is how to know when something is truly unattainable (or not worth the effort required to attain it). In truth, whenever the issue arises, it is impossible to be certain of the answer. To persevere may turn out to be glorious stupidity. To give up may turn out to be tragic loss. The well-known serenity prayer asks for "the wisdom to know the difference" between these cases. Whether the answer comes from a divinity or from a lifetime of experience, the ability to choose wisely (or at least believe that one has chosen wisely) and follow one's choice fully is also an important strength.

GROWTH AS HUMAN STRENGTH

A final human strength also concerns development in a sense, but does so from a very different angle. Specifically, people grow and evolve psychologically across time and experience. We were drawn to consider this aspect of human strength partly by our discovery of a developing literature on how people respond to jolts in life serious enough to be viewed as trauma. Consideration of responses to trauma led us to think more closely about growth more generally.

Discussions of trauma have noted that such events can have diverse long-term consequences. Sometimes people remain diminished in some way; sometimes they return to their prior levels of functioning. It's possible, though, for people to respond to trauma by surpassing their prior functioning. This possibility has been discussed under a number of labels, including thriving (O'Leary & Ickovics, 1995), post-traumatic growth (Calhoun & Tedeschi, 1998; Tedeschi & Calhoun, 1995), and stress-related growth (Park, Cohen, & Murch, 1996). A substantial number of people have begun to note the possibility that serious adversity can eventually bring about benefit (see also Affleck & Tennen, 1996; Aldwin, 1994; Antoni et al.,

2001; Ickovics & Park, 1998; Janoff-Bulman, 1992; Updegraff & Taylor, 2000).

There are several ways to think about the nature of such gains (Carver, 1998). People may emerge from disruptive and even traumatic events with new skills for managing the external world or for managing their distress. The "skill" may be an actual skill, it may be an enhanced knowledge base, it may be enhanced social support. With new skills, people are better prepared to deal with an unpredictable world. With new pathways to get from one place to another, people are more flexible in confronting the unknown.

Along with the ability to do something new can come a sense of mastery (Aldwin, 1994). Along with having gotten through a painful experience can come confidence ("I survived this, I can deal with other hard things too."). Having this confidence can also make subsequent difficulties easier to approach (Affleck, Tennen, & Rowe, 1991). Confidence is a key contributor to keeping people engaged in efforts to cope (indeed, this looks like precisely the sort of confidence that is most conducive to staying engaged through adversity).

In sum, gains following trauma appear to reflect one or another kind of growth: growth in skill, growth in knowledge, growth in confidence, greater elaboration and differentiation in one's ability to deal with the world. This leads to an interesting question: If thriving reflects growth in response to adversity, does this growth differ in principle from any other growth experience?

One possible difference is that thriving occurs in circumstances in which growth would be unexpected. On the other hand, it's noteworthy that many kinds of growth occur only in response to stress. Muscle development occurs when a muscle is systematically worked close to its limits. Without that, there's no change in strength. Similarly, cognitive skills develop because the person's existing understanding of reality is too limited to handle current experiences. It takes a mismatch between the person and the world—a disequilibration (Piaget, 1963, 1971) or a failure of prediction (Kelly, 1955)—to force the growth and elaboration to occur (see also Ruble, 1994).

These considerations suggest that thriving reflects an extreme case of the same growth processes. It is extreme in the sense that it occurs in circumstances at the outer limit of tolerability. Indeed, if circumstances are even more extreme, growth (thriving) may be precluded. Perhaps trauma changes the situation so much that growth (if it occurs at all) is speeded up. Thus, responses to trauma may provide observers a clearer window on processes that also take place in less extreme circumstances, but normally are more hidden from view because they are slower.

This idea is reminiscent of Kelly's (1955) discussion of two kinds of changes in people's construct systems. He distinguished between (gradual) elaboration of a system and a sudden reorganization that can occur when there has been a massive failure of prediction (usually, though not always, involving a traumatic event). The latter changes are in some respects the same as in normal evolution of the construct system, but they occur suddenly rather than gradually.

What is the nature of these changes? Our view of the tendency toward growth over time and experience—whether gradual or sudden—is a naïve position that echoes both Piaget (1963) and Kelly (1955), among others. We think humans continuously strive toward better prediction. Better prediction (both as an observer and as an actor) leads to better outcomes and more efficiency. We think a gradual shift toward efficiency occurs when people continue to pursue an activity over multiple repetitions. We regard gradual change toward greater efficiency as a self-adjusting process that is characteristic of the human cognitive machinery (see MacKay, 1956).

Piaget (1963) viewed growth as resting on the broad processes of differentiation (making greater distinctions among the elements of reality), organization (integrating simple elements into more complex wholes, which may have emergent properties), and adaptation (testing the structures so they fit the constraints of reality). The process of organization supplies the efficiency, adaptation ensures that the efficiency continues to predict accurately, and differentiation ensures that more and more subtle aspects of reality are taken into account over accumulated experience.

There are also resonances of this view in ideas about the function of consciousness. Some hold that consciousness is involved in making decisions under uncertainty, but that the repeated decisions made in some domain begin to form a pattern, gradually yielding default values for perception, thought, and action (Bargh, 1997; Norman & Shallice, 1986). As the defaults form, processing is more automatic and requires less attention. Automaticity attained in one domain frees attention for other domains or for more elaborate decision making in the same domain. The person thus evolves to become both more complex and more integrated. As people become capable of handling more and more complexity automatically, they take into account more and more variables at once, thereby stretching themselves yet further (Carver & Scheier, 1998, chapter 16).

The making of ever more subtle distinctions, the forming of organizations from elements, the testing of those organizations against reality, and the attainment of automaticity—taken together, they constitute a kind of growth. Taken together, as growth, they also represent an important core of human strength.

CONCLUSION

We described in this chapter three kinds of human strength: perseverance, giving up the unattainable, and growth. Unknown at present are the relations among them. Even perseverance and giving up, which seem so antithetical, may not be. Perhaps the reality is more that strength is expressed in the selection of some threads of life to pursue diligently while others wither away, much as the pruning that occurs among neural projections over time and experience.

In any event, we think it important to note that the strengths on which we have focused in this chapter do not belong only to a select few individuals. Rather, they are part of everyone's experience, to a greater or lesser degree. A psychology of human strengths is no less than a psychology of human nature. As such, it will remain important for the foreseeable future.

REFERENCES

Affleck, G., & Tennen, H. (1996). Construing benefits from adversity: Adaptational significance and dispositional underpinnings. *Journal of Personality, 64,* 899–922.

Affleck, G., Tennen, H., & Rowe, J. (1991). *Infants in crisis: How parents cope with newborn intensive care and its aftermath.* New York: Springer-Verlag.

Aldwin, C. M. (1994). *Stress, coping, and development: An integrative perspective.* New York: Guilford Press.

Amsel, A. (1967). Partial reinforcement effects on vigor and persistence: Advances in frustration theory derived from a variety of within-subject experiments. In K. W. Spence & J. T. Spence (Eds.), *The psychology of learning and motivation: Vol. 1* (pp. 1–65). New York: Academic Press.

Antoni, M. H., Lehman, J. M., Kilbourn, K. M., Boyers, A. E., Culver, J. L., Alferi, S. M., Yount, S. E., McGregor, B. A., Arena, P. L., Harris, S. D., Price, A. A., & Carver, C. S. (2001). Cognitive-behavioral stress management intervention decreases the prevalence of depression and enhances benefit finding among women under treatment for early-stage breast cancer. *Health Psychology, 20,* 20–32.

Aspinwall, L. G., & Richter, L. (1999). Optimism and self-mastery predict more rapid disengagement from unsolvable tasks in the presence of alternatives. *Motivation and Emotion, 23,* 221–245.

Atkinson, J. W. (1964). *An introduction to motivation.* Princeton, NJ: Van Nostrand.

Baltes, P. B. (1993). The aging mind: Potentials and limits. *Gerontologist, 33,* 580–594.

Baltes, P. B. (1997). On the incomplete architecture of human ontogeny: Selection, optimization, and compensation as foundation of developmental theory. *American Psychologist, 52,* 366–380.

Baltes, P. B., Cornelius, S. W., & Nesselroade, J. R. (1979). Cohort effects in developmental psychology. In J. R. Nesselroade & P. B. Baltes (Eds.), *Longi-*

tudinal research in the study of behavior and development (pp. 61–87). New York: Academic Press.

Bandura, A. (1997). *Self-efficacy: The exercise of control*. New York: Freeman.

Bargh, J. A. (1997). The automaticity of everyday life. In R. S. Wyer, Jr. (Ed.), *Advances in social cognition* (Vol. 10, pp. 1–61). Mahwah, NJ: Erlbaum.

Brandtstädter, J., & Greve, W. (1994). The aging self: Stabilizing and protective processes. *Developmental Review, 14,* 52–80.

Brandtstädter, J., & Renner, G. (1990). Tenacious goal pursuit and flexible goal adjustment: Explication and age-related analysis of assimilative and accommodative strategies of coping. *Psychology and Aging, 5,* 58–67.

Calhoun, L. G., & Tedeschi, R. G. (1998). Beyond recovery from trauma: Implications for clinical practice and research. *Journal of Social Issues, 54,* 357–371.

Carstensen, L. L., Hanson, K. A., & Freund, A. M. (1995). Selection and compensation in adulthood. In R. A. Dixon & L. Bäckman (Eds.), *Compensating for psychological deficits and declines: Managing losses and promoting gains* (pp. 107–126). Mahwah, NJ: Erlbaum.

Carver, C. S. (1998). Resilience and thriving: Issues, models, and linkages. *Journal of Social Issues, 54,* 245–265.

Carver, C. S., & Scheier, M. F. (1990). Origins and functions of positive and negative affect: A control-process view. *Psychological Review, 97,* 19–35.

Carver, C. S., & Scheier, M. F. (1998). *On the self-regulation of behavior*. New York: Cambridge University Press.

Carver, C. S., & Scheier, M. F. (1999). Several more themes, a lot more issues: Commentary on the commentaries. In R. S. Wyer, Jr. (Ed.), *Advances in social cognition* (Vol. 12, pp. 261–302). Mahwah, NJ: Erlbaum.

Carver, C. S., & Scheier, M. F. (2000). Scaling back goals and recalibration of the affect system are processes in normal adaptive self-regulation: Understanding "response shift" phenomena. *Social Science and Medicine, 50,* 1715–1722.

Feather, N. T. (1982). *Expectations and actions: Expectancy–value models in psychology*. Hillsdale, NJ: Erlbaum.

Freund, A. M., & Baltes, P. B. (1998). Selection, optimization, and compensation as strategies of life management: Correlations with subjective indicators of successful aging. *Psychology and Aging, 13,* 531–543.

Heckhausen, J., & Schulz, R. (1995). A life-span theory of control. *Psychological Review, 102,* 284–304.

Ickovics, J. R., & Park, C. L. (Eds.). (1998). Thriving [Special issue]. *Journal of Social Issues, 54*(2).

Janoff-Bulman, R. (1992). *Shattered assumptions*. New York: Free Press.

Kelly, G. A. (1955). *The psychology of personal constructs*. New York: W. W. Norton.

Klinger, E. (1975). Consequences of commitment to and disengagement from incentives. *Psychological Review, 82,* 1–25.

Kuhl, J. (1984). Volitional aspects of achievement motivation and learned helplessness: Toward a comprehensive theory of action control. In B. A. Maher (Ed.), *Progress in experimental personality research* (Vol. 13, pp. 99–170). New York: Academic Press.

Kukla, A. (1972). Foundations of an attributional theory of performance. *Psychological Review, 79,* 454–470.

Lewin, K. (1948). Time perspective and morale. In G. W. Lewin (Ed.), *Resolving social conflicts: Selected papers on group dynamics* (pp. 103–124). New York: Harper.

Linville, P. (1987). Self-complexity as a cognitive buffer against stress-related illness and depression. *Journal of Personality and Social Psychology, 52,* 663–676.

MacKay, D. M. (1956). Towards an information-flow model of human behaviour. *British Journal of Psychology, 47,* 30–43.

Marsiske, M., Lang, F. R., Baltes, P. B., & Baltes, M. M. (1995). Selective optimization with compensation: Life-span perspectives on successful human development. In R. A. Dixon & L. Bäckman (Eds.), *Compensating for psychological deficits and declines: Managing losses and promoting gains* (pp. 35–79). Mahwah, NJ: Erlbaum.

Norman, D. A., & Shallice, T. (1986). Attention to action: Willed and automatic control of behavior. In R. J. Davidson, G. E. Schwartz, & D. Shapiro (Eds.), *Consciousness and self-regulation: Advances in research and theory* (Vol. 4, pp. 1–18). New York: Plenum Press.

O'Leary, V. E., & Ickovics, J. R. (1995). Resilience and thriving in response to challenge: An opportunity for a paradigm shift in women's health. *Women's Health: Research on Gender, Behavior, and Policy, 1,* 121–142.

Orbuch, T. L. (Ed.). (1992). *Close relationship loss: Theoretical approaches.* New York: Springer-Verlag.

Park, C. L., Cohen, L. H., & Murch, R. L. (1996). Assessment and prediction of stress-related growth. *Journal of Personality, 64,* 71–105.

Piaget, J. (1963). *The child's conception of the world.* Patterson, NJ: Littlefield, Adams.

Piaget, J. (1971). *Biology and knowledge.* Chicago: University of Chicago Press.

Plomin, R., Pedersen, N. L., Lichtenstein, P., & McClearn, G. E. (1994). Variability and stability in cognitive abilities are largely genetic in later life. *Behavior Genetics, 24,* 207–216.

Powers, W. T. (1973). *Behavior: The control of perception.* Chicago: Aldine.

Pyszczynski, T., & Greenberg, J. (1992). *Hanging on and letting go: Understanding the onset, progression, and remission of depression.* New York: Springer-Verlag.

Ruble, D. N. (1994). A phase model of transitions: Cognitive and motivational consequences. In M. Zanna (Ed.), *Advances in Experimental Social Psychology, 26,* 163–214.

Ryff, C. D., & Singer, B. (1998). The contours of positive human health. *Psychological Inquiry, 9,* 1–28.

Scarr, S. (1993). Genes, experience, and development. In D. Magnusson & P.

Caesar (Eds.), *Longitudinal research on individual development: Present status and future perspectives* (pp. 26–50). Cambridge, England: Cambridge University Press.

Scheier, M. F., & Carver, C. S. (1992). Effects of optimism on psychological and physical well-being: Theoretical overview and empirical update. *Cognitive Therapy and Research, 16,* 201–228.

Schulz, R., & Heckhausen, J. (1996). A life span model of successful aging. *American Psychologist, 51,* 702–714.

Seligman, M. E. P. (1975). *Helplessness: On depression, development, and death.* San Francisco: Freedman.

Seligman, M. E. P. (1999). The president's address. *American Psychologist, 54,* 559–562.

Shah, J., & Higgins, E. T. (1997). Expectancy X value effects: Regulatory focus as determinant of magnitude and direction. *Journal of Personality and Social Psychology, 73,* 447–458.

Showers, C. J., & Ryff, C. D. (1996). Self-differentiation and well-being in a life transition. *Personality and Social Psychology Bulletin, 22,* 448–460.

Snyder, C. R. (1994). *The psychology of hope.* New York: Free Press.

Snyder, C. R., & Lopez, S. J. (Eds.). (2002). *Handbook of positive psychology.* New York: Oxford University Press.

Sprangers, M. A. G., & Schwartz, C. E. (1999). Integrating response shift into health-related quality of life research: A theoretical model. *Social Science and Medicine, 48,* 1507–1515.

Stroebe, M. S., Stroebe, W., & Hansson, R. O. (Eds.). (1993). *Handbook of bereavement: Theory, research, and intervention.* Cambridge, England: Cambridge University Press.

Taylor, S. E. (1989). *Positive illusions: Creative self-deception and the healthy mind.* New York: Basic Books.

Tedeschi, R. G., & Calhoun, L. G. (1995). *Trauma and transformation: Growing in the aftermath of suffering.* Thousand Oaks, CA: Sage.

Updegraff, J. A., & Taylor, S. E. (2000). From vulnerability to growth: Positive and negative effects of stressful life events. In J. H. Harvey & E. Miller (Eds.), *Loss and trauma: General and close relationship perspectives* (pp. 3–28). Philadelphia: Brunner-Routledge.

Vallacher, R. R., & Wegner, D. M. (1985). *A theory of action identification.* Hillsdale, NJ: Erlbaum.

Vroom, V. H. (1964). *Work and motivation.* New York: Wiley.

Wicklund, R. A., & Gollwitzer, P. M. (1982). *Symbolic self-completion.* Hillsdale, NJ: Erlbaum.

Wortman, C. B., & Brehm, J. W. (1975). Responses to uncontrollable outcomes: An integration of reactance theory and the learned helplessness model. In L. Berkowitz (Ed.), *Advances in experimental social psychology* (Vol. 8, pp. 277–336). New York: Academic Press.

Wright, R. A., & Brehm, J. W. (1989). Energization and goal attractiveness. In L. A. Pervin (Ed.), *Goal concepts in personality and social psychology* (pp. 169–210). Hillsdale, NJ: Erlbaum.

Wrosch, C., Scheier, M. F., Carver, C. S., & Schulz, R. (in press). The importance of goal disengagement in adaptive self-regulation: When giving up is beneficial. *Self and Identity*.

8

THE MALLEABILITY OF SEX DIFFERENCES IN RESPONSE TO CHANGING SOCIAL ROLES

ALICE H. EAGLY AND AMANDA B. DIEKMAN

The scientific study of sex differences and similarities is critical to understanding human behavior. Because gender is one of the most fundamental distinctions people make between human groups, scientific knowledge about the ways in which female and male behavior does or does not differ has far-reaching implications for explaining human functioning. The potential of such knowledge to promote understanding of human strengths emerges in part from the questions that it raises concerning the malleability of male and female behavior in response to changing conditions. As the roles and responsibilities of the sexes become more similar, as they have especially in many Western societies in the 20th century, do the psychological attributes of women and men become more similar as well? Or do people who differ by sex show divergent behavioral tendencies, regardless of changes in their social roles? In this chapter, we consider some answers to these questions.

Preparation of this chapter was supported by National Science Foundation Grant SBR-9729449 to Alice H. Eagly.

We use two lenses to view the malleability of sex differences in response to changing social roles. The first lens is social perceivers' experiences in their daily lives, which yield a common-sense psychology of everyday thinking about women and men.[1] The second lens is the observations produced by scientific research, which yield a scientific psychology of sex differences. In common-sense psychology, the flexibility of human sex differences in response to the changing life circumstances of women and men receives considerable emphasis. In scientific psychology, assumptions about the malleability of sex differences vary depending on researchers' theoretical positions, and empirical research has begun to address the question of whether sex differences in psychological dispositions have changed in response to changing social roles.

THE COMMON-SENSE PSYCHOLOGY OF SEX DIFFERENCES

That people believe that there are differences between the typical characteristics of men and women is a clear conclusion from research on gender stereotypes (see review by Kite, 2001). Nonetheless, people do not view the sexes as very different in the sense that they locate men and women on opposite ends of psychological dimensions (e.g., men are aggressive, women are unaggressive). Rather, the implicit statistical model underlying these beliefs consists of sex differences in central tendency, with distributions of women and men overlapping to a greater or lesser extent depending on the domain (Swim, 1994).

A very important aspect of the common-sense psychology of sex differences is the perceived malleability of these differences—that is, the extent to which people believe that the attributes of women and men change in response to a change in the typical life circumstances of each sex. In a research program addressing this issue, we examined the beliefs that social perceivers have about the characteristics of women and men at different time periods—the past, the present, and the future (Diekman & Eagly, 2000). We hypothesized that because of the increasing similarity of the lives of women and men, people would discern convergence in their characteristics. To the extent that women or men or, for that matter, members of any social group are perceived to change their characteristics over time, they should acquire a cultural representation that incorporates this change —in our terminology, a *dynamic stereotype*.

Why would members of a social group be viewed as changing their attributes? According to social role theory (Eagly, 1987; Eagly, Wood, & Diekman, 2000), the role behavior of group members shapes their stereo-

---

[1]Heider (1958) introduced the term *common-sense psychology* and maintained that scientific psychology has much to learn from the study of how people construe behavior in everyday life.

type because perceivers assume correspondence between people's behavior in their everyday social roles and their inner dispositions (see Gilbert, 1998). Perceivers fail to give much weight to the constraints of social roles in inferring the dispositions of role occupants. Therefore, groups should have dynamic stereotypes—that is, be perceived as changing their inner dispositions—to the extent that their typical social roles are perceived to change over time.

Applied to men and women, this theory predicts that perceivers should think that sex differences are eroding because of increasing similarity in the social roles of men and women. Moreover, the stereotype of women should be more dynamic than that of men, because much greater change has taken place in the roles of women than in those of men. The increasing similarity in the roles of women and men is thus primarily a product of women's increased wage labor, which has occurred without a commensurate change in men's domestic labor (Shelton & John, 1996), and of women's entry into male-dominated occupations, which has occurred without a similar shift of men into female-dominated occupations (Reskin & Roos, 1990).

In our studies examining contemporary perceivers' beliefs about the typical attributes of women and men of the past, present, or future, women and men were perceived to converge strongly in their masculine personality characteristics (e.g., competitive, dominant) from the years 1950 to 2050. Also, the sexes were perceived to converge moderately in their masculine cognitive characteristics (e.g., analytical, good with numbers) and masculine physical characteristics (e.g., rugged, muscular). This convergence in masculine characteristics reflected perceived change in women but not in men. Although there was no convergence in feminine cognitive characteristics (e.g., imaginative, intuitive) or physical characteristics (e.g., cute, petite), there was modest convergence in feminine personality characteristics (e.g., gentle, kind) that was a product of women's perceived loss of these characteristics and (only in some studies) of men's gain as well.

The common-sense psychology of gender thus features belief in considerable malleability over a 100-year time span, and the trends that people project over time primarily reflect the belief that women's attributes are changing. People believe that women of the present are more masculine than women of the past and that women of the future will be more masculine than women of the present, especially in their personality characteristics. This perceived shift in women's attributes encompassed even masculine personality characteristics that are unfavorably evaluated (e.g., egotistical, arrogant). Belief in complementary change by which men increase their feminine tendencies in personality, cognitive, and physical domains was not consistently demonstrated in this research, nor was belief in change by which women decrease their feminine tendencies. We predicted these results because the increasing similarity in the roles of women and men is primarily a product of change in women's roles. Because the modal situation for women now incorporates paid employment along with domestic responsibilities, perceivers should believe that women's attributes have shifted to incorporate the personal characteristics identified with men and employees.

Functioning as implicit role theorists, people apparently believe that personal characteristics, especially personality attributes, adapt to social structure. When change takes the form of a substantial proportion of a social group changing their social roles, people believe that the characteristics of these group members change as well to meet the requirements of the new roles. It is especially revealing that people extrapolate changes in women's roles and characteristics into the future. This common-sense belief that women will continue to change should foster continued upward change in the status of women.

Despite some resistance to the shifts in women's roles, especially among more politically conservative social groups, the shared belief that women will augment their masculine personality, cognitive, and physical characteristics in the future should expand women's access to male-dominated roles and to the socialization experiences and training opportunities that will allow them to assume these roles. It is thus likely that stereotypes' representation of change in group members' characteristics functions in the service of social change, despite the potential for stereotypes' representation of group members' present characteristics to justify the status quo (e.g., Jost & Banaji, 1994). Dynamic stereotypes may thus be an important part of the positive psychology of everyday life.

THE SCIENTIFIC PSYCHOLOGY OF SEX DIFFERENCES

How do social perceivers' beliefs about sex differences correspond to the findings of research psychologists who study these differences with scientific methods? Does research validate the common-sense psychological principles that men and women have stereotypic attributes and that these sex-typed attributes are converging, with women increasingly manifesting attributes previously associated with men? It is surely possible that this common-sense psychology is incorrect, perhaps even particularly illusory, in its understanding of the malleability of male and female characteristics.

Concerning the scientific psychology of sex differences, research psychologists have a somewhat complicated tale to tell. Many psychologists have been hesitant to use their research to produce conclusions about sex differences. This reluctance stems from understandable roots—in particular, from the fear that scientific validation of differences would suggest that one sex is inherently inferior to the other. Displaying ambivalence about investigating sex differences, psychologists have debated whether male and female data should even be separately reported and compared (see Kitzinger, 1994).

Given this disinclination of many research psychologists to study male–female differences, the gap in knowledge has been exploited by popular writers such as John Gray (1992), who offer the public accounts of sex differences that are grounded in personal experiences and informal observations. Regardless of whether such writers correctly discern sex differences and similarities, their generalizations do not have the credibility of research that uses scientific methods. Therefore, some researchers have responded to the public's quite insatiable interest in understanding female and male behavior by producing scientific knowledge that has begun to replace speculation.

Theories of Sex Differences

Scientific knowledge develops in conjunction with theories that are tested empirically. Therefore, it is not surprising that researchers have proposed theories of sex differences and similarities (see Eckes & Trautner, 2000). In social psychological theories, the causes of sex-differentiated behavior include sex-typed skills, beliefs, self-concepts, attitudes, and social expectations. In personality and developmental theories, the causes include the socialization experiences of girls and boys in conjunction with their interpretations of sex-typed environments. Theorists who have addressed the more ultimate causes of differences have taken primarily an essentialist or a social constructionist perspective. Essentialist perspectives emphasize the basic, stable sex differences that arise from inherent causes such as biological factors and evolved psychological dispositions (Buss & Kenrick, 1998). Social constructionist perspectives emphasize variation in sex differences across societies and across contexts within societies (e.g., Bohan, 1993). In this view, sex differences depend on the constraints that particular contexts place on social interaction.

Our preferred perspective is social role theory, which is an interactionist approach because it draws explicitly on both essentialist and constructionist ideas (see Eagly, Wood, & Diekman, 2000). In this analysis, sex differences in social behavior arise from the distribution of men and women into social roles within a society. In current industrial and postindustrial economies, these roles are organized so that women are more likely than men to assume domestic roles of homemaker and primary caretaker of children, whereas men are more likely than women to assume roles in the paid economy and to be primary family providers. The different positions of men and women in the social structure yield sex-differentiated behavior through a variety of proximal, mediating processes. One such process is the formation of gender roles, by which people of each sex are expected to have characteristics that equip them for the tasks that they typically carry out. Gender roles, along with the specific roles occupied by men and women (e.g., provider, homemaker), then guide social behavior. This guidance is mediated by sex-typed socialization practices, as well as by processes detailed in social psychological theory and research (e.g., expectancy confirmation, self-regulatory processes).

Social role theory is interactionist in its assumptions about the determinants of sex-typed roles within a society (Wood & Eagly, in press). These determinants include the variable factors represented by the social, economic, technological, and ecological forces present in a society and inherent sex differences represented by each sex's physical attributes and related behaviors, especially women's childbearing and nursing of infants and men's greater size, speed, and upper-body strength. These physical sex differences, in interaction with social and ecological conditions, influence the roles held by men and women because certain activities are more efficiently accomplished by one sex than by the other. The benefits of this greater efficiency emerge because women and men are often allied in cooperative relationships in societies and engage in a division of labor. In brief, then, we argue that psychological sex differences are a function of gender roles and other proximal causes, which in turn arise from the distal causes that define the positions of women and men in the social structure.

Scientific Descriptions of Sex Differences

What have research psychologists found when they compared men and women? Increasingly, psychologists have drawn their conclusions systematically by taking many studies into account. Faced with very large research bases composed of multiple studies (e.g., the hundreds of studies that have compared the self-esteem or leadership style of men and women), research psychologists have turned to the methods known as *quantitative synthesis* or *meta-analysis*, which provide statistically justified methods for synthesizing research (see Johnson & Eagly, 2000). Meta-analysts typically represent the comparison between male and female behavior for each relevant study in terms of its effect size (or d), which expresses the sex difference in units of the study's standard deviation. Calculating effect sizes places each study's sex difference on a continuum that ranges from no difference to large differences. With each finding represented by an effect size, multiple studies are collectively represented by taking an average of their effect sizes. This central tendency of effect sizes is also located along this quantitative continuum and thus does not provide a simple yes or no answer to the question of whether the sexes differed in general in the available studies. Also, because findings generally differ from one study to the other, this variability illuminates the conditions under which sex differences are larger, smaller, and sometimes reversed from their typical direction.

Given these sophisticated scientific methods for integrating research findings, have psychologists produced clear descriptions of sex differences and similarities? To some extent, the answer is yes. Psychologists have shown that differences between the sexes appear in research data as distributions that overlap to a greater or lesser extent. Some sex differences are relatively large compared with other psychological findings—for example, some cognitive performances (e.g., on the Shepard-Metzler test of mental rotation), some social behaviors (e.g., facial expressiveness, frequency of filled pauses in speech), some sexual behaviors (e.g., incidence of masturbation), and one class of personality traits (tender-minded and nurturant tendencies). However, most aggregated sex-difference findings are in the small-to-moderate range that appears to be typical of research findings in psychology. Nonetheless, even small differences are not necessarily inconsequential in everyday life. When small differences cumulate over time and individuals, they can produce substantial effects (e.g., Martell, Lane, & Emrich, 1995).

THE RELATION BETWEEN THE COMMON-SENSE PSYCHOLOGY AND THE SCIENTIFIC PSYCHOLOGY OF SEX DIFFERENCES

To understand the relation between the common-sense psychology and the scientific psychology of sex differences, researchers have examined the overall accuracy of gender stereotypes by comparing these stereotypes to the meta-analyzed results of research on sex differences. This research has shown that, for the most part, gender stereotypes match research findings on sex differences, thus yielding the conclusion that people are in general competent to correctly discern the typical or average behaviors of men and women in everyday life. For example, in a study examining 77 meta-analyzed traits, abilities, and behaviors, Hall and Carter (1999) found a correlation of .70 between the mean of student judges' estimates of sex differences and meta-analytic effect sizes in the 77 areas. These judges displayed an understanding of the relative magnitude of differences in addition to their male or female direction. However, as Hall and Carter showed, some people perceive sex differences more accurately than other people do; and, as Diekman, Eagly, and Kulesa (2002) showed, there are some systematic biases that affect the accuracy of perceptions of men and women. Nonetheless, one way of describing the sex differences established by scientific research is that they generally conform to people's ideas about men and women.

As we have explained, consistent with the ability of humans to adapt psychologically to changing social conditions, the common-sense theory that perceivers hold about sex differences incorporates malleability in the characteristics of men and women in response to changes in social roles.

Research has shown that the substantial change that has occurred in women's roles is itself reflected in shifts of attitudes toward greater approval of nontraditional roles for women (e.g., Twenge, 1997a) and of women's participation in the labor force, equal pay for women, and nonmaternal care for children (see Kahn & Crosby, 1985). Yet the critical question with respect to perceivers' assumptions about malleability is whether research on personality, social behavior, and cognitive abilities has produced evidence of actual change over time in the personal attributes of women and men. Such evidence is difficult to produce because it requires the collection of comparable data over long time periods. Also, if research methods or participant populations have changed as a research area matures, the effects of such shifts on findings must be controlled in order to discern genuine change in behavioral tendencies (Knight, Fabes, & Higgins, 1996). Despite these complexities, in research literatures in which studies extend over several decades, the hypothesis that sex differences are decreasing in size is amenable to testing by relating the year that the data were collected to the outcomes of the studies.

From the perspectives of the common-sense psychology of sex differences and of social role theory, convergent male and female secular trends should be observed most clearly in research areas that reflect masculine, but not feminine, personality, cognitive, and physical dispositions, and this convergence should be accounted for mainly by change in women. Some findings support these predictions. For example, the career plans of male and female university students showed a marked convergence from 1966 to 1996 that is accounted for mainly by changes in women's career aspirations (Astin, Parrott, Korn, & Sax, 1997). Also, a meta-analytic synthesis of sex differences in reports of job attribute preferences showed that job attributes such as freedom, challenge, leadership, prestige, and power became relatively more important to women, in comparison to men, from the 1970s to the 1980s and 1990s (Konrad, Ritchie, Lieb, & Corrigall, 2000). As the gender barriers to opportunity declined during this period, women's aspirations rose to obtain jobs with these attributes. Also, a meta-analysis of self-report measures of masculine and feminine personality traits found that women's masculinity increased linearly with the studies' year of publication (Twenge, 1997b). Men's masculinity showed a weaker increase with year, and their femininity increased slightly as well.

Some meta-analyses of sex differences in specific domains of stereotypically masculine behavior also showed a decrease in the magnitude of these differences. For example, a meta-analysis of sex differences in risk-taking behavior found a decrease over time in the tendency of men to engage in riskier behavior than women (Byrnes, Miller, & Schafer, 1999). A meta-analysis of leader emergence in small groups found a decrease over time in the tendency for men to emerge more than women (Eagly & Karau, 1991). One meta-analysis showed convergence over time in the aggressiveness of women and men (Hyde, 1984), although another did not show such convergence (Eagly & Steffen, 1986). Also, studies of performance on tests of cognitive abilities demonstrated some declines in the size of sex differences favoring men on tests of mathematics and science but no decline in the size of differences favoring women on tests of reading and writing (Campbell, Hombo, & Mazzeo, 2000; Hedges & Nowell, 1995; Hyde, Fennema, & Lamon, 1990). Also, the marked increase in women's athletic participation (National Collegiate Athletic Association, 1997) suggests that women may even be physically stronger than in the past. On balance, in view of some evidence of actual convergence in masculine personal characteristics, perceivers may be reasonably accurate observers not only of the current attributes of the sexes, but also of changes in these attributes.

CONCLUSION

The common-sense psychology of sex differences is compatible with the scientific psychology of social role theory because both emphasize the capacity of the sexes to change their characteristics as their social roles change. Both perspectives portray the sexes as converging in their psychological attributes mainly through women assuming some of the attributes that have traditionally been associated with men. The research literatures of psychology have produced some evidence that human behavior is actually changing in this manner in the United States. Such changes would probably also be evident in other nations in which the status of women has shown substantial upward change in recent decades. It is of course difficult to array the evidence of large research literatures to test overarching propositions about change over time, despite the advantages offered by meta-analysis. Yet, as research extends over longer periods of time and researchers refine their use of meta-analytic techniques, conclusions about the secular changes in sex differences will become more firmly grounded in empirical data.

Some readers may be surprised to find that change in men and women over time appears to be asymmetrical, with women adopting men's masculine characteristics without much reciprocal change whereby men adopt women's feminine characteristics. From a social role theory perspective, men's characteristics would not change until they change their social roles by accepting substantially more domestic responsibility and entering female-dominated occupations. Because any changes in this direction have been small, there is little basis for predicting that men would adopt more feminine characteristics. Groups alter their actual characteristics as they prepare for and occupy roles that have new demands: Women but not men have undergone such transitions on a major scale in recent decades in the United States and many other industrialized nations.

Another possible direction of social change is that roles change to accommodate new role occupants. For example, in relation to the managerial roles that women have entered in large numbers, rather than women conforming to the typical behaviors of male managers, the managerial role might change by encompassing the more relational qualities of women (see Eagly & Karau, 2002). Although many social roles are flexible enough to accommodate a range of behavioral styles, new role occupants' accommodation to the requirements of roles may override roles' accommodation to the characteristics of new role occupants, if only because the newcomers are at least initially only a small minority. However, if the proportion of new occupants of a social role increases very substantially, so that it becomes dominated by the new group, the role may change greatly in its wage structure and cultural representation (e.g., see Preston's [1995] analysis of the formation of public school teaching as a woman's profession).

Have psychologists proceeded in this research area in a manner that allows their research and theory to contribute to an understanding of human strengths? In showing that people are for the most part accurate observers of sex differences, the study of gender stereotypes has corrected the negative view that people are misguided in their everyday life about as fundamental a matter as the characteristics that are typical of women and men. In suggesting that dynamic stereotypes can foster upward change in the status of groups, this research has opened up the possibility that the universal tendency of people to stereotype social groups is not necessarily destructive to group members' aspirations for changing their situation.

The dynamic stereotypes that people hold about women can operate in the service of social change by opening doors to opportunities previously unavailable to women. Moreover, in demonstrating that the common-sense psychology of sex differences includes belief in their malleability in response to changes in social roles, our research has demonstrated a common-sense optimism about the ability of humans to adapt to changing conditions. Finally, in maintaining an open-minded perspective about the potential of men and women to develop characteristics that allow them to fulfill nontraditional as well as traditional roles, scientific investigators of sex differences have begun to produce evidence that people can fulfill their hopes and dreams without being seriously limited by sex-typed psychological characteristics.

REFERENCES

Astin, A. W., Parrott, S. A., Korn, W. S., & Sax, L. J. (1997). *The American freshman: Thirty year trends.* Los Angeles: Higher Education Research Institute, University of California at Los Angeles.

Bohan, J. S. (1993). Regarding gender: Essentialism, constructionism, and feminist psychology. *Psychology of Women Quarterly, 17,* 5–21.

Buss, D. M., & Kenrick, D. T. (1998). Evolutionary social psychology. In D. T. Gilbert, S. T. Fiske, & G. Lindzey (Eds.), *The handbook of social psychology* (4th ed., Vol. 2, pp. 982–1026). Boston: McGraw-Hill.

Byrnes, J. P., Miller, D. C., & Schafer, W. D. (1999). Gender differences in risk taking: A meta-analysis. *Psychological Bulletin, 125,* 367–383.

Campbell, J. R., Hombo, C. M., & Mazzeo, J. (2000). *NAEP trends in academic progress: Three decades of student performance* (No. NCES 2000-469). Washington, DC: U.S. Department of Education, Office of Educational Research and Improvement, National Center for Educational Statistics.

Diekman, A. B., & Eagly, A. H. (2000). Stereotypes as dynamic constructs: Women and men of the past, present, and future. *Personality and Social Psychology Bulletin, 26,* 1171–1188.

Diekman, A. B., Eagly, A. H., & Kulesa, P. (2002). Accuracy and bias in stereotypes about the social and political attitudes of women and men. *Journal of Experimental Social Psychology, 38,* 268–282.

Eagly, A. H. (1987). *Sex differences in social behavior: A social-role interpretation.* Hillsdale, NJ: Erlbaum.

Eagly, A. H., & Karau, S. J. (1991). Gender and the emergence of leaders: A meta-analysis. *Journal of Personality and Social Psychology, 60,* 685–710.

Eagly, A. H., & Karau, S. J. (2002). Role congruity theory of prejudice toward female leaders. *Psychological Review, 109,* 573–598.

Eagly, A. H., & Steffen, V. J. (1986). Gender and aggressive behavior: A meta-analytic review of the social psychological literature. *Psychological Bulletin, 100,* 309–330.

Eagly, A. H., Wood, W., & Diekman, A. (2000). Social role theory of sex differences and similarities: A current appraisal. In T. Eckes & H. M. Trautner (Eds.), *The developmental social psychology of gender* (pp. 123–174). Mahwah, NJ: Erlbaum.

Eckes, T., & Trautner, H. M. (Eds.). (2000). *The developmental social psychology of gender.* Mahwah, NJ: Erlbaum.

Gilbert, D. T. (1998). Ordinary personology. In D. T. Gilbert, S. T. Fiske, & G. Lindzey (Eds.), *The handbook of social psychology* (4th ed., Vol. 2, pp. 89–150). Boston: McGraw-Hill.

Gray, J. (1992). *Men are from Mars, women are from Venus: A practical guide for improving communication and getting what you want in your relationships.* New York: Harper Collins.

Hall, J. A., & Carter, J. D. (1999). Gender-stereotype accuracy as an individual difference. *Journal of Personality and Social Psychology, 77,* 350–359.

Hedges, L. V., & Nowell, A. (1995). Sex differences in mental test scores, variability, and numbers of high-scoring individuals. *Science, 269,* 41–45.

Heider, F. (1958). *The psychology of interpersonal relations.* New York: Wiley.

Hyde, J. S. (1984). How large are gender differences in aggression? A developmental meta-analysis. *Developmental Psychology, 20,* 722–736.

Hyde, J. S., Fennema, E., & Lamon, S. J. (1990). Gender differences in mathematics performance: A meta-analysis. *Psychological Bulletin, 107,* 139–155.

Johnson, B. T., & Eagly, A. H. (2000). Quantitative synthesis of social psychological research. In H. T. Reis & C. M. Judd (Eds.), *Handbook of research methods in social and personality psychology* (pp. 496–528). New York: Cambridge University Press.

Jost, J. T., & Banaji, M. R. (1994). The role of stereotyping in system-justification and the production of false consciousness. *British Journal of Social Psychology, 33,* 1–27.

Kahn, W. A., & Crosby, F. (1985). Discriminating between attitudes and discriminatory behaviors: Change and stasis. In L. Larwood, A. H. Stromberg, & B. A. Gutek (Eds.), *Women and work: An annual review* (Vol. 1, pp. 215–238). Thousand Oaks, CA: Sage.

Kite, M. (2001). Gender stereotypes. In J. Worrell (Ed.), *Encyclopedia of gender* (pp. 561–570). San Diego, CA: Academic Press.

Kitzinger, C. (Ed.). (1994). Special feature: Should psychologists study sex differences? *Feminism and Psychology, 4,* 501–546.

Knight, G. P., Fabes, R. A., & Higgins, D. A. (1996). Concerns about drawing causal inferences from meta-analyses: An example in the study of gender differences in aggression. *Psychological Bulletin, 119,* 410–421.

Konrad, A. M., Ritchie, J. E., Jr., Lieb, P., & Corrigall, E. (2000). Sex differences and similarities in job attribute preferences: A meta-analysis. *Psychological Bulletin, 126,* 593–641.

Martell, R. F., Lane, D. M., & Emrich, C. E. (1995). Male-female differences: A computer simulation. *American Psychologist, 51,* 157–158.

National Collegiate Athletic Association. (1997). *Participation statistics report: 1982–1996.* Overland Park, KS: Author.

Preston, J. A. (1995). Gender and the formation of a women's profession: The case of public school teaching. In J. A. Jacobs (Ed.), *Gender inequality at work* (pp. 379–407). Thousand Oaks, CA: Sage.

Reskin, B. F., & Roos, P. A. (1990). *Job queues, gender queues: Explaining women's inroads into male occupations.* Philadelphia: Temple University Press.

Shelton, B. A., & John, D. (1996). The division of household labor. *Annual Review of Sociology, 22,* 299–322.

Swim, J. K. (1994). Perceived versus meta-analytic effect sizes: An assessment of the accuracy of gender stereotypes. *Journal of Personality and Social Psychology, 66,* 21–36.

Twenge, J. M. (1997a). Attitudes toward women, 1970–1995: A meta-analysis. *Psychology of Women Quarterly, 21,* 35–51.

Twenge, J. M. (1997b). Changes in masculine and feminine traits over time: A meta-analysis. *Sex Roles, 36,* 305–325.

Wood, W., & Eagly, A. H. (in press). A cross-cultural analysis of the social roles of women and men: Implications for the origins of sex differences. *Psychological Bulletin.*

9

TOWARD A POSITIVE PSYCHOLOGY: SOCIAL DEVELOPMENTAL AND CULTURAL CONTRIBUTIONS

NANCY EISENBERG AND VIVIAN OTA WANG

Quite recently, there has been a flurry of interest in positive psychology. It has been argued that psychologists have focused on deficits in human functioning and that positive development and functioning have been neglected. Although problems in adjustment, including violence and psychopathology, have been more popular topics for study than healthy or positive development, research on positive aspects of psychological and behavioral development certainly is not new. What is new is the widespread use of the term *positive psychology*.

Many aspects of positive human functioning have been examined for decades (or longer) and in considerable depth. For example, research on prosocial behavior, that is, voluntary behavior motivated to benefit another, has been published for many decades, with a number of books on the topic written in the 1970s and early 1980s (e.g., Darley & Latane,

Writing of this chapter was supported by a grant and a Research Scientist Award from the National Institutes of Mental Health (R01 HH55052, R01 MH60838, and K05 M801321) to Nancy Eisenberg.

1968; Mussen & Eisenberg-Berg, 1977). In fact, the popularity and quantity of research on this topic has merited review chapters in the major handbooks in developmental (Eisenberg & Fabes, 1998; Radke-Yarrow, Zahn-Waxler, & Chapman, 1983) and social (Batson, 1998) psychology. Similarly, theory on emotional empathy—that is, feeling an emotion consistent with another's emotional state or situation—has been an important area of interest since the 1970s (see Batson, 1998; Eisenberg & Fabes, 1998; Feshbach, 1978; Hoffman, 1995, 2000). Moreover, there has been considerable work for decades on topics such as the development of social competence (see Rubin, Bukowski, & Parker, 1998) and subjective well-being (Diener, 1984; Diener, Suh, Lucas, & Smith, 1999). Thus, to some degree, the notion of positive psychology is not novel but is merely an effort to emphasize domains of psychology that may have been overshadowed by the current focus on maladjustment and the darker side of human nature.

The fact that positive psychology is not new does not mean that a stronger emphasis on the topic is unnecessary. In recent years in the United States, funding has been increasingly targeted toward work on mental health problems and relations between psychological processes or stress and poor physical health. In developmental psychology, more and more scholars have been drawn into research related to problem behaviors and maladjustment, such as work related to prevention and developmental psychopathology. Concurrently, in the domain of prosocial development, there has been a marked drop in the number of scholars working primarily on the topic in the last decade (Batson, 1998). Nonetheless, even in this work, there has been a focus on processes that promote positive adjustment despite stress and adversity, such as coping (e.g., Wolchik & Sandler, 1997) and resiliency (Masten & Coatsworth, 1995). Thus, human strengths are, and have been, a part of the study of human frailty.

PITFALLS IN STUDYING POSITIVE PSYCHOLOGY

Positive development can be intrapersonal (in terms of happiness and life satisfaction), as well as interpersonal. Whereas prosocial behavior and empathy-related responding seem central to the issue of positive development in the interpersonal domain, coping is an important topic if one wishes to understand human strengths in dealing with stress, interpersonal or otherwise. We will use these domains of research for examples of pitfalls when studying human strengths.

Discrepancies Between True and Apparent Prosocial Behavior

One potential pitfall in studying positive development and behavior has been the failure to clearly differentiate between what is and what merely appears to be positive functioning or behavior. Of course, it often is difficult to define what is genuinely "positive," much less develop ways of differentiating truly positive functioning from less positive functioning that merely appears positive. An apt example can be found in the study of altruism. Altruism is a type of prosocial behavior. *Prosocial behavior* generally is defined as voluntary behavior intended to benefit others. Prosocial behaviors such as helping, sharing, and comforting can be enacted for many reasons, from concern for another to attempts to curry favor or obtain rewards. Altruism is intrinsically motivated voluntary behavior intended to benefit another—acts motivated by internal motives such as concern for others or by internalized values, goals, and self-rewards rather than by the expectation of concrete or social rewards or the avoidance of punishment (Eisenberg & Fabes, 1998). Because of the emphasis on genuine caring and internalized motives and values, altruism has been highly relevant to an understanding of the development of morality and caring for others.

Unfortunately, because of the difficulties in differentiating between altruistically motivated actions and actions motivated by more ignoble concerns, people have often studied prosocial behaviors such as helping and sharing without knowing if the motives behind the given behaviors were altruistic. Investigators have often tried to increase the probability that an enacted prosocial behavior is altruistic by assessing the behavior in a context in which the likelihood of receiving material or social rewards for prosocial action is minimized. Moreover, a body of literature exists, primarily in social psychology, in which investigators have tried to differentiate between altruistically motivated prosocial behaviors (e.g., motivated by sympathy) and those motivated by the avoidance of guilt or aversive, self-focused distress, empathic positive emotion, or identification with another person (e.g., Batson, 1998). However, the manipulations involved in this work, such as whether the potential helper has to deal with the helpee in the future (which could induce distress) or whether the helper sees the aid recipient's reactions to the receipt of assistance (which could induce empathic positive emotion) have been subtle and difficult to implement and have resulted in inconsistent findings across studies (see Batson, 1998). Thus, in general it has been quite difficult to know if behaviors that appear to be positive are truly as moral as they seem.

Of course, one could argue that it doesn't matter much why people help one another, as long as they do so. But if people help for egoistic reasons, they will do so primarily in those circumstances in which they perceive some sort of self-gain. In contrast, if people assist others due to sympathetic concern or based on the desire to live up to internalized values, they are more likely to display altruistic behavior in circumstances in which others are in need, when there is little reason to expect self-gain. An extreme example is individuals in Europe who assisted Jews in Nazi-occupied territories during World War II. These individuals often seemed to provide assistance due to concern or internalized values that extended to individuals outside their immediate social world (Oliner & Oliner, 1988), and they would have been unlikely to do so if they wished to obtain rewards or approval (although some individuals no doubt assisted because of connections with other individuals—e.g., in their church—who asked them to assist).

Positive Behaviors With Negative Responses

A second difficulty in assessing human strengths and positive behavior has been that some behaviors that appear to be strengths or adaptive also may lead to behaviors or internal processes that are not especially positive or adaptive. Consider the example of *empathy*, defined as an affective response that stems from the apprehension or comprehension of another's emotional state or condition and which is identical or very similar to what the other person is feeling or would be expected to feel (Eisenberg & Fabes, 1998). For some time, theorists and researchers assumed that empathy generally engendered other-oriented concern and prosocial behavior toward others (Feshbach, 1978; Hoffman, 1995, 2000). However, as Batson (1998) pointed out, when empathy is experienced as aversive, people tend to become concerned about themselves rather than others. This may occur when individuals experience overly high levels of empathy with negative emotion—that is, empathic overarousal. We have argued that empathy is most likely to lead to sympathetic concern and to altruistic behavior when empathy is experienced at a moderate level. In fact, some evidence is consistent with the view that high empathic arousal is associated with lower levels of prosocial behavior (see Eisenberg & Fabes, 1998). Thus, the capacity to experience others' emotional states or empathize with their situation, which generally is considered a human strength, may sometimes undermine caring interpersonal reactions and behavior.

Contextual Considerations

A third difficulty in studying human strengths is that what is good for the individual may not be viewed as a strength by people around the individual. Thus, what is viewed as positive development or a human strength likely varies across individuals and, as a consequence, may engender immediate or long-term costs for behaviors or characteristics that are viewed as positive by others. For example, preschool children who cope with their negative emotion in peer interactions by avoiding the situation appear to be viewed positively (as socially appropriate) by adults (e.g., teachers or adult observers). However, such avoidant behavior in the preschool years is associated with externalizing problems 2 and 4 years later (Eisenberg et al., 1999). Moreover, the same coping behavior or style of coping may be viewed as a strength in some contexts and as a dysfunctional response in other situations. For example, instrumental or secondary coping —taking control of situations and trying to influence objective events or conditions—appears to be productive in contexts in which the individual has control but is associated with more negative outcomes (e.g., distress or frustration) in situations in which individuals do not have control (e.g., Altshuler & Ruble, 1989; Weisz, McCabe, & Dennig, 1994).

Cultural Considerations

Another issue to consider in conceptualizing and measuring human strengths is that what is seen as a strength undoubtedly differs across cultures. For example, achievement of personal happiness and well-being, as well as the maintenance and enhancement of one's overall evaluation of the self, is likely to be viewed more positively in individualistic cultures than in collective cultures (Diener et al., 1999; Kitayama, Markus, Matsumoto, & Norasakkunkit, 1997). Similarly, valuing of prosocial behavior may differ across cultures. Hindu Indians, school-aged and adult, tend to focus more than Americans on the importance of responsiveness to others' needs in discussing moral conflicts (Miller & Bersoff, 1992). In contrast, Americans tend to view interpersonal responsiveness and caring as less obligatory and more of a personal choice, particularly if the other person's need is moderate or minimal or if friends or strangers (rather than parents and children) are potential recipients (Miller, Bersoff, & Harwood, 1990). Thus, what is viewed as a strength or as positive behavior may be highly influenced by cultural norms and values.

IMPORTANT HUMAN STRENGTHS

Given that conceptions of human strengths differ within and across individuals and cultures, there is likely to be considerable disagreement about what are important human strengths. In thinking about human strengths and positive psychology, one can consider strengths that are important at the individual level and those significant for the functioning of the larger society. At the individual level, qualities that contribute to approaching life in a positive manner rather than to being overwhelmed by stress and negative emotion when dealing with the difficulties of everyday living are important. In addition, because of the centrality of human relationships for most aspects of functioning, including happiness and survival, social competencies are essential if individuals and groups are to cooperate, work, and live together in an affirming and constructive manner. Thus, strengths that foster positive interpersonal relationships, cooperation, peace, and understanding among people are especially worthy of study.

Regulation of Emotion and Emotion-Related Responding

What characteristics of people are especially important for enhancing interpersonal relationships, personal interactions, and adjustment? We would argue that the abilities to regulate emotions and cope effectively are essential strengths for achieving these outcomes. The abilities to effortfully regulate one's internal emotional and physiological states and one's overt behaviors (including those associated with internal emotion-related states; e.g., facial expressions, aggression, or venting of emotion) have been associated with adjustment and social competence (see Eisenberg, Fabes, Guthrie, & Reiser, 2000). Regulation is not the same as control; in our view, regulation is optimal control (with *control* defined as inhibition or restraint). Like a number of other investigators, we believe that well-regulated individuals are not overly controlled or undercontrolled; well-regulated people have the ability to respond to the ongoing demands of life experience with a range of responses that are socially acceptable and sufficiently flexible to allow for spontaneous as well as delayed reactions as needed (Cole, Michel, & Teti, 1994). Whereas regulation generally has been viewed as adaptive, it can be differentiated from *control* of behavior, which may be adaptive or maladaptive depending on its flexibility and if it can be voluntarily managed.

A key distinction in thinking about regulation and control may be voluntary or effortful versus involuntary (or less voluntary) control. Well-adjusted, regulated children would be expected to be relatively high in the ability to voluntarily control their attention and behavior as needed to respond in an adaptive manner. Rothbart and Bates (1998) defined *effortful control* as "the ability to inhibit a dominant response to perform a sub-dominant response" (p. 137). Effortful control involves both attentional regulation (e.g., the ability to voluntarily focus attention as needed) and behavioral regulation (e.g., the ability to inhibit or activate behavior as appropriate) and involves the notion of "will" or "effort." In contrast to effortful types of regulation, aspects of control, or the lack thereof exist, often appearing to be involuntary or so automatic that they are not usually under voluntary control. These might include some types of impulsivity or, at the other extreme, very low impulsivity as in overcontrolled children who are timid, restrained, and lacking in flexibility in novel or stressful situations. Extremes of involuntary control appear to be maladaptive.

Initial work has suggested that well-regulated individuals—not overly or undercontrolled but effortfully regulated—are likely to be resilient and to cope more effectively with life's stresses (Asendorpf & van Aken, 1999; Block & Block, 1980; Eisenberg et al., 2000). Recent work in other countries has suggested that children who appear to be optimally regulated or resilient, in comparison to undercontrolled or overcontrolled children, get along with others better in adolescence and adulthood, are more adjusted, and express less negative emotion (Asendorpf & van Aken, 1999; Hart, Hofmann, Edelstein, & Keller, 1997; Newman, Caspi, Moffitt, & Silva, 1997; Robins, John, Caspi, Moffitt, & Stouthamer-Loeber, 1996).

Thus, an important human strength that appears to influence many aspects of individuals' functioning is their ability to regulate themselves in an optimal manner. Indeed, effortful regulation has been positively associated not only with social competence but also with sympathy and prosocial behavior (see Eisenberg & Fabes, 1998). Moreover, people who can regulate themselves tend to experience more positive and less negative emotions (Derryberry & Rothbart, 1988; see Eisenberg & Fabes, 1992; Eisenberg, Fabes, Guthrie, & Reiser, 2000). Thus, the ability to effortfully regulate behavior when needed (but not extremes of control) seems to underlie a variety of positive aspects of human functioning and positive well-being.

Tolerance and Understanding: Requirements for Peace

Another critical human strength is the capacity of individuals for tolerance and understanding of people different from themselves—a capacity necessary for peaceful coexistence and cooperation among people from various cultures and racial or ethnic backgrounds. Although this human strength is related to sympathy and prosocial behavior, for many people it also involves extending personal and social boundaries in regard to who is a target of understanding, sympathy, and caring. Moreover, self-acceptance and self-understanding may be equally important contributors to acceptance of others (Carter & Helms, 1992; Johnson, 1987).

Recognizing the importance of such human qualities, some international organizations have launched programs to promote human strengths related to human rights and peace. For example, assuming a positivist approach for understanding human strengths, the United Nations has taken up the challenge of translating theoretical advancements in the understanding of human strengths into practice. By regarding individual and group peace and human rights as essential human strengths, the United Nations Educational, Scientific and Cultural Organization (UNESCO) has begun developing more psychologically responsive international peace and human rights programs. These programs reflect a perspective that values the importance of nurturing individual inner peace as a fundamental vehicle for meaningful and sustainable prosocial behaviors.

For example, UNESCO's Culture of Peace Program has developed and promoted educational efforts using "a holistic approach based on participatory methods and taking into account the various dimensions of education for a culture of peace: peace and non-violence; human rights; democracy; tolerance; international and intercultural understanding; cultural and linguistic diversity; gender related issues" (Savolainen, 1999, p. 53).

A case in point, their Asian-Pacific Network for International Education and Values Education (APNIEVE) curriculum has served as a culture-sensitive educational framework for contributing a more integrated psychological perspective of prosocial behaviors for personal, community, and social peace for the Asia-Pacific region (Quisumbing, 1999; UNESCO, 1995b, 1998a). This framework characterizes peace as a

> dynamic, holistic and lifelong process through which mutual respect, understanding, caring, sharing, compassion, social responsibility, solidarity, acceptance, and tolerance of diversity among individuals and groups ... are internalized and practiced together to solve problems and to work toward a just and free, peaceful and democratic society. ... This process begins with the development of inner peace ... of individuals engaged in the search for truth, knowledge, and understanding ... [and] requires that quality of relationships at all levels is committed to peace, human rights, democracy, and social justice in an ecologically sustainable environment. (Quisumbing, 1999, pp. 110–111)

UNESCO's initial peace education efforts have focused on individual and institutional racism, discrimination, structural injustices, and historical oppression. However, a growing number of people have become increasingly critical of some of these efforts because they have resulted in superficial "celebrations" of external and social cultural differences without a critical understanding of the relationship between the inner psychological dimensions of peace values and prosocial behaviors. Additionally, others have raised concerns over the primary focus on inner or personal peace. These critics have suggested that narrowly limiting the psychological development of inner personal peace may ultimately lead people to self-centered, overindividualistic states of mind or contentment with attaining personal peace instead of appreciating how inner peace can interact with subsequent work toward societal and global understanding.

In accordance with these concerns and challenges, the United Nations has recently developed a number of standard-setting instruments, declarations, and action plans that have provided the basic framework for promoting human strengths and peace worldwide (UNESCO, 1995a, 1999a) that are consistent with earlier directives advocating that "education shall be directed to the full development of the human personality and to the strengthening of respect for human rights and fundamental freedoms" (United Nations, 1948, Art. 26, Para. 2) that includes "principles of human diversity as a life-enhancing condition; conflict as a normal process to be managed constructively; and social responsibility as the human capacity ... to reflect and apply ethical norms to personal and public decisions" (UNESCO, 1999b, p. 56).

CONCLUSION

In many ways, nurturing peace, human strengths, and prosocial behaviors between and within similar and different cultures will eventually have to involve a new philosophy of thinking, learning, and being that must be capable of accommodating to the new and unforeseen demands and challenges of the 21st century. Major challenges for positive psychology include recognizing the reality of what exists versus the "appearance" of positive behavior and taking into account the diverse personal, social, and cultural contexts in which positive development is conceptualized, expressed, and regarded. Recognition of the difficulty in defining what is positive development, and according to which individuals or groups, is critical. In addition, the fact that positive development can be intra- or interpersonal and that positive development in these two domains can be complementary or conflicting is important to thinking about the costs and benefits of interventions designed to promote positive development, peace, and understanding.

With these issues in mind, positive psychology must consider how regulating inter- and intrapersonal relationships, interactions, and adjustment at the levels of the individual, organization, and larger society truly encourages and discourages human strengths and prosocial behaviors. In addition, psychologists will need to select and use findings from relatively individual-focused psychological perspectives (e.g., work on individual differences in prosocial behavior and regulation and their relation to developmental outcomes) in ways that are sensitive to what is known about group and cultural processes and interactions.

One key to lifelong learning and development is nurturing meaningful and sustainable relationships between individuals and communities by first helping people develop and sustain internally peaceful environments that allow honest exploration and understanding of real and perceived personal and group differences. Additionally, the development of psychological peace, although indeed essential, may need to be linked with empowerment for structural transformations across various levels of a person's life—personal, interpersonal, work, and institutional environments—so that collective prosocial actions can draw on inner values of peace. People do not live as isolated independent units; they are in fact interconnected and related to one another psychologically and socially.

As stated in the 1998 UNESCO *World Education Report* (1998b), because the world we leave to our children depends in large measure on the children we leave to our world, those concerned with peace must go beyond examining and negotiating conflicts. People and organizations will need to invest in accepting and understanding new and possibly unfamiliar ways as valid and valuable ways of knowing. Intervention procedures have been shown to foster tolerance; for example, Bohmig-Krumhaar,

Staudinger, and Baltes (2002) found that they could foster adults' value-relativistic thinking (i.e., tolerance, empathy) by sending participants on a virtual journey around the world and having them consider given difficult life problems at different places around the world. Additionally, individuals must consider the fact that learning about other cultural perspectives will not necessarily make one more culturally sensitive or competent. People must first understand that the self is related to others, so that they will become more flexible and capable of understanding similarities and differences. How to promote human strengths related to such an understanding is the challenge for everyone.

REFERENCES

Altshuler, J. L., & Ruble, D. N. (1989). Developmental changes in children's awareness of strategies for coping with uncontrollable stress. *Child Development, 60,* 1337–1349.

Asendorpf, J. B., & van Aken, M. A. G. (1999). Resilient, overcontrolled, and undercontrolled personality prototypes in childhood: Replicability, predictive power, and the trait-type issue. *Journal of Personality and Social Psychology, 77,* 815–832.

Batson, C. B. (1998). Altruism and prosocial behavior. In D. T. Gilbert, S. T. Fiske, & G. Lindzey (Eds.), *The handbook of social psychology* (Vol. 2, pp. 282–316). Boston: McGraw-Hill.

Block, J. H., & Block, J. (1980). The role of ego-control and ego-resiliency in the organization of behavior. In W. A. Collins (Ed.), *Development of cognition, affect, and social relations: The Minnesota Symposia on Child Psychology* (Vol. 13, pp. 39–101). Hillsdale, NJ: Erlbaum.

Böhmig-Krumhaar, S., Staudinger, U. M., & Baltes, P. B. (2002). Mehr Toleranz tut Not: Läßt sich wert-relativierendes Denken und Urteilen verbessern? [In need of more tolerance: Is it possible to facilitate vale relativism?]. *Zeitschrift für Entwicklungspsychologie und Pädagogische Psychologie, 34,* 30–43.

Carter, R. T., & Helms, J. E. (1992). The counseling process as defined by relationship types: A test of Helm's interactional model. *Journal of Multicultural Counseling and Development, 20,* 181–201.

Cole, P. M., Michel, M. K., & Teti, L. O. (1994). The development of emotion regulation and dysregulation: A clinical perspective. *Monographs of the Society for Research in Child Development, 59*(Serial No. 240), 73–100.

Darley, J. M., & Latane, B. (1968). Bystander intervention in emergencies: Diffusion of responsibility. *Journal of Personality and Social Psychology, 25,* 377–383.

Derryberry, D., & Rothbart, M. K. (1988). Arousal, affect, and attention as components of temperament. *Journal of Personality and Social Psychology, 55,* 958–966.

Diener, E. (1984). Subjective well-being. *Psychological Bulletin, 95,* 542–575.

Diener, E., Suh, E. M., Lucas, R. E., & Smith, H. L. (1999). Subjective well-being: Three decades of research. *Psychological Bulletin, 125,* 276–302.

Eisenberg, N., & Fabes, R. A. (1992). Emotion, regulation, and the development of social competence. In M. S. Clark (Ed.), *Review of personality and social psychology: Vol. 14. Emotion and social behavior* (pp. 119–150). Newbury Park, CA: Sage.

Eisenberg, N., & Fabes, R. A. (1998). Prosocial development. In W. Damon (Series Ed.) & N. Eisenberg (Vol. Ed.), *Handbook of child psychology: Vol. 3. Social, emotional, and personality development* (5th ed., pp. 701–778). New York: Wiley.

Eisenberg, N., Fabes, R. A., Guthrie, I. K., & Reiser, M. (2000). Dispositional emotionality and regulation: Their role in predicting quality of social functioning. *Journal of Personality and Social Psychology, 78,* 136–157.

Eisenberg, N., Guthrie, I. K., Murphy, B. C., Shepard, S. A., Cumberland, A., & Carlo, G. (1999). Consistency and development of prosocial dispositions: A longitudinal study. *Child Development, 70,* 1360–1372.

Feshbach, N. D. (1978). Studies of empathic behavior in children. In B. A. Maher (Ed.), *Progress in experimental personality research* (Vol. 8, pp. 1–47). New York: Academic Press.

Hart, D., Hofmann, V., Edelstein, W., & Keller, M. (1997). The relation of childhood personality types to adolescent behavior and development: A longitudinal study of Icelandic children. *Developmental Psychology, 33,* 195–205.

Hoffman, M. L. (1995). Developmental synthesis of affect and cognition and its implications for altruistic motivation. *Developmental Psychology, 11,* 607–622.

Hoffman, M. L. (2000). *Empathy and moral development: Implications for caring and justice.* Cambridge, England: Cambridge University Press.

Johnson, S. D. (1987). Knowing that versus knowing how: Toward achieving expertise through multicultural training for counseling. *Counseling Psychologist, 15,* 320–331.

Kitayama, S., Markus, H. R., Matsumoto, H., & Norasakkunkit, V. (1997). Individual and collective processes in the construction of the self: Self-enhancement in the United States and self-criticism in Japan. *Journal of Personality and Social Psychology, 72,* 1245–1266.

Masten, A. S., & Coatsworth, J. D. (1995). Competence, resilience, and psychopathology. In D. Cicchetti & D. J. Cohen (Eds.), *Developmental psychopathology: Vol. 2. Risk, disorder, and adaptation* (pp. 715–782). New York: Wiley.

Miller, J. G., & Bersoff, D. M. (1992). Culture and moral judgment: How are conflicts between justice and interpersonal responsibilities resolved? *Journal of Personality and Social Psychology, 62,* 541–554.

Miller, J. G., Bersoff, D. M., & Harwood, R. L. (1990). Perceptions of social responsibilities in India and in the United States: Moral imperatives or personal decisions? *Journal of Personality and Social Psychology, 58,* 33–47.

Mussen, P., & Eisenberg-Berg, N. (1977). *Roots of caring, sharing, and helping: The development of prosocial behavior in children*. San Francisco: Freeman.

Newman, D. L., Caspi, A., Moffitt, T. E., & Silva, P. A. (1997). Antecedents of adult interpersonal functioning: Effects of individual differences in age 3 temperament. *Developmental Psychology, 33*, 206–217.

Oliner, S. P., & Oliner, P. M. (1988). *The altruistic personality: Rescuers of Jews in Nazi Europe*. New York: Free Press.

Quisumbing, L. (1999). A framework for teacher education programmes in Asia and the Pacific. In *Korean Nation Commission for UNESCO's Education for International Understanding and Peace in Asia and the Pacific* (pp. 108–120). Bangkok, Thailand: UNESCO Principal Regional Office for Asia and the Pacific.

Radke-Yarrow, M., Zahn-Waxler, C., & Chapman, M. (1983). Prosocial dispositions and behavior. In P. Mussen (Series Ed.) & E. M. Hetherington (Vol. Ed.), *Manual of child psychology: Vol. 4. Socialization, personality, and social development* (pp. 469–545). New York: Wiley.

Robins, R. W., John, O. P., Caspi, A., Moffitt, T. E., & Stouthamer-Loeber, M. (1996). Resilient, overcontrolled, and undercontrolled boys: Three replicable personality types. *Journal of Personality and Social Psychology, 70*, 157–171.

Rothbart, M. K., & Bates, J. E. (1998). Temperament. In W. Damon (Series Ed.) & N. Eisenberg (Vol. Ed.), *Handbook of child psychology: Vol. 3. Social, emotional, and personality development* (5th ed., pp. 105–176). New York: Wiley.

Rubin, K. H., Bukowski, W., & Parker, J. G. (1998). Peer interactions, relationships, and groups. In W. Damon (Series Ed.) & N. Eisenberg (Vol. Ed.), *Handbook of child psychology: Vol. 3. Social, emotional, and personality development* (5th ed., pp. 619–700). New York: Wiley.

Savolainen, K. (1999). Education for a culture of peace. In *Korean Nation Commission for UNESCO's Education for International Understanding and Peace in Asia and the Pacific* (pp. 51–59). Bangkok, Thailand: UNESCO Principal Regional Office for Asia and the Pacific.

United Nations. (1948). *The universal declaration of human rights*. Paris: UNESCO.

United Nations Economic, Social and Cultural Organization. (1995a). *Declaration (Geneva, Switzerland, 1994) and integrated framework of action on education for peace, human rights and democracy (Paris, France, 1995)*. Paris: Author.

United Nations Economic, Social and Cultural Organization. (1995b). *The organizational meeting to form the network of regional experts in education for peace, human rights, and democracy*. Bangkok, Thailand: UNESCO Principal Regional Office for Asia and the Pacific.

United Nations Economic, Social and Cultural Organization. (1998a). *Learning to live together in peace and harmony—Values education for peace, human rights, democracy, and sustainable development for the Asia-Pacific region. A UNESCO-APNIEVE sourcebook for teacher education and tertiary level education*. Bangkok, Thailand: UNESCO Principal Regional Office for Asia and the Pacific.

United Nations Economic, Social and Cultural Organization. (1998b). *World education report*. Paris: Author.

United Nations Economic, Social and Cultural Organization. (1999a). *Declaration and programme of action on a culture of peace*. Paris: Author.

United Nations Economic, Social and Cultural Organization. (1999b). *Education for international understanding and peace in Asia and the Pacific*. Bangkok, Thailand: UNESCO Principal Regional Office for Asia and the Pacific.

Weisz, J. R., McCabe, M., & Dennig, M. D. (1994). Primary and secondary control among children undergoing medical procedures: Adjustment as a function of coping style. *Journal of Consulting and Clinical Psychology, 62*, 324–332.

Wolchik, S. A., & Sandler, I. N. (Eds.). (1997). *Handbook of children's coping: Linking theory and intervention*. New York: Plenum Press.

10

LIGHT AND DARK IN THE PSYCHOLOGY OF HUMAN STRENGTHS: THE EXAMPLE OF PSYCHOGERONTOLOGY

ROCÍO FERNÁNDEZ-BALLESTEROS

Positive psychology and *psychology of human strengths* are new combinations of key words that appear to be related to an emerging field in psychology and even in the social sciences in general. Over the past decade several outstanding and powerful psychologists have claimed to improve a psychology that is especially (or even exclusively) devoted to pathology by defining a new field of research and enquiry focusing on positive psychological attributes or characteristics at several levels:

The field of positive psychology at the *subjective level* is about valued subjective experiences: well-being, contentment, and satisfaction (in the past); hope and optimism (for the future); and flow and happiness (in the present). At the *individual level*, it is about positive individual traits: the capacity for love and vocation, courage, interpersonal skill, aesthetic sensibility, perseverance, forgiveness, originality, future mind-

The author expresses her gratitude to Idoya Barrenechea, expert on literature metrics, for her assistance in developing Figure 10.1.

131

edness, spirituality, high talent, and wisdom. At the *group level*, it is about the civic virtues and the institutions that move individuals toward better citizenship: responsibility, nurturance, altruism, civility, moderation, tolerance, and work ethic. (Seligman & Csikszentmihalyi, 2000a, p. 5; italics added)

This new approach can be seen to have a "light" and a "dark" side: light because its focus on positive human characteristics can illuminate, reinforce, and promote adaptive individual and social conditions; dark when this perspective hides relevant negative traits or neglects them or when its interpretations and theoretical developments are biased. The birth of positive psychology at the end of the millennium allowed it to take advantage of the positive millennial spirit that supposedly compensates for alarmist notions related to the millennium bug and all the other apocalyptic scenarios predicted for humankind. Psychologists appear to have joined the search for characteristics that are functional for human beings, society, the planet, and perhaps even the future of human life on Earth (e.g., Hay, 2000).

This chapter examines some aspects of the light and dark in this psychological frame of reference. I discuss two core questions affecting positive psychology: Is psychology focused on negative conditions? And are positive constructs new in psychology? I then suggest some conceptual dimensions that should be helpful to the scientific study of human strengths. Finally, I analyze the field of aging from the point of view of successful aging and positive psychogerontology.

HUMAN STRENGTHS OR POSITIVE PSYCHOLOGY AS A "NEW" FIELD OF RESEARCH

The recent literature has cited "the exclusive focus on pathology that has dominated so many of our discipline's results" (Seligman & Csikszentmihalyi, 2000a, p. 5.) Two questions arise from the thesis of positive psychology that should be reviewed and answered: Is psychology focused exclusively on pathology? And are strengths or positive constructs totally new in psychology?

Is Psychology Focused on Negative Conditions?

Throughout the history of human thought (across cultures, religions, and philosophies), forces influencing human life have usually been defined in terms of opposition: good and evil, Eros and Thanatos, yin and yang. Philosophical systems have adopted opposing perspectives on the nature of the human being and on life in general and social life in particular: for example, whereas for Hobbes people are like wolves in their relations with others, Rousseau held that humans are good by nature; whereas Leibniz argued that this world is the best of all possible worlds, Schopenhauer considered that the only true fact of the real world is suffering. Thus, throughout history, the qualities of the human being, the nature of life, and the status of the external world have been conceptualized from different and polar perspectives or as opposite forces.

Psychology is a scientific discipline defined, depending on the different theoretical frameworks, as the science of consciousness, behavior, or the mind as emergent operations of the human being. In any case, because it is devoted to the study of behavior and psychological processes and structures (e.g., attention, perception, learning, memory, problem-solving, reasoning, intelligence, emotion, and personality), it cannot be claimed that psychology is devoted to "positive" or "negative" conditions, given that both terms refer to evaluative and ethical concepts and are thus inapplicable to scientific subjects. At the end of the 20th century, psychology is a science with more than 100 years behind it, and one cannot say that it has had a "negative" bias.

Nevertheless, although it is true that general psychology is searching for the basic principles applicable to "normal" behavior or psychological structures and processes, there may be "abnormal" versions of them, and in this sense psychologists might talk about "negative" behavior, processes, or structures. Some branches of psychology—such as psychopathology and clinical psychology—are precisely devoted to the study, assessment, and treatment of abnormal psychological conditions. Of course, these subdisciplines of psychology (mainly applied) are devoted to behavioral disorders that are negative in the sense that they are linked to human suffering. However, can one criticize psychopathology or clinical psychology for emphasizing and being devoted to negative processes or structures? It would be the same as criticizing clinical biology for dealing with abnormal developments of organisms.

In the lay or public arena, psychology is usually reduced to psychopathology and to clinical psychology dominated by "negative" or psychopathological constructs and conditions. In no way should psychologists generalize from the lay perspective on psychopathology and clinical psychology to the entire science and profession of psychology. Scientific psychology is not devoted to "positive" or "negative" human conditions; these are evaluative rather than scientific terms.

Are Human Strengths and Positive Constructs New in Psychology?

The proponents of the "new" field of positive psychology place emphasis on its novelty. The key words *positive psychology*[1] and *psychology of*

---

[1] In Spanish, "positive psychology" ("*psicología positiva*") means psychology that is developed with the positivistic method proposed by Comte as the basic tool of science.

human strengths are indeed relatively new. Nevertheless, throughout the history of applied psychology and through several paradigms, research participants' strengths have been taken into consideration as resources, or "competence." For example, in work and organizational psychology, several abilities (other than basic human skills) have formed the basis for personnel selection (e.g., intrinsic motivation, self-determination); in educational psychology, creativity, giftedness, and talent in children have been carefully studied; finally, in psychotherapy and other clinical settings, *assets, abilities, outcome expectancies, self-efficacy, self-actualization,* and other human strengths have been considered human resources from several theoretical perspectives, including behavioral psychology (e.g., Tolman, 1938; Bandura, 1977), gestalt psychology (e.g., Lewin, 1938), and humanistic models (e.g., self-actualization, Maslow, 1954).

Is the content claimed as the core of this field really new? To answer this question, I selected the following constructs from common scientific literature databases: creativity, emotional intelligence, empathy, giftedness, happiness, optimism, prosocial behavior, self-determination, solidarity, well-being (including its variants well being and wellbeing), and wisdom. Constructs such as courage, spirituality, and "civil virtues" in general do not appear in the scientific literature, perhaps because they come from scholastic philosophy, catechisms, or civil and religious rhetoric and have never reached the status of scientific subjects. Nevertheless, they are human "virtues," and once they can be operationalized and submitted to scientific criteria, they may become psychological constructs.

A search on the selected constructs in PsycLIT from 1930 to February 2000 yielded interesting results. As shown in Table 10.1, the constructs, with the exception of prosocial behavior, are present in the very earliest references. Several of the key words have shown rapid growth in many cases doubling from one decade to the next. However, if one compares the evolution of the four most frequently cited strengths constructs (well-being, creativity, empathy, happiness) with the general evolution of the psychology literature since the 1980s, only well-being has grown more than the scientific literature in general (see Figure 10.1). Thus, the constructs at the core of this "new" field have been in use for decades, and of the most frequently cited constructs, the possibility of an increased emphasis in the literature was borne out only for well-being.

CONCEPTUAL DIMENSIONS IN THE STUDY OF PSYCHOLOGICAL HUMAN STRENGTHS

Leaving aside possible criticisms, psychological characteristics that can be considered as human strengths are undoubtedly a subject for scientific psychology. However, as mentioned above, Seligman and Csik-

TABLE 10.1

The number of articles in PsycLIT per decade on selected strengths constructs from 1930 to February 2000, compared to the total number of documents in PsycLIT divided by 100

Strengths construct	Decade							
	30–39	40–49	50–59	60–69	70–79	80–89	90–00
Creativity	0	91	256	1,362	1,997	2,754	3,321
Emotional Intelligence	6	4	3	3	6	14	45
Empathy	40	29	169	284	813	1 579	2,148
Giftedness	8	5	129	50	54	280	427
Happiness	131	129	132	106	323	772	1,118
Optimism	26	47	42	68	164	319	885
Prosocial Behavior	0	0	0	3	95	481	748
Self-Determination	10	9	27	19	73	208	558
Solidarity	40	50	45	43	103	253	344
Well-Being	51	59	78	104	401	2,220	5,871
Wisdom	38	34	38	40	96	349	699
Total	584.6	501.26	812.03	1,025.57	2,105.1	3,625.48	5,104.78

Note. The total number of documents in PsycLIT was divided by 100 because of the large number of documents in PsycLIT and to facilitate comparisons of the growth of specific constructs with the growth of the total psychological literature.

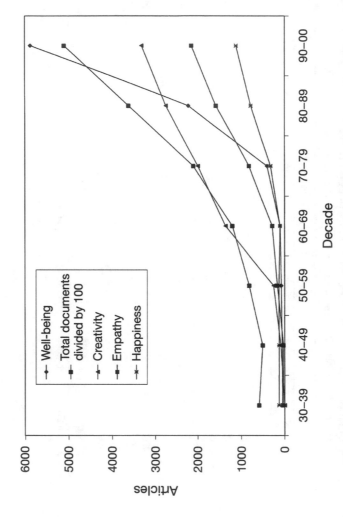

Figure 10.1. The number of articles in PsycLIT per decade on the four most frequently cited strengths constructs (well-being, creativity, empathy, and happiness) from 1930 to February 2000, compared with the total number of documents in PsycLIT divided by 100.

szentmihalyi's proposed list (quoted in the first paragraph of this chapter) includes a mixture of cognitive, affective, and social psychological attributes and other moral virtues with different epistemological and methodological significance. It is therefore important to analyze the scientific status of the items in this provisional list and to decide on which criteria to base a consideration of psychological characteristics as "human strengths" or as "positive."

Criteria for Structuring the Concept of Human Strengths

From the provisional list proposed by Seligman and Csikszentmihalyi (2000a), and taking into account other publications on positive psychology (Seligman & Csikszentmihalyi, 2000b), two types of human strengths characteristics can be identified: (a) psychological and (b) ethical or moral. Psychological characteristics are those with an epistemological and methodological scientific status, whereas ethical or moral characteristics remain within the philosophical, civil, or religious arena. Of course, there is an overlap between scientific and ethical characteristics—for example, *solidarity* could be considered a civil virtue, and *prosocial behavior* is one of the latest psychological characteristics in the field of social and personality psychology (Caprara, 1987). The only difference between the two categories lies in their differential scientific status.

It may be premature to try to develop a conceptual network with all the scientific constructs listed. A first classification has been proposed by Seligman and Csikszentmihalyi (2000): subjective level, individual level, and group level. The first group of this classification system could be considered a homogeneous (in that they are subjective) set of variables, all of them with very close relationships and all of them referring to positive experience (i.e., well-being, contentment, satisfaction, hope, optimism, happiness). In contrast, the second group involves a mixture of moral virtues (e.g., capacity for love and forgiveness, courage, spirituality, etc.) and scientific cognitive characteristics (originality, talent and wisdom). Finally, at the group level, the classified items could all be considered as civil virtues, and cannot be accepted at least until they are operationalized in an appropriate way.

Moreover, there are other psychological characteristics that could be taken into consideration because of evidence of their positive role in the development or status of human beings: intelligence, creativity, self-efficacy, self-determination, empathy, spontaneity, intrinsic motivation, self-determination, and life satisfaction (among others). These elements can be classified in five classical categories: emotional, motivational, intellectual, social interaction, and social structure. Table 10.2 lists the five categories of human strengths and examples of potential positive psycho-

TABLE 10.2
Classification System and Examples of Potential Human Strengths

Category	Examples
Emotional	Optimism
	Well-being
	Happiness
	Satisfaction
Motivational	Self-efficacy
	Self-determination
	Intrinsic motivation
	Self-realization
Intellectual	Originality
	Creativity
	Talent or giftedness
	Wisdom
	Emotional intelligence
Social interaction	Empathy
	Interpersonal skills
	Prosocial behavior
	Spontaneity
Social structure	Social network and social support
	Social opportunities
	Physical and social diversity
	Egalitarian socio-economic resources

logical conditions. It should be noted that there are often strong relationships between different characteristics in the same category.

In the first category, *optimism*, *well-being*, *happiness*, and *satisfaction* refer to positive subjective (reported) emotions and have been discussed under the concept of "positive emotionality" (Depue & Spoont, 1986; Hammer, 1996; Lykken & Tellegen, 1996). The motivational category refers to self-perceived ways of controlling external situations, and these will probably covary considerably. The intellectual category refers to cognitive skills that, even in the case of emotional intelligence, are strongly related to intelligence or cognitive abilities. The social interaction category includes psychological characteristics that facilitate human relationships, such as empathy, interpersonal skills, prosocial behavior, and spontaneity. The social structure category refers to the external world in which microsocial structures (social network and support) and macrosocial ones (social opportunities and egalitarian socio-economic resources) allow the development of human strengths.

The classification system suggested is not exhaustive, has a rational basis, and should be empirically tested. In subsequent iterations, it should be complemented with inclusion criteria. In other words, researchers should attempt to arrive at agreement on a definition of the concept equipped with norms for considering certain characteristics as "human strengths."

Criteria for Defining Psychological Human Strengths

To define a new configuration of psychological constructs considered human strengths or positive characteristics, criteria for inclusion should be first proposed and then evaluated. The most important criterion for considering a psychological condition as a human strength may be that it is instrumental or functional in both biological and sociocultural success. The search for the best criteria for measuring biological and sociocultural success is important in establishing a theory of human strengths. Human behavior and psychological characteristics, processes, and structures are, in principle, neither positive nor negative, but they can be considered as adaptive or maladaptive. As sociobiology and evolutionary psychology have indicated, current mental mechanisms and behavioral conditions are outcomes of a selective process and therefore involve inherited biological mechanisms (Buss, 1999).

Looking at human history—and attempting to remain parsimonious—there is a sociodemographic indicator that could be considered as an index of human and social development: life expectancy. Life expectancy at birth refers to mortality, and consequently to morbidity; thus, all human characteristics that relate positively to life expectancy and negatively to mortality or morbidity (and are also positively related to quality of life) could be considered as positive or as human strengths, at least from a biological point of view.

However, life expectancy is not a purely biological indicator of human success: It depends on social and cultural factors. Estimations of life expectancy across the history of humanity suggest that there were no changes until approximately the 20th century. From 1900 to 2000 average life expectancy doubled; for example, at the beginning of the 20th century, average life expectancy in Spain was 36; in the year 2000, it was 77—74.5 for men and 81.5 for women (Fernández-Ballesteros, Díez-Nicolás, & Ruíz Torres, 1999), but this is not the case in many developing countries. Over the same period, life expectancy in Sierra Leone, Somalia, and Zimbabwe, for example, did not increase at all. Even within the same country, this indicator may fail to reflect differences between social groups; in South Africa, for example, until the 1990s White people had significantly higher life expectancy than Black people (United Nations, 1999). Life expectancy in a given country may thus be an index of unequal conditions between groups. Social and environmental conditions determining increases in life expectancy are well known: education, hygiene, nutrition, access to health care, and economic development are among the socio-economic variables associated with such improvement.

Are there psychological conditions related to life expectancy? This is undoubtedly a possibility. In principle, researchers should look for empirical evidence about all the psychological characteristics included in Table 10.2.

A first source of evidence links human strengths with "salutogenic" biological conditions or health functioning. For example, there is strong evidence supporting the direct effects of positive (and negative) emotional experience and expression on physiology, especially in the enhancement of the immune system, with implications for health outcomes (e.g., Salovey, Rothman, Detweiler, & Steward, 2000). Also, with respect to motivational characteristics, there is experimental evidence that perception of self-efficacy can activate a wide range of biological processes that mediate human health and disease (e.g., Bandura, 1997).

A second source of evidence relating life expectancy to psychological conditions comes from longitudinal studies in which psychological characteristics are taken as predictors of survival or longevity. Bearing in mind that no single variable can explain longevity, several psychological conditions have been associated with survival. For example, intelligence and cognitive measures were predictors of survival in several longitudinal studies (for a review, see Schroots, 1993) and of mortality due to accidents and suicide (O'Toole & Stankov, 1992). Also, life satisfaction (more positive mood or morale), greater social participation, activities outside the family, and involvement in community activities characterized survivors in the Bonn longitudinal study (Lehr, 1982).

A final source of evidence linking psychological characteristics with mortality and life prolongation comes from the relationships identified between emotional states and physical health. Positive thinking and positive emotional states such as positive emotionality, optimism, and self-efficacy appear to be psychological resources related to health protection, illness prevention, and life prolongation (Affleck, Tennen, Croog, & Levine, 1987; Kemeny & Gruenewald, 2000; Salovey et al., 2000; Scheier & Carver, 1987; Taylor, Kemeny, Reed, Bower, & Gruenewald, 2000).

In sum, several cognitive, emotional, and social characteristics can be considered human strengths in the sense that they are linked to criteria of biological success such as mortality, morbidity, life expectancy, and health functioning. However, the human being and his or her psychological equipment are also social products, and human evolution and social evolution are interacting, mutually interdependent isomorphic processes. Thus, the behavior and psychological attributes of human beings are governed not only by biological (or Darwinian) laws, but also by cultural and social conditions (Boyd & Richerson, 1985; Dawkins, 1976; Gould, 1977). As several authors have pointed out, even if it is difficult to evaluate independently the relative influence of biological and cultural factors on the characteristics of human beings, it is accepted that there are causal relationships among human behavior, biology, and culture (Massimini & Delle Fave, 2000; Richerson & Boyd, 1978). Thus, human strengths would be those psychological characteristics associated with both biological evolution and cultural and social progress. It is therefore extremely important to establish a link between human strengths and sociocultural evolution.

What are the criteria for evaluating social and cultural progress? International organizations such as the United Nations, UNESCO, and the World Health Organization have developed hundreds of socio-economic, educational, cultural, and health indicators to evaluate the comparative status of different countries and cultures in terms of development. It is of great importance to know how and how much psychological characteristics such as intelligence, creativity, originality, self- and collective efficacy, interpersonal relationships, and optimism contribute to national development to set up inclusion criteria. As yet there are no empirical data about this important question, but without doubt psychological human strengths are behind socio-economic, cultural, and social progress.

Returning to our previous proposal about the inclusion criteria for the category of human strengths, there is important and easily accessible experimental evidence supporting the idea that psychological conditions are strongly linked to health promotion and illness prevention, and therefore to health functioning and morbidity and, in turn, to life prolongation and life expectancy. The continued search for the best criteria to determine those psychological characteristics that could be considered as human strengths is an essential task.

HUMAN STRENGTHS IN OLD AGE, OR POSITIVE PSYCHOGERONTOLOGY

Positive psychogerontology, as an applied field of psychology, constitutes a good example for positive psychology, because it includes both the light and the dark characteristics of the field of psychology. Psychogerontology is the psychological subdiscipline devoted to the study of age (stage of life), aging (the lifespan process), and the aged population (older persons with needs for support and help; Birren, 1996). Even though several positive characteristics emerge from the aging process, psychogerontology has been devoted mainly to the study of the decline of and damage to psychological structures, processes, and behavior; in other words, the study of the aged population has been more important than the study of the process of aging or the stage of age. Moreover, in the study of aging and age, the targets of psychological study have been the conditions that are likely to decline or become damaged through age.

In the 1990s[2] gerontologists began working on a new perspective called "successful aging," "aging well," "vital aging," and "competent ag-

---

[7]There are antecedents of the search for positive characteristics in old age, for example, in Hall (1922) or Mira y Lopez (1961).

ing" (e.g., Baltes & Baltes, 1990b; Fernández-Ballesteros, 1986; Fries, 1989; Klein & Bloom, 1997; Rowe & Kahn, 1987). This perspective has been extremely successful, at least from the point of view of the scientific literature produced. For this reason it is very difficult to summarize, but let me begin by referring to some empirical antecedents.

The successful aging perspective emerged from three well-observed facts: (a) the substantial heterogeneity (variability) in the process of aging; (b) the lack of a clear distinction between changes due to age and changes due to illness (as a covariate of age); and (c) the positive effects on the aging process of manipulating behavioral factors such as diet, exercise, personal habits, and psychosocial dimensions (Fernández-Ballesteros, 1997). The majority of authors would agree with the proposal of Rowe and Kahn (1997) (based on the MacArthur Foundation Midlife study) that successful aging includes three main components: low probability of disease and disease-related disability, high cognitive and physical capacity, and active engagement in life.[3]

The successful aging perspective has two main purposes. The first is to increase successful aging—that is, to develop and implement strategies with the purpose of promoting successful aging, attempting to change modifiable (negative) physical characteristics linked to illness, optimizing or compensating for cognitive and physical capacities, and increasing social interactions and engagement in life (see Baltes & Baltes, 1990a). The second purpose is to search for positive conditions of aging (Fernández-Ballesteros, 1997). This second field of research has uncovered psychological characteristics linked to the aging process, such as wisdom, philosophy of life, serenity, coping strategies, adaptive capacities, prosocial behavior, social and civic involvement, and so forth.

Strategies for Aging Well

Changes in mortality and life expectancy have occurred at the same time as changes in morbidity and morbimortality; as Fries (1989) pointed out, acute disease has been replaced as a cause of death by chronic diseases. Chronic diseases are strongly associated with behavioral factors such as lifestyle (e.g., diet, exercise), coping mechanisms, social networks, and social support. In other words, pathological aging is moving from biology to psychology. Aging well basically means "doing" well; to counter problems linked to age, behavioral solutions can improve health (by optimizing and compensating using the selective optimization with compensation model by Baltes & Baltes, 1990a; see also Baltes & Freund, chapter 2, this volume), as well as cognitive, emotional, and social functioning (see Fernández-Ballesteros, 1997).

---

[3]The model proposed by Rowe and Kahn does not take into consideration any environmental or external variables, such as health and social services (see Fernández-Ballesteros, 2001).

Development Versus Decline During Later Adulthood

As Atchley (1999) pointed out, "Development can be defined as movement toward evolutionary possibilities.... Most scholars agree that biological development is completed in young adulthood but also agree that most aging adults retain their capacity for psychological and social growth" (p. 12). Biological models of aging cannot be transferred to psychological aging because psychological development continues throughout the life span. It is true that there are decrements in cognitive functioning (fluid intelligence), but such declines can be compensated for by cognitive training and, where they occur, have little effect on everyday functioning (Baltes & Willis, 1982; Fernández-Ballesteros & Calero, 1995; Schaie, 1996). Also, empirical evidence suggests that personality characteristics are quite stable across the life span (e.g., Costa & McCrae, 1994), and the development of internal patterns such as self-concept, value systems, social roles, and other internal or external behavioral patterns appear to support the continuity theory (Atchley, 1999): We age as we have lived!

If researchers listen to the elderly population, becoming older would appear to lead to thousands of positive experiences. For example, in the 20-year Ohio Longitudinal Study of Aging and Adaptation, most participants reported finding aging to be generally a positive experience. From an emotional point of view, people usually reported feeling much more serene and relaxed than at other stages of life; from a cognitive perspective, elderly people reported having a broader capacity for the analysis of problems (both intellectual and social); from a social viewpoint, a new type of relationship—with grandchildren—begins, one they described as extremely pleasant. Perhaps because they have followed the biological model of aging, psychologists have not taken an interest in these positive characteristics or human strengths that increase during old age; these and other positive descriptions should stimulate psychologists to study this area of development and growth in old age.

Heckhausen, Dixon, and Baltes (1989) studied gains and losses perceived by different age groups throughout adulthood. Participants ($N = 112$, three age groups) were asked to rate a list of person-descriptive adjectives with respect to three aspects of developmental increase: the degree to which it occurs over the adult life span, its desirability, and the age at which it is expected to start and finish. Results yielded a consensus on beliefs within and across adult age groups, but older adults had a more complex conception of development throughout adulthood than younger adults. When the authors analyzed their data to establish the relative numbers of desirable attributes (gains) and undesirable ones (losses) accrued over the adult life span, perceived losses were found to increase; however, even up to age 80, about 20% of the expected changes were considered to be gains. Perceived developmental gains greatly outnumbered perceived losses throughout adulthood, with the exception only of advanced age (beyond 80), when more losses than gains were expected. Most importantly, from this and other studies there emerges a consensus not only on the fact that there are positive characteristics linked to the process of aging, but also that perhaps the most important of them is wisdom.

Thus, one of the paradigmatic human characteristics for this field of research is wisdom. Until about 10 years ago, wisdom belonged to the field of philosophy; it was little more than an implicit theory in people's minds. In the past decade psychogerontologists and developmental psychologists, under the auspices of the Max Planck Institute of Berlin (for reviews, see Baltes & Staudinger, 1993, 2000), have taken on a worthwhile challenge in developing a complex research program on wisdom. *Wisdom* has been defined as an expert knowledge system concerning the fundamental pragmatics of life. It has been operationalized through qualitative methods of data collection, such as think-aloud protocols during which participants complete several tasks related to problems occurring in life (e.g., life planning, life review, life management). Wisdom-related performance is associated with intelligence, creativity, cognitive style, social intelligence, and personality. Currently, wisdom is gradually becoming, without doubt, a positive psychological characteristic that can be considered as the peak of human evolution and therefore as a human strength.

Philosophers sometimes indicate the best path: Epicurus (341–270 BC) ended his *Maxims for a Happy Life* with advice along the following lines: Search for wisdom, you shall drink from an inexhaustible well for the health of the soul.... Wisdom is the seed of happiness.... Those who declare that they are still not of an age to love wisdom, to philosophize, or that such a time is passed, are like those who state that it is still not time for them to be happy, or that it is too late for that now. Epicurus was concerned with human strengths 2,300 years ago. Today, it is psychology that is responsible for researching these human characteristics. Its methods, as epistemic activity, have been developed more as a positive product of phylogenesis than of our genes!

REFERENCES

Affleck, G., Tennen, H., Croog, S., & Levine, S. (1987). Causal attribution, perceived benefits, and morbidity after a heart attack: An eight-year study. *Journal of Consulting and Clinical Psychology, 55,* 29–35.

Atchley, R. C. (1999). *Continuity and adaptation in aging.* Baltimore, MD: Johns Hopkins University Press.

Baltes, P. B., & Baltes, M. M. (1990a). Psychological perspectives on successful aging: Methodological and theoretical issues. In P. B. Baltes & M. M. Baltes (Eds.), *Successful aging* (pp. 1–34). New York: Cambridge University Press.

Baltes, P. B., & Baltes, M. M. (Eds.). (1990b). *Successful aging*. New York: Cambridge University Press.

Baltes, P. B., & Staudinger, U. M. (1993). The search for a psychology of wisdom. *Current Directions in Psychological Science, 2*, 75–80.

Baltes, P. B., & Staudinger, U. M. (2000). Wisdom. *American Psychologist, 55*, 122–136.

Baltes, P. B., & Willis, S. L. (1982). Plasticity and enhancement of intellectual functioning in old age: Penn State's adult development and enrichment program (ADEPT). In F. I. M. Craik & S. E. Trehub (Eds.), *Aging and cognitive processes* (pp. 353–389). New York: Plenum Press.

Bandura, A. (1977). Self-efficacy: Toward a unifying theory of behavioral change. *Psychological Review, 84*, 191–215.

Bandura, A. (1997). *Self-efficacy: The exercise of control*. New York: W. H. Freeman.

Birren, J. (Ed.). (1996). *Encyclopedia of gerontology*. New York: Academic Press.

Boyd, R., & Richerson, P. J. (1985). *Culture and the evolutionary process*. Chicago: Chicago University Press.

Buss, D. M. (1999). *Evolutionary psychology: The new science of the mind*. Boston: Allyn & Bacon.

Caprara, G. V. (1987). The disposition/situation debate and research on aggression. *European Journal of Personality, 1*, 1–16.

Costa, P. T., & McCrae, R. R. (1994). Set like plaster? Evidence for the stability of adult personality. In T. F. Heatherton & J. L. Weinberger (Eds.), *Can personality change?* (pp. 21–40). Washington, DC: American Psychological Association.

Dawkins, R. (1976). *The selfish gene*. Oxford, England: Oxford University Press.

Depue, R. A., & Spoont, M. R. (1986). Conceptualizing a serotonin trait: A behavioral dimension of constraint. *Annals of the New York Academy of Sciences, 487*, 47–62.

Fernández-Ballesteros, R. (1986). Hacia una vejez competente: Un desafío a la ciencia y a la sociedad [Toward competent aging: A challenge for science and society]. In M. Carretero, J. Palacios, & A. Marchesi (Eds.), *Psicología evolutiva [Developmental psychology]* (pp. 197–215). Madrid: Alianza.

Fernández-Ballesteros, R. (1997). *Vejez con éxito, vejez competente: Un reto para todos* [Successful aging, competent aging: A challenge for everyone]. Barcelona, Spain: Asociación Multidisciplinar de Gerontología.

Fernández-Ballesteros, R. (2001). Environmental conditions, health and satisfaction among the elderly: Some empirical results. *Psicothema, 13*, 40–49.

Fernández-Ballesteros, R., & Calero, M. D. (1995). Training effects on intelligence of older persons. *Archives of Gerontology and Geriatrics, 20*, 135–148.

Fernández-Ballesteros, R., Díez-Nicolás, J., & Ruíz Torres, A. (1999). Spain. In J. J. F. Schroots, R. Fernández-Ballesteros, & G. Rudinger (Eds.), *Aging in Europe* (pp. 107–121). Amsterdam: IOS Press.

Fries, J. F. (1989). *Aging well*. Reading, MA: Addison-Wesley.

Gould, R. L. (1977). *Ontogeny and phylogeny*. New York: Appleton.

Hall, G. S. (1922). *Senescence: The last half of life*. New York: Appleton.

Hammer, D. H. (1996, October). The heritability of happiness. *Nature Genetics, 14*, 125–126.

Hay, L. L. (Ed.). (2000). *Millennium 2000: A positive approach*. Carlsbad, CA: Hay House.

Heckhausen, J., Dixon, R. A., & Baltes, P. B. (1989). Gains and losses in development throughout adulthood as perceived by different adult age groups. *Developmental Psychology, 25*, 109–121.

Kemeny, M. E., & Gruenewald, T. L. (2000). Affect, cognition, the immune system and health. In E. A. Mayer & C. Saper (Eds.), *The biological basis for mind body interactions* (pp. 122–147). Amsterdam: Elsevier Science.

Klein, W., & Bloom, M. (1997). *Successful aging: Strategies for healthy living*. New York: Plenum Press.

Lehr, U. (1982). Socio-psychological correlates of longevity. *Annual Review of Gerontology and Geriatrics, 3*, 102–147.

Lewin, K. (1938). *The conceptual representation and the measurement of psychological forces*. Durham, NC: Duke University Press.

Lykken, D., & Tellegen, A. (1996). Happiness is a stochastic phenomenon. *Psychological Science, 7*, 186–189.

Maslow, A. H. (1954). *Motivation and personality*. New York: Harpers.

Massimini, F., & Delle Fave, A. (2000). Individual development in a bio-cultural perspective. *American Psychologist, 55*, 24–33.

Mira y Lopez, E. (1961). *Hacia una vejez joven* [Toward a young old age]. Buenos Aires: Kapelusz.

O'Toole, B. J., & Stankov, L. (1992). Ultimate validity of psychological tests. *Personality and Individual Differences, 13*, 699–716.

Richerson, P. J., & Boyd, R. (1978). A dual inheritance model of human evolutionary process: Basic postulates and a simple model. *Journal of Social and Biological Structures, 1*, 127–154.

Rowe, J. W., & Kahn, R. L. (1987). Human aging: Usual and successful. *Science, 237*, 143–149.

Rowe, J. W., & Kahn, R. L. (1997). Successful aging. *Gerontologist, 37*, 433–440.

Salovey, P., Rothman, A. J., Detweiler, J. B., & Steward, W. T. (2000). Emotional states and physical health. *American Psychologist, 55*, 110–121.

Schaie, K. W. (1996). Intellectual development in adulthood. In J. E. Birren & K. W. Schaie (Eds.), *Handbook of psychology of aging* (4th ed., pp. 266–286). New York: Academic Press.

Scheier, M. F., & Carver, C. S. (1987). Dispositional optimism and physical well-being: The influence of generalized outcome expectancies on health. *Journal of Personality, 55*, 169–210.

Schroots, J. J. F. (Ed.). (1993). *Aging, health and competence: The next generation of longitudinal research*. Amsterdam: Elsevier.

Seligman, M. E. P., & Csikszentmihalyi, M. (2000a). Positive psychology: An introduction. *American Psychologist, 55*, 5–14.

Seligman, M. E. P., & Csikszentmihalyi, M., eds. (2000b). Special issue on happiness, excellence, and optimal human functioning [Special issue]. *American Psychologist, 55*(1).

Taylor, S. E., Kemeny, M. E., Reed, G. M., Bower, J. E., & Gruenewald, T. L. (2000). Psychological resources, positive illusions and health. *American Psychologist, 55*, 99–109.

Tolman, E. C. (1938). The determiners of behavior at a choice point. *Psychological Review, 45*, 1–41.

United Nations. (1999). *World population.* New York: Author.

11

INTERVENTION AS A MAJOR TOOL OF A PSYCHOLOGY OF HUMAN STRENGTHS: EXAMPLES FROM ORGANIZATIONAL CHANGE AND INNOVATION

DIETER FREY, EVA JONAS, AND TOBIAS GREITEMEYER

Psychology is a science that studies the attitudes, emotions, motivation, cognition, and behavior of individuals, as well as interaction processes within and between groups. Furthermore, psychology studies the structures and cultures individuals and groups establish. It is a fascinating science, because its practitioners have the basic knowledge necessary to diagnose mentalities, attitudes, and patterns of behavior and to change them. Psychology has a deeper understanding than other disciplines of the subjective experiences of people and their behavior as individuals and in groups. It has many elaborate theories that classify, describe, explain, and predict behavior on the individual as well as group level.

Using these theories and this knowledge, psychologists can design intervention programs for achieving positive goals and aims, and it is this activity that lies at the heart of the term "positive psychology." Psychological theories and knowledge can be applied directly to the analysis of organizational cultures, structures, and teams in social and commercial organizations for the purposes of managing change processes and promoting innovation in processes, products, and services.

In this chapter we describe some areas of our own research relevant to organizational change and innovation. The success of social and commercial organizations in modern societies depends on how well individuals, as well as teams, can be motivated and how successfully their potential for creativity and innovation is activated. These processes depend on the application of psychological knowledge to change the mentalities and behaviors of members of organizations, as well as organizations' structures, values, and cultures. This chapter describes how psychology can contribute to these endeavors.

MISUNDERSTANDINGS ABOUT PSYCHOLOGY

Laypeople, and also many scientists outside the field of psychology, think that psychology has to do only with abnormal and pathological behavior and emotional problems and with psychotherapy. Outsiders (and even some psychologists) often have a very narrow-minded view of the field. Psychologists have much to say concerning prevention, rehabilitation, and intervention techniques in all settings of society, and those settings include commercial as well as social organizations. The challenge psychologists face is to better communicate the relevance of their research, of their knowledge and theories, to people who have misconceptions about the field. Psychologists must show that they can solve real-life problems, and not just problems of theoretical interest.

In addition, it is very important to convey to our psychology students that we have knowledge that we can be proud of, and that—although we do not have all the wisdom we would like to have—psychological theories provide considerable knowledge about how individuals and groups function. Furthermore, there are lots of opportunities for applying psychological understanding. To neglect to teach these concepts would be extremely costly for individuals, organizations, and society as a whole. From a Lewinian perspective, basic research, applied research, and the application of research findings should always be done according to the philosophy "Nothing is as practical as a good theory."

APPLYING PSYCHOLOGY TO CHANGE-MANAGEMENT PROCESSES IN ORGANIZATIONS

Psychology has a lot to say about the important problems of our time, including globalization, change processes in organizations, mergers, and a rapidly changing marketplace. A lot of psychological theories can contribute to efforts to increase organization members' motivation and innovation in facing these challenges, including control theory (Skinner, 1996), social learning theory (Bandura, 1977), goal setting theory (Locke & Latham, 1990a, 1990b), self-determination theory (Deci & Ryan, 1985), theories of fair treatment (Tyler, 1994), and theories about the self (Dweck, 1991).

Success Factors for Change Management

Psychological theories and research clearly reveal that it is not simply a matter of chance whether organizational changes, including mergers between organizations with different cultures, are successful and accepted by the organizations' members. People are willing to accept change processes wholeheartedly if certain factors are considered (e.g., Frey & Schnabel, 1999).

People have to see that the change process is definite, inevitable, and irreversible, and they must understand why the change is necessary. It is of great importance that they know what awaits them; they must be able to foresee the process and to be clear about rules and responsibilities. They have to feel as if they are a part of the decision-making process—that is, they have to be able to participate in the change process. The whole process must be communicated professionally.

People have to feel they are being treated fairly, for example, in decisions concerning resources and positions. Further, it is important that they see that human aspects count as well. Therefore, anxieties, stress in the workplace, and similar topics have to be discussed explicitly. They have to see that they are not mere "instruments" for success and that the employer is interested in the employees' future as well—inside and outside the company. In addition, employees must see the utility of the change for themselves and for the team, in the short run as well as in the long run. The closer the cultural fit between the old culture and the new culture, the higher the probability that those involved will accept the change process and identify with the emerging culture. Finally, people have to see that changing themselves is part of their duties, and the top managers must serve as role models.

Very often, people who are responsible for changing processes in organizations, who have to make the relevant decisions, and who are responsible for the implementation of those decisions have a poor understanding of how human beings and groups function on a psychological level. So many mergers, takeovers, and change processes ultimately fail because of the inability of those responsible to correctly assess the anxieties, hopes, and expectations of employees and to communicate what changes are necessary and why and how.

Work Motivation, Top Performance, and Innovation

The globalization of markets is leading to increased competition between companies. To be internationally successful, companies depend more than ever on the top performance of their employees. To motivate employees for high performance, a high level of leadership skills from managers is required.

Wendt and Frey (Wendt, 1998; Wendt & Frey, 2002) identified central factors that are responsible for high performance and high satisfaction in the workplace. Their findings show that motivation, as well as identification with the organization and with individual leadership figures, depends on the following principles, which are summarized from Frey's Principles of Leadership and Motivation (Frey, 1998):

- *Principle of providing meaning and vision.* People must feel that their work has meaning and makes sense. A vision of their work as part of a larger picture, such as a joint aim pursued by the whole company, is even more motivating. When these conditions are fulfilled, employees are likely to identify with their place of work and to do their work with enthusiasm.
- *Principle of transparency.* Employees have to be informed about conditions that affect the context of their work, including the company's aims and impending changes. People who feel that they are not sufficiently well informed do not feel motivated, lack a feeling of control, and cannot react adequately to changing conditions. Transparency cannot be achieved only via abstract information; direct, specific communication is the best way to prevent misunderstandings, reduce uncertainty, and build trust and loyalty.
- *Principle of participation and autonomy.* The more people feel they participate from the beginning in workplace decisions, the higher their identification and satisfaction with their work and the greater their willingness to take on responsibility will be.
- *Principle of a sense of fit.* The closer the fit between the skills and personal interests of individuals and the demands of their job, the likelier they are to find their work fun and to be intrinsically motivated.
- *Principle of goal setting and goal negotiation.* Clear, specific, high, and realistic goals increase performance. Goals have informational as well as motivational value. When goals are set in an authoritarian fashion, employees are less likely to accept and identify with the goals. Employees also need periodic feedback about progress toward goal achievement.

- *Principle of constructive feedback and appreciation.* Praise and constructive criticism can increase motivation and performance when it is done correctly. Just like all people, employees strive for positive appreciation and respect from leadership figures. The slogan "Tough on the issue, soft on the person" summarizes the philosophy behind this principle. Being "tough on the issue" means being very clear about goals, standards, and rules. Being "soft on the person" means being highly tolerant of individual variation, showing appreciation for individuals, and avoiding the violation of human dignity—in other words, treating people as partners.
- *Principle of professional and social integration.* A challenging job that one can feel proud of and positive social relationships within the working group provide employees with emotional support and a feeling of emotional and social integration, resulting in a commitment to the organization. The burnout literature describes numerous strategies for avoiding burnout, including celebrating successes, integrating social networks by holding organizational "family days," revising procedures to avoid waste of time and energy, and improving work routines.
- *Principle of personal growth.* People must have room for development and for growth. When employees, especially those who are achievement-oriented, do not see a future orientation in the organization, their motivation suffers.
- *Principle of situational leadership.* Leadership style must fit the situation and the person. When called for, leadership must be very directive, clear, and even authoritarian, but it must also be very partnership-oriented. Situational leadership has a lot to do with the so-called androgynous leadership style, which involves a mixture of "masculine" and "feminine" leadership. Masculine leadership styles mean saying no and being tough, whereas feminine or "soft" leadership involves asking questions, listening, showing emotions, standing aside and letting others be heard, admitting faults, and being a mentor and trainer instead of being the boss.
- *Principle of fair and equitable material reward.* Top performance calls for top rewards. However, when the reward is seen as being sufficient and fair, additional rewards do not increase motivation.

Our research among service and industrial companies shows that when these principles are fulfilled in the eyes of employees, their satisfaction with work and work performance are higher, illness and turnover rates are lower, and employees make more suggestions for improvement (Frey, 1998; Frey & Ludorf, 2002; Wendt, 1998; Wendt & Frey, 2002).

Research on innovation and idea management, too, shows how important psychological processes are. We studied the reasons for the varying numbers of suggestions for improvements across the departments of an organization. The more employees perceived that they were given independence in their work, the more they felt informed and perceived that they could participate in decisions, and the more satisfied they were with their work, the higher the number of suggestions for improvement their departments made (cf. Frey, Raabe, & Jonas, 2002; Kauffeld, Jonas, & Frey, 2002).

Our research demonstrates that the quality of communication and the existence of trust, which are important components of the atmosphere at work, are correlated with the sickness rates of the employees, their performance and degree of goal attainment, and their evaluation by customers (Frank, Maier, Frey, & Wendt, 2002). So communication, as well as the existence of trust, seem to be key variables not only for satisfaction and identification, but also for economic success.

In view of the globalization of the markets and the increasing competition among companies, it could be advantageous for companies, at least in Western countries, to take this psychological research into account to motivate their employees to give their best performance at work and to prevent disengagement, burnout, and resignation. Existing psychological research on the subject of how to increase work identification, satisfaction, and performance is important not only for economic reasons; it also goes hand in hand with humanitarian considerations. Furthermore, top performance, innovation, and humanitarian considerations are interdependently related: When employees see that words and deeds are not consistent with each other, when they see inconsistency, hypocrisy, and dishonesty, they do not activate their full potential.

At least in Germany, but also in many other countries, schools provide no direct education in the professionalism of leadership—that is, how to communicate, how to praise, how to constructively criticize, how to convince others, how to solve conflicts, and so forth. There is thus a great deal of room for improvement in the application of psychological knowledge to increasing motivation, identification, creativity, and innovation in social and commercial organizations, as well as in administration.

Top Performance of Teams

Companies depend on the top performance not only of single employees, but also of teams. Moreover, many important decisions in organizations, as well as in everyday life, are made by small groups rather than by individuals. Groups are assumed to have access to a wider range of information relevant to the decision. Interestingly, the main focus of research so far has been on the negative aspects of group decision making and has suggested that group decisions are seldom better than decisions made by individuals, mainly due to a lack of critical discussion in groups (e.g., Janis, 1982; Steiner, 1972; Stroebe & Diehl, 1994).

However, there is growing evidence that top performance can be achieved in groups under certain conditions (Levine & Moreland, 1998; West, 1994). Those conditions include the following:

- Team members agree on the rules for dealing with each other, are able to communicate honestly, and respect each other and display loyalty.
- Team membership represents a heterogeneity of talents, experiences, education, and background.
- The team has a vivid commitment to excellent output and an ethos for achievement.
- All members take responsibility for the team's success.
- The team sets itself clear, specific, and high goals.
- Team members fit together on a technical and personal level.
- Team members are able to profit from their individual strengths.
- The team is able to use the tool of team reflection (i.e., regular joint reflection about social and task matters) to discuss what is good and should be sustained and what is bad and should be improved.

In reality, group decision making does not always take place under these conditions. Instead, most groups strive for group harmony and unanimity, fostering an uncritical attitude that can result in the "groupthink" phenomenon, or an excessive tendency among group members to strive for concurrence (Janis, 1982). Such groups suppress opinions and arguments that go against the present majority position, leading to quick decision making and high confidence of group members in the correctness of their joint decision but also to disastrously wrong decisions. Hence, a high degree of harmony and certainty among group members does not guarantee that the chosen course of action is a good one. All signs of a phony peace (e.g., absence of critical discussion and controversial debate) should be taken as a warning signal.

The groupthink effect is relevant in all decision-making processes, including the identification of problems, analysis of causes, development of decision alternatives, evaluation of alternatives, decision making, decision implementation, and control of decisions. For this reason, much of the research on groupthink has dealt with disclosing the conditions under which successful group decisions can occur (for a summary, see Frey, Schulz-Hardt, & Stahlberg, 1996). Our research on group decision making shows that homogeneity in group member preferences leads groups to select supporting over nonsupporting information, whereas heterogeneous groups seek information in a much more balanced way (see Schulz-Hardt, Frey, Lüthgens, & Moscovici, 2000).

Moreover, Brodbeck, Kerschreiter, Mojzisch, Frey, and Schulz-Hardt (2002) found that heterogeneous groups made somewhat better decisions than homogenous groups by basing them on a more thorough exchange of information. Groupthink distortions are more likely to occur—and will be more pronounced—if groups are homogeneous. Thus, heterogeneity in groups can lead to a higher decision quality by optimizing flexibility and creativity in the decision-making process (Levine & Moreland, 1998). Further, effects of groupthink are stronger when the group is hierarchically structured and weaker when the group functions along egalitarian lines.

Another line of research in the group decision-making literature deals with motivation effects in groups. Again, most of the existing literature focuses on loss of motivation in groups (for a review, see Shepperd, 1993). Recent evidence, however, suggests that group decision making can also give rise to increases in motivation, and when at least some group members work harder, group performance is enhanced (e.g., Hertel, Kerr, & Messé, 2000).

What does this have to do with positive psychology? The message is that there is considerable empirical evidence supporting strategies for promoting individual and group decision making in organizations: The group leader should take the role of impartial coordinator, the self-confidence of minority members should be built, external experts should be called in, artificial conflicts should be incorporated into the group decision process (for instance, through devil's advocacy or dialectical inquiry), and group members should be made responsible for the decision-making process and outcome (for a summary of these interventions, see Frey et al., 1996).

Center of Excellence Cultures

Research in psychology has shown that attitudes and norms are important in predicting behavior. The culture of a company and the philosophy its managers communicate shape the attitudes and standards of its other members and accordingly strongly influence their behavior. To achieve top performance as a global player in the international market, all employees must have a high achievement ethos, must constantly learn and improve processes, and must show responsibility and courage. According to Frey (1996a, 1996b, 1998; Frey & Schulz-Hardt, 2000b), these characteristics are included in the framework of "center of excellence cultures." (The terms 'culture' and 'subculture' here are used in the sense of a system of generally accepted norms, expectations, and behavior patterns.)

Center of excellence cultures are the most important cultures and philosophies of an organization and seem to be the most important for high performance in social and commercial organizations. These cultures have been found relevant in investigations of "hidden champions," which are relatively small companies in Germany that have achieved excellence with their products (Simon, 1996; see also Frey & Schulz-Hardt, 2000a). The more these center of excellence cultures are present, the more successful an organization's products, procedures, and services will be (Simon, 1996; Frey & Schulz-Hardt, 2000a). The following are examples of center of excellence cultures:

- *Customer orientation culture.* The expectations of internal as well as external clients must be fulfilled, and employees must understand what needs to be done to increase the satisfaction of the customer.
- *Competitor orientation and benchmarking culture.* Organizations must be guided by the best in the world, and the best in one's own field—and, also, by the best within one's own organization. A competitor orientation leads an organization to learn the best practices in all fields and on all levels.
- *Net production and entrepreneurial culture.* All employees must be conscious of the entire production process to which they themselves make only partial and specific contributions. They have to consider the economic implications of their actions; they must bear in mind costs and benefits. The intention behind the culture of net production is for employees to develop an attitude akin to that of an entrepreneur in the enterprise—that is, an attitude of responsibility and initiative. To foster such an attitude, employees must have contextual information and must be enabled to make decisions, factors described in control theory (Skinner, 1996).
- *Culture of permanent improvement and innovation.* To achieve improvements and innovations, several subcultures have to be established that shape the attitudes of employees. A "problem-solving culture" fosters the development of solutions to problems and discourages mere complaining about problems. A "mistakes-as-learning-opportunity culture" focuses on viewing mistakes as opportunities or even "gifts" that can be connected with causal analysis (i.e., five "why" questions) and promotes the realization that each mistake is an opportunity to improve things. A "creativity and fantasy culture" seeks to increase innovation by having employees "dream" about ideal states of the organization and consider how could these could be achieved. A "questioning and curiosity culture" focuses on asking questions, being curious, and leading by questioning, as well as supporting the asking of questions in general. Finally, a "courage culture" places

value on the courage to criticize when things go wrong and to stick to one's own opinions and beliefs.

- *Recognition-of-diversity and synergy culture.* Organizations benefit greatly by selecting people (and combining them) in a way that promotes a high degree of diversity within teams in members' talents, experiences, and abilities, but at the same time promotes homogeneity in team rules and values. In addition, such a culture welcomes new ways of thinking and establishes something like a cosmopolitan environment with intercultural talents, personalities, and mentalities represented within the organization.

- *Constructive confrontation and conflict culture.* The best organizational decisions are made when different views are discussed constructively and false harmony is avoided. An open, critical discussion culture tolerates open confrontation, constructive criticism, critical analysis, and a culture of open debate. This communication style helps to settle differing views and use conflict to the organization's benefit. The social life of human beings will always entail certain conflicts, simply because people have different interests, backgrounds, and values. It is not conflict itself that causes problems; the central question is how such conflicts are dealt with. Social and organizational psychological research demonstrates that conflicts that are discussed on the factual level improve the quality of decision-making processes. Even if people with different opinions are not right, they stimulate the discussion, lead to divergent thinking, and thus increase creativity and decision quality.

Center of excellence cultures are implemented more easily when employees have a motivational leadership culture characterized by meaning and transparency, participation and autonomy, and constructive feedback. The more an employee is motivated, the more he or she is eager to implement these cultures.

WHAT CAN WE LEARN FROM PHILOSOPHY?

The success of a social or commercial organization has a lot to do with how it treats human beings. This in turn has a lot to do with the "*Menschenbild,*" or view of humanity, and values held by the company's leadership. This leads to the question, Where do people derive their values? In our view, five philosophers who emphasize specific aspects of the *Men-*

schenbild help provide an answer to this question. Many elements of the center of excellence cultures can be deduced from these philosophers.

Immanuel Kant

Kant's philosophy emphasized the release of humans from adolescence and the importance of emancipation and responsibility for one's actions. Kant's categorical imperative states, "Always act in such a way that you can also will that your maxim should become a universal law" (Kant, 2000/1788, p. 140). This imperative includes the necessity to change one's perspective—for example, a leadership figure's aim should be to treat others in ways he or she wants to be treated or to lead others as he or she wants to be led. The same holds true with regard to clients: Employees should treat clients as they would like to be treated as a client. Kant's philosophy set forth the ideas of autonomy, independence, and responsibility, as well as the necessity to change one's perspective and to show regard for others.

Gotthold Ephraim Lessing

In *Nathan der Weise*, Lessing proclaimed tolerance for different value systems and cultures (Lessing, 1919). He emphasized that variety is a blessing. Applied to social and commercial organizations, Lessing's work urges groups to strive for heterogeneity instead of homogeneity, to accept different personalities, and to use synergies.

Hans Jonas

Jonas held that human beings are obliged to take responsibility because they are the only organism on this planet able to take responsibility for the planet, as well as for their own rights and dignity (Jonas, 1989). Managers from social and commercial organizations can find support for the relevance of responsibility for future, for the team, and for the organization in the ideas of Jonas.

Sir Karl Raimund Popper

In his philosophy of critical reasoning, Popper showed that living is problem solving. In society as in science, he argued, humans can eliminate deficits by means of critical rational discussion (Popper, 1992). Popper also emphasized that eliminating deficits may be a better strategy than striving to achieve an ideal state. According to Popper, progress is learning from mistakes. Social and commercial organizations can learn from Popper's philosophy the relevance of critical rational discussion in solving problems, the relevance of viewing mistakes as opportunities, and the idea of a constructive conflict culture.

Confucius

Many centuries ago Confucius spoke of the value of lifelong learning and continuous improvement. A person, a group, or a nation who does not learn from its mistakes will make even greater mistakes, according to Confucius (Konfuzius, 2000). The ideas of Confucius have not lost their importance for organizations.

Philosophy's Contribution to Psychology

Psychology can help us understand how to realize the teachings of these philosophers. Tolerance, responsibility, lifelong learning, critical rational discussion, and change of perspectives do not come about by chance. The more people are treated according to solid leadership principles, the more people are willing to behave in line with the philosophers' postulates.

Organizations that are active in different regions and markets of the world will have to incorporate the philosophers' teachings into their cultures. The reason is this: A global player has to act on two fronts. On the one hand, organizations have to implement certain universal fundamental values and principles that are valid across all locations. On the other hand, organizations have to adapt to different regional identities. To implement fundamental values worldwide, a global player cannot accept many heterogeneous value systems. The philosophers have pointed out substantial values that are relevant for all locations in the world: how people are treated, what rules of negotiations apply, and so forth.

Only the global players with the best and most qualified employees will be successful. To develop the best employees, organizations must be guided by a view of the person that involves individual emancipation, responsibility, and respect and the principles emphasized by the philosophers. Thus, the globalizing market is leading to the implementation of values proclaimed by these philosophers, and a globalized economy may be a substantial step towards the development of a so-called world ethics.

Some view globalization as leading to Westernization and therefore as limiting the available points of view. But this may be only a short-run consideration. In the long run, especially as the underdeveloped countries continue to develop, globalization will increase our horizons.

CONCLUSION

Psychology is a science that seeks to analyze, explain, and predict human behavior. Psychological theories provide its practitioners with methods not only to explain human behavior (e.g., Why does someone become aggressive? Why is a person unmotivated?), but also to predict human behavior (e.g., How will a person's motivation and performance change?). Psychological theories and knowledge are very important for changing mentalities, attitudes, climates, structures, and behavior in social and commercial organizations. Hence, psychological theories can be used to launch intervention programs.

Many in leading positions in science, politics, and economics are not well-informed about the relevant psychological mechanisms that lead to identification with an organization's work. A great deal of inner resignation, burnout, and low performance in organizations can be explained by the fact that fundamental psychological aspects are neglected in the day-to-day interactions and communication in social and commercial organizations. Because of this neglect, and partly because of a corresponding arrogance (in ignoring fundamental knowledge about human functioning, such as wishes, anxieties, sorrows, and hopes), many organizations are a long way from realizing their potential. Ignoring psychological knowledge is very expensive.

Psychologists must communicate their knowledge to the public more than is currently the case, and they must introduce it into companies, social organizations, and administrations. Psychologists should become more adept at using their methodology and theories in politics, as well as in economics. The factors that increase internal resignation, burnout, and depression have been clearly specified. Thus, psychologists have the tools to take a more active role in forming the structures and conditions in social and commercial organizations; organizations that do not function adequately are a cause of many personal and social disorders. Present psychological knowledge has the potential to bring about substantive change. Therefore, the cooperation of scientists and practitioners, a science market, and action research are needed.

Courageous promoters are needed to convey psychology's knowledge and ideas to leading figures in social and commercial organizations, in politics, and in science. But more contributions are also needed from practitioners in the field in the form of asking questions and articulating problems that need to be solved. This would help to center research in problems of reality rather than those of the literature.

Thus, we think it would be very helpful to introduce "science markets" where psychologists could build a dialogue between the practical field (e.g., teachers, managers, organizational leaders) and the field of scientific psychology. One component of the science market could be a "problem exchange market," where participants would identify which problems exist and what solution ideas are being developed and where practitioners would formulate their questions and problems and could establish contacts with scientists. Another component could be a "psychological science market," in which psychologists would present their research findings and the knowledge they consider relevant for solving actual problems.

The idea behind the science market is that the science, psychology, would have a forum for communicating its knowledge and solving practical problems and practitioners would have the opportunity to discuss problems and generate solutions together with researchers. In addition, it would be worthwhile to have as science "traders" or "brokers" social engineers who carry out interventions and evaluate them and who convey the results of the social sciences to the practical field to help solve practical problems. Well-trained social engineers are needed who are familiar with psychological research, who are able to communicate it to heterogeneous social and commercial organizations, and who can implement it there. This process could be very similar to that described by Lewin, who referred to this as "action research" (Lewin, 1951).

Lewin's saying "Nothing is as practical as a good theory" is also applicable to the field of positive psychology. Psychology's many theories and a great deal of psychological knowledge can be directly applied to solve existing problems and to increase satisfaction, identification, and acceptance of change management processes, as well as innovations in social and commercial organizations.

A final word to those working in universities: The research we have presented in this chapter involves social and commercial organizations. All of this knowledge can also be applied to universities and the researchers working there. The productivity and creativity of psychology could be much better if we would apply our own psychological knowledge to optimize processes and services.

REFERENCES

Bandura, A. (1977). *Social learning theory*. Englewood Cliffs, NJ: Prentice Hall.

Brodbeck, F. C., Kerschreiter, R., Mojzisch, A., Frey, D., & Schulz-Hardt, S. (2002). The dissemination of critical, unshared information in decision-making groups: The effect of pre-discussion dissent. *European Journal of Social Psychology, 32*, 35–56.

Deci, E. L., & Ryan, R. M. (1985). *Intrinsic motivation and self-determination in human behavior*. New York: Plenum Press.

Dweck, C. (1991). Self theories and goals: Their role in motivation, personality, and development. In K. Dienstbier (Ed.), *The Nebraska symposium on motivation* (pp. 199–235). Lincoln, NE: University of Nebraska Press.

Frank, E., Maier, G., Frey, D., & Wendt, M. (2002). *Führung, Kommunikation und Krankheit* [Leadership, communication, and illness rates]. Unpublished manuscript, University of Munich, Germany.

Frey, D. (1996a). Notwendige Bedingungen für dauerhafte Spitzenleistungen in der Wirtschaft und im Sport: Parallelen zwischen Mannschaftssport und kommerziellen Unternehmen [Necessary conditions for permanent top performance in the economy and in sports: Parallels between team sport and commercial organizations]. In A. Conzelmann, H. Gabler, & W. Schlicht (Eds.), *Soziale Interaktionen und Gruppen im Sport* (pp. 3–28). Cologne, Germany: bps.

Frey, D. (1996b). Psychologisches Know-how für eine Gesellschaft im Umbruch —Spitzenunternehmen der Wirtschaft als Vorbild [Psychological knowledge for a changing society—Top companies in the economy as models]. In C. Honegger, J. M. Gabriel, R. Hirsig, J. Pfaff-Czarnecka, & E. Poglia (Eds.), *Gesellschaften im Umbau: Identitäten, Konflikte, Differenzen* (pp. 75–98). Zurich, Switzerland: Seismo.

Frey, D. (1998). Center of Excellence—Ein Weg zu Spitzenleistungen [Center of excellence—A way to top performance]. In P. Weber (Ed.), *Leistungsorientiertes Management: Leistungen steigern statt Kosten senken* (pp. 199–233). Frankfurt, Germany: Campus.

Frey, D., & Ludorf, S. (2002). *Über Selbsteinschätzung und Fremdeinschätzung: Überprüfung des Prinzipienmodells der Führung* [About self-assessment and assessment by others: An inspection of the principles of leadership]. Unpublished manuscript, University of Munich, Germany.

Frey, D., Raabe, B., & Jonas, E. (2002). *Zur kognitiv-affektiven Landkarte von Change Agents* [Toward a cognitive-affective map of change agents]. Unpublished manuscript, University of Munich, Germany.

Frey, D., & Schnabel, A. (1999). Change Management—Der Mensch im Mittelpunkt. [Change management—Humankind in the center]. *Die Bank—Zeitschrift für Bankpolitik und Bankpraxis, 1*, 44–49.

Frey, D., & Schulz-Hardt, S. (Eds.) (2000a). *Vom Vorschlagswesen zum Ideenmanagement—Zum Problem der Änderung von Mentalitäten, Verhalten und Strukturen* [From improvement suggestions to idea management—The problem of changing mentalities, behavior, and structures]. Göttingen, Germany: Hogrefe.

Frey, D., & Schulz-Hardt, S. (2000b). Zentrale Führungsprinzipien und Center of Excellence-Kulturen als notwendige Bedingungen für ein funktionierendes Ideenmanagement [Central principles of leadership and center of excellence cultures as necessary conditions for the functioning of idea management]. In D. Frey & S. Schulz-Hardt (Eds.), *Vom Vorschlagswesen zum Ideenmanagement—Zum Problem der Änderung von Mentalitäten, Verhalten und Strukturen* (pp. 15–46). Göttingen, Germany: Hogrefe.

Frey, D., Schulz-Hardt, S., & Stahlberg, D. (1996). Information seeking among individuals and groups and possible consequences for decision-making in business and politics. In E. Witte & J. H. Davis (Eds.), *Understanding group behavior: Small group processes and interpersonal relations* (Vol. 2, pp. 211–225). Mahwah, NJ: Erlbaum.

Hertel, G., Kerr, N., & Messé, L. A. (2000). Motivation gains in performance groups: Paradigmatic and theoretical developments on the Köhler effect. *Journal of Personality and Social Psychology, 79*, 580–601.

Janis, I. L. (1982). *Groupthink* (2nd rev. ed.). Boston: Houghton Mifflin.

Jonas, H. (1989). *Das Prinzip Verantwortung. Versuch einer Ethik für die technologische Zivilisation* [The imperative of responsibility]. Frankfurt, Germany: Suhrkamp.

Kant, I. (2000). *Kritik der praktischen Vernuft* [Critique of practical reason]. Frankfurt, Germany: Suhrkamp. (Original work published 1788)

Kauffeld, S., Jonas, E., & Frey, D. (2002). *Effects of flexible work time designs.* Manuscript submitted for publication.

Konfuzius (2000). *Die Weisheit des Konfuzius* [The wisdom of Confucius]. Frankfurt, Germany: Insel.

Lessing, G. E. (1919). *Nathan der Weise* [Nathan the wise]. Bielefeld, Germany: Velhagen & Klasing.

Levine, J. M., & Moreland, R. L. (1998). Small groups. In D. T. Gilbert, S. T. Fiske, & G. Lindzey (Eds.), *The handbook of social psychology* (Vol. 2, pp. 415–469). New York: McGraw Hill.

Lewin, K. (1951). *Field theory in social science: Selected theoretical papers.* New York: Harper.

Locke, E. A., & Latham, G. P. (1990a). *A theory of goal setting and task performance.* Englewood Cliffs, NJ: Prentice Hall.

Locke, E. A., & Latham, G. P. (1990b). Work motivation and satisfaction: Light at the end of the tunnel. *Psychological Science, 1,* 240–246.

Popper, K. R. (1992). *Die offene Gesellschaft und ihre Feinde* [The open society and its enemies]. Stuttgart, Germany: UTB.

Schulz-Hardt, S., Frey, D., Lüthgens, C., & Moscovici, S. (2000). Biased information search in group decision making. *Journal of Personality and Social Psychology, 78,* 655–669.

Shepperd, J. A. (1993). Productivity loss in performance groups: A motivation analysis. *Psychological Bulletin, 113,* 67–81.

Simon, H. (1996). *Hidden champions: Lessons from 500 of the world's best unknown companies.* Boston: Harvard Business School Press.

Skinner, E. A. (1996). A guide to constructs of control. *Journal of Personality and Social Psychology, 71,* 549–570.

Steiner, I. D. (1972). *Group process and productivity.* New York: Academic Press.

Stroebe, W., & Diehl, M. (1994). Why groups are less effective than their members: On productivity losses in idea-generating groups. *European Review of Social Psychology, 5,* 271–303.

Tyler, T. R. (1994). Psychological models of the justice motive: Antecedents of distributive and procedural justice. *Journal of Personality and Social Psychology, 67,* 850–863.

Wendt, M. (1998). *Die Überprüfung des Prinzipienmodells der Führung* [The assessment of the principles of leadership]. Unpublished doctoral dissertation, University of Kiel, Germany.

Wendt, M., & Frey, D. (2002). *Empirische Forschungen zum Prinzipienmodell der Führung* [Empirical research toward the principles of leadership]. Unpublished manuscript, University of Munich, Germany.

West, M. A. (1994). *Effective teamwork.* Exeter, England: BPC Wheatons.

12

JUDGMENTAL HEURISTICS: HUMAN STRENGTHS OR HUMAN WEAKNESSES?

DALE GRIFFIN AND DANIEL KAHNEMAN

Everyone complains of his memory and nobody complains of his judgment.

—La Rochefoucauld

Few would claim that human behavior or physical performance defines optimal behavior or performance. Similarly, few would claim that human perceptual performance is optimal. The statement that observed performance in these domains is inferior to optimal models will not stir controversy. In the domain of judgment, however, such claims violate the *rationality presumption* and are subject to intense and often hostile scrutiny. Many philosophers, economists, and political scientists, as well as quite a few psychologists, hold the strong belief that normal educated human judgment is rational. We believe that this rationality presumption is unduly constraining and that descriptive models of judgment that abandon this presumption do indeed belong in a psychology of human strengths. Good and poor judgments are both normal, and the processes that produce brilliant intuitive insights are also the cause of systematic biases. The study of judgment errors provides a map of the regions of danger where fast and confident intuition should give way to slower reasoning processes and where automatized cognitive skills should give way to formal rules and guidelines.

In this chapter, we consider how one descriptive approach to human judgment, the heuristics and biases (HB) program, fits into the positive psychology perspective. From its beginning (Tversky & Kahneman, 1971), the heuristics and biases tradition of research on human judgment included both descriptive and critical research agendas. The descriptive agenda of HB research was to identify and characterize the "judgmental heuristics" of intuitive thinking about probability and likelihood. The critical agenda was to identify the "biases" that distinguish intuitive thinking from idealized formal models of probability and statistical inference. The study of systematic judgment errors was not intended to document a pessimistic view of human nature. The idea of cognitive biases was intended as a corrective to two separate ideas that were prevalent at the time: (a) that idealized models of inference and decision (e.g., statistical decision theory) are adequate descriptive theories of how people actually think and choose and (b) that errors of judgment and choice are due primarily to motivated thinking, not to the inherent biases of intuition.

The general issue of human rationality was not addressed in the early studies of heuristics and biases (e.g., Tversky & Kahneman, 1973), although other investigators with a similar agenda were perhaps less restrained. The rationality presumption was bypassed by an emphasis on the similarities between intuitive judgment and perceptual processes. Nonetheless, the perspective on human rationality that is suggested by demonstrations of cognitive biases has been the subject of some sharp criticism. Critics have argued that the HB perspective offers an unjustifiably pessimistic view of humans as irrational, and accused researchers in this tradition of promoting a distorted view of human reason by focusing selectively on entertaining examples of foolish thinking.

Defenders of the rationality presumption and critics of cognitive biases were motivated by two distinct ideas. One generic claim for optimality is that rationality does not exist outside of human thought, and therefore (normal) human thought must be rational (e.g., Cohen, 1981). A second and increasingly common claim comes from the logic of evolutionary optimization: A priori, it is suggested, pressures of natural selection will guarantee that surviving organisms will hold mostly true beliefs and make rational decisions (Dennett, 1984). Note that these positions do not require that people demonstrate rational judgments in all situations. They recognize that people make mistakes for a variety of reasons but view these errors as rather uninteresting failures of performance, rather than as consequences of flaws in basic cognitive competence. These claims imply a "true score plus error" model in which optimal judgment can be distorted by inadequate attention, effort, or consideration. The heuristics and biases perspective is qualitatively different from these positions in proposing that truth and systematic error are produced by the same cognitive mechanisms.

BACKGROUND TO THE HEURISTICS AND BIASES PROGRAM

The HB program was directly influenced by ideas and observations from two quite distinct sources: the use of visual illusions as a diagnostic tool for the understanding of perceptual processing and the demonstrations of systematic flaws in clinical reasoning (e.g., Goldberg, 1959; Hoffman, 1960; Meehl, 1954). The ground for the HB program was prepared by Simon in his Nobel-winning research on bounded rationality and organizational economics and by a variety of others working at the same time (see Griffin, Gonzalez, & Varey, 2001, for a review). Simon (1956, 1957) challenged the predominant notion that "economic man" should be modeled as an unbiased processor of prodigious memory and effortless calculation and argued that people "satisfice" (by achieving limited goals) rather than optimize (by achieving the best possible outcome).

Because of cognitive limitations, Simon argued, people sought to do "well enough" rather than to optimize their outcomes. The same limitations led people to use relatively simplistic "heuristics," or rules of thumb, rather than exhaustive normative methods of decision making, but such heuristic approaches were often good enough for survival in both life and the marketplace. In this view people are "substantively rational" in the sense of planning, reasoning, and goal setting, but because of the bounds of computational limitations, people fail the tests of "procedural rationality," which demands exhaustive consideration of alternatives and coherence among related judgments and decisions. Simon stressed that evolutionary pressures on both organisms and organizations led to local ("better than") rather than global ("best of") optimization, and he dismissed arguments that natural selection or economic competition would lead to—or even encourage—behavior that meets the formal definitions of rationality. Instead of full-blown rationality, Simon argued, people needed and demonstrated "myopic rationality," a combination of reasoned deliberation in planning and goal-setting and inconsistency among preferences and beliefs that was in sharp violation of the coherence principles central to rational models (Simon, 1983).

The critical or negative message from Simon's work was simply that idealized multiattribute models of rational decision making dominant in economics were much too complex to describe not only limited-capacity human information processors but even the most powerful computer. His positive message was that simple heuristics could take advantage of environmental regularities and perform pretty well in a range of environments. Furthermore, because both marketplace and evolutionary success required local satisficing (beating the immediate competition) rather than global optimization, performing pretty well was often good enough to survive and prosper.

Empirical programs inspired by Simon's positive message are flourishing in a number of areas, including computer science, artificial intelligence, and psychology. For example, the Adaptive Decision Making program (Payne, Bettman, & Johnson, 1993) explores how people selectively invest their limited attentional resources according to the importance of various tasks; people are assumed to selectively raise the standard of their satisficing heuristics when solving more important problems. Gigerenzer and his ABC (Adaptive Behavior and Cognition) colleagues have studied how presumably evolved "fast and frugal" processes can exploit the structure of the environment (summarized in Gigerenzer, Todd, & the ABC Research Group, 1999). Gigerenzer's position has developed in two distinct phases, moving from a firm defense of the rationality presumption to a strong advance of bounded rationality. Gigerenzer initially argued that biases in judgment disappeared in ecologically (and evolutionarily) valid conditions and that people naturally reason according to normative methods (Gigerenzer, 1991, 1994). These claims, which are not in the spirit of Simon's original critique, have received little empirical or theoretical support (see, e.g., Griffin & Buehler, 1999). However, the current ABC research on heuristics of choice is very much in the spirit of Simon's positive message, starting as it does with assumptions about simplicity and efficiency.

The HB program also adopted the idea that intuitive thinking is simplifying—though not necessarily simple—and generally efficient. The guiding idea was that the processes of intuitive thinking are an evolutionary development of the processes that serve perception (Kahneman & Frederick, 2002). The early HB work reflected experiences acquired in laborious efforts to overcome erroneous intuitions in teaching statistics to undergraduates. Intuitions about probability seem closer to direct perceptions of likelihood (e.g., in immediately experienced "feelings" of surprise) than to logical consideration of set inclusion relations that define the extensional rules of probability theory. Demonstrations of the persistence of sample-size neglect in the intuitive thinking of trained statisticians (Tversky & Kahneman, 1971) and of the prevalence of base-rate neglect and illusions of validity in clinical judgment (Meehl & Rosen, 1955; Kahneman & Tversky, 1973) suggested that these errors represent fundamental characteristics of the human mind that education can override, but not eradicate (Kahneman & Frederick, 2002).

THE HB RESEARCH STRATEGY

Heuristics and Cognitive Illusions

The term *heuristic* was used in the HB program to distinguish the uncontrolled strategies of intuitive statistical judgment from the algorithmic solutions proposed in formal treatments of probability and prediction.

Heuristics were shortcuts relative to the optimal algorithmic solution, but they were nonetheless built on complex cognitive processes such as the computation of the prototypicality of an instance (the representativeness heuristic) or the ease of retrieving and generating multiple instances (the availability heuristic). These judgmental heuristics were used to describe how people evaluated the frequency, commonness, or probability of some outcome. (In contrast, Simon had focused on decision heuristics for selecting which action to choose.) *Judgmental biases* served as the diagnostic markers of judgmental heuristics—deviations from ideal or optimal judgments were used to pinpoint phenomena that needed to be explained. Both the heuristic processes and the biases used to diagnose them were modeled on studies of human perception, especially the study of visual illusions.

The human visual system comprises an impressive and efficient set of analytical processes. It allows us to recognize a face or a shape despite tremendous changes in light, shadow, color, and viewing angle. More remarkably, these flexible processes occur extremely quickly and without perceived effort. However, the same extremely efficient shortcuts used to organize information in the visual system lead to predictable mistakes, or illusions. Simple manipulations of context make shorter lines appear longer, white backgrounds appear colored, and straight lines appear bent. These visual illusions offer insights into how the visual system operates by identifying the ways in which the cues provided by the world are weighted and combined to construct a representation of the environment (Brunswik, 1955; Coren & Girgus, 1978). Finding the ways in which the visual system can be "fooled" is a useful part of the tool kit of visual scientists. More generally, of course, many psychological processes are studied by examining their failures: Much of what is known about memory is drawn from studies of forgetting and misremembering. "The focus on bias and illusion is a research strategy that exploits human error, although it neither assumes nor entails that people are perceptually or cognitively inept" (Tversky & Kahneman, 1983, p. 313).

The vignettes that were a prominent tool in HB research were designed to fool the judgment system. The metaphor of visual illusions was used at many levels and mapped onto the concept of "cognitive illusions." The visual system is quick, efficient, and usually accurate, but it shows predictable biases in specific situations. Visual illusions can be measured against the actual stimulus information and the bias revealed, but even when the perceiver "knows" an illusion to be false, the subjective appeal of the illusion remains. Reason and rules can be decisive, but they do not make the visual experience less compelling. Similarly, cognitive illusions often remain compelling even when normative rules of reasoning are brought to bear. Visual illusions differ in robustness—some are relatively easy to overcome; others are persistent even for the informed viewer. Cognitive illusions also differ in the ease with which they can be overcome and in the accessibility of the relevant logical rules.

The vignettes and other short problems that were used in early HB research were simultaneously tests and demonstrations of the role of judgmental heuristics. Scenarios were couched in everyday terms and settings rather than in the traditional metaphors of urn sampling and dice throwing, both because the former settings were more interesting and because they were less transparently a test of mathematical or logical reasoning. Readers of academic articles were faced with the same puzzles as the original subjects of the experiments, and the true test of the heuristics and biases account was whether the cognitive illusion "worked" on the sophisticated reader. This method was borrowed from the classic works of gestalt psychology, in which illustrations of the rules of grouping or figure-ground organization served both as a description of an experimental method and as an implicit report of the results. Cognitive illusions are not as compelling, of course, and the demonstrations were accompanied by statistics of responses, but the approach was much the same.

One of the earliest demonstration studies was this word problem:

> The frequency of appearance of letters in the English language was studied.... Consider the letter R. Is R more likely to appear in ____ the first position? ____ the third position? (check one). (Tversky & Kahneman, 1973, pp. 211–212)

R is more frequent in the third than the first position. However, the first letter of a word is a better search cue than the third letter, and words beginning with r are easier to bring to mind than words with r in the third letter. Subjects estimated that such letters were twice as common in the first than the third position, and readers were given the chance to "feel" the operation of the availability heuristic in action.

A common question about such demonstrations is whether the phenomenon has "ecological validity"—whether such judgmental biases are characteristic of consequential real-world judgments. There are two distinct answers to that question. The first is that several judgment biases have been observed both in the laboratory and in ecological studies of the performance of experts (see reviews in Gilovich, Griffin, & Kahneman, 2002; Kahneman, Slovic, & Tversky, 1982). The second is that the frequency of errors in the real world is no more relevant to the study of cognitive illusions than to the study of visual illusions. Both types of illusions are valid objects of study even if both the visual system and the cognitive system work well—and even if few people complain about the qualities of their perceptual or cognitive systems. Illusions, whether visual or cognitive, provide cues to processes that also deliver impressively accurate representations of the world.

Many laboratory studies of perception have been inspired by observations of illusions in the real world; the moon illusion is a salient example. There are parallel phenomena in the study of judgment. In particular, the analysis of intuitive prediction in terms of representativeness (Kahneman & Tversky, 1973) was drawn from three real-world observations: (a) the "interview illusion"—the tendency to make strong inferences about an individual on the basis of a short personal interview; (b) the "illusion of validity"—the high confidence that people have in their judgments, even when they know that their judgments are generally invalid; and (c) base-rate neglect—the willingness of people to predict the occurrence of rare events on the basis of weak evidence (Meehl & Rosen, 1955). Evidently, intuitive predictions do not follow the rules of Bayesian inference or regression analysis. It seems that people often make predictions by choosing the outcome that is most representative of the image they formed, regardless of the quality of the evidence on which the match is based.

To capture these characteristics of intuitive prediction, Kahneman and Tversky (1973) used the following vignette:

> Tom W. is of high intelligence, although lacking in true creativity. He has a need for order and clarity, and for neat and tidy systems in which every detail finds its appropriate place. His writing is rather dull and mechanical, occasionally enlivened by somewhat corny puns and by flashes of imagination of the sci-fi type. He has a strong drive for competence. He seems to have little feel and little sympathy for other people and does not enjoy interacting with others. Self-centered, he nonetheless has a deep moral sense. (p. 238)

One group of participants was asked to rank the relative frequency of nine fields of graduate education. A second group of participants was asked to rank Tom's similarity to the typical graduate student in each graduate specialization. Finally, a third prediction group was told that the description was based on projective psychological tests and was asked to rank the nine fields in terms of the likelihood that Tom was a graduate student in that field. The correlation between the mean ranks in the similarity group and the rankings of the likelihoods was almost perfect. Differences in the base rates of outcomes had no distinguishable effects on judgments unless predictions were made for an individual about whom no information was provided. The representativeness heuristic could not be applied in the absence of case-specific information. This experiment accomplished two objectives: It provided experimental confirmation for hypotheses derived from informal observations in the real world, and it provided direct evidence for the explanation of these observations in terms of representativeness by demonstrating a perfect correlation between predictions and judgments of representativeness.

Judgmental Heuristics: Not "Effort-Saving Devices"

The HB approach to intuitive reasoning differs from the "cognitive miser" perspective in social psychology. The latter approach is similar to one of the possible interpretations of Simon's notion of bounded rationality: It focuses on the individual's unwillingness to think deeply or carefully as an explanation of errors. Failures of reasoning or overreliance on salient cues are treated as manifestations of energy-saving strategies. The implicit assumption is that people could do better if they were willing to pay the "costs of thinking" associated with getting an accurate answer. In contrast, the standard HB assumption would be that confidence in intuitive judgment is often so high that people do not feel any need to improve their judgments, and even when people are very motivated to be accurate, they may be unable to perform the operations that would minimize likely errors. Incentives and attention may matter when the individual knows logical or statistical rules that could prevent errors and the situation provides cues that evoke the relevant rules.

Multiple Levels of Reasoning: Heuristics, Rules, and Algorithms

According to the representativeness model, intuitive statistical inference and statistical prediction are sensitive only to the similarity between a target individual and the prototype of a category, or between a sample and a population; information about base rate, sample size, and cue validity is simply neglected. This model is an oversimplification: There is ample evidence that people have many valid intuitions about statistical rules, although they often fail to apply these rules to particular problems. The relevance of base rates and sample sizes is quite intuitive—in principle, if not always in practice. Indeed, some everyday maxims are actually statistical rules in a memorable form. The physicians' guideline "When you hear hooves, think horses, not zebras" means nothing other than "Remember the base rate: rare events are unlikely." There is also considerable evidence that people trained in formal statistics can transfer concepts and rules when reasoning in new domains (Nisbett, Krantz, Jepson, & Kunda, 1983). Overall, the heuristics and biases tradition fits a three-level model of reasoning: automatic, associative heuristic reasoning in system 1 (exemplified by judgmental heuristics); controlled rule-based reasoning (including rule-based heuristics) in system 2; and external cognition using formal rules and decision models in system 3. This scheme extends the distinction between the two modes of thinking that Stanovich and West (2000; see also Sloman, 1996) labeled system 1 and system 2.

Judgmental heuristics make use of the outputs of even lower-level judgment processes termed "natural assessments" (Tversky & Kahneman, 1983). The natural assessments continuously compute attributes such as similarity, prototypicality, causal potency, retrieval fluency, and affective value. For an example, consider the statements "Woody Allen's aunt wished him to be a dentist" and "Madonna's mother wished her to be a nun." It appears impossible to comprehend the meaning of those phrases without also going beyond the literal meaning by computing the fit (representativeness) of the individual and the relevant social stereotype. The misfit between target and category gives rise to astonished amusement in the first case and a sense of disquiet in the second case.

The examples of Woody Allen and Madonna suggest that the relation of representativeness is computed automatically, even in the absence of any particular cognitive goal. However, natural assessments are highly accessible and readily recruited by the goal of making a relevant judgment. Kahneman and Frederick (2002) offered an "attribute-substitution model" of heuristic judgments, in which attributes that are highly accessible and relevant to the task are substituted for the relevant attribute that the individual intends to evaluate. Thus, an assessment of representativeness may be mapped onto the probability scale, or an assessment of availability may be transformed into a judgment of frequency. More generally, any highly accessible attribute may be substituted for a target attribute if the target attribute is difficult to assess and if the potential heuristic attribute passes a threshold of relevance.

Natural assessments and judgmental heuristics form what Sloman (1996) called the "associative system" of reasoning, also referred to as system 1 (Stanovich & West, 2000). This system is closely tied to the perceptual system and provides output that is directly experienced as a property of the stimulus. However, the heuristics and biases tradition also recognizes a role for the "rule-based" system of thought, or system 2. Consider the following scenario (Tversky & Kahneman, 1983, pp. 297–300):

> Linda is 31 years old, single, outspoken, and very bright. She majored in philosophy. As a student, she was deeply concerned with issues of discrimination and social justice, and also participated in anti-nuclear demonstrations. Please rank the following statements by their probability, using 1 for the most probable.
> Linda is active in the feminist movement. (F)
> Linda is a bank teller. (T)
> Linda is a bank teller and active in the feminist movement. (T & F)

When only three items are ranked, the problem is "transparent" for those who are trained in the conjunction rule of probability: Statistically sophisticated subjects (but not untrained subjects) find the logical rule that bank tellers (T) must be more common than feminist bank tellers (T & F) decisive, even though the representativeness heuristic makes the conjunction "feel" more likely. However, when eight items are ranked, or when the conjunction is ranked separately from the general category, both statistically sophisticated and statistically naïve subjects rank the items in accord with representativeness and are not constrained by the rules of logic. The rules of set inclusion are most compelling in a within-subjects design when the question is asked in terms of relative frequency (number of people) rather than probability.

In many cases, the associative and rule-based systems work together and lead to the same answer, but setting up conflicts between the systems can reveal fundamental contradictions between the outputs of the two systems. As Sloman (1996) noted, disagreements between the associative and rule-based systems are characterized by the subjective state of "simultaneous conflicting belief": In cases such as the Linda example, most people agree, on reflection, that the conjunction must be less likely than the constituents but cannot shake the feeling that Linda really is more likely to be a feminist bank teller than a bank teller.

The rule-based system (system 2), characterized by limited capacity, deliberate attention, and serial processing, is not synonymous with normative or rational thought. The majority of deliberate reasoning processes are best characterized as "system 2 heuristics," or simplifying rules of thumb that are consistently applied and logically defensible. For example, people can recognize that a larger sample size increases the reliability of a poll result (a statistical heuristic corresponding to the law of large numbers) but nonetheless find the notion of predicting the votes of millions of people from samples of hundreds to be highly counterintuitive (because intuitions are not statistically based). The "fast and frugal" decision heuristics posited by the ABC group are system 2 heuristics, in that they refer to deliberate decision strategies. The same holds true for the evaluation heuristics identified in the study of consumer behavior (e.g., the price–quality heuristic, or the assumption that expensive products are better products) or the persuasion heuristics identified in social psychology (e.g., the length means strength heuristic, or the assumption that long messages are more informative, information held constant).

System 2 thought can override the associative heuristics when the problem structure or content activates the relevant logical rules or heuristics, but such overriding will usually provide qualitative guidelines rather than the precise quantitative adjustments required to match formal normative models. Formal rationality is best thought of as a third external system that requires explicit calculation and is not captured by either system of human intuition. This is underlined by the remarkable fact that the most basic rules of probability were not codified until the past 300 years, which in turn helps explain the striking difficulty that introductory statistics students have in thinking about the basic rules of probability.

The associative system of natural assessments and judgmental heuristics is a fast, efficient, and well-tested system that compresses a great deal of information into a simple output and therefore yields many correct inferences at the cost of some systematic biases. The rule-based system, in contrast, may be seen as an evolutionary work in progress. Its limited capacity for abstract manipulation of symbols provides the basis for discovering and using formal models and calculations, but it is generally too slow and cumbersome for everyday reasoning (Sloman, 1996). The cognitive miser metaphor in social psychology is a good description of the effortful rule manipulation of system 2, but a better characterization of system 1 would be a "cognitive busybody": Due to its more parallel, automatic nature, the problem is that too many associations are triggered, not too few. The heuristics and biases approach does not see human reasoning as a "true score plus error" model in which formal rationality is somehow hidden inside distorted judgments. Rather, good and bad judgments follow from the same basic processes and can occur within both systems of reasoning.

RATIONALITY AND POSITIVE PSYCHOLOGY

Simon (1983) described formal models of rationality as "jewels of intellectual accomplishment" (p. 3). Any positive perspective on human thought and reason must celebrate the immense step forward represented by formal models and by the capacity of humans to reason using abstract logic and symbols. As we have suggested, there is also much to be celebrated in the efficiencies of system 1 thought, especially the immensely efficient ability of the system to easily and effortlessly "pattern-match" an instance with such complex categories as "nerdy computer student" or "comedian dentist."

However, it is neither productive nor positive to succumb to the temptation to assume that because humans have "made it to the moon," thanks to the use of formal models, optimal modes of reasoning are in some way "natural." Neither is it correct to confuse evolutionary adaptations with optimal models of reasoning. As Gould noted, "even the strictest operation of pure Darwinism builds organisms full of nonadaptive parts and behaviors.... All organisms evolve as complex and interconnected wholes, not as loose alliances of separate parts, each independently optimized by natural selection" (Gould, 1997, p. 51). High-level systems such as reasoning are typically built on the foundations of earlier mechanisms; evolution cannot throw out (all) the old to make room for the new. When a qualitatively new system arises, such as the abstract language-based system 2, it shows an uneasy coexistence with what came before, both cooperating and competing with the earlier system. Both systems show considerable intelligence, and individual differences in both kinds of intelligence are likely. Simon spoke of the expert chess player as one with a huge repertoire of domain-specific patterns available for pattern-matching (system 1) heuristics (Chase & Simon, 1973).

Is there any particular value in searching for the positive message of human strengths in the heuristics and biases tradition? One attempt to hold the middle ground argues that the apparently competing visions of the HB approach and the evolutionary adaptationists differ primarily in rhetoric but agree in core claims (Samuels, Stich, & Bishop, 2002). Thus, it is tempting to invoke the refrain that the glass of human cognition may be seen as half full or half empty. However, we believe there is more to the debate on rationality than differing perspectives, and more to considering how visions of human rationality fit into a psychology of human strengths than simply searching for the most positive angle or "spin." The true challenge in amplifying human abilities, we believe, is helping people distinguish between the amazingly efficient human ability to form opinions and the less developed ability to evaluate those opinions. Creativity, spontaneity, and other celebrated strengths of human thought and feeling are integral to the ability to form opinions, to develop hunches, and even to dream of someday traveling to the moon. But it is the societal system of formal thought—a human strength to be celebrated in its own right—based on thousands of years of shared intellectual tradition that provides the testing ground for those opinions and hunches, as well as the tools for making the moon voyage a reality.

Stanovich and West (2000) contrasted the "meliorist" perspective of the heuristics and biases program with the "Panglossian" perspective of its main critics. These labels, although fanciful, do have some merit in defining the kind of positive psychology each side brings to bear. The positive psychology of the meliorists is the message that the intellectual tools to improve judgment exist as a kind of external intelligence. Paradoxically, a Panglossian message that people are perfectly rational animals when in the right environment leaves little scope for improving the multitude of judgments required of those who do not live in small hunter-gatherer groups on the savannah. Based on advances in formal methods in optics, some research teams now believe that human vision could be surgically altered to yield twice the acuity of normal 20-20 vision. Great advances in formal theories of decision-making have taken place in the past century, and although no surgical procedures will be available to improve judgment (in the near future, anyway), there are exciting challenges ahead in designing other ways to increase the acuity of human judgment.

REFERENCES

Brunswik, E. (1955). Representative design and probabilistic theory in a functional psychology. *Psychological Review, 62*, 193–217.

Chase, W. G., & Simon, H. A. (1973). Perception in chess. *Cognitive Psychology, 4*, 55–81.

Cohen, L. J. (1981). Can human irrationality be experimentally demonstrated? *Behavioral and Brain Sciences, 4,* 317–370.

Coren, S., & Girgus, J. S. (1978). *Seeing is deceiving: The psychology of visual illusions.* Hillsdale, NJ: Erlbaum.

Dennett, D. (1984). *Brainstorms: Philosophical essays on mind and psychology.* Boston: MIT Press.

Gigerenzer, G. (1991). How to make cognitive illusions disappear: Beyond heuristics and biases. *European Review of Social Psychology, 2,* 83–115.

Gigerenzer, G. (1994). Why the distinction between single-event probabilities and frequencies is important for psychology (and vice versa). In G. Wright & P. Ayton (Eds.), *Subjective probability* (pp. 129–161). New York: Wiley.

Gigerenzer, G., Todd, P. M., & the ABC Research Group. (1999). *Simple heuristics that make us smart.* New York: Oxford University Press.

Gilovich, T., Griffin, D., & Kahneman, D. (2002). *Heuristics and biases: The psychology of intuitive judgment.* Cambridge, England: Cambridge University Press.

Goldberg, L. R. (1959). The effectiveness of clinicians' judgments: The diagnosis of organic brain damage from the Bender-Gestalt Test. *Journal of Consulting Psychology, 23,* 25–33.

Gould, S. J. (1997, June 26). Evolution: The pleasures of pluralism. *New York Review of Books,* 46–52.

Griffin, D. W., & Buehler, R. (1999). Probability, frequency, and prediction: Easy solutions to cognitive illusions? *Cognitive Psychology, 38,* 48–78.

Griffin, D. W., Gonzalez, R., & Varey, C. A. (2001). The heuristics and biases approach to judgment under uncertainty. In A. Tesser & N. Schwarz (Eds.), *The Blackwell handbook of social psychology: Intrapersonal processes* (pp. 207–235). Malden, MA: Blackwell.

Hoffman, P. J. (1960). The paramorphic representation of clinical judgment. *Psychological Bulletin, 57,* 116–131.

Kahneman, D., & Frederick, S. (2002). Representativeness revisited: Attribute substitution in intuitive judgement. In T. Gilovich, D. Griffin, & D. Kahneman (Eds.), *Heuristics and biases: The psychology of intuitive judgment* (pp. 49–81). Cambridge, England: Cambridge University Press.

Kahneman, D., Slovic, P., & Tversky, A. (1982). (Eds.). *Judgment under uncertainty: Heuristics and biases.* Cambridge, England: Cambridge University Press.

Kahneman, D., & Tversky, A. (1973). On the psychology of prediction. *Psychological Review, 80,* 237–251.

Meehl, P. E. (1954). *Clinical versus statistical prediction.* Minneapolis: University of Minnesota Press.

Meehl, P. E., & Rosen, A. (1955). Antecedent probability and the efficacy of psychometric signs, patterns, or cutting scores. *Psychological Bulletin, 52,* 194–216.

Nisbett, R. E., Krantz, D. H., Jepson, D., & Kunda, Z. (1983). The use of statistical heuristics in everyday inductive reasoning. *Psychological Review, 90,* 339–363.

Payne, J. W., Bettman, J. R., & Johnson, E. J. (1993). *The adaptive decision maker*. New York: Cambridge University Press.

Samuels, R., Stich, S., & Bishop, M. (2002). Ending the rationality wars: How to make disputes about human rationality disappear. In R. Elio (Ed.), *New directions in cognitive science: Vol. 11. Common sense, reasoning, and rationality* (pp. 236–268). New York: Oxford.

Simon, H. A. (1956). Rational choice and the structure of the environment. *Psychological Review, 63*, 129–138.

Simon, H. (1957). *Models of man: Social and rational*. New York: Wiley.

Simon, H. (1983). *Reason in human affairs*. Stanford, CA: Stanford University Press.

Sloman, S. A. (1996). The empirical case for two systems of reasoning. *Psychological Bulletin, 119*, 3–22.

Stanovich, K. E., & West, R. F. (2000). Individual differences in reasoning: Implications for the rationality debate? *Behavioral and Brain Sciences, 23*, 645–665.

Tversky, A., & Kahneman, D. (1971). The belief in the "law of small numbers." *Psychological Bulletin, 76*, 105–110.

Tversky, A., & Kahneman, D. (1973). Availability: A heuristic for judging frequency and probability. *Cognitive Psychology, 5*, 207–232.

Tversky, A., & Kahneman, D. (1983). Extensional versus intuitive reasoning: The conjunction fallacy in probability judgment. *Psychological Review, 90*, 293–315.

13

POSITIVE AFFECT AS A SOURCE OF HUMAN STRENGTH

ALICE M. ISEN

In recent years there has been increasing interest in affect or emotion as a topic of scientific investigation in psychology, and there appears to be an increasing tendency to consider affect in a way that is integrated with cognition, motivation, and neurophysiological functioning (see Isen, 2000, 2002a, for discussion). In earlier decades, affect was not typically a major focus of investigation, and was certainly not considered as an integrated component of cognition or motivation. In fact, affect was generally omitted from cognitive theories and models, or was considered only as "arousal" (e.g., Duffy, 1934; Lindsley, 1951), or as a mechanism for interruption in case of a need for redirection of attention (e.g., Simon, 1967; see Isen & Hastorf, 1982, for further discussion). Although intense affect can surely serve such an alerting function, a growing body of work now shows that even mild, and even positive, affect has important influences on cognition and behavior and that affect's influence goes far beyond that gross, alerting function and is more subtle, complex, and multifaceted, as well.

Not only has the field's understanding of affect increased greatly, as a result of the newfound legitimacy of studying affect, but this affective revolution, because it has integrated affect with cognition and motivation, has enriched understanding of those subfields as well. Researchers now know, for example, that positive affect (but not negative affect) is a category in memory used spontaneously by people to organize their thoughts. This knowledge comes from studies published in the late 1970s and early 1980s showing that induced mild positive affect served as a retrieval cue for positive material learned during an experimental session—without any instruction to use affective state as an organizational scheme—but that the same was not as true for induced negative affect, particularly sadness (e.g., Isen, 1987; Isen, Shalker, Clark, & Karp, 1978; Snyder & White, 1982; Teasdale & Fogarty, 1979; Teasdale & Russell, 1983; Teasdale, Taylor, & Fogarty, 1980).

Even the emerging new neuroscience fields are being integrated with the study of affect, contributing to understanding of affect, and benefiting from application of information learned from the affect literature (see, e.g., Ashby, Isen, & Turken, 1999; Depue & Collins, 1999). The realization that affect is a regular part of thought processes and motivation or processing goals has enriched conceptualizations in those fields, and they have grown more realistic and complex as a result. In addition, by identifying ways in which affect influences well-researched processes in, for example, cognitive psychology, researchers have learned a great deal about affect that would not have been learned by introspection or only by focusing more obviously on affect, how it feels, and how people describe the experience of it.

Thus, the past three decades have seen a great enrichment in psychologists' understanding of affect and a great enrichment of the entire field, because of the field's recognition of affect as a regular influence on, or part of, all other processes. However, as a field, psychology still carries some baggage from its older affectless theories and approaches and past attitudes toward affect; and these represent challenges that must be overcome if researchers are to make further progress. Therefore, in this chapter I will point out what I think are some of these assumptions and approaches that, although outdated, may still infuse the field's thinking about affect, for the most part unwittingly.

The purposes of this chapter are, to present some of the research findings indicating that positive affect is a source of human strength—that it encourages and supports flexible, open-minded cognitive processing that enables people to do what needs to be done and make the most of the situations they are in—and to explore these findings in more detail, considering their implications and the circumstances in which they are most likely to occur or not occur. In addition, a goal will be to address some misconceptions or puzzles that have grown up about these findings and that may relate to some of the outdated assumptions surrounding the concept of affect.

Some of these misconceptions include, (a) that affect—even mild positive affect—typically, by its nature, distorts or disrupts orderly, effective thinking; (b) that the goals or processes induced by affect are unlike other goals, and as a result that they are in some sense more singular and more irresistible; (c) that positive and negative affect have similar or parallel effects; and (d) that true influences of affect can arise only from long-term, stable affective dispositions, whereas induced affect produces only very short-lived, inconsequential impacts.

Before discussing these misconceptions in detail, I will first suggest a broader conceptual issue that may be responsible for many of them.

TOWARD DISPELLING SOME MISCONCEPTIONS ABOUT AFFECT

Viewing Affect and Cognition as Separate

Many of these misconceptions themselves stem from the legacy of psychology's past orientation that viewed affect and cognition as separate, even opposite or opposing, forces or as characterized by fundamentally different kinds of processes. This orientation is sometimes referred to as the "hot–cold" dichotomy (e.g., Abelson, 1963; see also Lepper, 1994) and is represented in many ways in both the basic theoretical literature and the applied literatures as, for example, contrasts between "thinking versus feeling" approaches to persuasion. In neuroscience, as well, it is often assumed that affect and cognition compete for brain resources. In this chapter, I will suggest that such conceptualizations of affect and cognition as by nature different, even opposing, forces are not necessary and, in fact, hold back progress in understanding human functioning.

This view of affect as separate had its roots in the tripartite conceptualization of psychological processes, or mind, which posited three basic components of mind—cognition, conation ("will," corresponding to motivation and behavior), and affect or affection (see also, Hilgard, 1980; Isen & Hastorf, 1982; Isen, 2002b, for discussion and application). As others had before us, we called for the integration of these three functions, rather than their maintenance as separate "faculties," to develop a modern view of human functioning.

The data that have now accumulated regarding the impact of affect reveal some specific ways in which the assumption that affect, cognition, and motivation are separate is holding the field back. In particular, the view fosters three of the four misconceptions mentioned earlier: that all affect disrupts orderly thinking, that positive and negative affect have similar or parallel effects, and that the fundamental goals and processes associated with affect are, by nature, different from those of cognition (e.g., that they are more irresistible). To consider why I am suggesting that these are misconceptions and need to be abandoned or at least modified substantially, let us consider what the research literature has found.

Misconception That Positive Affect Disrupts Thinking

Positive Affect Facilitates Cognitive Flexibility

A growing body of research indicates that positive affect (happy feelings) has important facilitating effects on thinking and on people's ability to function. For example, it promotes the sought-after abilities underlying innovation and creativity, creative problem solving, and indeed problem solving more generally (e.g., Carnevale & Isen, 1986; Estrada, Isen, & Young, 1994, 1997; George & Brief, 1996; Greene & Noice, 1988; Hirt, Melton, McDonald, & Harackiewicz, 1996; Isen, 1999, 2002b; Isen, Daubman, & Nowicki, 1987; Isen, Johnson, Mertz, & Robinson, 1985; Isen, Rosenzweig, & Young, 1991; Kahn & Isen, 1993; Lee & Sternthal, 1999; Staw & Barsade, 1993). This has been found for both children and adults, in research laboratory tasks and in applied settings, and among managers, consumers, medical students, and physicians performing a diagnostic task, to name just a few.

This finding has also been obtained in a face-to-face negotiation situation where, without the introduction of mild positive affect, the session became very hostile, angry, unpleasant, and unproductive. In contrast to the situation of the control condition, people in whom mild positive affect had been induced were more likely to take a problem-solving approach (rather than contending for their own position, withdrawing, or yielding), to reason constructively, and thus to achieve the optimal solution possible in the situation for both parties (Carnevale & Isen, 1986).

Compatibly with these findings and the results showing that positive affect promotes cognitive flexibility and the ability to take different perspectives, very recent work is showing that positive affect, and its first cousin, optimism, may also be a source of self-control and a resource for coping ability in difficult situations (e.g., Aspinwall, 1998, 2001; Aspinwall & Brunhart, 1996; Aspinwall & Richter, 1999; Taylor & Aspinwall, 1996; Trope & Neter, 1994; Trope & Pomerantz, 1998). Optimism and positive affect have been shown to reduce "defensiveness" and to lead people to be more open to seeing things as they really are: more accepting where things cannot be changed, but more active in changing them where they can be changed (e.g., Scheier, Weintraub, & Carver, 1986).

In addition, not only has positive affect been found to facilitate innovation and creative problem solving, as noted, but it has also been shown to guide and facilitate organization in memory (e.g., Isen et al., 1978; Lee & Sternthal, 1999; Teasdale & Fogarty, 1979), to enable cognitive efficiencies that result from this organization (e.g., Estrada et al., 1997; Isen et al., 1991; Lee & Sternthal, 1999), and thus to facilitate thinking and judgment and enable them to be more flexible (e.g., Barone, Miniard, & Romeo, 2000; Dovidio, Gaertner, Isen, & Lowrance, 1995; Isen, Niedenthal, & Cantor, 1992; Kahn & Isen, 1993; Urada & Miller, 2000; just to name a few). For example, studies have now shown that people in positive affect consider more alternative ways of solving problems or meeting needs (e.g., try more solutions to difficult problems, Isen et al., 1987; have larger consideration sets in decision making about safe, enjoyable products, Kahn & Isen, 1993); engage in more reasonable processes and have better outcomes in an integrative bargaining situation, as described earlier (Carnevale & Isen, 1986); are more responsive to negotiation partners' moves in a zero-sum type of negotiation (Labroo & Isen, 2000); are more comfortable with reasonable (but not with unrealistic) extensions of existing concepts or categories; and can think about people and social groups, as well as other concepts, in more flexible ways (Barone et al., 2000; Dovidio et al., 1995; Isen & Daubman, 1984; Isen et al., 1992; Urada & Miller, 2000).

These data show significant interactions with the type of stimuli or materials, indicating that such effects are not simply mindless elevations of evaluation, akin to those that would result from putting on "rose-colored glasses," nor thoughtless categorization of all stimuli together. Rather, the effects of positive affect vary with particulars of the situations and materials and indicate that positive affect fosters careful, though flexible, consideration of the materials and concepts, in the situation.

Positive Affect Promotes Helpfulness

Also relating to the misconception that positive affect disrupts thinking, it should be recalled that there is a large literature indicating that positive affect promotes reasonable helpfulness, generosity, and social responsibility (see Isen, 1987, for review). Compatibly, Baron (1984) has also reported that mild positive affect leads to reduced conflict in organizational settings. It has been proposed that this social behavior may itself result from the impact of positive affect on memory and thinking (Isen et al., 1978); and, importantly, empirical work shows that these effects, too, are not mindless, but reflect the person's decision about the most appropriate course of action in the situation (e.g., Isen & Simmonds, 1978; see Isen, 1987, for review).

Thus, the main thing that is wrong with the assumption that affect —even mild, positive affect—typically disrupts orderly thinking is, first and foremost, that the evidence does not support such a view. This is not to say that there may not be times when some affects may disrupt some processes. But to assume that any positive affect, by its nature, will interfere with systematic processing whenever it has impact is to ignore a great deal of data showing that positive affect often facilitates cognitive processing, and to miss much of positive affect's potential for benefiting human functioning (e.g., Forgas, 2002; Mackie & Worth, 1991; Schwarz & Bless, 1991; but see Bless et al., 1996, for a modified view). Although some studies have reported effects that appear to show that positive affect interferes with thinking carefully or with reasoning (e.g., Melton, 1995), as noted, many others indicate that positive affect enhances many cognitive abilities and processes.

Therefore, it will be important to try to determine under what conditions positive affect interferes with task performance and under what conditions it is facilitating, rather than just to assert that by its nature it typically disrupts systematic processing if it has any effect at all. In fact, current work is addressing this question, and it appears that when a task is both unpleasant or annoying, and unimportant, people in positive affect may be less likely than controls to engage the task or to work on it carefully (Isen, Christianson, & Labroo, 2001). These studies also found that the kind of task used by Melton (1995) is one that is perceived by experimental participants to be very annoying and that when the reasoning task was made either more pleasant or more important, people in positive affect performed better than controls on it. The fact that people in positive affect are less likely to work on an unpleasant, unimportant task may relate to the fact that, more than controls, they themselves determine what is appropriate to do in the situation.

Misconception That Affect Always Takes Precedence or That Goals Induced by Affect Are Always More Influential

In view of these accumulating data, it is now possible to consider in more detail the question of what it may mean for affect and cognition to be integrated or not fundamentally distinct. To think of affect as a component of cognitive and motivational processes (and cognition and motivation as integral components of affect, at the same time), rather than as an outside, separate process, involves a subtle but meaningful change in the way many people currently think about affect, but one that is supported by the data. First, it would mean recognition that the basic nature of affect, cognition, and motivation is similar or at least compatible and integratable, if not identical, and that the processes involved in these functions are not fundamentally different. One implication of this view is that these functions can influence one another. A second is that all three of these functions are seen to be integrated by a person's purposive determination of the appropriate response to the situation as the person sees it.

Consequently, for example, motives engendered by mild positive affect would be considered no more irresistible or urgent than motives fostered by other plans and considerations. Bearing in mind the general principle that behavior is multidetermined and that motives operate in concert to produce behavior, one expects that people will always be determining courses of action based on combinations of goals, situational considerations, and motives or plans arising out of many aspects of the situation. Even when affect is playing a role and fosters some motive, this will simply be one of many in the situation and may or may not be acted on, depending on the other factors in the situation. For instance, although there is evidence that positive affect engenders a motive to maintain the positive state (e.g., Isen, Nygren, & Ashby, 1988; Isen & Patrick, 1983; Isen & Simmonds, 1978), this motive may not take precedence over other motives, goals, or plans and may be no more likely than any of a host of other considerations to determine behavior. Thus, people in positive affect should not be expected to distort or ignore useful negative, threatening, or disconfirming information in an effort to maintain their good mood, although they may avoid unnecessary exposure to risks, danger, or unpleasant material (see Isen, 2002a, for discussion).

Indeed, this is what data from several domains are now showing: positive affect has been reported to lead to *less* distortion or ignoring of information that did not fit with a preliminary hypothesis in a diagnostic task, and to *more* thoughts about losing when a real, meaningful risk was being contemplated (e.g., Aspinwall, 1998; Estrada et al., 1997; Isen & Geva, 1987). That is, people have motives that result from affective states, but these are not necessarily more pressing or more urgent or more determining of behavior than other considerations in the situation. For another example, it has been found that positive affect leads to greater persistence on tasks, especially tasks that are enjoyable or functional (e.g., Erez & Isen, in press), and it is commonly assumed that optimists will persist longer than pessimists on unsolvable tasks; but a recent study has found that optimists switched from the unsolvable task sooner if there were alternative tasks to work on in the situation (Aspinwall & Richter, 1999).

Conversely, there can be plans or interests that are just as captivating, or more so, than motives stemming from positive feelings. For example, seeing a newspaper article headline on a topic that is of interest prompts the person to pay attention to the article and to turn to read it. It does not need to be "emotional" to capture attention or motivate behavior. For another example, wanting to attend a meeting sets in motion a whole series of behaviors designed to get the person to the right place at the right time. Even without affect generated, one makes plans and acts on them.

Thus, the processes involved in affect, cognition, and motivation are not necessarily or fundamentally different. This relates to the "hot-cold" or "hot-cool" distinction that is sometimes drawn in the literature to describe thinking under different circumstances (e.g., Abelson, 1963), and is sometimes assumed to correspond to emotional versus nonemotional processing. What I am suggesting is that the hot-cool or "go versus know" system, as it is called by Mischel and colleagues (e.g., Mischel & Mendoza-Denton, chapter 17, this volume), should not be assumed to map directly onto "emotional" versus "non-emotional" decision making or thinking.

This suggestion, of course, is perfectly compatible with the way Mischel and colleagues have used the terms "hot" and "cool," speaking of two different kinds or levels of motivation, or two different ways of resolving a motivational dilemma, not necessarily relating to emotion. Many people assume that the "go" system corresponds to "emotion," and the "know" system to "cognition." But the evidence shows that, using the terminology of this dichotomy, sometimes mild positive affect can "cool" things down, in the sense that "cooling" means enabling people to be more reasonable and reasoning, more careful and thorough and organized in their thinking and evaluating of their long-term best interests, better able to switch perspectives, and even better able to build and branch out and self-regulate (e.g., Aspinwall, 1998; Fredrickson, 1998; Fredrickson, Mancuso, Branigan, & Tugade, 2000; Isen & Geva, 1987; Isen et al., 1991; Trope & Neter, 1994; Trope & Pomerantz, 1998). Thus, even if it turns out that strong emotion does sometimes energize the "go" system or orientation or approach, mild positive affect would not be similar to intense affect or negative affect or the other systems that are discovered to foster that kind of responding. (At the same time, it should be noted that pressing, nonaffective motives may also prompt the "go" system, as for example if one wants to be finished with the present task and move on to something else, or a participant in a study wants to finish the session and go to class. Then one may not be as careful or as willing to wait for rewards, but not because of emotion.)

This line of reasoning points out, in still another context, that all affect is not the same in its effects, that different feeling states have different effects on thinking and behavior, and that these effects themselves usually depend on the context of the task and behavior. And, just as all affect does not have the same influence on thinking, affect need not be considered fundamentally different from cognition, at least in the processes it sets in motion or utilizes.

Misconception That Positive Affect and Negative Affect Are Symmetrical

Another misconception stemming from a simplified, unitary view of affect, and related to the idea that affect is separate from cognition, is the notion that positive affect and negative affect should have opposite or parallel effects. Again, it was the empirical evidence that first led to the realization that such preconceptions about negative and positive affect are misleading. For example, in the helping literature, as noted above, it was discovered that positive affect, induced in a variety of ways (e.g., finding a small amount of money unexpectedly, receiving a small free sample or gift, receiving a report of success on a task) increased a person's tendency to help others, also measured in several different ways (e.g., Cunningham, 1979; see Isen, 1987, for review). However, negative affect was not regularly found to have the same effect, as might be expected by theories that considered all affect as simply "arousal" and therefore as alike in impact. Neither did negative affect always decrease helping, as one might expect if one conceptualized these two states as opposites or as reciprocally related. To the contrary, negative affect was found to be much more variable than positive affect, sometimes increasing helping, sometimes decreasing it, and sometimes having no effect (e.g., Cialdini, Darby, & Vincent, 1972; Cunningham, Steinberg, & Grev, 1980; Isen, 1970).

Similarly, in the cognitive domain, positive affect and negative affect were not found to have the same effects or parallel effects. For example, induced positive affect was found to cue positive material in memory, but negative affect, especially sadness, the presumed "opposite" of positive affect, was typically not found to serve as an effective retrieval cue for negative material in memory or was found to be much less effective as a cue (for more extensive discussion of this asymmetry between positive and negative affect, see, e.g., Isen, 1987, 1990, 1999).

Misconception That Small Positive Affect Inductions Cannot Have Important, Potentially Enduring Effects

A fourth misconception that needs to be addressed involves the assumption that induced positive affect is too fleeting to have real significance, along with the corollary assumption that stable affective traits or dispositions are the only important sources of affective impact on thinking and behavior. This assumption seems to be gaining application, especially in organizational settings, where there has been some effort to base personnel decisions on measured affective traits or dispositions. It should be noted, however, that the data do not support such a view regarding induced affect versus dispositional affect.

First, the results discussed above, showing strong effects of induced affect on several aspects of cognition, social cognition, and social behavior have been observed in studies where seemingly very mild occurrences were used to induce affect and where participants were randomly assigned to the experimental condition. This means that whatever people's affective predispositions, they were apparently overridden by small, subtle affect inductions, such as seeing 5 minutes of a nonaggressive, nonsexual comedy film, receiving a report of success on an unimportant task, receiving a small bag of 10 wrapped candies, receiving a useful free sample or a small gift worth under $1.00, and so forth. Further, these studies involved small numbers of participants per condition (15 to 30), indicating that the effects observed are statistically powerful. Third, the idea that these effects typically last only a few minutes has been shown not to be true, as some studies reported significant effects of these affect inductions even after 45 minutes had elapsed and two complex intervening tasks had been performed (e.g., Estrada et al., 1994, 1997). In addition, studies that have used measured (dispositional) positive affect or optimism have obtained very similar results to those obtained with induced positive affect (e.g., Aspinwall & Richter, 1999; Staw & Barsade, 1993). Further, a recent study that looked specifically at the relative effects of dispositional versus situational affect on job satisfaction in a work setting found that reported pleasant mood on the job made a significant and independent contribution, beyond affective disposition, to overall job satisfaction (Weiss, Nicholas, & Daus, 1999). Although this is only one context, it is illustrative of the fact that temporary feeling states may have an impact beyond that of dispositional affect. Further, it adds to the evidence showing that affect occurring in response to situational factors can have important and potentially lasting influence.

That induced positive affect should be maintained and continue to influence thought and behavior for more than a few minutes makes theoretical sense, as well. Because positive affect promotes a tendency to maintain the positive state and induces cognitive and social vehicles for doing so, all else equal, people who are feeling happy should be expected to retain those feelings, or at least to be more likely to experience them than others, until something happens specifically to disrupt them. That is, all else equal, people in whom positive affect has been induced have easier access to positive material in memory, perform better on tasks that are important or interesting, and have more pleasant social interactions with the people they encounter. These capabilities may, in addition, cause reciprocity of helping from others, which can contribute to maintaining one's own positive affective state. It may even set up a chain reaction in organizations or other settings, or influence "organizational culture" in the direction of being more pleasant, helpful, and enjoyable. As just one illustration, in the negotiation study reported by Carnevale and Isen (1986), not only did the bargainers in the positive-affect condition demonstrate a problem-solving approach and obtain better joint and individual outcomes, but also, for that group, the whole session was more pleasant, enjoyable, and devoid of conflict than it was for controls.

TOWARD UNDERSTANDING HOW THESE EFFECTS OCCUR

In trying to understand how positive affect has these far-reaching effects on cognition and behavior, we have proposed that this may occur because of positive affect's influence on the content of cognition. That is, positive affect cues positive material in memory (e.g., Isen et al., 1978; Teasdale & Fogarty, 1979), and this material is diverse and extensive (e.g.,

Cramer, 1968; Isen et al., 1985). Thus, people who are feeling happy have access to a wide range of positive thoughts and a great variety of thoughts. Additionally, a neurological model for the influence of positive affect on cognitive processes has recently been proposed to supplement this earlier view. This model suggests that the effects of positive affect are mediated by the dopamine system in the brain (Ashby et al., 1999; Isen, 2002a).

The suggestion of a neuropsychological model, or a role for neurological processes in these effects, may at first seem to add fuel to the assumption that meaningful effects of positive affect can come only from affect traits or dispositions. Although some researchers have proposed that individual differences in brain dopamine correspond to affective dispositions, particularly extroversion (e.g., Depue & Collins, 1999; Depue, Luciana, Arbisi, Collins, & Leon, 1994), and that both extraversion and the brain dopamine system are genetically determined or established by early adulthood (Depue & Collins, 1999), recent evidence is suggesting that even the brain itself can change in its receptor and neurochemical makeup in response to stimuli, events, and the presence or absence of other neurochemicals (e.g., Heller, 1997; Isom & Heller, 1999; Katz, 1999; see Isen, 2002a for further discussion). This would mean that even if extroversion or other "traits" or dopamine receptors in the brain may have some genetic or early childhood basis, they may also be malleable, depending on the circumstances.

CONCLUSION

In summary, this review has indicated that positive affect can facilitate effective cognitive processing and improved human interaction and thus can be a source of human strength. In some ways, these kinds of results make perfect sense to people and seem obvious. Everyone knows, on some level, that people (and even animals) who are mistreated become mean and selfish and fearful and regimented, and that people who are afraid are "defensive." Similarly, we understand that people who are loved become loving and are more understanding and open-minded. Thus, the temptation to use intuition when thinking about affect and its effects is enormous. However, on reflection, everyone also knows many contrasting examples —of people who suffered yet became or remained kind, for example, or people who were treated so well that they became selfish and self-centered. Thus, intuition alone cannot be relied on to understand affect.

In some ways, also, the beneficial influence of positive affect seems surprising to people, in part because happy feelings seem so simple and frequent that it is hard to imagine that their impact is so strong and of so much potential consequence. Another reason that the beneficial effects of positive affect surprise people may be that people in general do not look for reasons or explanations when things go smoothly (Weiner, 1985). In addition, and possibly for these reasons, psychology itself typically looks for negative things to study, problems to fix. As a result, people in the field become accustomed to looking for the negative side of any seemingly positive event, even if it does not involve a problem to be fixed.

To some extent, this tendency may stem in part from Freudian theory, which emphasized the negative; delineated a negative view of human nature and held firmly to it, despite abundant observations of simple, everyday generosity, kindness, sympathy, helpfulness, caring, honesty, diligent work, friendliness, comfort, social responsibility, and the like; and explained away any positive tendencies as "defensive" or disguised, distorted negative tendencies. Unfortunately, this theory has had disproportionate influence in many domains of psychology, despite its lack of scientific formulation or verification by evidence.

In contrast, I am proposing that it is legitimate, and beneficial, to study positive affect and its effects in their own right, without needing to focus on negative affect or negative states in order to understand positive ones. In fact, I suspect that limiting the study of positive affect by considering it only in the context of negative affect may be misleading, and I suggest that it is beneficial to study positive affect without the typical nod to the negative that usually accompanies mention of positive affect.

It is my hope that the current interest in human strengths and constructive tendencies will not fall prey to the kinds of unsupported theoretical assumptions and preconceptions or habits described earlier in this chapter, but that the field will progress to studying human strengths, constructive tendencies, and positive affect fully, in their own right. This is especially my hope for positive affect, which I believe merits further investigation and holds the potential to enhance human functioning. Research has shown it to be a powerful influence that, even though down-to-earth and simple to induce, holds great potential as a source of human strength. It is important especially for people who supervise employees in organizations or students in classrooms to understand that many of the small everyday things over which they have control in people's daily lives can have important facilitating effects on the people in these groups, and to try to figure out the best ways to apply this understanding.

REFERENCES

Abelson, R. P. (1963). Computer simulation of "hot cognitions." In S. Tomkins & S. Messick (Eds.), *Computer simulation of personality* (pp. 277–298). New York: Wiley.

Ashby, F. G., Isen, A. M., & Turken, A. U. (1999). A neuropsychological theory of positive affect and its influence on cognition. *Psychological Review, 106,* 529–550.

Aspinwall, L. G. (1998). Rethinking the role of positive affect and self-regulation. *Motivation and Emotion, 23,* 1–32.

Aspinwall, L. G. (2001). Dealing with adversity: Self-regulation, coping, adaptation, and health. In A. Tesser & N. Schwarz (Eds.), *Blackwell handbook of social psychology: Intraindividual processes* (pp. 591–614). Malden, MA: Blackwell.

Aspinwall, L. G., & Brunhart, S. M. (1996). Distinguishing optimism from denial: Optimistic beliefs predict attention to health threats. *Personality and Social Psychology Bulletin, 22,* 99–103.

Aspinwall, L. G., & Richter, L. (1999). Optimism and self-mastery predict more rapid disengagement from unsolvable tasks in the presence of alternatives. *Motivation and Emotion, 23,* 221–245.

Baron, R. A. (1984). Reducing organizational conflict: An incompatible response approach. *Journal of Applied Psychology, 69,* 272–279.

Barone, M. J., Miniard, P. W., & Romeo, J. B. (2000). The influence of positive mood on brand extension evaluations. *Journal of Consumer Research, 26,* 386–400.

Bless, H., Clore, G. L., Schwarz, N., Golisano, V., Rabe, C., & Wolk, M. (1996). Mood and the use of scripts: Does a happy mood really lead to mindlessness? *Journal of Personality and Social Psychology, 71,* 665–679.

Carnevale, P. J. D., & Isen, A. M. (1986). The influence of positive affect and visual access on the discovery of integrative solutions in bilateral negotiation. *Organizational Behavior and Human Decision Processes, 37,* 1–13.

Cialdini, R. B., Darby, B., & Vincent, J. (1972). Transgression and altruism: A case for hedonism. *Journal of Experimental Social Psychology, 9,* 502–516.

Cramer, P. (1968). *Word association.* New York: Academic Press.

Cunningham, M. R. (1979). Weather, mood, and helping behavior: Quasi-experiments in the sunshine Samaritan. *Journal of Personality and Social Psychology, 37,* 1947–1956.

Cunningham, M. R., Steinberg, J., & Grev, R. (1980). Wanting to and having to help: Separate motivations for positive mood and guilt induced helping. *Journal of Personality and Social Psychology, 38,* 181–192.

Depue, R. A., & Collins, P. F. (1999). Neurobiology of the structure of personality: Dopamine, facilitation of incentive motivation, and extraversion. *Behavioral and Brain Sciences, 22,* 491–569.

Depue, R. A., Luciana, M., Arbisi, P., Collins, P., & Leon, A. (1994). Dopamine and the structure of personality: Relation of agonist-induced dopamine activity to positive emotionality. *Journal of Personality and Social Psychology, 67,* 485–498.

Dovidio, J. F., Gaertner, S. L., Isen, A. M., & Lowrance, R. (1995). Group representations and intergroup bias: Positive affect, similarity, and group size. *Personality and Social Psychology Bulletin, 21,* 856–865.

Duffy, E. (1934). Emotion: An example of the need for reorientation in psychology. *Psychological Review, 41*, 184–198.

Erez, A., & Isen, A. M. (in press). The influence of positive affect on the components of expectancy motivation. *Journal of Applied Psychology.*

Estrada, C. A., Isen, A. M., & Young, M. J. (1994). Positive affect influences creative problem solving and reported source of practice satisfaction in physicians. *Motivation and Emotion, 18*, 285–299.

Estrada, C. A., Isen, A. M., & Young, M. J. (1997). Positive affect facilitates integration of information and decreases anchoring in reasoning among physicians. *Organizational and Human Decision Processes, 72*, 117–135.

Forgas, J. P. (2002). Feeling and doing: Affective influences on interpersonal behavior. *Psychological Inquiry, 13*, 1–28.

Fredrickson, B. L. (1998). What good are positive emotions? *Review of General Psychology, 2*, 300–319.

Fredrickson, B. L., Mancuso, R. A., Branigan, C., & Tugade, M. M. (2000). The undoing effect of positive emotions. *Motivation and Emotion, 24*, 237–258.

George, J. M., & Brief, A. P. (1996). Motivational agendas in the workplace: The effects of feelings on focus of attention and work motivation. In L. L. Cummings & B. M. Staw (Eds.), *Research in organizational behavior* (Vol. 18, pp. 75–109). Greenwich, CT: JAI Press.

Greene, T. R., & Noice, H. (1988). Influence of positive affect upon creative thinking and problem solving in children. *Psychological Reports, 63*, 895–898.

Heller, W. (1997). Emotion. In M. Banich (Ed.), *Neuropsychology: The neural bases of mental function.* (pp. 398–429). Boston: Houghton Mifflin.

Hilgard, E. R. (1980). The trilogy of mind: Cognition, affection and conation. *Journal of the History of the Behavioral Sciences, 16*, 107–117.

Hirt, E. R., Melton, R. J., McDonald, H. E., & Harackiewicz, J. M. (1996). Processing goals, task interest, and the mood-performance relationship: A mediational analysis. *Journal of Personality and Social Psychology, 71*, 245–261.

Isen, A. M. (1970). Success, failure attention and reactions to others: The warm glow of success. *Journal of Personality and Social Psychology, 17*, 107–112.

Isen, A. M. (1987). Positive affect, cognitive processes and social behavior. In L. Berkowitz (Ed.), *Advances in experimental social psychology* (pp. 203–253). New York: Academic.

Isen, A. M. (1990). The influence of positive and negative affect on cognitive organization: Implications for development. In N. Stein, B. Leventhal, & T. Trabasso (Eds.), *Psychological and biological processes in the development of emotion* (pp. 75–94). Hillsdale, NJ: Erlbaum.

Isen, A. M. (1999). On the relationship between affect and creative problem solving. In S. Russ (Ed.), *Affect, creative experience, and psychological adjustment* (pp. 3–17). Philadelphia: Taylor & Francis.

Isen, A. M. (2000). Positive affect and decision making. In M. Lewis & J. M. Haviland-Jones (Eds.), *Handbook of emotions* (2nd ed., pp. 417–435). New York: Guilford Press.

Isen, A. M. (2002a). A role for neuropsychology in understanding the facilitating influence of positive affect on social behavior and cognitive processes. In C. R. Snyder & S. J. Lopez (Eds.), *Handbook of positive psychology* (pp. 528–540). New York: Oxford University Press.

Isen, A. M. (2002b). Missing in action in the AIM: Positive affect's facilitation of cognitive flexibility, innovation, and problem solving. *Psychological Inquiry, 13,* 57–65.

Isen, A. M., Christianson, M., & Labroo, A. A. (2001). *A role for the nature of the task in determining whether positive affect facilitates task performance.* Unpublished manuscript, Cornell University, Ithaca, NY.

Isen, A. M., & Daubman, K. A. (1984). The influence of affect on categorization. *Journal of Personality and Social Psychology, 47,* 1206–1217.

Isen, A. M., Daubman, K. A., & Nowicki, G. P. (1987). Positive affect facilitates creative problem solving. *Journal of Personality and Social Psychology, 52,* 1122–1131.

Isen, A. M., & Geva, N. (1987). The influence of positive affect on acceptable level of risk: The person with a large canoe has a large worry. *Organizational Behavior and Human Decision Processes, 39,* 145–154.

Isen, A. M., & Hastorf, A. H. (1982). Some perspectives on cognitive social psychology (pp. 1–31). In A. H. Hastorf & A. M. Isen (Eds.), *Cognitive social psychology.* New York: Elsevier North-Holland.

Isen, A. M., Johnson, M. M., Mertz, E., & Robinson, F. G. (1985). The influence of positive affect on the unusualness of word association. *Journal of Personality and Social Psychology, 48,* 1413–1426.

Isen, A. M., Niedenthal, P., & Cantor, N. (1992). The influence of positive affect on social categorization. *Motivation and Emotion, 16,* 65–78.

Isen, A. M., Nygren, T. E., & Ashby, F. G. (1988). The influence of positive affect on the perceived utility of gains and losses. *Journal of Personality and Social Psychology, 55,* 710–717.

Isen, A. M., & Patrick, R. (1983). The influence of positive feelings on risk taking: When the chips are down. *Organizational Behavior and Human Performance, 31,* 194–202.

Isen, A. M, Rosenzweig, A. S., & Young, M. J. (1991). The influence of positive affect on clinical problem solving. *Medical Decision Making, 11,* 221–227.

Isen, A. M., Shalker, T., Clark, M., & Karp, L. (1978). Affect, accessibility of material in memory, and behavior: A cognitive loop? *Journal of Personality and Social Psychology, 36,* 1–12.

Isen, A. M., & Simmonds, S. (1978). The effect of feeling good on a helping task that is incompatible with good mood. *Social Psychology Quarterly* (formerly *Sociometry), 41,* 346–349.

Isom, J., & Heller, W. (1999). Neurobiology of extraversion: Pieces of the puzzle still missing. *Behavioral and Brain Sciences, 22,* 524.

Kahn, B., & Isen, A. M. (1993). The influence of positive affect on variety seeking among safe, enjoyable products. *Journal of Consumer Research, 20,* 257–270.

Katz, L. D. (1999). Dopamine and serotonin: Integrating current affective engagement with longer-term goals. *Behavioral and Brain Sciences, 22,* 527.

Labroo, A. A., & Isen, A. M. (2000, November). *The influence of positive affect on strategic decision making in "Prisoner's Dilemma" situations.* Paper presented at the annual meeting of the Society for Judgment and Decision Making, New Orleans.

Lee, A., & Sternthal, B. (1999). The effects of positive mood on memory. *Journal of Consumer Research, 26,* 115–127.

Lepper, M. R. (1994). "Hot" versus "cold" cognition: An Abelsonian voyage. In R. C. Schank & E. Langer (Eds.), *Beliefs, reasoning, and decision making: Psycho-logic in honor of Bob Abelson* (pp. 237–275). Hillsdale, NJ: Erlbaum.

Lindsley, D. B. (1951). Emotion. In S. S. Stevens (Ed.), *Handbook of experimental psychology* (pp. 473–516). New York: Wiley.

Mackie, D. M., & Worth, L. (1991). Feeling good but not thinking straight: The impact of positive mood on persuasion. In J. P. Forgas (Ed.), *Emotion and social judgment* (pp. 201–220). Oxford, England: Pergamon.

Melton, R. J. (1995). The role of positive affect in syllogism performance. *Personality and Social Psychology Bulletin, 21,* 788–794.

Scheier, M. F., Weintraub, J. K., & Carver, C. S. (1986). Coping with stress: Divergent strategies of optimists and pessimists. *Journal of Personality and Social Psychology, 51,* 1257–1264.

Schwarz, N., & Bless, H. (1991). Happy and mindless, but sad and smart? The impact of affective states on analytic reasoning. In J. P. Forgas (Ed.), *Emotion and social judgment* (pp. 55–71). Oxford, England: Pergamon.

Simon, H. A. (1967). Motivational and emotional controls of cognition. *Psychological Review, 74,* 29–39.

Snyder, M., & White, E. (1982). Moods and memories: Elation, depression, and remembering the events of one's life. *Journal of Personality, 50,* 149–167.

Staw, B. M., & Barsade, S. G. (1993). Affect and managerial performance: A test of the sadder-but-wiser vs. happier-and-smarter hypotheses. *Administrative Science Quarterly, 38,* 304–331.

Taylor, S. E., & Aspinwall, L. G. (1996). Mediating and moderating processes in psychosocial stress: Appraisal, coping, resistance and vulnerability. In H. B. Kaplan (Ed.), *Psychosocial stress: Perspectives on structure, theory, life-course, and methods* (pp. 71–110). San Diego, CA: Academic Press.

Teasdale, J. D., & Fogarty, S. J. (1979). Differential effects of induced mood on retrieval of pleasant and unpleasant events from episodic memory. *Journal of Abnormal Psychology, 88,* 248–257.

Teasdale, J. D., & Russell, M. L. (1983). Differential aspects of induced mood on the recall of positive, negative and neutral words. *British Journal of Clinical Psychology, 22,* 163–171.

Teasdale, J. D., Taylor, R., & Fogarty, S. J. (1980). Effects of induced elation-depression on the accessibility of memories of happy and unhappy experiences. *Behavior Research and Therapy, 18,* 339–346.

Trope, Y., & Neter, E. (1994). Reconciling competing motives in self-evaluation: The role of self-control in feedback seeking. *Journal of Personality and Social Psychology, 66,* 646–657.

Trope, Y., & Pomerantz, E. M. (1998). Resolving conflicts among self-evaluative motives: Positive experiences as a resource for overcoming defensiveness. *Motivation and Emotion, 22,* 53–72.

Urada, M., & Miller, N. (2000). The impact of positive mood and category importance on crossed categorization effects. *Journal of Personality and Social Psychology, 78,* 417–433.

Weiner, B. (1985). "Spontaneous" causal thinking. *Psychological Bulletin, 97,* 74–84.

Weiss, H. M., Nicholas, J. P., & Daus, C. S. (1999). An examination of the joint effects of affective experiences and job beliefs on job satisfaction and variations in affective experiences over time. *Organizational Behavior and Human Decision Processes, 78*(1), 1–24.

14

THE PARAMETRIC UNIMODEL OF HUMAN JUDGMENT: A FANFARE TO THE COMMON THINKER

ARIE W. KRUGLANSKI, HANS-PETER ERB, SCOTT SPIEGEL, AND
ANTONIO PIERRO

Is human everyday thinking rational? Or is it prone to error and riddled by shortcomings? Imagine the example of the "village idiot" (adopted from Gigerenzer, 1996b, p. 324): In a small town there lives a village idiot. He was once offered a choice between one pound and one shilling. He took the shilling, and his choice may appear irrational according to rules of maximizing utility. However, having heard about this, all of the townspeople in turn offered him the choice, and he always took the shilling. Taking into account the consequences of the first choice, the village idiot's behavior does not seem to be irrational anymore.

This example demonstrates that judgments of human rationality are relative to the standard against which they are compared. When judging the rationality of the lay thinker, researchers mostly come up with either a glowingly positive or a starkly negative conclusion. For example, when mathematicians started developing models of probability calculus, they were influenced by the Enlightenment view that the laws of probability are nothing else but the "laws of the mind" (see Gigerenzer & Hoffrage, 1995).

Probability theory represented common sense reduced to calculus, and discrepancies between probability theory and intuition meant that the theory rather than the intuition was wrong. Since that time, psychologists have developed theories that dramatically reverse this positive image. On the one hand, the lay thinker was assumed to be driven by motivational goals rendering judgments erroneous by biasing reasoning toward desired outcomes. On the other hand, an even more "negative" view grew out of the image of the human thinker as a "cognitive miser" (Taylor, 1981). In this vein, empirical evidence has accumulated allegedly demonstrating that "people do not appear to follow the calculus of chance or statistical theory in prediction. Instead, they rely on a limited number of heuristics which sometimes yield reasonable judgments and sometimes lead to severe and systematic errors" (Kahneman & Tversky, 1973, p. 237).

Today, the catalog of "fallacies" appears almost unlimited. They are said to result from a variety of inferential shortcuts people are assumed to use. Thus, the judgment and decision making literature discusses the "representativeness heuristic," the "availability heuristic," and many others (cf. Kahneman, Slovic, & Tversky, 1982), whereas the persuasion literature discusses the "experts are right heuristic," the "consensus implies correctness heuristic," and so on (cf. Chaiken, Liberman, & Eagly, 1989). Whereas the heuristically driven reasoning process was thought to occasionally lead to reasonable judgments, by and large it was portrayed as prone to bias and error and, hence, definitely inferior and less rational as compared to the normative models and systematic judgmental operations assumed to guide the scientist in his or her work.

In recent years, this negative view of the lay knower has been challenged from several perspectives. Systematic errors were attributed to the overload of complex environmental stimuli with which the individual may be burdened. Accordingly, it seemed quite rational that humans allocate their limited cognitive resources in a strategic manner and in accordance with the "principle of least effort" (Allport, 1954). Further commentaries suggested that researchers sometimes applied formal models incorrectly to assess the quality of human judgments (e.g., Cosmides & Tooby, 1996; Gigerenzer, 1996a), that some tasks required computational operations that simply exceed human cognitive capacity (e.g., Fiedler, 1988; Gigerenzer & Hoffrage, 1995), and that participants may have misinterpreted experimental tasks because experimenters' presentation of information contradicted conversational rules (Grice, 1975) that usually guide the understanding of communication (e.g., Hilton, 1995; Schwarz, Strack, Hilton, & Naderer, 1991). Finally, it has also been shown that even very simple judgmental strategies can result in accurate judgments and even outperform elaborate formal models (e.g., Gigerenzer, Czerlinski, & Martignon, 1999). In short, the answers to the question of human rationality varied widely depending on the standard of rationality one adopted (a formal model, desirable outcomes, the limits of human potential, etc.). From that perspective, it makes sense to ask whether a "scientific" mode of reasoning, or the application of formal statistical models, can be regarded as the proper standard against which to evaluate everyday thinking.

Logically prior to the question of whether the "scientific" mode is more rational than the lay thinker's mode is the question of whether qualitatively different modes of reasoning even exist. The question is whether lay persons' and scientists' reasoning modes are qualitatively different. The received answer to this question within the cognitive and social psychological literatures has been a resounding yes (for reviews, see Chaiken & Trope, 1999; Kahneman et al., 1982). Typically, theorists distinguished between two separate modes of reasoning, even though different authors identified highly distinct modes as "partners" in the duality. For example, within the "heuristics and biases" approach (e.g., Kahneman et al., 1982), the use of heuristics was contrasted with judgments guided by formal rules whose appropriateness to a given problem rested on "consensus among formal scientists" (Nisbett & Ross, 1980, p. 13).

Tversky and Kahneman (1983, p. 293) distinguished between "extensional" and "intuitive" reasoning, the former describing the cognitive process of analyzing "an exhaustive list of possibilities" including formal operations, and the latter subsuming heuristic reasoning processes characterized by a "relative neglect of other considerations" and based on "natural assessment" as a vehicle of judgment (Tversky & Kahneman, 1983, p. 294). Similarly, Epstein and colleagues (e.g., Epstein & Pacini, 1999) distinguished between a "rational" and an "experiential" cognitive system. They described the rational system as analytic, intentional, effortful, and logically oriented (hence leading to rational judgments) and the experiential system as associative, automatic, effortless and driven by affect (hence capable of error). Similar distinctions have been put forth in other domains of human judgment, such as impression formation, attribution (e.g., Fiske, Lin, & Neuberg, 1999; Trope & Gaunt, 1999), and persuasion (e.g., Chaiken et al., 1989; Petty & Cacioppo, 1986). For a source book on these and other dualistic models of human judgment, see Chaiken and Trope (1999).

THE PARAMETRIC UNIMODEL

In contrast to these dualistic approaches, in this chapter we outline a uniform model of human judgment whereby all of its instances can be understood in terms of an intersection of several fundamental parameters at different levels. According to our parametric unimodel, the popular dualistic frameworks have rested in each case on a confounding between two specific content domains of judgment on the one hand and a given intersection of the fundamental parameters (at specific levels) on the other.

According to the present argument, it is the specific content that lends the different "modes" an air of qualitative distinctiveness. However, there is no necessary relation between contents and parameter values. The parameters are orthogonal to one another and are continuous or dimensional. Their values can combine in a quasi-infinite number of ways, and each combination of parameters can be attached to any judgmental content. As one can see, then, our present conception is very different from the dualistic modes, for our approach allows for a quasi-infinite number of parametric intersections rather than only two as in the dual-process models.

Furthermore, our parameters are assumed to be "fundamental" in the sense of being represented (at some of their possible levels) in every instance of judgment, whether scientific or lay, guided by formal rules or "heuristics," and so forth. Thus, instead of focusing on differences between instances of judgment, we focus on their commonalities. We propose, moreover, that such a focus is capable of furnishing a general answer to the question besetting the cognitive and social literatures on human judgment: the conditions under which a given judgmental outcome (rather than another) will obtain (e.g., an outcome derived from statistical reasoning rather than based on a "heuristic").

In furnishing a uniform alternative to dualistic conceptions, our parametric unimodel parts ways with the notion that the lay thinker is often irrational and hence inferior to the "professional" thinker (for discussion, see Kruglanski, 1989a, chapter 10). In other words, we will be able to understand in the same terms both the idiot's choice and the scientist's assessment of this behavior. This portrayal of the lay thinker is more "positive" than even the argument for the evolutionary adaptiveness of heuristic thinking (Gigerenzer, 1996b) that still admitted (however implicitly) the logical inferiority of heuristic thinking to formal models of human judgment. In contrast, we argue against the proposed qualitative distinctions in judgmental modes. To present our case, we first identify what we believe are the parameters of human judgment and show how, in the extant judgmental literature, their intersections at various levels were often confounded or left uncontrolled in regard to specific contents of judgments.

Fundamental Parameters of Human Judgment

We assume that *judgments* constitute conclusions rendered on the basis of pertinent evidence. Such evidence is roughly syllogistic in form. Specifically, it consists of contextual information serving as a minor premise of the syllogism—for example, "Laura is a graduate of MIT." This information may serve as evidence for a conclusion if it instantiates an antecedent condition of a major premise in which the individual believes—for example, "All MIT graduates are engineers" or "If one is an MIT graduate, one is an engineer." Jointly, the major and the minor premises yield the conclusion "Laura is an engineer."

Relevance

By *relevance* we mean the degree to which the individual believes in a linkage between the antecedent and the consequent terms in the major premise. For example, one may believe strongly the proposition that "All MIT graduates are engineers" or believe it only weakly, with all the different shades of belief or disbelief in between. A strong belief in the linkage (between graduation from MIT and being an engineer) renders the antecedent, and the information that instantiates it (in our example, the knowledge that "Laura is a graduate of MIT"), highly relevant to the conclusion. Similarly, complete disbelief renders the information irrelevant as evidence. Consider the statement "All persons weighing above 150 lb are medical doctors." An individual may not believe this particular statement and hence consider the information that a target weighs 162 lb as completely irrelevant to the judgment of whether he or she is a doctor. Degrees of belief in the linkage between the antecedent and the consequent terms in a given rule (a major premise) may be thought of as a continuum defining a dimension of perceived relevance that a given bit of evidence possesses in regard to a conclusion.

To concretize a bit our discussion of relevance, consider the reasoning from statistical base rates in the famous lawyer/engineer problem (Kahneman & Tversky, 1973). Consider specifically a case in which the base rates in the sample are 98 to 2 (say, 98 lawyers to 2 engineers or vice versa) as compared to 50 to 50. An individual may believe more that a given member of this sample is a lawyer (rather than an engineer) in the former than in the latter sample. More formally speaking, he or she may believe more in the statement that "if 98% of a sample are X, then someone taken out of this sample is extremely likely to be an X" than in the statement where 98% is substituted by 50%. To say it differently, different base rates may correspond to different inference rules in which the individual may have different degrees of belief (e.g., Ginosar & Trope, 1980; Wells & Harvey, 1977, but see also Lyon & Slovic, 1976).

Similarly, various types of "representativeness" information could be associated with inference rules in which the individual may have different degrees of belief. For example, information that a target reads technical journals and constructs airplanes as a hobby could correspond to a highly credible inference rule suggesting this person is an engineer, more so than information, say, that the target enjoys skiing.

From this perspective, it is important to realize that the degree of participants' beliefs in different inference rules has not been controlled in the experimental literature comparing the use of "heuristics" with that of base-rate information, so that these types of information could well be confounded with different degrees of belief participants had in the corresponding inference rules. Specifically, it is possible that the reason why in some research participants tended to use "heuristic information" more than they did the base-rate information was simply that in these experimental contexts the heuristic information appeared more relevant—that is, more closely tied to the required judgment according to participants' "if-then" inference rule—than did the base rate.

One way of increasing the relevance of an inference rule, or a set of rules, may be by promoting the acquisition of those rules via teaching. Indeed, research has shown that statistical reasoning can be taught and that it can result in the increased use of formal information (e.g., Cheng, Holyoak, Nisbett, & Oliver, 1986, 1993). Similarly, it should be possible to teach individuals nonstatistical if-then rules, including rules that depict particular attributes as representative of particular categories, as in the socialization of children to various cultural stereotypes.

Humans are also capable of constructing inference rules *de nouveau* according to particular needs and motivations. This is related to the process of hypothesis generation (Kruglanski, 1989a; Trope & Liberman, 1996) and the creative linkage of alternative judgmental categories (the hypotheses) with subjectively relevant types of information (the evidence). Such constructive flexibility represents a process that accounts for humans' considerable problem-solving abilities as compared with other species.

Accessibility

Even if a given inference rule were available in a person's memory, it might not be readily accessible at the moment of judgment. The accessibility of a rule depends on the recency and frequency of its activation, as well as on its motivational significance (Higgins, 1996). A rule will not be used if it is not accessed by the individual. Thus, the degree of a rule's accessibility, again thought of as a continuum or a dimension, is presently considered a major parameter affecting the outcomes of judgment. For demonstration, the reader may recall his or her first impression of the village idiot's preference for the shilling over the pound. The rule "if one makes a seemingly irrational choice, then one may get the chance to choose again" was not accessible when the idiot's behavior was initially judged to be irrational.

In research on human judgment and decision making, accessibility might have been confounded with specific contents of rules, and in particular with the rule being related to characteristics of the individual (as in the representativeness heuristic) or of the sample (as in case of the base rates). For example in the lawyer/engineer problem, the framing of a given reasoning problem as "psychological" might have activated the notion of individual characteristics and rendered accessible various rules linking such characteristics with the required judgment of the target's profession. Similarly, framing of the same problem as "statistical" might have activated for the participants the notion of sample characteristics rendering accessible various rules linking those characteristics with the required judgment. Indeed, research has established that the framing of a given problem as "statistical" or "scientific" reduced the base-rate neglect effect found in the original Kahneman and Tversky (1973) work, whereas framing it as "psychological" or "clinical" replicated the original finding (Schwarz et al., 1991; Zukier & Pepitone, 1984). Thus, the original differences in the use of base-rates or representativeness information may have reflected differences in rule accessibility (confounded with statistical and nonstatistical contents) rather than principled differences between "extensional" and "intuitive" reasoning.

Beyond affecting accessibility, the framing manipulations may have lent greater motivational desirability to the use of some rules rather than others. The issue of motivation is relevant to judgmental parameters related to motivational states of the perceiver.

Motivational States of the Perceiver

Momentary or chronic motivational states of the perceiver may interact with characteristics of the information given to determine the inferential rule to be used and, hence, the outcome of the judgmental process. Two types of motivation are pertinent in this regard: (a) nondirectional motivation to process the information in depth or only superficially and (b) directional motivation to arrive at a specific conclusion (Kruglanski, 1989a). We consider these in turn, followed by a brief discussion of the cognitive capacity parameter that has effects similar to those of nondirectional motivation.

Nondirectional Effects

Strong nondirectional motivation allows the individual to cope with complex, lengthy information that requires extensive processing and increases the probability that such information will figure as evidence and affect the judgment. For example, in research on the "dual modes" of persuasion (Chaiken et al., 1989; Petty & Cacioppo, 1986), lengthy and complex information was often contained in the message, whereas superficial and brief information pertained to "peripheral" or "heuristic" aspects of the context (e.g., the communicator's expertise). In such research (e.g., Petty, Cacioppo, & Goldman, 1981), the message typically exerted impact under strong processing motivation (e.g., high involvement in the persuasion issue), whereas peripheral or heuristic information exerted impact under low processing motivation (i.e., low involvement).

However, there is no necessary relation between the contents of information (e.g., their being peripheral to the message versus constituting a part of the message) and its length and complexity. These two have been typically confounded in prior persuasion research, but they can be readily unconfounded. Indeed, Kruglanski and Thompson (1999a, 1999b) performed such an unconfounding in a series of studies. They found that what matters is the length or complexity of the information in interaction with nondirectional motivation (and capacity constraints) rather than its content or type (peripheral cue or message argument). Specifically, when persuasive evidence, whether a peripheral cue or a message argument, was presented in a lengthy and complex format, it had impact only under high processing motivation (and high cognitive capacity) encouraging extensive processing, but not under low motivation (and low cognitive capacity).

Similar to the effects of the nondirectional motivation to process information are the effects of cognitive capacity to do so. For example, the unintentional covariation of capacity requirements and specific types of information (or contents) of judgments figures in the work of Trope and Alfieri (1997) on the dual-phase model of dispositional attribution. These authors posited a qualitative difference between the processes of identification and of inference. Specifically, they adduced evidence that the identification process is automatic and effortless and hence insensitive to cognitive load, whereas the inference process is deliberative, controlled, and hence sensitive to load. But the present unimodel affords a reinterpretation of these results.

Specifically, a principal difference between the identification and inference stages discussed by Trope and Alfieri (1997) might be in the contents of the respective judgment required at these phases. In the identification phase the judgmental question is, "What is it?" (i.e., what is the identity of the behavior emitted by the target), whereas in the inference phase the question is, "What caused it?" (i.e., whether the behavior may be causally attributed to the target's disposition or to the situation). According to the parametric unimodel, each of those judgments is guided by the same process wherein specific types of evidence and the corresponding judgmental rules (e.g., rules deriving an identity judgment about "sadness" from a "down-turned mouth" based on an if-then rule connecting the two in the perceiver's belief repertory) play a role.

In a series of experiments, Chun, Spiegel, and Kruglanski (2002) obtained evidence for the proposition that in the Trope and Alfieri (1997) research the identification question was easy to answer (in that its relevant evidence was readily accessible), whereas the inference question was relatively difficult to answer. Specifically, Chun et al. varied independently the difficulty of the identification and the inference questions, showing that, contrary to Trope and Alfieri's findings, under difficult conditions both were affected by a cognitive load, whereas neither was so affected under easy conditions. Of interest, recent research from Trope's laboratory (Trope & Gaunt, 2000) has also demonstrated that the inference process need not be affected by cognitive load under some conditions, consistent with the present unimodel, whereby the same judgmental process is at work at both the identification and the inference stages.

The unintentional covariation between type and content of information and its level of difficulty isn't unique to the persuasion and attribution domains; it appears also in research on impression formation in particular reference to the distinction between "category-based" and "individuating" processing (e.g., Neuberg & Fiske, 1987). Our analysis suggests that it is not the contents or type of information (i.e., categorical or individuating) that matter but rather its level of difficulty (as determined by length, complexity, and ordinal position) as it interacts with the individual's degree of processing capacity or motivation. Presumably one could reverse Neuberg and Fiske's findings by presenting the individuating information briefly and up front and the categorical information subsequently and at greater length (for a similar view, see Kunda, 1999).

Directional Effects

In addition to the effects of processing effort, the use of different inferential rules can be influenced by the individual's directional motivations (Kruglanski, 1989a; Kunda, 1999). Some such motivations may lend desirability to the contents of desirable conclusions, whereas others may lend such desirability to the use of specific rules per se. Again, according to the parametric unimodel, such directional motivations would affect all contents of judgments that happen to be motivationally pertinent in the same (directional) way.

In this vein, research by Sanitioso and Kunda (1991) demonstrated that the use of the statistical rule whereby predictability increases sharply with sample size was greater where it allowed the participants to conclude what they wished to conclude, "namely that smaller samples would suffice for their predictions" (p. 161). Similar conclusions were reached by Ginosar and Trope (1987) where the use of base-rate information was affected by its pertinence to the participants' directional motivations. In a different line of work, Sanitioso, Freud, and Lee (1996) demonstrated that the use of stereotypical (or category-based) and individuating information is similarly affected by participants' directional motivations. Specifically, participants' needs to perceive their potential partner as competent and their potential competitor as incompetent increased or decreased the use of stereotyping information and increased or decreased the use of individuating information.

The framing effects of reasoning tasks in terms of "statistical" or "psychological" problems discussed above (Schwarz et al., 1991) may also be interpreted in terms of directional motivations. Specifically, framing a reasoning problem as statistical may suggest to the participants that the experimenter desires or expects that they will use the statistical rule, whereas framing it as psychological suggests that the experimenter desires that they use the "individuating" information. To the extent that participants are motivated to please or positively impress the experimenter, they may use the rule believed to be expected. Such motivational interpretation of "conversational relevance" (Grice, 1975) may account for the greater tendency of participants in Schwarz et al.'s research to use the statistical information under statistical framing.

CONCLUSION

Whereas the received views of human judgment emphasized differences and argued for the existence of two qualitatively separate judgmental modes, our analysis has stressed the similarities in all instances of human judgment. According to this portrayal, all judgments are determined by an intersection of fundamental parameters whose values have been confounded in past research with specific content categories of judgment. Specifically, we assume that judgments are made on the basis of evidence connected to rules of the if-then variety, lending present information its evidential status. The degree to which the individual believes in a given if-then linkage can vary, and so may the momentary accessibility of a particular linkage (the major premise) and the accessibility of relevant situational information (the minor premise). Moreover, different if-then rules can be more or less complex or difficult to acquire. Gigerenzer and Hoffrage (1995), for example, argued that rules involving frequencies of events are acquired more readily than rules involving ratios. Rules may also be constructed *de nouveau* from the individual's background knowledge in the course of a flexible hypothesis generation process.

The application of specific rules may also differ across different circumstances. This variation may have to do with the accessibility of the rule and the accessibility of the situational information that may fit the rule, hence serving as evidence for a given conclusion. Such information may be "packaged" in a way that requires more or less effortful "unpacking" depending on the degree to which it is buried amid irrelevant detail, visible, audible, and so forth.

States of the perceiver, such as the degree of (nondirectional) processing motivation, the (directional) motivation to arrive at specific conclusions, and the cognitive capacity at the moment of judgment formation would determine the likelihood that a perceiver will acquire a given rule and use it to arrive at a conclusion. For instance, the more difficult, complex, or counterintuitive a given rule, the greater the motivation and capacity required for its acquisition. Similarly, the more difficult the application of a rule in a given context, the more processing motivation and capacity would be required for its use. Rule use also may be influenced by the degree to which it, or the conclusion it mediates, is desirable given the perceiver's directional motivations.

The present parametric analysis permits two types of integration: an integration of the two proposed modes into one, and an integration across different content domains of judgments (e.g., across domains of persuasion, impression formation, causal attribution and heuristics and biases). Moreover, it serves to organize the vast empirical literatures in these domains regarding the conditions under which given judgments are rendered.

Of particular relevance to the present volume, our analysis has implications for the general issue of human rationality. From the present perspective, the notion that the very same process underlies all instances of human judgment is inconsistent with the argument that distinct instances of judgment are characterized by different degrees of rationality, as well as with the kindred notion that the thinking of the common person is qualitatively different and inferior to that of the scientist (for comparison of lay and scientific modes of thinking, see Kruglanski, 1994).

Nor is a given set of parameter values necessarily superior to another set. Gigerenzer and colleagues (Gigerenzer & Hoffrage, 1995; Gigerenzer, 1996a; Gigerenzer & Goldstein, 1996), for instance, have demonstrated that the application of formal models presumably requiring considerable processing motivation and cognitive capacity may in some instances yield inferior judgmental outcomes to those afforded by the use of simple heuristics. Whether a given judgment will ultimately be anointed as correct should depend on the external reality criterion, unknowable at the time the judgment is rendered (cf. Kruglanski, 1989b), as nicely demonstrated by the village idiot's choice. Over time, humans have evolved knowledge based on extensive prior feedback that works well to permit survival, effective functioning, and development (Gigerenzer & Hoffrage, 1995).

The great advantage of the human reasoning process (employed by laypersons and scientists alike) and the one justly deserving of fanfare is its flexibility and responsiveness. Thus, whereas all humans can produce subjectively justifiable conjectures, when those are met by refutations dished out by the external realities, they are capable of constructing new inference rules whereby additional promising hypotheses can be tested (cf. Popper, 1959, 1963).

From the present perspective, it is the fundamentally uniform judgmental process, characterized by its considerable flexibility and openness to feedback, that accounts for the considerable achievements of humankind (cf. Kruglanski, 1992; Tuchman, 1984). Rather than remaining bogged down in superficial distinctions about degrees of rationality, we may do well to move ahead with a careful study of the uniform process of human reasoning in order to better understand its considerable potential.

REFERENCES

Allport, G. W. (1954). *The nature of prejudice*. Reading, MA: Addison-Wesley.

Chaiken, S., Liberman, A., & Eagly, A. H. (1989). Heuristic and systematic processing within and beyond the persuasion context. In J. S. Uleman & J. A. Bargh (Eds.), *Unintended thought* (pp. 212–252). New York: Guilford Press.

Chaiken, S., & Trope, Y. (Eds.). (1999). *Dual process theories in social psychology*. New York: Guilford Press.

Cheng, W. P., Holyoak, K. J., Nisbett, R. E., & Oliver, L. M. (1986). Pragmatic versus syntactic approaches to training deductive reasoning. *Cognitive Psychology, 18*, 293–328.

Cheng, W. P., Holyoak, K. J., Nisbett, R. E., & Oliver, L. M. (1993). Pragmatic versus syntactic approaches to training deductive reasoning. In R. E. Nisbett (Ed.), *Rules for reasoning* (pp. 165–203). Hillsdale, NJ: Lawrence Erlbaum.

Chun, W. Y., Spiegel, S., & Kruglanski, A. W. (2002). *Assimilative behavior identification can also be resource-dependent: A unimodel perspective on personal attribution*. Manuscript submitted for publication.

Cosmides, L., & Tooby, J. (1996). Are humans good intuitive statisticians after all? Rethinking some conclusions from the literature on judgment under uncertainty. *Cognition, 58*, 1–73.

Epstein, S., & Pacini, R. (1999). Some basic issues regarding dual-process theories from the perspective of cognitive-experiential self-theory. In S. Chaiken & Y. Trope (Eds.), *Dual process theories in social psychology* (pp. 462–482). New York: Guilford Press.

Fiedler, K. (1988). The dependence of the conjunction fallacy on subtle linguistic factors. *Psychological Research, 50*, 123–129.

Fiske, S. T., Lin, M., & Neuberg, S. L. (1999). The continuum model: Ten years later. In S. Chaiken & Y. Trope (Eds.), *Dual process theories in social psychology* (pp. 231–254). New York: Guilford Press.

Gigerenzer, G. (1996a). The psychology of good judgment: Frequency formats and simple algorithms. *Medical Decision Making, 16*, 273–280.

Gigerenzer, G. (1996b). Rationality: Why social context matters. In P. B. Baltes & U. M. Staudinger (Eds.), *Interactive minds: Life-span perspectives on the social foundation of cognition* (pp. 319–346). Cambridge, England: Cambridge University Press.

Gigerenzer, G., Czerlinski, J., & Martignon, L. (1999). How good are fast and frugal heuristics? In J. Shanteau, B. A. Mellers, & D. A. Schum (Eds.), *Decision science and technology: Reflections on the contributions of Ward Edwards* (pp. 81–103). Boston: Kluwer.

Gigerenzer, G., & Goldstein, D. G. (1996). Reasoning the fast and frugal way: Models of bounded rationality. *Psychological Review, 103,* 665–669.

Gigerenzer, G., & Hoffrage, U. (1995). How to improve Bayesian reasoning without instruction: Frequency formats. *Psychological Review, 102,* 684–704.

Ginosar, Z., & Trope, Y. (1980). The effects of base rates and individuating information on judgments about another person. *Journal of Experimental Social Psychology, 16,* 228–242.

Ginosar, Z., & Trope, Y. (1987). Problem solving in judgment under uncertainty. *Journal of Personality and Social Psychology, 52,* 464–474.

Grice, H. P. (1975). Logic and conversation. In P. Cole & J. L. Morgan (Eds.), *Syntax and semantics 3: Speech acts* (pp. 41–58). San Diego, CA: Academic Press.

Higgins, E. T. (1996). Knowledge activation, application, and salience. In E. T. Higgins & A. W. Kruglanski (Eds.), *Social psychology: Handbook of basic principles* (pp. 133–168). New York: Guilford Press.

Hilton, D. J. (1995). The social context of reasoning: Conversational inference and rational judgment. *Psychological Bulletin, 118,* 248–271.

Kahneman, D., Slovic, P., & Tversky, A. (1982). *Judgment under uncertainty: Heuristics and biases.* Cambridge, England: Cambridge University Press.

Kahneman, D., & Tversky, A. (1973). On the psychology of prediction. *Psychological Review, 80,* 237–251.

Kruglanski, A. W. (1989a). *Lay epistemics and human knowledge: Cognitive and motivational bases.* New York: Plenum Press.

Kruglanski, A. W. (1989b). The psychology of being "right": On the problem of accuracy in social perception and cognition. *Psychological Bulletin, 106,* 395–409.

Kruglanski, A. W. (1992). On methods of good judgment and good methods of judgment: Political decisions and the art of the possible. *Political Psychology, 13,* 455–475.

Kruglanski, A. W. (1994). The social-cognitive bases of scientific knowledge. In W. R. Shadish & S. Fuller (Eds.), *The social psychology of science* (pp. 197–213). New York: Guilford Press.

Kruglanski, A. W., & Thompson, E. P. (1999a). The illusory second mode or, the cue is the message. *Psychological Inquiry, 10,* 182–193.

Kruglanski, A. W., & Thompson, E. P. (1999b). Persuasion by a single route: A view from the unimodel. *Psychological Inquiry, 10,* 83–109.

Kunda, Z. (1999). Parallel processing of stereotypes and behaviors. In S. Chaiken & Y. Trope (Eds.), *Dual process theories in social psychology* (pp. 314–322). New York: Guilford Press.

Lyon, D., & Slovic, P. (1976). Dominance of accuracy information and neglect of base-rates in probability estimations. *Acta Psychologica, 40,* 287–298.

Neuberg, S. L., & Fiske, S. T. (1987). Motivational influences on impression formation: Outcome dependency, accuracy-driven attention, and individuating processes. *Journal of Personality and Social Psychology, 53,* 431–444.

Nisbett, R. E., & Ross, L. (1980). *Human inference: Strategies and shortcomings of social judgment*. Englewood Cliffs, NJ: Prentice Hall.

Petty, R. E., & Cacioppo, J. T. (1986). The elaboration likelihood model of persuasion. In L. Berkowitz (Ed.), *Advances in experimental social psychology* (Vol. 19, pp. 123–205). San Diego, CA: Academic Press.

Petty, R. E., Cacioppo, J. T., & Goldman, R. (1981). Personal involvement as a predictor of argument-based persuasion. *Journal of Personality and Social Psychology, 41*, 847–855.

Popper, K. R. (1959). *The logic of scientific discovery*. New York: Basic Books.

Popper, K. R. (1963). *Conjectures and refutations*. New York: Harper.

Sanitioso, R., Freud, K., & Lee, J. (1996). The influence of self-related goals on the use of stereotypical and individuating information. *European Journal of Social Psychology, 26*, 751–761.

Sanitioso, R., & Kunda, Z. (1991). Ducking the collection of costly evidence: Motivated use of statistical heuristics. *Journal of Behavioral Decision Making, 4*, 161–178.

Schwarz, N., Strack, F., Hilton, D. J., & Naderer, G. (1991). Base-rates, representativeness, and the logic of conversation. *Social Cognition, 9*, 67–84.

Taylor, S. E. (1981). The interface of cognitive and social psychology. In J. Harvey (Ed.), *Cognition, social behavior, and the environment* (pp. 189–211). Hillsdale, NJ: Erlbaum.

Trope, Y., & Alfieri, T. (1997). Effortfulness and flexibility of dispositional judgment processes. *Journal of Personality and Social Psychology, 73*, 662–674.

Trope, Y., & Gaunt, R. (1999). A dual-process model of overconfident attributional inferences. In S. Chaiken & Y. Trope (Eds.), *Dual process theories in social psychology* (pp. 161–179). New York: Guilford Press.

Trope, Y., & Gaunt, R. (2000). The use of situational information in dispositional inference: Correction or integration? *Journal of Personality and Social Psychology, 79*, 344–354.

Trope, Y., & Liberman, A. (1996). Social hypothesis testing: Cognitive and motivational mechanisms. In E. T. Higgins & A. W. Kruglanski (Eds.), *Social psychology: Handbook of basic principles* (pp. 239–270). New York: Guilford Press.

Tuchman, B. W. (1984). *The march of folly: From Troy to Vietnam*. New York: Alfred A. Knopf.

Tversky, A., & Kahneman, D. (1983). Extensional versus intuitive reasoning: The conjunction fallacy in probability judgment. *Psychological Review, 91*, 293–315.

Wells, G. L., & Harvey, J. H. (1977). Do people use consensus information in making attributional judgments? *Journal of Personality and Social Psychology, 35*, 279–293.

Zukier, H., & Pepitone, A. (1984). Social roles and strategies in prediction: Some determinants of the use of base-rate information. *Journal of Personality and Social Psychology, 47*, 349–360.

15

TURNING ADVERSITY TO ADVANTAGE: ON THE VIRTUES OF THE COACTIVATION OF POSITIVE AND NEGATIVE EMOTIONS

JEFF T. LARSEN, SCOTT H. HEMENOVER, CATHERINE J. NORRIS, AND JOHN T. CACIOPPO

Although health psychology has long been concerned with the interplay of emotions and health, research has overwhelmingly focused on negative, rather than positive, emotions. Why the preoccupation with the negative? Negative, compared to positive, emotions have a larger impact on affective judgments (Ito, Cacioppo, & Lang, 1998), beliefs and behavior (Cacioppo, Gardner, & Berntson, 1997; Skowronski & Carlston, 1989; Taylor, 1991), the viscera (Cacioppo, Berntson, Larsen, Poehlmann, & Ito, 2000), and even event-related potentials (Ito, Larsen, Smith, & Cacioppo, 1998). Given the traditional conceptualization of the substrates underlying positive and negative emotions as falling at opposite ends of a single bipolar affective mechanism (e.g., see Russell & Carroll, 1999), health psychology's

Preparation of this chapter was supported by a grant to JTC from the Mind-Body Integration Network of the John D. and Catherine T. MacArthur Foundation and by a National Research Service Award to JTL from the National Institute of Mental Health.

focus on potent and disruptive negative emotional processes to the relative exclusion of positive emotional processes made much sense. It followed from the assumed reciprocity of positive and negative hedonic processes that reducing negative feelings was equivalent to increasing positive feelings. Thus, what was learned from the study of negative emotional processes was thought to transfer directly and completely to positive emotional processes (but see Ito & Cacioppo, 1999).

Given this theoretical context, it is understandable that the vast majority of research on health and emotion has studied the impact of negative emotional experiences on disease processes. Such studies have in fact outnumbered those investigating positive, health-promoting factors by 11 to 1 (Mayne, 1999). A long-standing area of interest has focused on the impact of psychological stress on cardiovascular activity (e.g., Tomaka, Blascovich, Kibler, & Ernst, 1997), neuroendocrine response (e.g., Cacioppo et al., 1995), and immune function (Glaser, Pearl, Kiecolt-Glaser, & Malarkey, 1994), as well as on mental (Folkman, Lazarus, Gruen, & DeLongis, 1986) and physical health (Cohen, Tyrrell, & Smith, 1991). A second major area of research has focused on the effects on physical health of such negative emotions as depression, anxiety, loneliness, hostility, and anger, as well as on emotional personality traits such as neuroticism (e.g., Friedman & Booth-Kewley, 1987). These areas of study have been productive in identifying negative emotional factors that act as health risk factors and in developing models explicating how such factors may contribute to disease outcomes. Given that negative emotions do affect health outcomes, it is likewise understandable that these lines of research have treated negative emotions as something to be avoided or at least diminished, rather than dwelled on.

Nevertheless, recent theoretical developments in the areas of emotions and affective neuroscience call into question the long-standing assumption that the processes underlying positive and negative affect are identical. Elsewhere, we have suggested that the characteristics of the affect system differ across the levels of the nervous system as a function of the unique constraints acting on each level (Cacioppo, Gardner, & Berntson, 1999; Ito & Cacioppo, 1999). Although physical limitations constrain behavioral expressions and incline behavioral predispositions toward a bipolar organization (e.g., good vs. bad; approach vs. withdraw), a central tenet of our evaluative space model (ESM; Cacioppo & Berntson, 1994, 1999; Larsen, McGraw, & Cacioppo, 2001) is that these limiting conditions may lose their power at the level of underlying mechanisms. Activation of positivity (appetition) may therefore be partially distinct and separate from activation of negativity (aversion) at the earliest stages of evaluative processes, even though these processes typically result in bipolar evaluative responses.

The ESM has two important implications here. First, the ESM raises the possibility that reducing negative feelings may not be equivalent to enhancing positive feelings. Accordingly, what has been learned from the study of negative emotional processes may not transfer completely to positive emotional processes. As such, the study of linkages between positive emotions and health may be expected to yield associations, mechanisms, and successful interventions that the exclusive study of negative emotions would fail to reveal. The various chapters in this book are testimony to this point.

Second, by conceptualizing the affect system within a bivariate space rather than a bipolar continuum, the ESM allows several modes of evaluative activation, each possessing distinct antecedents, processing properties, and consequences (Cacioppo & Berntson, 1994, Table 1). Bipolar conceptualizations assume that stimuli affect positivity and negativity in opposite directions, such that increases in one system are accompanied by decreases in the other. A bivariate conceptualization allows for such reciprocal activation as well as additional modes of activation. Uncoupled activation occurs when stimuli affect positivity or negativity, but not both. Stimuli may also affect positivity and negativity in the same direction. Coinhibition occurs when a stimulus reduces activation of both systems. Similarly, coactivation occurs when a stimulus increases activation of both systems.

The ambivalence associated with coactivation provides indeterminate behavioral guidance and is therefore presumed to be unstable and unpleasant (Cacioppo & Berntson, 1994, 1999). The thesis of this chapter, however, is that this discomfitting mode of coactivation may allow individuals to make sense of stressors, to gain mastery over future stressors, and to transcend traumatic experiences. That is, coactivation may allow individuals to transform adversity to advantage. More generally, we will point out that the traditional focus on the negative aspects of health and well-being (e.g., Cannon, 1929), as well as the more contemporary focus on the positive aspects (e.g., Ryff & Singer, 1998), need to be complemented by a consideration of the conditions for and consequences of the several modes of evaluative activation.

PRIOR RESEARCH ON THE EFFECTS OF EMOTIONAL REACTIONS TO STRESSORS ON HEALTH

Psychological stress has been known to have negative effects on health since the work of Cannon (1929) and Selye (1956). Contemporary research suggests that negative emotional reactions to stressors can also be detrimental to health, but that emotion management can foster healthy coping (Lazarus & Folkman, 1984). Those who ignore the occasional aggressive driver on the morning commute, for example, avoid the negative health outcomes often associated with perseverating on daily hassles. But not all stressors are small. Given that extreme, persistent negative events cannot always be ignored, effective coping may require acceptance of the stressor and the negative emotions it evokes. In other words, individuals facing severe traumas must grapple and come to grips with the negative event.

A number of investigations have examined the role of emotional reactions to stressors in healthy coping in the context of the disclosure paradigm. In the disclosure paradigm (e.g., Pennebaker, 1993), participants are asked to write several brief daily essays on their thoughts and feelings about a stressor. A typical finding is that experimental participants subsequently show better health outcomes than control participants who write about nonstressful topics. Importantly, disclosure participants typically express both positive and negative emotional reactions to the stressor in such studies. King and Miner (2000), for instance, found that participants given the standard disclosure instructions used just as many positive and negative words in their essays as those explicitly instructed to focus on the traumatic and beneficial aspects of the stressful event. Work by Spiegel and colleagues (Spiegel, Bloom, Kraemer, & Gottheil, 1989) further shows that individuals who express little or no emotion when faced with dire stressors typically suffer worse health outcomes than individuals who are more emotionally expressive.

These studies were important in calling into question the focus on reducing the negative emotions felt by individuals in periods of dire stress. In one of the initial disclosure studies, Pennebaker, Kiecolt-Glaser, and Glaser (1988) asked participants to write about severe, personally relevant traumas. Pennebaker (1993) later found that those participants in the Pennebaker et al. study who subsequently showed improved health outcomes (e.g., fewer trips to the student health center, superior immune function) used more negative emotion words in their essays (e.g., *sad, angry*; M = 3.0) than did those who showed no improvement (M = 2.7). Moreover, those who improved also used fewer positive emotion words (e.g., *happy, joy*; M = 2.5) than those who did not improve (M = 3.1).

What was not clear from this study was whether it was the increased negativity, decreased positivity, or some optimal balance of the two (i.e., coactivation) that was fundamentally related to the subsequent improvements in health outcomes. Interestingly, subsequent studies examining the relationship between disclosure of positive and negative emotions have not consistently replicated Pennebaker's (1993) initial findings. In one study, Pennebaker and Francis (1996) found that undergraduates who disclosed their thoughts and feelings about the relatively mild stressor of entering college made fewer illness-related physician visits over the following 2 months than did control participants. As in Pennebaker et al. (1988), the experimental participants in Pennebaker and Francis typically used both positive emotion words (M = 3.2 words) and negative emotion words (M = 1.9 words) in their essays, consistent with their writing about the stress of entering college leading to a coactivation of positivity and negativity. Contrary to the findings of Pennebaker (1993), Pennebaker and Francis found that the use of negative words was uncorrelated with physician visits, whereas the use of positive emotion words was negatively correlated with physician visits.

The use of relatively more positive emotion words has also been shown to benefit individuals facing traumas and other severe stressors. Stein, Folkman, Trabasso, and Richards (1997) examined spoken narratives of caregivers whose partners had recently died of AIDS. Each participant provided narratives 2 weeks, 4 weeks, and 12 months after bereavement. Unlike the undergraduates who were dealing with their transition to college (Pennebaker & Francis, 1996), the bereaved caregivers used nearly twice as many negative emotion words (M = 13.7) as positive emotion words (M = 7.8). Though Stein et al. did not relate health outcomes to the use of negative and positive words in separate analyses, they did find that those caregivers who used a higher proportion of positive emotion words to total emotion words (i.e., positive + negative) showed more positive health outcomes, including more positive morale and less depressed mood.

In sum, beneficial physical and psychological health outcomes have been associated in some studies with the use of more negative and fewer positive emotion words (Pennebaker, 1993) and in other studies with use of more positive emotion words (e.g., Pennebaker & Francis, 1996) or a higher proportion of positive words (Stein et al., 1997). In light of such seemingly inconsistent findings, it may be useful to consider factors that were held constant within studies but varied across studies. For example, the studies seem to differ in the severity of the traumatic event. How might severity affect the relationship between emotional reactions and health outcomes? Moreover, it may be useful to further consider the psychological significance of the proportion of positive emotion words used (Stein et al., 1997). Participants in disclosure studies wrote essays about salient stressors in their lives, so the use of positive emotion words can be viewed in the context of the negative affect associated with the stressor. Thus, the proportion of positive to total emotions may provide a surrogate measure of the configuration of positive and negative reactions. Whereas high and low proportions denote predominantly positive and negative emotions, respectively, middling proportions denote coactivation of both positive and negative emotions. Rather than examining whether those who express more positive and fewer negative emotions show better or worse health outcomes, this approach allows one to examine the circumstances under which various configurations of positive and negative emotions are associated with beneficial health outcomes.

THE COACTIVATION MODEL OF HEALTHY COPING

We are not suggesting that there is a specific configuration of positive and negative emotions that is most beneficial in all circumstances. Drawing on the literature relating emotional disclosure to coping, Figure 15.1 depicts a model relating emotional reactions to beneficial health outcomes. The model contains a number of features, such as the prediction that health outcomes tend to be worse for severe than for mild stressors and worse when individuals respond with entirely negative rather than entirely positive emotions. In this chapter, however, we focus on the two features that are most relevant to the disclosure literature. First, the relationship between positive or negative emotions and health outcomes is depicted as a series of curvilinear functions, rather than a single linear function. Second, the optimal balance of positive and negative emotions for healthy coping is lower for more severe stressors. That is, effective coping with trivial stressors is associated with primarily positive thoughts and emotions, whereas effective coping with major traumas requires dealing with and working through much more negative information and, hence, is associated with a higher proportion of negative thoughts and emotions.

How does this model account for the extant data? First, we assume that bereavement and one's most traumatic experience, the disclosure topics used by Stein et al. (1997) and Pennebaker (1993), respectively, represent particularly severe stressors and can therefore be depicted on the curve in the bottom panel. The Stein et al. participants used a lower proportion of positive words (M = 0.4) than did the Pennebaker participants (M = 0.5), which places the Stein et al. study to the left of the Pennebaker et al. study on the curve. These studies produced seemingly inconsistent results, such that the proportion of positive emotions and beneficial health outcomes were directly related in the Stein et al. study but inversely related in the Pennebaker study. The data from these studies are compatible, however, if participants in the Stein et al. study fell to the left of the optimal proportion of positive emotions, whereas participants in the Pennebaker study fell to the right.

In the Pennebaker and Francis (1996) study, participants wrote about entering college. We assume that entering college represents a less severe stressor than bereavement (Stein et al., 1997) or one's most traumatic experience (Pennebaker, 1993). The Pennebaker and Francis study would therefore be expected to reflect the middle panel of Figure 1. The participants in the Pennebaker and Francis study used a higher proportion of positive words (M = 0.6) in their essays than did participants in the Pennebaker study (M = 0.5). In contrast to Pennebaker, however, Pennebaker and Francis found a direct relationship between proportion of positive emotions and health outcomes. Though these results seem discrepant, they can also be reconciled if the Pennebaker and Francis study fell to the left of

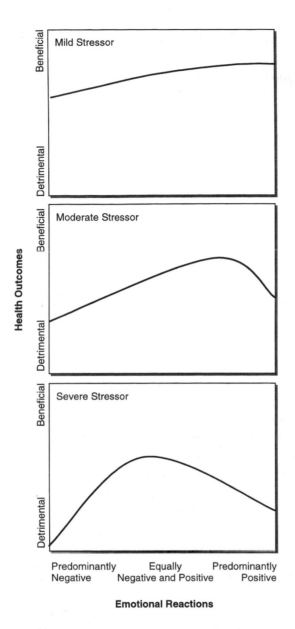

Figure 15.1. The coactivation model of healthy coping. The curves depict a series of curvilinear relationships between emotional reactions to stressors and health outcomes. Beneficial health outcomes are not necessarily associated with entirely positive or entirely negative emotions, but rather with some optimal proportion of positive to total (i.e., positive + negative) emotions. The top, middle, and bottom panels represent stressors of increasing severity. As severity increases, the optimal proportion of positive emotions decreases.

the optimal proportion of positive emotions depicted in the middle panel of Figure 15.1.

Implicit in the coactivation model's prediction that healthy coping is associated with some optimal balance of positive and negative emotions is the additional prediction that the health benefits of disclosure are associated more strongly with coactivation than with neutrality (i.e., the absence of positive and negative emotions). Yet the proportional measure we have used fails to distinguish between individuals experiencing coactivation and neutrality. Evidence for the role of coactivation comes from the basic and often-replicated finding from the disclosure literature that disclosure participants, who typically express more emotions than control participants, also show more beneficial health outcomes than controls. In addition, Spiegel (1998) reviewed evidence that whereas emotional expression can be beneficial among cancer patients (e.g., Spiegel et al., 1989), emotional repression has been associated with detrimental health outcomes (e.g., Jensen, 1987). The extant evidence therefore suggests that beneficial health outcomes are associated more strongly with coactivation than with neutrality.

COACTIVATION AS A CONTRIBUTORY STEP TOWARD COPING

To this point we have argued that the coactivation of positive and negative emotions may be associated with healthy coping. We now consider whether coactivation represents a contributory step toward healthy coping. Although health has typically been conceptualized as the avoidance of stress or disease, positive psychology has begun to reconceptualize health as the possession of the goods in life (Ryff & Singer, 1998). Both models can be seen as providing strategies for healthy coping. To borrow the words of songwriter Johnny Mercer, the former view suggests that individuals dealing with stressful events and the resulting negative emotions must eliminate the negative; the latter view, that such individuals must accentuate the positive. We consider these strategies and their potential limitations for emotion-focused coping, then propose an alternative strategy.

Eliminate the Negative?

The ability to inhibit emotions has been treated as a developmental milestone (e.g., Kopp, 1989) and as an important skill among healthy adults (Tomkins, 1984). Emotional suppression may therefore represent a useful coping strategy. A variety of research, however, including findings that use of negative words during disclosure can be associated with beneficial health outcomes, suggests that emotional suppression may not always be most effective. Gross and Levenson (1997), for example, found that undergraduates could suppress their overt emotional reactions to amusing or sad films when instructed to do so, but only at the physiological cost of increased sympathetic activation.

Additional research by Wegner, Erber, and Zanakos (1993) suggests that suppression of negative emotions not only is difficult under cognitive load, but can also have the ironic effect of making negative emotions more accessible. In their study, participants first wrote a brief essay about a personal failure, then tried to either think about or avoid thinking about the failure. In a subsequent Stroop-type color-naming task, words related to failure were more accessible among those participants who had avoided thinking about failure, thus raising the possibility that individuals' attempts to suppress the negative emotions associated with stressors can have insidious effects on affect and cognition. Moreover, theorists have recently implicated thought suppression in the etiology and maintenance of posttraumatic stress disorder, phobias, and other mental disorders (Purdon, 1999).

Accentuate the Positive?

A viable alternative to eliminating the negative may be to accentuate the positive. For example, Folkman and Moskowitz's (2000) review suggests that positive reappraisal (focusing on the good in what is happening or what has happened), problem-focused coping (focusing on thoughts and instrumental behaviors that manage or solve the underlying cause of the distress), and creation of positive events (creating a positive psychological time-out by infusing ordinary events with positive meaning) can benefit coping. Indeed, one of positive psychology's most impressive lines of research has examined the beneficial effects of optimism on health and well-being. Scheier et al. (1989), for example, found that dispositional optimism predicted problem-focused coping, physical recovery, and postsurgical quality of life among coronary surgery patients.

Taylor and Brown's (1988) work on positive illusions shows that even those with unrealistically optimistic outlooks enjoy better psychological health outcomes. Taylor and Brown also argued, however, that although the social environment fosters mild illusions, it does not tolerate extreme illusions (Taylor, 1989; Taylor & Brown, 1994). Supportive evidence comes from Epstein and Meier's (1989) development of the Constructive Thinking Inventory (CTI), which contains factors termed Behavioral Coping and Naïve Optimism, among others. Behavioral Coping entails maintaining an optimistic outlook and planning and carrying out effective action; Naïve Optimism entails simplistic, overly positive thinking. Whereas Behavioral Coping was positively correlated with various indicators of successful living (e.g., academic achievement), Naïve Optimism provided a mixed bag

(Epstein & Meier, 1989). Those high in Naïve Optimism did enjoy more effective social relationships, but they also suffered more physical symptoms of illness.

Take the Good With the Bad?

A third strategy, which is similar to the approach articulated by Folkman and Moskowitz (2000), follows from the notion that healthy coping is associated with some optimal proportion of positive and negative emotions. That is, we suggest that coactivation can play a crucial role in the resolution of stressful events. Turning adversity to advantage requires planning and problem solving, which are served by working memory. Working memory, in turn, involves both an active maintenance of information in short-term memory and an executive control governing the activation of, suppression of, and operation on this information. The activation of memories of stressful events can itself be aversive, thereby reducing the likelihood of subsequent activation. Consistent with this hypothesis, traumatic events appear to be particularly disorganized (Foa & Riggs, 1993) and fail to be integrated into the personal narratives that characterize the processing of memories for ordinary events (Christianson, 1992). If these memories are to be organized, integrated into one's personal narratives, and ultimately transformed into something beneficial, they must be retained in working memory. A key to maintaining stressful negative information in working memory sufficiently long, and with sufficient clarity of mind to grapple with the stressor, may be the simultaneous activation of positive emotional processes—that is, a coactivation of positivity and negativity.

As mentioned above, the ESM holds that coactivation provides indeterminate behavioral guidance and therefore tends to be unstable and aversive (Cacioppo & Berntson, 1994). Nevertheless, unavoidable negative events must be resolved, and coactivation in the short run may be an important step toward instigating the cognitive mediators of healthy coping in the long run. Recent research by Taylor and her colleagues has investigated two such cognitive mediators, specifically, engagement in the stressor and meaning making. Rivkin and Taylor (1999) found that a group of participants who visualized an ongoing stressful event, as well as their own behavioral and emotional reactions to the stressful event, subsequently reported greater engagement coping (Carver, Scheier, & Weintraub, 1989), including greater acceptance of the reality of the event and more positive reinterpretations of the event.

The ability to engage or confront stressors may also promote the ability of individuals to find meaning in the event (cf. Folkman & Moskowitz, 2000). In a study of bereaved HIV-seropositive men, Bower, Kemeny, Taylor, and Fahey (1998) found that effortful, deliberative cognitive processing about traumas was necessary but not sufficient for improved health outcomes; only those men who were also able to find meaning in the trauma had better immune function and lower AIDS-related mortality. These findings suggest that coping depends not only on grappling with the stressor, but also on coming to grips with and gaining insight into it.

CONCLUSION

Positive psychology has blazed a new trail across the landscape of contemporary psychology, bringing with it an emphasis on positive factors that promote health and well-being. Although it has long been suspected that the reduction of negative emotions can reduce illness and disease, positive psychology has added the important complement that positive emotions can independently promote health and well-being. What is missing in both literatures is a further consideration of the configuration of positive and negative affective processing, especially when dealing with a major life stressor. Although brooding over trivial failures and tribulations or fixating on the negative aspects of more significant life stressors can be detrimental to health, negative emotions are often aroused for a reason— to interrupt ongoing activity, to counteract a threat, to modify one's actions, or to change one's environment. Although emotion management (Lazarus & Folkman, 1984) may be seen as the ability to reduce negative and enhance positive emotions, we suggest that emotion management might often entail experiencing and working through, rather than simply reducing, negative emotions (see also Gross, 1998). Reflexive withdrawal or denial may improve one's immediate mood but will do little to increase adaptability—a feature of a good life that may be just as important as happiness.

Among those with terminal illness, confronting and overcoming negative emotions may be critical not only to a good life, but to extending life itself. In a landmark study on the relationship between coping and health outcomes, Spiegel et al. (1989) found that breast cancer patients randomly assigned to a support group where they were encouraged to express their feelings about their illness survived on average 37 months, twice as long as control patients survived. Spiegel (1998) reported that breast cancer patients in support-expressive group therapy "came to realize that happiness and sadness are not two poles of one dimension," a point that is central to our coactivation model and to the ESM from which it has been derived (p. 67). These women achieved happiness not by eliminating their negative emotions, but by confronting them. One woman finally attended the Santa Fe Opera only after accepting that she might not be able to wait until she felt better. She later remarked, "I brought my cancer with me and put it in the seat next to me. It was there but I had a wonderful time" (Spiegel, 1998, p. 67). To say that this woman had neutralized her negative emotions is to miss the point. She did not eliminate her fear; rather, she accepted it. As a result, she engaged her illness, found meaning in it, and ultimately adapted to it.

Spiegel's research also makes clear, however, that it is often not enough to experience negative emotions. Indeed, we have argued that it may be necessary to experience positive emotions if one is to be able to grapple with the negative emotions associated with a stressor. The coactivation of positive and negative affective processes is unstable, unpleasant, and disharmonious, however (Cacioppo et al., 1997, 1999), and thus is best viewed not as a frequent or commonplace affective state but only as a means to a more enduring affective endpoint. Thus, it is conceivable that the ability to experience coactivation and withstand its ambiguous implications for behavior enhances the likelihood that one can work through and transcend major life stressors. As such, the ability to withstand the tension of feeling both positive and negative emotions may represent an important human strength. More generally, although positive psychology has made it clear that an exclusive focus on negative emotions is insufficient, the present perspective implies that an exclusive focus on positive emotions may also ultimately prove insufficient.

REFERENCES

Bower, J. E., Kemeny, M. E., Taylor, S. E., & Fahey, J. L. (1998). Cognitive processing, discovery of meaning, CD4 decline, and AIDS-related mortality among bereaved HIV-seropositive men. *Journal of Personality and Social Psychology*, 66, 979–986.

Cacioppo, J. T., & Berntson, G. G. (1994). Relationship between attitudes and evaluative space: A critical review, with emphasis on the separability of positive and negative substrates. *Psychological Bulletin*, 115, 401–423.

Cacioppo, J. T., & Berntson, G. G. (1999). The affect system: Architecture and operating characteristics. *Current Directions in Psychological Science*, 8, 133–137.

Cacioppo, J. T., Berntson, G. G., Larsen, J. T., Poehlmann, K. M., & Ito, T. A. (2000). The psychophysiology of emotion. In M. Lewis & J. M. Haviland-Jones (Eds.), *Handbook of emotions* (2nd ed., pp. 173–191). New York: Guilford Press.

Cacioppo, J. T., Gardner, W. L., & Berntson, G. G. (1997). Beyond bipolar conceptualizations and measures: The case of attitudes and evaluative space. *Personality and Social Psychology Review*, 1, 3–25.

Cacioppo, J. T., Gardner, W. L., & Berntson, G. G. (1999). The affect system has parallel and integrative processing components: Form follows function. *Journal of Personality and Social Psychology*, 76, 839–855.

Cacioppo, J. T., Malarkey, W. B., Kiecolt-Glaser, J. K., Uchino, B. N., Sgoutas-

Emch, S. A., Sheridan, J. F., Berntson, G. G., & Glaser, R. (1995). Heterogeneity in neuroendocrine and immune responses to brief psychological stressors as a function of autonomic cardiac activation. *Psychosomatic Medicine, 57,* 154–164.

Cannon, W. B. (1929). *Bodily changes in pain, hunger, fear, and rage.* New York: Appleton.

Carver, C. S., Scheier, M. F., & Weintraub, J. K. (1989). Assessing coping strategies: A theoretically based approach. *Journal of Personality and Social Psychology, 56,* 267–283.

Christianson, S. (1992). *Handbook of emotion and memory.* Hillsdale, NJ: Erlbaum.

Cohen, S., Tyrrell, D. A., & Smith, A. P. (1991). Psychological stress and susceptibility to the common cold. *New England Journal of Medicine, 325,* 606–612.

Epstein, S., & Meier, P. (1989). Constructive thinking: A broad coping variable with specific components. *Journal of Personality and Social Psychology, 57,* 332–350.

Foa, E., & Riggs, D. (1993). Post-traumatic stress disorder in rape victims. In J. Oldham, M. B. Riba, & A. Tasman (Eds.), *American Psychiatric Press review of psychiatry* (Vol. 12, pp. 273–303). Washington, DC: American Psychiatric Press.

Folkman, S., Lazarus, R. S., Gruen, R. J., & DeLongis, A. (1986). Appraisal, coping, health status, and psychological symptoms. *Journal of Personality and Social Psychology, 50,* 571–579.

Folkman, S., & Moskowitz, J. T. (2000). Stress, positive emotion, and coping. *Current Directions in Psychological Science, 9,* 115–118.

Friedman, H. S., & Booth-Kewley, S. (1987). Personality, Type A behavior, and coronary heart disease: The role of emotional expression. *Journal of Personality and Social Psychology, 53,* 783–792.

Glaser, R., Pearl, D. K., Kiecolt-Glaser, J. K., & Malarkey, W. B. (1994). Plasma cortisol levels and reactivation of latent Epstein-Barr virus in response to examination stress. *Psychoneuroendocrinology, 19,* 765–772.

Gross, J. J. (1998). The emerging field of emotion regulation: An integrative review. *Review of General Psychology, 2,* 271–299.

Gross, J. J., & Levenson, R. W. (1997). Hiding feelings: The acute effects of inhibiting negative and positive emotions. *Journal of Abnormal Psychology, 106,* 95–103.

Ito, T. A., & Cacioppo, J. T. (1999). The psychophysiology of utility appraisals. In D. Kahneman, E. Diener, & N. Schwartz (Eds.), *Understanding quality of life: Scientific perspectives on enjoyment and suffering* (pp. 453–469). New York: Russell Sage.

Ito, T. A., Cacioppo, J. T., & Lang, P. J. (1998). Eliciting affect using the international affective picture system: Trajectories through evaluative space. *Personality and Social Psychology Bulletin, 24,* 855–879.

Ito, T. A., Larsen, J. T., Smith, N. K., & Cacioppo, J. T. (1998). Negative information weighs more heavily on the brain: The negativity bias in evaluative categorizations. *Journal of Personality and Social Psychology, 75,* 887–900.

Jensen, M. R. (1987). Psychobiological factors predicting the course of breast cancer. *Journal of Personality, 55,* 317–342.

King, L. A., & Miner, K. N. (2000). Writing about the perceived benefits of traumatic events: Implications for physical health. *Personality and Social Psychology Bulletin, 26,* 220–230.

Kopp, C. B. (1989). Regulation of distress and negative emotions: A developmental view. *Developmental Psychology, 25,* 343–354.

Larsen, J. T., McGraw, A. P., & Cacioppo, J. T. (2001). Can people feel happy and sad at the same time? *Journal of Personality and Social Psychology, 81,* 684–696.

Lazarus, R. S., & Folkman, S. (1984). *Stress, appraisal, and coping.* New York: Springer.

Mayne, T. J. (1999). Negative affect and health: The importance of being earnest. *Cognition and Emotion, 13,* 601–635.

Pennebaker, J. W. (1993). Putting stress into words: Health, linguistic, and therapeutic implications. *Behaviour Research and Therapy, 31,* 539–548.

Pennebaker, J. W., & Francis, M. E. (1996). Cognitive, emotional, and language processes in disclosure: Physical health and adjustment. *Cognition and Emotion, 10,* 601–626.

Pennebaker, J. W., Kiecolt-Glaser, J. K., & Glaser, R. (1988). Disclosure of traumas and immune function: Health implications for psychotherapy. *Journal of Consulting and Clinical Psychology, 56,* 239–245.

Purdon, C. (1999). Thought suppression and psychopathology. *Behaviour Research and Therapy, 37,* 1029–1054.

Rivkin, I. D., & Taylor, S. E. (1999). The effects of mental simulation on coping with controllable stressful events. *Personality and Social Psychology Bulletin, 25,* 1451–1462.

Russell, J. A., & Carroll, J. M. (1999). On the bipolarity of positive and negative affect. *Psychological Bulletin, 125,* 3–30.

Ryff, C. D., & Singer, B. (1998). The contours of positive human health. *Psychological Inquiry, 9,* 1–28.

Scheier, M. F., Matthews, K. A., Owens, J. F., Magovern, G. J., Sr., Lefebvre, R. C., Abbott, R. A., & Carver, C. S. (1989). Dispositional optimism and recovery from coronary artery bypass surgery: The beneficial effects on physical and psychological well-being. *Journal of Personality and Social Psychology, 57,* 1024–1040.

Selye, H. (1956). *The stress of life.* New York: McGraw-Hill.

Skowronski, J. J., & Carlston, D. E. (1989). Negativity and extremity biases in impression formation: A review of explanations. *Psychological Bulletin, 105,* 131–142.

Spiegel, D. (1998). Getting there is half the fun: Relating happiness to health. *Psychological Inquiry, 9*, 66–68.

Spiegel, D., Bloom, J. R., Kraemer, H. C., & Gottheil, E. (1989). Effects of psychosocial treatment on survival of patients with metastatic breast cancer. *Lancet, 2*, 888–891.

Stein, N., Folkman, S., Trabasso, T., & Richards, T. A. (1997). Appraisal and goal processes as predictors of psychological well-being in bereaved caregivers. *Journal of Personality and Social Psychology, 72*, 872–884.

Taylor, S. E. (1989). *Positive illusions: Creative self-deception and the healthy mind.* New York: Basic Books.

Taylor, S. E. (1991). Asymmetrical effects of positive and negative events: The mobilization-minimization hypothesis. *Psychological Bulletin, 110*, 67–85.

Taylor, S. E., & Brown, J. D. (1988). Illusion and well-being: A social psychological perspective on mental health. *Psychological Bulletin, 103*, 193–210.

Taylor, S. E., & Brown, J. D. (1994). Positive illusions and well-being revisited: Separating fact from fiction. *Psychological Bulletin, 116*, 21–27.

Tomaka, J., Blascovich, J., Kibler, J., & Ernst, J. M. (1997). Cognitive and physiological antecedents of threat and challenge appraisal. *Journal of Personality and Social Psychology, 73*, 63–72.

Tomkins, S. (1984). Affect theory. In K. R. Scherer & P. Ekman (Eds.), *Approaches to emotion* (pp. 163–195). Hillsdale, NJ: Erlbaum.

Wegner, D. M., Erber, R., & Zanakos, S. (1993). Ironic processes in the mental control of mood and mood-related thought. *Journal of Personality and Social Psychology, 65*, 1093–1104.

16

A HOLISTIC PERSON APPROACH FOR RESEARCH ON POSITIVE DEVELOPMENT

DAVID MAGNUSSON AND JOSEPH L. MAHONEY

Human strengths represent a relatively new area of research. After a period during which the focus of much developmental research was concerned with negative aspects of individual development and functioning, an increasing number of researchers have pointed to the need to investigate positive aspects (e.g., Cowen, 1991; Ryff & Singer, 1998). Now is the ideal time to discuss the basic requirements for successful empirical research in this area.

In principle, individual functioning can be investigated from three different perspectives: a current, synchronic perspective; a developmental, diachronic perspective; and an evolutionary perspective. This chapter addresses the first two. The *synchronic perspective* attempts to explain individual functioning in terms of current psychological and biological dispositions. This perspective is not concerned with developmental processes that

The research presented in this chapter was supported by grants from the Swedish Council for Social Research and the Swedish Council for Planning and Coordination of Research to David Magnusson. We thank Michael Bohman, Lars Nystedt, and Amanda Schweder for valuable comments on an early version of the manuscript.

precede an individual's present functioning. The *diachronic perspective*, on the other hand, is concerned with current functioning in terms of an individual's developmental history. Such models are concerned with the ontogeny of the individual, the timing and expression of significant environmental events, and the ways these factors interact over time.

The synchronic and diachronic perspectives imply different scientific models and methods. Research on human strengths has emphasized the current, synchronic perspective. For a fuller understanding of human strengths and their role in individuals' lives and in society, a developmental, diachronic perspective is indicated (see, e.g., the seminal work on successful aging by Baltes & Baltes, 1990). This chapter focuses on positive development from a developmental perspective. It should be kept in mind, however, that the two perspectives are not contradictory; they are complementary. Proper models for positive individual development presuppose reference to models for current functioning.

The establishment of this new area of research requires a discussion of three issues: (a) a definition of the concept to delineate the space of phenomena under investigation; (b) a careful, descriptive analysis of the nature of the space of phenomena; and (c) a formulation of a theoretical framework that serves to hold studies on specific issues together to synthesize knowledge in the field. Until now, most of the contributions to the field of positive development are theoretical discussions and propositions under different headings. They lack a commonly agreed on definition of what constitutes "positive" functioning. Consequently, proponents of positive development research have discussed and applied the concept in different ways. In empirical research, this has led to a fragmented set of results from well-planned and -implemented studies on specific aspects of human strengths such as resilience and ego control (Luthar, Cicchetti, & Becker, 2000), competence (Strayhorn, 1988), self-efficacy (Bandura, 1997), and other studies on so-called protective factors. A commonly accepted definition of positive development would promote scientific progress by making the debate on theoretical issues more constructive and the design, implementation, and interpretation of empirical studies more coherent.

This chapter aims to contribute to the other two requirements for progress in empirical research on what has been designated positive development in very general terms. Scientific theorizing and the selection of research strategies and methodological tools should be grounded in an understanding and careful description of the nature of the phenomena being investigated. Accordingly, we first present a descriptive analysis of the structures and processes in individual development that are of interest. This serves as a basis to discuss three issues: (a) the task for research on positive development, (b) a holistic theoretical framework needed to meet the challenges of this task, and (c) the consequences of that perspective for research methods and strategies.

In the proposed framework, the individual serves as the organizational principle for scientific inquiry into positive development. As such, individual functioning defines the space of phenomena of interest. This principle, forming the essence of what has been designated a "person approach," is basically the same as that proposed for research on "normal" as well as negative aspects of development (Magnusson, 1999). Therefore, much of what is proposed is valid for research on different aspects of individual development, regardless of how positive development is defined. What we propose, however, emphasizes what may be particularly important for research on positive development. These propositions are intended to facilitate productive research. To that end, some of the pitfalls in research on other aspects of individual development (e.g., a lack of careful analysis of the phenomena) may be avoided.

In this chapter we offer a programmatic analysis of positive development rather than an overview and discussion of current empirical research in this area (see, e.g., Kahneman & Diener, 1999; Mahoney & Bergman, 2002; Seligman & Csikszentmihalyi, 2000). Making explicit the basic conditions for empirical research in any field forms a necessary basis for contributing to real scientific progress.

BASIC PROPOSITIONS IN RESEARCH ON POSITIVE DEVELOPMENT

Four descriptive propositions about the nature of the phenomena in research on positive development form the starting point for our further remarks (Magnusson, 1999; Magnusson & Stattin, 1998).

- *Proposition 1.* The individual functions and develops as an active, intentional part of an integrated, complex, dynamic, and adaptive person–environment system. The nature of this system changes through the individual's life course as a result of individual developmental processes, societal changes, and continuous individual–environment interaction processes.
- *Proposition 2.* The individual develops as an integrated, undivided organism in a complex, dynamic, and adaptive process of maturation and learning over time. Mental, biological, and behavioral factors in the individual and social, cultural, and physical properties of the environment are involved in this interactive process.
- *Proposition 3.* The conditions that the individual's environment offers, including the potentialities, restrictions, demands, and expectations it places on the individual, are of special importance for research on positive development.

- *Proposition 4.* A theoretical model aimed at explaining the processes guiding individual positive development must incorporate and integrate mental, biological, and behavioral aspects of the individual and the physical, social, and cultural aspects of his or her environment.

Although the individual is the main concern, these propositions emphasize that the positive development of an individual cannot be understood in isolation from the environment. As such, theories and empirical research on human strengths must center on a person who functions and develops as an active part of an integrated person–environment system. Metaphorically speaking, the individual is the cell of the societal body. The better we understand the functioning of the cell, the better we understand the functioning of the body. Understanding the functioning of the cell presupposes consideration of the framework—the body—to which the cell belongs. Accordingly, a definition of positive development cannot be made with reference to an isolated individual; it must be formulated with reference to the characteristic features, resources, and restrictions of the individual considered and the social, cultural, physical, and historical contexts in which he or she is embedded.

INDIVIDUAL DEVELOPMENT

The extent to which human strengths characterize an individual's functioning at a certain age involves a developmental process initiated at conception. From the beginning, constitutional factors form potentialities and set restrictions on the nested developmental processes of maturation and learning. The early system is not, however, closed. It is open to change across the life span. Development occurs in a continuous, interactive process of mental, biological, and behavioral factors in the individual and of social, cultural, and physical factors in the environment.

Two characteristics make the complex processes involved in the development of individual strengths accessible to scientific analysis. First, developmental processes are regulated by specific psychological and biological principles. Among other things, these principles serve to maintain the individual's integrity as a biological and psychological being. A central task for research on positive development is to identify the specific principles and mechanisms guiding these processes. Second, individual developmental processes operate within structures organized to best serve the functioning of the organism as an integrated whole. This functional organization is a characteristic of individual structures and processes at all levels, including mental, biological, and behavioral factors. The organism's active role in maintaining organization is a prerequisite for developmental processes to function well and adapt to situational conditions.

The development of functionally organized systems that preserve the integrity of the individual's total functioning is guided by the self-organization. Self-organization is a property of open systems and refers to a process by which new structures and patterns emerge, and it is a guiding principle from the outset of development. The operating components of each subsystem organize themselves to maximize their functioning with respect to each other. At higher levels, subsystems organize themselves toward optimal functioning of the total system. The self-organization principle has been applied in discussions of developmental processes in general (e.g., Thelen, 1989), the organization of the brain (Schore, 1997), the development of temperament (Derryberry & Rothbart, 1997), and the development and functioning of sensory and cognitive systems and manifest behavior (Carlson, Earls, & Todd, 1988).

In empirical research on positive development, two characteristic features of developmental processes have to be considered: (a) the holistic nature of the processes and (b) the principle of synchronization of operating elements in the processes. Both have specific and fundamental implications for strategy and methodology in research on positive development.

The Holistic, Integrated Nature of Developmental Processes

The integrated nature of developmental processes implies that they are holistic—that is, that they function and develop as irreducible wholes. This characteristic is found at all levels of the total person–environment system. Each level of the system derives its characteristic features and properties from the functional interaction of the elements involved, not from the effect of each isolated part on the totality. At the individual level, each aspect of the operating structures and processes (e.g., brain and physiological systems, perceptions, values, goals, motives, conduct), and each aspect of the proximal and distal environment (e.g., social relationships, home, school, neighborhood, culture) takes on meaning from its role in the total functioning of the individual. An element of the system derives its significance not from its structure, but from its role in the system it forms a part of (Magnusson, 1990).

The holistic nature of developmental processes implies that they cannot be determined by a single factor. If development were primarily influenced by a single aspect (e.g., a single gene in the case of Huntington's disease or poisoning in the case of the environment), the processes would go astray and lead to pathological processes in other systems. Accordingly, the normal functional role of a single variable in the processes of positive development cannot be understood by studying it in isolation from other, simultaneously operating factors. Most traditional research on individual development has focused on the role of single variables. It is only the integrated individual, however, that remains distinct and identifiable across time. This holds also when the focus of analysis is human strength and positive development.

Synchronization of Elements in Processes

In the developmental processes of an individual, an enormous number of dynamic, interacting elements are involved. For the processes to operate and change in an effective way that maintains the total integrity of the organism, all elements must be synchronized. Synchronization characterizes the interactive processes within subsystems, between subsystems at the same level, and between systems at different levels. Individual positive development is dependent on how well intraorganism functioning (mental, biological, and behavioral) and extraorganism activity (environmental opportunities, demands, rules, and regulations) are functionally synchronized.

A good illustration of the holistic nature of developmental processes and the role of synchronization in such processes is girls' transition from childhood to adulthood. Girls differ from each other remarkably with respect to the timetable for biological maturation. Thus, girls of the same chronological age, but at very different biological maturation levels, have different biologically and psychologically motivated needs and goals, with respect to ways of living, not least social and sexual relations (Stattin & Magnusson, 1990). However, they are expected to adapt to the same societal system of social regulations based on chronological age (e.g., attending the same class at school) and to the same expectations and norms with regard to appropriate and acceptable behaviors (e.g., social and sexual relations). The integration and synchronization of mental, biological, and behavioral aspects of the girl, and social and cultural aspects of the environment, become critical for her positive development. The way the environment functions and the role it plays in this synchronization process vary across societies and cultures. As a consequence, the organization and functional synchrony of developmental processes varies between societies and cultures.

Individual Differences

Thus far, we have argued that human strengths should be conceptualized from a holistic, interactionistic developmental perspective. In this view, the important information about an individual is found in the organization of patterns of functioning—that is, typical configurations of operating mental, biological, and behavioral factors at different levels of individual functioning. Patterning of operating factors characterizes current and developmental processes involved in psychological and biological functioning. For example, Stryker (1994) discussed the role of patterns of neural activity in the developing nervous system and how these patterns of activity vary among individuals. Weiner (1989) suggested that the oscillations produced by the natural pacemakers of the heart, the stomach, and the brain are patterned (cf. Kelso, 1997). Thus, at all levels of organization, individual developmental processes occur and change in terms of patterns of operating factors, not in terms of single variables that operate independent of other simultaneously working variables.

This perspective advocates studying patterns of individual functioning over time rather than measuring predictive relations between discrete variables. In identifying the relevant operating factors in positive functioning, their interrelations, and their patterning, exceptional or positive behavior may show qualitatively different patterns from both nonnegative and problematic adjustment behaviors (Cowen, 1994).

An empirical longitudinal study of adult social behavior can help elucidate this issue. The study showed that a majority of 12- and 13-year-old boys who later became persistent criminals (i.e, who had a criminal record up to the age of 30) had a characteristic pattern of a lack of concentration, motor restlessness, and low sympathetic nervous system activity as measured by adrenaline excretion in stressful and nonstressful situations at school (Magnusson, 1996a). This pattern was not found for boys who had no criminal record up to the age of 30 or for boys who had a criminal record only during the teenage years. Accordingly, distinct patterns of biological and psychosocial factors characterized the long-term trajectories of boys showing persistent, transient, and no criminal offending. This raises two related questions for research on human strengths and positive development: (a) Are the life trajectories for adults who are functioning positively different from the life trajectories of other individuals? and (b) If so, what are the unique patterns of operating factors in the life trajectories of individuals who demonstrate human strengths and positive functioning, and when can they be identified?

Basic properties of the organism's way of functioning at any stage of life are the result of a coherent process from conception through the prenatal period and onward. Patterns of perceptions, cognitions, emotions, and behaviors are established early during the fetal and infant period. A prerequisite for an optimal organization of these individual capabilities is the establishment of an effective biological system. In particular, the brain is organized as the central organ for interpretation and appraisal of external information, for attaching emotions and values to this information, and for activating and interacting with biological autonomic, endocrine, and muscular systems. The early psychobiological system is a basis for developmental processes in the future and has consequences for the character of the individual's future life course. A central issue for research on positive development is to what extent and under what conditions the organism is open for change in positive and negative directions over the life span. New results indicate that the brain is particularly open to change during adolescence (Spear, 2000), making this period critical for understanding positive development in a lifespan perspective.

This description of the psychobiological system implies a difference between the developmental processes taking place early in its establishment and those operating during childhood, adolescence, and adulthood. Establishment of the psychobiological system early on occurs in a very open biological system during a brief time frame. These processes are fundamentally different from those during childhood, adolescence, and adulthood, which occur in the context of an established psychobiological system. Once this system has been established, the individual develops under the correlated constraints of the existing features and properties of the total person–environment system. For an understanding of developmental processes in general, and in this case positive development, the two kinds of processes require partly different analyses.

Theoretically, the hypothesis of personality crystallization may shed light on the particular developmental paths that characterize human strengths and positive development. The hypothesis implies that persons whose developmental system is organized differently at one point in time will take partly different directions at the next time point. Thus, for example, the early establishment of the integrated psychobiological system is particularly important because it is the foundation for further developmental processes. Each step confirms future developmental alternatives, and eventually an increasingly stable personality "type" appears over time. If this view is correct, it should show up in clearer homogenization within categories of individuals and clearer differentiation among categories of individuals across time. The empirical study by Magnusson (1996a) is illustrative of this process in that different patterns of operating factors among men reflected differential stability in antisocial behavior over time. It should be equally plausible for crystallization processes involved in positive development. In this regard, identifying early patterns of individual functioning could serve as "entry points" into the developmental process of crystallization of human strengths.

It should be clear that from a holistic perspective, the specific pattern and functional meaning of the operating factors involved in positive development vary as a consequence of individual resources and abilities and of social and cultural conditions. As such, the interpretation of whether a given behavior or characteristic is indicative of positive functioning will vary across persons and contexts. It is an important task for researchers to identify the homogeneity of patterns of positive functioning that applies to different subgroups of persons and how these patterns may differ across social and cultural conditions and historical time. Accordingly, positive development cannot be limited to exceptional ability in specific domains. Exceptional creativity in a certain area does not constitute a criterion of positive development. Some of the most prominent individuals in the history of science would not be referred to as examples of positive development. Even villains and criminals can show exceptional creativity in designing their crimes. We suggest that positive functioning characterizes an individual whose overall pattern of functioning is indicative of the individual's ability to adapt to environmental opportunities, demands, and restrictions in a way that best satisfies the individual's needs and also benefits society. This definition must be made with reference to the individual's available resources and opportunities (e.g., Luthar & Burack, 2000).

THE GOAL FOR RESEARCH ON POSITIVE DEVELOPMENT: THE NEED FOR A SYNTHESIS

A holistic perspective on positive development necessitates an integrated consideration of individual and environmental factors operating over time. Nonetheless, fragmentation has characterized psychological research over the last century. In spite of attempts toward integration, for example, in the interface of the biology of the brain and mental factors, a characteristic feature of psychological research is fragmentation. Generally, fragmentation is reflected in differences in theoretical models, conceptual spaces, and research designs used to study psychological development. As a result, empirical studies on specific aspects of individual development have essentially been conducted and interpreted in different scientific worlds.

One explanation for this fragmentation relates to the purported goal and criterion for success in empirical research in psychology during the past century. In defending psychology as a natural science, Watson in 1913 formulated the scientific goal for psychological research as being "to predict and control" behavior. Since then high prediction has been considered a worthwhile criterion for successful psychological research in general, including developmental research. This emphasis is reflected, for example, in empirical research on developmental processes whereby single variables are examined according to their statistical relation with an outcome. To some extent, a lack of distinction between statistical prediction in an experimental design and prediction over the life course of individuals has contributed to this fragmentation.

Indeed, the complex, dynamic nature of developmental processes does not permit strict prediction of individuals' life courses over time. Most contemporary developmentalists see the goal of developmental research as identifying the principles and mechanisms underlying and guiding developmental processes. A prerequisite for meeting that goal is to synthesize knowledge from all fields concerned with the study of individual developmental processes. Developmental processes cannot be understood at a particular level of the total person–environment system without an integrated synthesis of knowledge of all simultaneously operating factors at that level.

Importantly, a synthesis is different than mere accumulation and summation of facts, and this reflects the essence of a holistic perspective; namely, that the whole is more than the sum of the parts. Synthesizing knowledge on the emerging field of human strengths is necessary from the outset to overcome the detrimental effects of fragmentation. This activity will ultimately lead to a richer understanding of how and why individuals function and develop as totalities in the processes of positive development.

The Task for Research on Positive Development

The descriptive analysis of structures and processes involved in positive development leads to the following interrelated, empirical questions:

- How and under what conditions is the integrated individual system of mental, biological, and behavioral aspects established early in the lives of individuals? What role does the early established system play in the development of human strengths in the subsequent developmental processes of the individual?
- How and under what conditions are positive developmental processes facilitated and maintained in the life course of an individual? What kind of individually bound factors drive the emergence and maintenance of positive functioning?
- To what extent is the early integration of mental, biological, and behavioral factors of an individual open to change in a positive direction during the life course? Conversely, to what extent do life-course trajectories that have started in a positive direction provide resistance to change in a negative direction?
- Which are the relevant patterns of positive functioning that apply to subgroups of individuals and how do those patterns differ across social and cultural conditions and historical time?

Scientifically solid, empirically based answers to these questions require a common theoretical framework and the application of appropriate methodological tools and research strategies that are consistent with that framework.

A COMMON THEORETICAL FRAMEWORK FOR EMPIRICAL RESEARCH ON POSITIVE DEVELOPMENT

Our fourth general proposition for research on positive development is that a theoretical model aimed at explaining the processes guiding individual positive development must incorporate and integrate mental, biological, and behavioral aspects of the individual and physical, social, and cultural aspects of his or her environment.

The natural sciences illustrate the importance of a common theoretical framework for empirical research on specific aspects of complex, dynamic systems. Commonly accepted, general models of nature have been major prerequisites for the remarkable scientific progress in these fields. These models have served two purposes that are the same for a general, holistic model of human functioning and development, including research on human strength and positive development. First, through design, implementation, and interpretation of empirical studies on specific issues under a common theoretical frame of reference, results can be amalgamated and synthesized. An amalgamation of findings is a necessary step to understanding and explicating the principles and mechanisms guiding positive development and will overcome the detrimental effects of fragmentation. Second, a theoretical framework based on the holistic nature of structures and processes involved in positive development permits communication among scientists in different subfields of research on developmental processes.

To avoid misinterpretation, a point of clarification is pertinent: A holistic model does not imply that the entire individual system has to be the target of investigation in each study. In the natural sciences, the acceptance of a common model of nature has never implied that the whole universe should be investigated in every study. Indeed, scientific progress often necessitates empirical studies that are initially conducted on specific mental, biological, and behavioral aspects of development. Thus, for example, studies of particular protective factors that promote resilience contribute to an understanding of positive development. On this score, Mayr's (1976) warning with respect to biology is also applicable to research on positive development: "The past history of biology has shown that progress is equally inhibited by an anti-intellectual holism and a purely atomistic reductionism" (p. 72). However, an integrating framework must exist for a later synthesis of findings on these specific factors. Results from empirical research under a common, holistic framework will gain a surplus meaning and contribute more effectively to understanding the processes involved in positive development.

Commentary on a Holistic Theoretical Perspective

A common criticism of the holistic theoretical framework for psychological research is that it is too general, self-obvious, or even trivial to serve as a meaningful framework for conducting empirical research. In response to this criticism, the following comments are in order. First, either the basic propositions outlined in this chapter are incorrect, or they reflect the real nature of the phenomena. If they are incorrect, it is up to those who criticize them to argue for their standpoint and demonstrate empirically that they are false. If the propositions are accepted, then they must be taken seriously and should guide the conceptual basis, research strategy, and methodology involved in research on human strengths and positive development. Second, the claim that the integrated, dynamic, complex, and adaptive processes of individual development are accessible to systematic, scientific analysis is based on the fact that these processes are not random; they follow basic principles and proceed within functionally organized structures. These circumstances make developmental processes in general—including processes underlying human strengths and positive development—a natural target for scientific analysis.

One possible reason that a holistic theoretical framework has been avoided is that although developing subsystems operate interdependently, they often function on different spatial and temporal scales and subsume multiple levels of organization. This makes the identification of operating mechanisms and underlying principles extremely difficult. However, this must not deter empirical studies on specific aspects of the processes.

Methodological Implications

Measurement models, the type of data collected, and the methods for data treatment in research on the processes of positive development must match the character of the phenomenon under investigation. The holistic nature of the processes involved formulates specific demands on the application of methodological tools and research strategies. These specifications differ in some important respects from those that are commonly applied. They have been dealt with at length elsewhere (e.g., Bergman, 1998; Magnusson, 1998). Pattern analysis and longitudinal investigation are of special relevance for research on positive development.

Pattern Analysis

To assess human strengths and positive developmental processes, the simultaneous synchronized functioning of factors involved must be considered by studying patterns of operating factors at the appropriate level. Accordingly, methodological tools for the study of individual differences in patterns of data for relevant variables are required. The study on the developmental background of antisocial behavior among men offers a good example (Magnusson, 1996a). In the first stages of that study, standard methods were applied at the group level to study statistical relations among data for each of the three variables (i.e., a lack of concentration, motor restlessness, and sympathetic activity) and data for long-term registered criminal offenses. In terms of an understanding of the development of adult antisocial behavior, these results had limited value. The really interesting results were found only when the patterning of data for the three variables was used to characterize individual trajectories of functioning.

A pattern-analytic strategy should be equally useful for identifying the processes involved in attaining and maintaining human strengths (Bergman, 2002). Subgroups of individuals with distinct profiles of psychological, biological, social, and demographic characteristics relevant to the phenomenon of interest can be identified early in the developmental process and tracked forward in time (e.g., Bergman & Magnusson, 1991). These subgroups can then be linked to the future attainment of positive functioning, and the processes by which individuals in a given subgroup develop strength mechanisms can be evaluated (Gest, Mahoney, & Cairns, 1999; Mahoney, 2000). On this score, it is encouraging to note that person-centered and pattern-oriented approaches to the study of positive functioning have been successfully used (e.g., Singer, Ryff, Carr, & Magee, 1998).

Longitudinal Investigation of Developmental Processes

The existing research on human strengths typically begins by identifying persons who are already functioning positively in some area. This permits the correlates of positive functioning to be identified and provides clues as to how positive functioning may or may not be maintained over time. The conditions that give rise to positive functioning, however, remain largely unaccounted for. This will remain the case until representative samples of persons are followed over time and the emergence of positive functioning is assessed from a developmental perspective (e.g., Horowitz & O'Brien, 1985). Current positive functioning cannot be understood and promoted until its developmental course is investigated and understood. Thus, conducting longitudinal studies of processes that drive the emergence of human strengths is a primary task for research on human strengths and positive development.

Implicit in the character of processes is that they must be followed over time: A picture does not tell the whole story of a process. Cross-sectional studies are necessary for many purposes, including research on positive development, but they must be complemented with longitudinal designs. Over time, developmental changes occur with respect to which factors are involved and operating, the relative role of single factors in the total functioning of the individual, and the simultaneous operation of the factors and pattern of their functional synchronization. Accordingly, central issues such as stability and change and causal mechanisms in individual positive development cannot be investigated without observing the individual over time.

To summarize, the absence of a holistic, developmental approach to studying human strengths leads to measurement models that emphasize isolated variable relationships at one or a few occasions. This has the potential to oversimplify the more complex, interactive processes that operate differently depending on the individual, context, and developmental time frame considered.

Strategic Implications for Research on Positive Development

Cross-Disciplinary Research

One implication of the holistic nature of developmental processes is that research on positive development must go beyond what is represented in traditional developmental psychology. Knowledge from all scientific fields concerned with developmental processes must be integrated and synthesized, including developmental psychology, neuroscience, molecular biology, genetics, physiology, social psychology, sociology, anthropology, and other neighboring disciplines. As a consequence, research progress on human strengths and positive development requires interdisciplinary collaboration. This proposition has led to the establishment of "developmental science" as a domain for scientific inquiry with its own needs for theory, methodology, and research strategy (Magnusson, 2000; Magnusson & Cairns, 1996). The importance of planning research on developmental processes within the framework of developmental science was manifested in the organization of a Nobel Symposium in Stockholm in 1994 under the auspices of the Royal Swedish Academy of Sciences (Magnusson, 1996b).

Cross-Cultural and Cross-Generational Research

Each element of a complex, adaptive process gains meaning from its role in the process to which it belongs. Cultural and historical contexts form critical aspects of the processes involved in positive adaptation. Accordingly, cross-cultural research and cross-generational research are critical to understanding the extent to which principles and mechanisms in positive development can be generalized over time and place.

A characteristic of Western psychological research is ethnocentrism. Too often the results obtained in the context of Western cultures are assumed to hold for the rest of the world. However, these conditions apply, at best, to one sixth of the global population. Because culture forms one critical element in the total processes of positive development, the motivation for cross-cultural research from a holistic perspective is not cross-validation of results obtained in one culture by results obtained in another. Rather, cross-cultural differences provide potentially important information on the role of contextual factors in the holistic, developmental processes of positive development. This conclusion also holds for generalization across generations, as demonstrated in the research presented by Elder and his colleagues (e.g., Elder, Modell, & Parke, 1993).

CONCLUSION

Viewing the individual as an undivided target for analysis in research and application has old roots. However, only in the last part of the 20th century was the holistic model enriched by scientific contributions to the extent that it now offers a solid platform for empirical research (Magnusson, 1999). Included in this enrichment is a sound basis for conducting studies of positive development from a holistic, developmental perspective.

For further constructive discussions about positive development— how its boundaries shall be defined, which research strategies and methodologies will give the most effective answers to relevant questions, and which means are appropriate to promote positive development—it is noteworthy that a holistic framework for research on individual development is part of a broader scientific zeitgeist. It falls in line with strong trends in other scientific disciplines concerned with dynamic, complex processes, including biology, meteorology, ecology, and the life sciences in general. Thus, a holistic perspective for theorizing and empirical research on positive development enables psychology to fall into step with recent promising developments in other disciplines in the life sciences.

REFERENCES

Baltes, P. B., & Baltes, M. M. (1990). Psychological perspectives on successful aging: The model of selective optimization with compensation. In P. B. Baltes & M. M. Baltes (Eds.), *Successful aging: Perspectives from the behavioral sciences* (pp. 1–34). Cambridge, England: Cambridge University Press.

Bandura, A. (1997). *Self-efficacy: The exercise of control.* New York: Freeman.

Bergman, L. R. (1998). A pattern-oriented approach to studying individual development. In R. B. Cairns, L. R. Bergman, & J. Kagan (Eds.), *Methods and models for studying the individual* (pp. 217–241). Thousand Oaks, CA: Sage.

Bergman, L. R. (2002). Studying processes: Some methodological considerations. In L. Pulkkinen & A. Caspi (Eds.), *Paths to successful development. Personality in the life course* (pp. 177–199). Cambridge, England: Cambridge University Press.

Bergman, L. R., & Magnusson, D. (1991). Stability and change in patterns of extrinsic adjustment problems. In D. Magnusson, L. R. Bergman, G. Rudinger, & B. Törestad (Eds.), *Problems and methods in longitudinal research: Stability and change* (pp. 323–346). Cambridge, England: Cambridge University Press.

Carlson, M., Earls, F., & Todd, R. D. (1988). The importance of regressive changes in the development of the nervous system: Towards a neurobiological theory of child development. *Psychiatric Developments, 1,* 1–22.

Cowen, E. L. (1991). In pursuit of wellness. *American Psychologist, 46,* 404–408.

Cowen, E. L. (1994). The enhancement of psychological wellness: Challenges and opportunities. *American Journal of Community Psychology, 22,* 149–179.

Derryberry, D., & Rothbart, M. K. (1997). Reactive and effortful processes in the organization of temperament. *Development and Psychopathology, 9,* 633–652.

Elder, G. H., Jr., Modell, J., & Parke, R. D. (Eds.). (1993). *Children in time and place: Developmental and historical insights.* New York: Cambridge University Press.

Gest, S. D., Mahoney, J. L., & Cairns, R. B. (1999). A developmental approach to prevention research: Configural antecedents of early parenthood. *American Journal of Community Psychology, 27,* 543–565.

Horowitz, F. D., & O'Brien, M. (1985). Perspectives on research and development. In F. D. Horowitz & M. O'Brien (Eds.), *The gifted and talented: Developmental perspectives* (pp. 437–445). Washington, DC: American Psychological Association.

Kahneman, D., Diener, E., & Schwarz, N. (Eds.). (1999). *Well-being: The foundations of hedonic psychology.* New York: Russell Sage Foundation.

Kelso, J. A. (1997). *Dynamic patterns: The self-organization of brain and behavior.* Cambridge, MA: MIT Press.

Luthar, S. S., & Burack, J. A. (2000). Adolescent wellness: In the eye of the beholder? In D. Cicchetti, J. Rappaport, I. Sandler, & R. P. Weissberg (Eds.), *The promotion of wellness in children and adolescents* (pp. 101–132). Washington, DC: CWLA Press.

Luthar, S. S., Cicchetti, D., & Becker, B. (2000). The construct of resilience: A critical evaluation and guidelines for future work. *Child Development, 71,* 543–562.

Magnusson, D. (1990). Personality from an interactional perspective. In L. A. Pervin (Ed.), *Handbook of personality: Theory and research* (pp. 193–222). New York: Guilford Press.

Magnusson, D. (1996a). Interactionism and the person approach in developmental psychology. *European Journal of Adolescent Psychiatry, 5*(Suppl. 1), 18–22.

Magnusson, D. (Ed.). (1996b). *The life-span development of individuals: Behavioral, neurobiological and psychosocial perspectives: A synthesis.* Cambridge, England: Cambridge University Press.

Magnusson, D. (1998). The logic and implications of a person approach. In R. B. Cairns, L. R. Bergman, & J. Kagan (Eds.), *Methods and models for studying the individual* (pp. 33–63). Thousand Oaks, CA: Sage.

Magnusson, D. (1999). Holistic interactionism: A perspective for research on personality development. In L. A. Pervin & O. P. John (Eds.), *Handbook of personality: Theory and research* (2nd ed., pp. 219–247). New York: Guilford Press.

Magnusson, D. (2000). Developmental science. In A. E. Kazdan (Ed.), *Encyclopedia of psychology* (Vol. 3, pp. 24–26). New York: APA & Oxford Press.

Magnusson, D., & Cairns, R. B. (1996). Developmental science: Toward a unified framework. In R. B. Cairns, G. H. Elder, Jr., & J. Costello (Eds.), *Developmental science* (pp. 7–30). New York: Cambridge University Press.

Magnusson, D., & Stattin, H. (1998). Person–context interaction theories. In W. Damon & R. M. Lerner (Eds.), *Handbook of child psychology. Vol. 1: Theoretical models of human development* (pp. 685–759). New York: Wiley.

Mahoney, J. L. (2000). Participation in school extracurricular activities as a moderator in the development of antisocial patterns. *Child Development, 71*, 502–516.

Mahoney, J. L., & Bergman, L. R. (2002). Conceptual and methodological considerations in a developmental approach to the study of positive adaptation. *Journal of Applied Developmental Psychology, 23*, 195–217.

Mayr, E. (1976). *Evolution and the diversity of life.* Cambridge, MA: Harvard University Press.

Ryff, C. D., & Singer, B. (1998). The contours of positive human health. *Psychological Inquiry, 9*, 1–28.

Schore, A. N. (1997). Early organization of the non-linear right brain and development of a predisposition to psychiatric disoders. *Development and Psychopathology, 9*, 595–631.

Seligman, M. E. P., & Csikszentmihalyi, M. (2000). Positive psychology: An introduction. *American Psychologist, 55*, 5–14.

Singer, B., Ryff, C. D., Carr, D., & Magee, W. J. (1998). Linking life histories and mental health: A person-centered strategy. *Sociological Methodology, 28*, 1–51.

Spear, L. P. (2000). Neurobiological changes in adolescence. *Current Directions in Psychological Science, 9*, 111–114.

Stattin, H., & Magnusson, D. (1990). Pubertal maturation in female development. *Paths through life* (Vol. 2). Hillsdale, NJ: Erlbaum.

Strayhorn, J. M. (1988). *The competent child: An approach to psychotherapy and preventive mental health.* New York: Guilford Press.

Stryker, M. P. (1994). Precise development from imprecise rule. *Science, 263*, 1244–1245.

Thelen, E. (1989). Self-organization in developmental processes: Can systems approaches work? In M. R. Gunnar & E. Thelen (Eds.), *Systems and development* (pp. 77–117). Hillsdale, NJ: Erlbaum.

Watson, J. B. (1913). Psychology as the behaviorist views it. *Psychological Review, 20*, 158–177.

Weiner, H. (1989). The dynamics of the organism: Implications of recent biological thought for psychosomatic theory and research. *Psychosomatic Medicine, 51*, 608–635.

17

HARNESSING WILLPOWER AND SOCIOEMOTIONAL INTELLIGENCE TO ENHANCE HUMAN AGENCY AND POTENTIAL

WALTER MISCHEL AND RODOLFO MENDOZA-DENTON

The field of psychology has long been burdened by the baggage of disease and trait models of human vulnerability, generating sad catalogs of deficits, pathologies, and constraints that undermine the quality and possibilities of life. The psychology of human strengths promises an exciting alternative to this heritage—more than a welcome breath of optimism, it invites ways of thinking about the science that focus on the potential for human agency and freedom. But the psychology of human strengths also risks becoming little more than a fashionable form of advocacy for the power of positive thinking unless it pursues its goals within a rigorous framework and avoids a naïve denial of the constraints and tragedies that also characterize the human condition.

Accordingly, our focus in this chapter is on the limited but quintessentially human quality that enables personal agency in the face of temp-

Preparation of this article was supported by grant MH39349 from the National Institute of Mental Health.

tation and vulnerability, allowing persons to exert control and enhance their quality of life—at least sometimes. What enables, for example, the angry parent to be patient with a difficult child and provide a productive lesson, rather than allow the situation to deteriorate into an angry tirade? What are the mechanisms through which the recovering alcoholic can maintain a self-imposed resolution to stay clean, warding off the temptation to have another drink? Our goal is to demystify the essentials of willpower and socioemotional intelligence so that the strategies that underlie them can be harnessed in the service of self-direction and the enhancement of quality of life. The aim is to understand how people, while remaining capable of great rashness, also become able to deal with tasks that require them to delay gratification, exercise self-control, and utilize socioemotional intelligence for the sake of their long-term goals and well-being.

OVERCOMING "STIMULUS CONTROL"

Much of psychology in the past century viewed the person as pushed by impulses and conflicts from within (as in Freudian theory) or as pulled by rewards and incentives from external sources that control behavior (as in classic behaviorism). These traditions view people as victims either of their unfortunate biographies and socialization histories or of the constraints imposed by their DNA and the pressures of the situational forces in their lives. The influence of internal needs and external rewards on behavior and the importance of both our genes and our social worlds have been convincingly and repeatedly documented (Bargh, 1996, 1997; Plomin, DeFries, McClearn, & Rutter, 1997). But those findings coexist with evidence that people can transform external stimulus conditions and, by changing the ways they represent those stimuli cognitively, overcome their power to activate automatic, reflexive reactions.

From Hot-System Activation to Cool-System Mediation

Recognizing the human capacity for impulsivity as well as control, and consistent with diverse areas of research on self-regulation, a framework has been proposed that distinguishes between a "cool" or "know" system, and a "hot" or "go" system (Metcalfe & Mischel, 1999). The cool system is attuned to the informational and spatial aspects of stimuli and has the potential of generating rational, planned, and strategic behavior. It is characterized as cognitive rather than emotional, complex rather than simple, and reflective rather than reflexive. The hot system, on the other hand, is an emotional system specialized for quick reactions to strong, emotion-provoking stimuli that trigger pleasure and pain. The hot system elicits impulsive reactions to appetitive and sexual stimuli and the automatic enactment of defensive reactions when faced with threatening and fear-inducing stimuli (Metcalfe & Jacobs, 1996). Once activated, hot system processing triggers rapid action. As such, the hot system is largely under "stimulus control."

Whether the challenge is to resist eating the steaming slice of pizza when one is on a diet, to continue working on a frustrating and seemingly interminable project, or to practice safe sex despite strong situational inducements, volition and willpower require a person to effectively regulate the activation of the hot and cool systems in the service of long-term goals. How is the regulation of these systems—quite literally a self-regulation—achieved?

The ancient Greeks attributed failures in self-regulation to a character trait, *akrasia*, or deficiency of the will. In the same vein, psychology has traditionally invoked traits such as ego control or conscientiousness to describe how people manage to overcome the power of stimuli to elicit automatic reactions. Although these classifications may accurately describe differences among individuals in self-regulatory strength or capacity, they are not any more informative now than they were 2,500 years ago regarding the processes involved in this strength. Understanding these processes brings social science one step closer to harnessing the human potential to overcome the myriad of adverse conditions that can lead to health and adjustment problems, including substance abuse and addiction, eating disorders and failure to follow one's diet, and procrastination and pathological gambling.

A Paradigm for the Study of Self-Regulatory Processes

Initial insights into self-regulatory processes came from a series of studies on children's ability and willingness to delay gratification (Mischel, Cantor, & Feldman, 1996; Mischel, Shoda, & Rodriguez, 1989), a quality that appears to be central for the development of socioemotional intelligence and effective behavior over the life span (Mischel et al., 1996). In the delay-of-gratification paradigm (Mischel, 1974), popularly referred to as the "marshmallow test" (Goleman, 1995), a young child is shown a treat that he or she likes, for example, marshmallows or pretzel sticks. A dilemma is presented: wait until the experimenter returns and get two of the desired treats, or, alternatively, ring a bell and the experimenter will come back immediately—but then only one treat will be obtained. The child clearly prefers the larger outcome and commits himself or herself to wait for it. The child begins to wait for the experimenter to return to the room, but the delay soon becomes very difficult due to the growing temptation of the immediately available treat. For the young child this type of conflict is utterly real and involving and has yielded a route to examining the underlying processes systematically.

The Role of Attention Control

One of the most striking findings from the delay of gratification studies is that the same children who are unable to wait even a minute when left to their own devices are able to wait for almost 20 minutes when the situation is represented or framed in different terms or when the conditions are changed even in seemingly minor ways. Research shows that even young children can mentally "transform" the delay situation in ways that can dramatically enhance or undermine their own self-imposed waiting goal. For example, thinking about the hot, consummatory aspects of the rewards, such as the crunchiness of the pretzels or the chewiness of the marshmallows, led children to wait only for about 5 minutes, whereas thinking about their cool, abstract, and informational qualities (i.e., the appearance of the pretzels as little logs or of the marshmallows as puffy clouds) increased delay time to 13 minutes (Mischel, 1974; Mischel & Baker, 1975). Thus, the way the child represented the same stimuli mentally during the delay period profoundly transformed the impact of the stimuli and potentially enabled the child to effectively exert control over powerful temptations in order to pursue and attain a more valuable but distant goal (Moore, Mischel, & Zeiss, 1976; Mischel & Moore, 1973; Mischel et al., 1996).

As any dieter facing a sweet-smelling chocolate cake can attest, however, sometimes it can be very difficult to effectively focus on the abstract, informational, or cognitive aspects of particularly hot stimuli for very long. In such cases, a more effective cooling strategy seems to involve focusing one's attention away from the stimulus itself. Thus, the dieter might more successfully avoid succumbing to the chocolate cake not by transforming it mentally, but instead by putting it out of sight, leaving the kitchen, and going to watch a movie. Indeed, in studies in which children were given toys that they could play with while they waited, delay time was considerably longer than for children who were instructed to think about the rewards themselves. Moreover, the extent of the human potential for volition is suggested by the fact that the distraction can occur solely in the mind: When children were cued to think about fun thoughts ("If you want to, while you're waiting, you can think about Mommy pushing you on a swing") rather than the rewards, delay time was as long as when children were given actual toys to play with (Mischel, Ebbesen, & Zeiss, 1972).

Agency and Volition Through the Life Span

Do the results from the playroom—with cookies, marshmallows, and pretzels—speak to the real dilemmas of life? In fact, the same research program revealed stable individual differences in the ability to overcome stimulus control pressures in the purposeful pursuit of long-term goals. For example, those 4-year-old children who delayed longer became more socially and cognitively competent adolescents, also achieving higher levels of scholastic performance as reflected in their SAT verbal and quantitative scores. In a second follow-up, these children also were rated by their parents as more planful, persistent, and able to cope with stress (Mischel, Shoda, & Peake, 1988; Shoda, Mischel, & Peake, 1990). These long-term relations might be read—or misread—by some as supporting the view that an appreciable degree of destiny becomes visible early in life and reflects inborn immutable traits. However, research on delay of gratification also makes clear that specific mental operations can make self-regulation difficult or easy: The same child who cannot delay for even a minute can wait or work successfully for goal attainment by thinking differently about the situation. Such reframing and reconstrual can be activated by relatively simple cues and self-instructions (Mischel et al., 1996).

OVERCOMING THE COSTS AND CONSEQUENCES OF CHRONIC PERSONAL VULNERABILITIES

People differ characteristically in the particular "trigger" features that typically elicit hot, automatic, impulsive responses in them. There is evidence to suggest that strategic attention control can protect individuals against personal vulnerabilities involving tendencies to react in extreme and maladaptive ways. Recently, we examined the role of preschool delay of gratification in buffering individuals in adulthood against the maladaptive outcomes associated with *rejection sensitivity*, a cognitive–affective processing disposition to anxiously expect, readily perceive, and intensely react to rejection (Downey & Feldman, 1996; Feldman & Downey, 1994).

Rejection sensitive people may see even innocent or ambiguous behavior from a significant other as intentional rejection, which activates further thoughts and feelings of rejection (e.g., "She doesn't love me") and fears of betrayal and abandonment. In turn, the person's scripts for coercive or controlling behaviors may become activated, leading to angry, hostile, and even abusive reactions. Over time such hostility is likely to lead to actual rejection even when there was none before, further strengthening the cycle that characterizes this dynamic. Research has linked this vulnerability to a variety of maladaptive outcomes, including lower self-esteem and depression (Ayduk, Downey, & Kim, 2001), reactive hostility (Ayduk, Downey, Testa, Yen, & Shoda, 1999; Downey, Feldman, & Ayduk, 2000), and the early dissolution of close relationships (Downey, Freitas, Michealis, & Khouri, 1998).

Attention Control as a Protective Factor Against Rejection Sensitivity

In terms of basic mechanisms, the self-regulatory task for the rejection sensitive person may be similar to that of the 4-year-old waiting for marshmallows. In both cases the task involves the inhibition of reflexive, hot reactions by accessing cool representations and information processing. Strategies such as focusing attention away from the silent phone when expecting a romantic partner to call or reconstruing the partner's inability to spend the evening together as his or her being busy rather than as a sign of intentional rejection can help rejection sensitive individuals exert volition when their goals are to prevent themselves from impulsively lashing out and to maintain and uphold their romantic relationships constructively.

Theoretically, then, the attentional processes that enable people to delay gratification and inhibit impulsive reactions in the face of temptation may also help protect them from their own tendencies to react maladaptively in situations that activate their rejection concerns (Lang, Bradley, & Cuthbert, 1990; Metcalfe & Mischel, 1999). There is now reason to think that if individuals have cooling strategies available to them, they can use these as protective buffers against their own personal vulnerabilities.

Individuals who have similar levels of rejection expectations but who differ in the ease with which they access cooling strategies under high-stress conditions were recently compared on many measures of personal strength and adaptive life outcomes over the course of development. Across a variety of age groups and populations, rejection-sensitive individuals who were unable to access cooling strategies in the face of their hot vulnerability were more susceptible to a host of maladaptive outcomes, including low self-esteem, depression, and aggression, as well as lower educational levels and higher drug use. By contrast, vulnerable individuals who were able to access effective cooling strategies were better protected against their own maladaptive behavioral tendencies and on outcome measures resembled individuals without the vulnerability (Ayduk et al., 2000).

Thus, people need not become victims of their biographies. These findings underscore Kelly's (1955) principle of "constructive alternativism," which emphasized the individual's own power to alter his or her circumstances through reframing and reconstruing events. People's ability to flexibly encode, transform, and interpret stimuli and events can serve as a key source of human strength to optimize their potential for self-realization and positivity.

Emotional Regulation Through Interactionist Self-Encoding

Even the "self" can be construed in alternative ways in the service of agency and well-being. Importantly, this can be done honestly, without self-deception or the negation of adverse experiences. For example, following setbacks, encoding the self in unconditional trait terms (e.g., "I'm a failure") can amplify depressive responses to stressful experiences, leading the individual to generalize negative outcomes to the self as a whole and eliciting maladaptive coping patterns (e.g., Abramson, Metalsky, & Alloy, 1989; Mueller & Dweck, 1998). Conversely, discriminative encodings of the self that highlight the interaction and relationship between behavior and the situations or conditions to which it is bound (e.g., "I'm a failure when I wait until the last minute to study") can help bind the experience to its context (Chiu, Hong, Mischel, & Shoda, 1995). This, in turn, can attenuate the tendency to catastrophize failure—and conversely to glorify successes—beyond the contexts to which they apply. Consequently, such interactionist encoding may protect people against the emotional swings and distresses that can readily diminish the quality of life (Linville, 1985, 1987).

In a series of recent studies testing this idea (Mendoza-Denton, Ayduk, Mischel, Shoda, & Testa, 2001), college students were asked to listen to and to deeply imagine themselves as protagonists in a series of age-relevant failure or success experiences. Following each scenario, half of the participants encoded the self in unconditional terms by completing the sentence "I'm a _____." The other half of the participants were induced to encode the self in interactionist terms by completing the sentence "I'm a _____ when _____." The results showed that students in the interactionist encoding condition—regardless of whether they had imagined themselves succeeding or failing—subsequently felt less extreme affect than students who had encoded themselves in unconditional terms. These findings provide support for a causal role of interactionist self-encoding in helping people maintain an even keel and in buffering them against affective swings.

Knowledge of Self in the Service of Human Potential

Recognizing one's own patterns of stable behavioral variability across situations can empower individuals by allowing them to recognize the things they may be doing—or could be doing differently—to lead to desired outcomes. A student who stays up all night writing a term paper and then gets a failing grade is in a better position to improve his or her grade if he or she encodes the situation as "I'm a failure when I try to write term papers the night before" than if he or she encodes the situation as "I'm a failure." Just as importantly, the student who encodes the self after receiving a high grade as "I'm a great student when I keep up with the reading" also may be in a better position to know the strategy required to repeat this desired outcome than a student who encodes a similar event simply as "I'm a great student."

Attention to the close interplay between the psychological features of situations and the characteristic patterns of behavior that they tend to activate within oneself may additionally provide a window into self-awareness of one's particular "trouble spots." For example, the rejection-sensitive person who can discriminatively encode his or her maladaptive behavior in relation to its specific trigger features (e.g., "I become hostile when I feel like my partner is ignoring me") may subsequently be able to develop effective coping strategies, such as the enactment of implementation plans, in the presence of those trigger features (Gollwitzer, 1999). Implementation plans specify where, when, and how to pursue a goal intention by linking a specific situation to a specific response (e.g., "when I feel hurt, I should go running to cool down"); such plans facilitate the inhibition of unwanted habitual responses as well as resistance to temptation (Gollwitzer & Brandstätter, 1997; Gollwitzer & Schaal, 1998).

DEMYSTIFYING THE PRELIMINARIES UNDERLYING HUMAN STRENGTHS

A century ago, the philosopher and psychologist William James (1890/1981) opened his discussion on the will with the following words:

> Desire, wish, will are states of mind which everyone knows and which no definition can make plainer. . . . If with the desire there goes a sense that attainment is not possible we simply *wish*; but if we believe the end is in our power, we *will* that the desired feeling, having, or doing shall be real . . . and real it presently becomes, either immediately upon the willing or after certain preliminaries have been fulfilled. (p. 486)

James' analysis foreshadowed much of what proved to be the research agenda on the topic of human strengths for the next 100 years—and much that may still characterize that agenda for the new century. In differentiating "wish" from "will" by whether or not one believes the end is in one's power, James recognized the significance of perceptions of control and of self-efficacy that have rejuvenated interest in basic self-regulatory processes and indeed in the centrality of the construct of self (e.g., Bandura, 1986; Cantor & Kihlstrom, 1987; Dweck, 1999; Markus & Nurius, 1986; Mischel & Shoda, 1995). He also anticipated what would become the study of self-regulatory strategies and socioemotional intelligence in stressing that often people can realize their intentions only after having fulfilled certain "preliminaries." In this chapter we have attempted to clarify and demystify one of those preliminaries by describing how individuals can control hot reactions and instead engage in strategic cool information processing.

Willpower is often construed as stoic self-denial in the service of a distant goal, a capacity to deliberately endure and suffer while "biting the bullet." But a less heroic approach, in which one is able to support one's self-regulatory effort through distractions and cooling strategies that help one achieve a goal without becoming too frustrated or discouraged, seems to characterize successful goal-directed delay and effective realization of what one values. Rather than strive to be a stoic during such goal pursuit, the individual can convert an aversive delay situation into a more manageable one through strategic construal, thought, and action that focus attention on the cooling features of the stimuli. And in the pursuit of long-term goals requiring sustained self-regulatory effort, such as earning a graduate degree or becoming a better athlete, the ability to encode setbacks and successes in relation to the contexts in which they unfold can serve as a buffer against overly emotional, hot reactions, potentially preventing people from becoming derailed and helping them achieve their goals.

IMPLICATIONS FOR A POSITIVE PSYCHOLOGY

Humans are not simply "driven" organisms: Although people may not always be able to change the course of events, they can construe and conceptualize them differently and more constructively, viewing them in ways that can enhance the possibility of freedom, agency, and volition, as Kelly (1955) recognized long ago. Yet Kelly also soberly noted that life events often play out in negative, distressing, and even calamitous ways. The potential for human strengths lies not in turning away and ignoring negative events, but in reconstruing them in ways that are more constructive, creative, and adaptive. A psychology of human strengths—however positive in its emphasis—must recognize the tragedies and pitfalls of human existence, even if mostly to identify the potential to overcome them.

As Seligman and Czikszentmihalyi (2000) recently noted, positive psychology is an idea with a long history, but previous attempts have failed to take root within psychology. In our view, the prospects of the current effort depend on psychology's ability to move beyond a rosy emphasis on the positive, which risks becoming a "spin" more than a deep and useful perspective on human nature. The challenge will be to illuminate those psychological processes that enable positive functioning, strength, and well-being. The examples presented in this chapter are merely illustrative of some of these processes.

REFERENCES

Abramson, L. Y., Metalsky, G. I., & Alloy, L. B. (1989). Hopelessness-depression: A theory-based subtype of depression. *Psychological Review, 96,* 358–372.

Ayduk, O., Downey, G., & Kim, M. (2001). Rejection sensitivity and depressive symptoms in women. *Personality and Social Psychology Bulletin, 27,* 868–877.

Ayduk, O., Downey, G., Testa, A., Yen, Y., & Shoda, Y. (1999). Does rejection elicit hostility in high rejection sensitive women? *Social Cognition, 17,* 245–271.

Ayduk, O., Mendoza-Denton, R., Mischel, W., Downey, G., Peake, P., & Rodriguez, M. (2000). Regulating the interpersonal self: Strategic self-regulation for coping with rejection sensitivity. *Journal of Personality and Social Psychology, 79,* 776–792.

Bandura, A. (1986). *Social foundations of thought and action: A social cognitive theory.* Englewood Cliffs, NJ: Prentice Hall.

Bargh, J. A. (1996). Principles of automaticity. In E. T. Higgins & A. W. Kruglanski (Eds.), *Social psychology: Handbook of basic principles* (pp. 169–183). New York: Guilford Press.

Bargh, J. A. (1997). The automaticity of everyday life. In R. S. Wyer (Ed.), *Advances in social cognition* (Vol. 10, pp. 1–61). Mahwah, NJ: Erlbaum.

Cantor, N., & Kihlstrom, J. F. (1987). *Personality and social intelligence.* Englewood Cliffs, NJ: Prentice Hall.

Chiu, C., Hong, Y., Mischel, W., & Shoda, Y. (1995). Discriminative facility in social competence: Conditional versus dispositional encoding and monitoring-blunting of information. *Social Cognition, 13,* 49–70.

Downey, G., & Feldman, S. (1996). Implications of rejection sensitivity for intimate relationships. *Journal of Personality and Social Psychology, 70,* 1327–1343.

Downey, G., Feldman, S., & Ayduk, O. (2000). Rejection sensitivity and male violence in romantic relationships. *Personal Relationships, 7,* 45–61.

Downey, G., Freitas, A. L., Michealis, B., & Khouri, H. (1998). The self-fulfilling prophecy in close relationships: Rejection sensitivity and rejection by romantic partners. *Journal of Personality and Social Psychology, 75,* 545–560.

Dweck, C. (1999). *Self-theories: Their role in motivation, personality, and development.* Philadelphia: Psychology Press/Taylor and Francis.

Feldman, S., & Downey, G. (1994). Rejection sensitivity as a mediator of the impact of childhood exposure to family violence on adult attachment behavior. *Development and Psychopathology, 6,* 231–247.

Goleman, D. (1995). *Emotional intelligence.* New York: Bantam Books.

Gollwitzer, P. M. (1999). Implementation intentions: Strong effects of simple plans. *American Psychologist, 54,* 493–503.

Gollwitzer, P. M., & Brandstätter, V. (1997). Implementation intentions and effective goal pursuit. *Journal of Personality and Social Psychology, 73,* 186–199.

Gollwitzer, P. M., & Schaal, B. (1998). Metacognition in action: The importance of implementation intentions. *Personality and Social Psychology Review, 2,* 124–136.

James, W. (1981). *The principles of psychology* (Vol. 2). Cambridge, MA: Harvard University Press. [Original work published 1890]

Kelly, G. A. (1955). A theory of personality: The psychology of personal constructs. New York: Norton.

Lang, P. J., Bradley, M. M., & Cuthbert, B. N. (1990). Emotion, attention, and the startle reflex. Psychological Review, 97, 377–395.

Linville, P. W. (1985). Self-complexity and affective extremity: Don't put all of your eggs in one cognitive basket. Social Cognition, 3, 94–120.

Linville, P. W. (1987). Self-complexity as a cognitive buffer against stress-related illness and depression. Journal of Personality and Social Psychology, 52, 663–676.

Markus, H., & Nurius, P. (1986). Possible selves. American Psychologist, 41, 954–969.

Mendoza-Denton, R., Ayduk, O., Mischel, W., Shoda, Y., & Testa, A. (2001). Person × situation interactionism in self-encoding (I am ... when ...): Implications for affect regulation and social information processing. Journal of Personality and Social Psychology, 80, 533–544.

Metcalfe, J., & Jacobs, W. J. (1996). A "hot-system/cool-system" view of memory under stress. PTSD Research Quarterly, 7, 1–6.

Metcalfe, J., & Mischel, W. (1999). A hot/cool system analysis of delay of gratification: Dynamics of willpower. Psychological Review, 106, 3–19.

Mischel, W. (1974). Processes in delay of gratification. In L. Berkowitz (Ed.), Advances in experimental social psychology (Vol. 7, pp. 249–292). New York: Academic Press.

Mischel, W., & Baker, N. (1975). Cognitive appraisals and transformations in delay behavior. Journal of Personality and Social Psychology, 31, 254–261.

Mischel, W., Cantor, N., & Feldman, S. (1996). Principles of self-regulation: The nature of willpower and self-control. In E. T. Higgins & A. W. Kruglanski (Eds.), Social psychology: Handbook of basic principles (pp. 329–360). New York: Guilford Press.

Mischel, W., Ebbesen, E. B., & Zeiss, A. (1972). Cognitive and attentional mechanisms in delay of gratification. Journal of Personality and Social Psychology, 21, 204–218.

Mischel, W., & Moore, B. (1973). Effects of attention to symbolically-presented rewards on self-control. Journal of Personality and Social Psychology, 28, 172–179.

Mischel, W., & Shoda, Y. (1995). A cognitive-affective system theory of personality: Reconceptualizing situations, dispositions, dynamics and invariance in personality structure. Psychological Review, 102, 246–268.

Mischel, W., Shoda, Y., & Peake, P. (1988). The nature of adolescent competencies predicted by preschool delay of gratification. Journal of Personality and Social Psychology, 54, 687–696.

Mischel, W., Shoda, Y., & Rodriguez, M. L. (1989). Delay of gratification in children. Science, 244, 933–938.

Moore, B., Mischel, W., & Zeiss, A. (1976). Comparative effects of the reward stimulus and its cognitive representation in voluntary delay. *Journal of Personality and Social Psychology, 34,* 419–424.

Mueller, C. M., & Dweck, C. S. (1998). Praise for intelligence can undermine children's motivation and performance. *Journal of Personality and Social Psychology, 75,* 33–52.

Plomin, R., DeFries, J. C., McClearn, G. E., & Rutter, M. (1997). *Behavioral genetics* (3rd ed.). New York: W. H. Freeman.

Seligman, M. E. P., & Csikszentmihalyi, M. (2000). Positive psychology: An introduction. *American Psychologist, 55,* 5–14.

Shoda, Y., Mischel, W., & Peake, P. (1990). Predicting adolescent cognitive and self-regulatory competencies from preschool delay of gratification: Identifying diagnostic conditions. *Developmental Psychology, 26,* 978–986.

18

THE MOTIVATIONAL SOURCES OF CREATIVITY AS VIEWED FROM THE PARADIGM OF POSITIVE PSYCHOLOGY

JEANNE NAKAMURA AND MIHALY CSIKSZENTMIHALYI

Appearing at the dawn of a new paradigm, this volume affords a chance to reflect about the goals of the emerging psychology of strengths, its promise, and its limits. With Seligman, Csikszentmihalyi elsewhere has discussed psychology's long neglect of positive functioning and identified some of the key problems that a positive psychology ought to address in the coming years (Seligman & Csikszentmihalyi, 2000). In the present chapter, we draw on work on optimal experience and development, in particular work on creativity, to illustrate the promise of a strengths approach.

Positive psychology extends an umbrella over multiple existing, emerging, and envisioned programs of research. Its current core consists in the study of particular strengths or dimensions of positive functioning: optimism, hope, resilience, wisdom, happiness—in our case, creativity,

The Creativity in Later Life study was generously supported by the Spencer Foundation.

intrinsic motivation, flow. But beyond specific research directions, the emerging paradigm enriches the discipline by foregrounding a different perspective from the one most psychologists are in the habit of using.

The topic of creativity's motivational underpinnings provides an excellent example of such a shift in perspective. From Freud's earliest writings on the subject, it has been tacitly accepted that the single-minded dedication of such geniuses as Leonardo or Michelangelo must be the result of the displacement of repressed needs. For creativity, as in most areas of human behavior, a deficit was the prime mover, and everything that needed to be explained had to be reduced and assimilated to it. The deficit model of creativity has added necessary depth to the conventional view of behavior and has helped illuminate human motivations with greater complexity. At the same time, as the sole paradigm it runs the risk of flattening the field's perspective once again, substituting a one-dimensional explanatory framework based on deficit for the earlier and equally one-dimensional Victorian view of complacent rationalism.

Creativity, or the process by which new ideas, objects, or processes are introduced into the evolution of culture (Csikszentmihalyi, 1992, 1996; Simonton, 1984), is in large part a function of a specific kind of motivation. Even more than particular cognitive abilities, a set of motivational attributes—childlike curiosity, intrinsic interest, perseverance bordering on obsession—seem to set individuals who change the culture apart from the rest of humankind. Already in one of the earliest studies of creative geniuses, Cox (1926) concluded that in predicting which of two young people would make a creative contribution, one who was intellectually brilliant but not very motivated and another who was less brilliant but more motivated, the better bet would be on the latter person. But what are the sources of this motivation? It is in answering this question that positive psychology can provide a different and complementary account from traditional interpretations, which often stress the morbidly pathological sources of the motivation that leads to creativity.

To illustrate what difference it makes to use one or the other paradigm, it may be useful to apply the deficit and strengths perspectives to a recent biographical account of a creative individual. This is not intended to be a weighing of the two perspectives' relative merits; rather, we are interested in juxtaposing them in order to understand the phenomenon of creativity better. The particulars may be of interest to researchers studying creativity or intrinsic motivation; more generally, however, it serves as an exploration into whether, and how, the strengths perspective on a phenomenon broadens understanding as a whole.

The analysis was stimulated by a recent article in *The Atlantic Monthly* entitled "Fame: The Power and Cost of a Fantasy" by psychotherapist Sue Erikson Bloland (1999). She is the late Erik Erikson's daughter and, like her father, a gifted writer. The article is an eloquent, personal discussion of the costs of celebrity, which was inspired by and describes the case of her father on the one hand and those around him on the other. In an account embraced by others (e.g., Eckersley, 2000), Bloland analyzed the phenomenon of fame and the idealization of the famous in deficit terms, as pathologies of narcissism. As the child of a celebrity, she discussed with particular clarity the collateral damage to family members of individuals caught up in the pursuit of fame.

Briefly, Bloland argued that the pursuit of fame is "a defense against shame" (1999, p. 55). It is an attempt to overcome "a sense that the self is deeply flawed or deficient" through the particular means—destined to fail —of gaining from others the admiring attention that the parents did not adequately or appropriately provide (p. 55). An individual's full development of significant talent is "always" energized by this drive to become famous.

Bloland (1999) viewed others' idealization and pursuit of the celebrated individual through the lens of deficit as well: "The purpose of setting up figures who seem superpowerful, infinitely wise or infinitely kind, larger than life itself, is to make us feel safe" (p. 62). Other people's relationships to a celebrated individual are energized by their need to find a hero and thereby deny death and helplessness (Becker, 1973).

Bloland's analysis of her father's pursuit of fame consistently located motive force in deficit and in human relationships. Relationships with others are the cause of deficits (in Erikson's case, abandonment by the father and narcissistic needs of the mother), the place where the costs of these deficits are felt (for Erikson, in his relationships with Bloland and his other children), the arena in which one tries to overcome them (by winning attention and admiration), and the only sphere where true repair of self-esteem can occur (by revealing feelings of shame and inadequacy to another person and finding that one can still be accepted).

CREATIVE ACCOMPLISHMENT AND ITS MOTIVATION

Deficit-Based Motivations

Bloland's (1999) article, with its emphasis on deficit and human relationships, remains almost entirely silent about the interest in and enjoyment of the cultural and natural worlds, which are such powerful motives in any creative process. It is likely that the single-minded pursuit of fame has a basis in narcissistic deficit. In addition, we defer to Bloland's insight into her father's inner life when she ascribes to him a lack of self-confidence and, rooted in that deficit, a profound hunger for recognition. Human motivation is complex, however; it is rarely an either-or proposition. Research on accomplished creators (Csikszentmihalyi, 1996) leads us to question her analysis of Erikson's motivations, and more importantly her generalization beyond them, on two points: (a) her downplaying of his enjoyment of the work process and (b) her silence about the content of his work, meaning the specific questions with which he grappled throughout his lifetime as a psychologist.

In her one passing allusion to Erikson's subjective experience of the work itself, Bloland (1999) observed that the exercise of skills at a high level is a source of joy. A large body of research has documented the intense enjoyment found in demanding activities and has shown that it is intrinsically motivating—no other reason is needed to engage in activities that produce it (Csikszentmihalyi, 1975/2000; Deci, 1975). Through the lens of deficit, however, this is viewed as merely a gratifying by-product of the pursuit of fame and is quickly passed by in Bloland's analysis:

> Of course, there is enormous gratification in exercising one's talents for their own sake—a joy in one's mastery of any highly skilled activity. But I would suggest that *extraordinary talent is characteristically fueled by a desperate longing for human connection.* (Bloland, 1999, p. 58, italics added)

Thus, Erikson's work is reduced to a defense, a futile effort at repairing early deficits. This reductionism characterizes an established tradition within the study of creativity (for a discussion, see Ochse, 1990). The tradition is often but not exclusively identified with psychoanalytic psychology, where it reaches back to Freud's pathographies. It describes a troubled individual whose motivation for creative work is fundamentally negative and for whom the work lacks transformative power. It ignores the psychoanalytic notion of healthy narcissism that exists within the very paradigm drawn on by Bloland.

It is particularly problematic to pathologize creative accomplishment in general, as Bloland does when she extends the argument beyond the specific case of her father:

> Family friends learned to treat with good humor his disappearances from picnics or parties to find a quiet place where he could read or write. His brilliance was coupled with an overwhelming need to achieve. *I suspect that the full realization of great talent is always fueled by such an intense need. And what, exactly, is the source of this drive? An early experience of shame* so overwhelming to the sense of self that to become someone extraordinary seems the only way to defend against it. (Bloland, 1999, p. 55, italics added)

Passion for the Work

Erikson's behavior at family gatherings sounds strikingly similar to stories we heard many times in interviews with eminent older creators. Such behavior, however, can be interpreted very differently in the context of those accomplished individuals' lives. The emphasis in such accounts was on the passion for the work itself, one of two positive motivations that are evident from a strengths perspective on creativity. For example, the 83-year-old inventor Jack Rabinow invents because it's "a lot of fun" and selects problems because they "move" him. He struggled to answer our question about how he has balanced work and family life:

> I remember once at one of our parties here, we had a big party and Gladys [his wife] said that Jack sometimes walks to a different drummer. In other words, he's so involved in an idea he's working on, he's so carried away, that he is all by himself. He's not listening to what anybody says. This sometimes happens. That you're so—you've got a new idea and you feel that it's very good, and you're so involved that you're not paying attention to anybody. And you tend to drift away from people.... I'm social, I like people, I like to tell jokes, I like to go to theater. But it's probably true that there are times when Gladys would have liked me to pay more attention to her and to the family than I do.... I love Gladys and I love my children. But it could be that I sometimes am in a different world ... there's not much you can do about it. I'm sure this is true of most people who love their job. That they can be carried away. (Creativity in Later Life Project, 1993)

Another example involves the tumor biologist George Klein. Once he described the feeling he gets when working at the bench in his lab as "the happiness of a deer running through a meadow." But he violently dislikes small talk, parties, and idle social encounters. One evening in the early 1970s, everyone in the lab at the Karolinska Institute in Stockholm went to a traditional celebration of Midsummer's Eve, involving a party that lasts till dawn. Horrified at the thought of having to waste all that time, Klein excused himself by telling his colleagues that a shipment of Burkett's lymphoma cultures had just arrived by plane from South Africa, and he had to process them before they spoiled. So he stayed in the laboratory alone to carry out the delicate procedures that previously had been performed by his assistants. He found that he was completely inept at this task and ruined all the specimens. This is how he described the conclusion of that day:

> I remained into the wee hours studying tube after tube and could only confirm that everything was spoiled. At four in the morning I admitted total defeat and gave up. I was in a total state of euphoria. While driving home that bright Midsummer's morning, I wondered how I could be so happy after having destroyed the excellent samples. The answer was obvious: I had been excused from participating in the Midsummer's dance. (Klein, 1990, p. 154)

Should we consider the attitude decried by Bloland, and exemplified by many creative individuals, "antisocial," "selfish," and "defensive"? Why do we ascribe a higher moral purpose to being bored than to being happy?

And are the fruits of creativity to be accounted for less than satisfying the emotional needs of others?

Focusing on narcissistic pathology can create a susceptibility to interpreting as deficit-based and extrinsically motivated an undertaking that instead arises from intrinsic interest and coexists with positive human relationships. Within psychoanalytic psychology, White (1959) and others —including Erik Erikson himself—have written in this vein about ego processes, and Kohut (1966) has analyzed creativity as a positive transformation of narcissism. Research on flow, interest, and intrinsic motivation has addressed the creator's enjoyable absorption in the work itself (Collins & Amabile, 1999; Csikszentmihalyi, 1996). Put more generally, the strengths perspective perceives the creator's strivings in terms of proactive, constructivist tendencies of the organism (cf. Brandstädter, 1998) rather than reaction, coping, and repair.

Meaningful Purpose

A meaningful purpose is a second possible positive motivation for engaging a domain. Lifelong vocations are often based on goals formulated to make sense of an experienced threat or stress (Csikszentmihalyi & Beattie, 1979). A pressing existential problem encountered early in life (e.g., poverty, marginality, social injustice) inspires first a process of meaning construction, and then the channeling of energy into a sphere that is construed as addressing the problem. Frequently, the motivation for engaging the domain becomes functionally autonomous of its origins as a transformational response to threat, evolving into intrinsic interest in the work itself. A young person who has lost a family member to illness thus might frame the problem as one of inadequate medical knowledge and therefore decide to become a medical researcher. Along the way, the individual might discover that the process of scientific discovery is inherently enjoyable.

Despite the superficial resemblance to the narcissistic deficit model invoked by Bloland, the differences are critical. In the latter, creative accomplishment is traced to one kind of problem only: a sense of personal inadequacy. Only one solution to the problem is identified: securing fame. The work is pursued as a means of undoing a deep sense of inadequacy by garnering attention; the work's specific content is unimportant. In other words, the deficit model leaves out the role of meaning-making in motivating action. Erikson never knew the father who abandoned him—indeed, his mother refused even to reveal the father's identity. Erikson was haunted by this throughout his life. His daughter contends that his life's work was a tool to secure the attention he never got from his father.

The strengths model is more general in the sense that any problem is possible and any solution might be conceived. It is also more specific:

The solution chosen is organically rooted in the nature of the particular problem, as formulated by the individual, and in the particular resources that the person deploys to solve it. Further, it is possible for the individual to generalize the personal problem and try to solve it in more universal terms. Rather than simply being a bid for attention, it may have been in this manner that Erikson's lifelong intellectual exploration of identity crisis and identity development was animated by his early loss.

INTEGRATING THE DEFICIT AND STRENGTHS PERSPECTIVES: THE SYSTEMS MODEL

To see more clearly the different implications of the strengths and deficit perspectives, it may help to introduce at this juncture a model of creativity that encompasses both the interpersonal sphere on which the deficit view focuses and the work activity on which the strengths view focuses. The systems model (Csikszentmihalyi, 1988, 1999) depicts creativity not as an exclusively intrapsychic process, but as the outcome of interactions among three components of a system: (a) the innovating individual, whose motivation is the focus of this chapter; (b) the domain of knowledge about the empirical world, or ways of shaping it, to which the individual contributes (e.g., psychology, science, art); and (c) the social field of teachers, gatekeepers, and practitioners who respond to and judge the individual's contributions to the domain (i.e., praising, rejecting, ignoring, or embracing them). A given contribution is creative insofar as it gains the acceptance of the field and becomes part of the corresponding domain of knowledge by extending or transforming it.

Within this framework, the medium of *attention* (Csikszentmihalyi, 1978) bridges the deficit and strengths perspectives. Investment of attention provides the basis for exchange between the individual and the environment, including the interpersonal environment (the social field, in the systems model) and the symbolic sphere that mediates understanding of the world (the cultural domain, in the systems model). Both perspectives ascribe a key role to attentional processes. Figure 18.1 shows the creator's investment of attention from the two perspectives. Arrows represent flows of attention within the system. Solid lines represent the creator's investment of attention in a sphere for its own sake, whereas broken lines represent the investment of attention in a sphere instrumentally in the service of other goals. The thickness of a line suggests the amount of attention invested.

Attention might be considered the essential commodity in the psychology of narcissism. In the narcissistic deficit model, receiving inadequate or inappropriate attention from parents results in a lasting hunger for attention from others, a channeling of energy into its pursuit, and a sense of

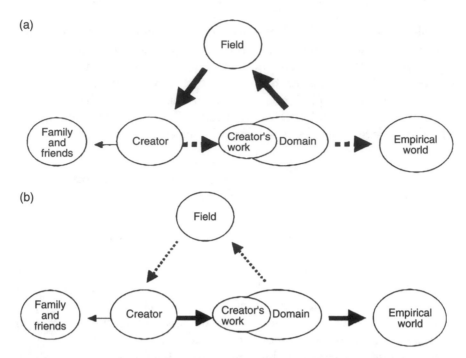

Figure 18.1. The creator's investment of attention in deficit and strengths models of creativity. Arrows represent the flow of attention. Solid lines represent investment of attention in something for its own sake. Broken lines represent investment of attention instrumentally in the service of other goals. Thickness of a line represents amount of attention invested. (a) In a (narcissistic) deficit model, attention is heavily invested in the sphere of creativity (versus other possible life spheres). Although attention is invested in using the domain to understand the empirical world, this activity is instrumental to eliciting feedback from the field (hopefully, acclaim). (b) In a strengths model, attention is heavily invested in the sphere of creativity (versus other possible life spheres). Attention is invested in understanding the empirical world, through use of the domain, as an end in itself. Feedback from the field is attended to secondarily and instrumentally as one source of information about the adequacy of current understanding.

gratification or despair depending on the success in attracting it. From a deficit perspective (Figure 18.1a), the creator's attention is heavily invested in using the domain to understand or shape the empirical world; however, this activity is in the service of winning favorable attention from the various audiences that constitute the field. From a strengths perspective (Figure 18.1b), the creator's attention is again heavily invested in understanding or shaping the empirical world through use of the domain. From this perspective, however, the activity is an end in itself. Attention to the domain, motivated by interest, is eager and undivided. When the activity goes well, attention becomes focused and effortless and the creator may enter a state of complete involvement, or *flow* (Csikszentmihalyi, 1996,

1997); this is what Bloland (1999) referred to in passing as the joy accompanying the mastery of highly skilled activities.

What are the implications of adopting one perspective rather than the other? We briefly identify three illustrative points of divergence. First, the two perspectives differ with respect to the creator's use of feedback to guide activity. From the deficit perspective, the creator pays close attention to the field, seen as a potential source of affirmation. Lack of affirmation, whether this means being rejected or ignored, might discourage persistence even if there has been promising feedback from the work itself. On the other hand, a positive reception by the field might lead the creator to persist in a line of work even if interest or enjoyment wanes or the work stagnates, because the creator's fundamental need for attention continues to be met. The underlying principle is that the creator is motivated to adjust involvement in the domain in the ways that maximize others' admiring attention.

From a strengths perspective, creators attend to the field's reception of their work instrumentally, as a form of feedback about their work's progress (cf. Collins & Amabile, 1999). The negative as well as the positive reactions from the field are therefore valued as sources of information. The more primary and more immediate source of feedback is the progress of the work itself, however (e.g., Is the medium expressing the artist's intentions? Is the theory fitting the empirical data?). Focusing on feedback from the activity itself might lead the creator to persist when things are going well despite receiving negative or no attention from the field.

A second point of divergence concerns the creator's relationship to other people. Bloland (1999) discussed the costs of fame for the people around an accomplished individual, particularly the immediate circle of family and friends. Creators devote enormous amounts of attention to their work (Ochse, 1990; Roe, 1952). Because attention is a finite resource (Csikszentmihalyi, 1978), individuals who choose to invest a great deal of attention in work necessarily have less attention to devote to other commitments, including family and friends (see Figure 18.1). This is true regardless of whether the accomplished creator's work life is viewed from a deficit perspective or a strengths one.

The differences emerge when other relationships are considered, as in the accomplished individual's relationship to students or followers. Both perspectives might suggest that the creator's attention is focused elsewhere (on the wider field, in the case of deficits; on the work itself, in that of strengths) more than on education of students. Beyond this, however, they differ. From the narcissistic deficit perspective, creators may view students as another potential source of affirmation and may actively seek students' admiration rather than directing their attention to the domain. Furthermore, regardless of the creator's intentions, the student motivated by the need for a hero may independently fix idealizing attention on the creator rather than focusing on the domain. Other ways of relating to accomplished individuals may be obscured when limited to a deficit perspective like Bloland's.

An alternative reading of teacher–student interactions, from the strengths perspective, is that the creative individual invests attention in the domain for its own sake, and so does the student. The motivation of the student, like the teacher, lies in curiosity, interest, and enjoyment of the activity. Rather than feeling neglected because of the creator's absorption in the work, the student relishes their joint involvement in the domain based on shared interest. Furthermore, students eager to learn an approach may do so regardless of the teacher's attentiveness to them by investing their own attention well in becoming keen observers of how the teacher approaches the domain.

Finally, deficit and strengths perspectives on the motivational underpinnings of creativity imply divergent therapeutic models. From the first perspective, the creator's absorption in work is motivated by deficit and signals a need for therapeutic treatment; in the latter, the creator's absorption illustrates what therapeutic treatment might seek to make possible. To return to the systems model, from the narcissistic deficit perspective, the individual's involvement with the domain represents a futile attempt to bolster self-worth through direct pursuit of affirmation (i.e., winning the regard of the field). The origin of the person's sense of inadequacy is relational, and treatment correspondingly must occur within an affirming therapeutic relationship. Activity in the domain is a barometer of the pathological need for attention; however, the relationship with the therapist is the medium of cure.

An alternative therapeutic model is associated with the strengths perspective. In it, involvement with a domain of activity is viewed as a route to engagement and a legitimate pathway to an increased sense of self-worth. Massimini and colleagues developed therapeutic interventions guided by flow principles (Delle Fave & Massimini, 1992; Inghilleri, 1999; Massimini, Csikszentmihalyi, & Carli, 1987). They sought to identify activities that a person enjoys and oriented therapy toward building on those interests and strengths, taking advantage of the growth of skill and confidence that attends flow experience (Csikszentmihalyi, 1997), and enabling the individual to reduce dysphoric experience as a by-product of this growth. The therapist serves as a source of feedback and a guide in reflecting on experience; however, involvement in the domain is the key medium of cure. The continuity between this therapeutic course and naturally occurring developmental processes is illustrated by Erikson's (1968) own notion of "self-chosen therapies," in which a person's identification and mastery of meaningful challenges leads them out of an identity crisis. His work is consistent with the view that people are capable of showing considerable initiative and ingenuity in fostering their own development.

The systems model helps put the deficit and strengths perspectives in contact with one another. In each of the illustrative areas identified in this chapter—the creator's use of feedback, the creator–student relationship, the approach to therapy—the implications of the two approaches largely diverge. Considering both perspectives yields a fuller, potentially more generative picture of the complex dynamics of creativity.

CONCLUSION

A paradigm based on deficit assumptions alone can give only a limited view of creativity. It cannot explain why some persons dedicate their energies to the pursuit of activities that bring them no external recognition, yet provide great joy. On the broader canvas of human evolution, the deficit perspective cannot adequately explain why people run risks to defy tradition and convention in order to experiment with new ways of seeing, describing, or understanding the world. Positive psychology assumes that the rewards of creativity—and more generally, of any behavior that stretches and enlarges the self—are as genuine and as primary as those homeostatic rewards that reduce discomfort and disease.

Within psychology's own field of creativity, those adopting deficit and strengths views rarely talk to each other, with a resultant loss to each in terms of stimulation and context for their research. Either focus, in isolation, runs the risk of finding only what it is looking for. As one example of the fruitfulness of an open stance, King (2001) brought a strengths perspective to bear on the literature concerning the benefits of self-disclosive writing. As long as subjects were asked only to write about past trauma, the health benefits of writing could be plausibly explained by catharsis, a deficit account. Because King questioned the completeness of this analysis, she proceeded to ask whether writing about positive events also carries health benefits. The finding that health improved after writing about either positive futures or negative pasts led her to frame a higher-order account in terms of writing's effect on self-understanding.

Those who pursue a psychology of strengths need not place borders around it and fix attention on strengths in a rigid way. There are clear examples of evolving research programs in which the study of strengths was stimulated by or grew out of the study of deficit. These include Bandura's transition from a concern with social learning of aggression to an interest in self-efficacy (Bandura, 1973, 1997); Seligman and colleagues' move from the study of helplessness and depression to the study of optimism and hope (Peterson, 2000; Seligman, 1990); and Haidt's (2000) passage from research on disgust to research on elevation, the response to witnessing moral acts. In each case, the established line of research suggested the study of strengths. Clearly, human behavior includes both positive and negative aspects, and what is important is to be open to the reality of both.

Through a psychology of strengths, the field hopes to overcome reductionist treatments of positive functioning, such as the reading of all creative accomplishment as a bid for attention (discussed in this chapter) or the interpretation of optimism as a form of denial (discussed in Aspinwall & Brunhart, 2000). At the same time, a psychology that denies the existence and dynamics of deficit, in practice even if not by design, would be equally reductionistic. In the case we have sketched, we found it helpful to identify a conceptual tool (the systems model) that bridges the deficit and strengths perspectives and thereby affords the possibility of ultimately integrating the two perspectives in a more encompassing model.

REFERENCES

Aspinwall, L. G., & Brunhart, S. M. (2000). What I do know won't hurt me: Optimism, attention to negative information, coping, and health. In J. Gillham (Ed.), *The science of optimism and hope: Research essays in honor of Martin E. P. Seligman* (pp. 163–200). Philadelphia: Templeton Foundation Press.

Bandura, A. (1973). *Aggression: A social learning analysis.* Englewood Cliffs, NJ: Prentice Hall.

Bandura, A. (1997). *Self-efficacy: The exercise of control.* New York: Freeman.

Becker, E. (1973). *The denial of death.* New York: Free Press.

Bloland, S. E. (1999, November). Fame: The power and cost of a fantasy. *The Atlantic Monthly,* pp. 51–62.

Brantdstädter, J. (1998). Action perspectives in human development. In R. M. Lerner (Ed.), *Handbook of child psychology, Vol. 1: Theoretical models of human development* (pp. 807–863). New York: Wiley.

Collins, M. A., & Amabile, T. (1999). Motivation and creativity. In R. J. Sternberg (Ed.), *Handbook of creativity* (pp. 297–312). Cambridge, England: Cambridge University Press.

Cox, C. (1926). *The early mental traits of three hundred geniuses.* Stanford, CA: Stanford University Press.

Creativity in Later Life Project. (1993). [Interview]. Unpublished interview.

Csikszentmihalyi, M. (1978). Attention and the holistic approach to behavior. In K. S. Pope & J. L. Singer (Eds.), *The stream of consciousness: Scientific investigations into the flow of human experience* (pp. 335–358). New York: Plenum.

Csikszentmihalyi, M. (1988). Society, culture, and person: A systems view of creativity. In R. J. Sternberg (Ed.), *The nature of creativity* (pp. 325–339). New York: Cambridge University Press.

Csikszentmihalyi, M. (1992). Motivation and creativity. In R. S. Albert (Ed.), *Genius and eminence* (pp. 19–34). Oxford, England: Pergamon.

Csikszentmihalyi, M. (1996). *Creativity: Flow and the psychology of discovery and invention*. New York: HarperCollins.

Csikszentmihalyi, M. (1997). *Finding flow*. New York: Basic Books.

Csikszentmihalyi, M. (1999). Implications of a systems perspective for the study of creativity. In R. J. Sternberg (Ed.), *Handbook of creativity* (pp. 313–335). New York: Cambridge University Press.

Csikszentmihalyi, M. (2000). *Beyond boredom and anxiety: The experience of play in work and games*. San Francisco: Jossey-Bass. (Original work published 1975)

Csikszentmihalyi, M., & Beattie, O. (1979). Life themes: A theoretical and empirical exploration of their origins and effects. *Journal of Humanistic Psychology, 19*, 45–63.

Deci, E. (1975). *Intrinsic motivation*. New York: Plenum Press.

Delle Fave, A., & Massimini, F. (1992). The ESM and the measurement of clinical change: A case of anxiety disorder. In M. deVries (Ed.), *The experience of psychopathology* (pp. 280–289). Cambridge, England: Cambridge University Press.

Eckersley, R. (2000). The mixed blessings of material progress: Diminishing returns in the pursuit of happiness. *Journal of Happiness Studies, 1*, 267–292.

Erikson, E. (1968). *Identity: Youth and crisis*. New York: Norton.

Haidt, J. (2000). The positive emotion of elevation. *Prevention and Treatment, 3*. Retrieved August 15, 2002 from http://journals.apa.org/prevention/volume3/pre0030003c.html.

Inghilleri, P. (1999). *From subjective experience to cultural change*. Cambridge, England: Cambridge University Press.

King, L. (2001). The health benefits of writing about life goals. *Personality and Social Psychology Bulletin, 27*, 798–807.

Klein, G. (1990). *The atheist and the holy city: Encounters and reflections*. Cambridge, MA: MIT Press.

Kohut, H. (1966). Forms and transformations of narcissism. *Journal of the American Psychoanalytic Association, 14*, 243–272.

Massimini, F., Csikszentmihalyi, M., & Carli, M. (1987). The monitoring of optimal experience: A tool for psychiatric rehabilitation. *Journal of Nervous and Mental Disease, 175*, 545–549.

Ochse, R. (1990). *Before the gates of excellence: The determinants of creative genius*. Cambridge, England: Cambridge University Press.

Peterson, C. (2000). The future of optimism. *American Psychologist, 55*, 44–55.

Roe, A. (1952). *The making of a scientist*. New York: Dodd, Mead.

Seligman, M. (1990). *Learned optimism*. New York: Knopf.

Seligman, M., & Csikszentmihalyi, M. (2000). Positive psychology: An introduction. *American Psychologist, 55*, 5–14.

Simonton, D. K. (1984). *Genius, creativity, and leadership*. Cambridge, MA: Harvard University Press.

White, R. (1959). Motivation reconsidered: The concept of competence. *Psychological Review, 66*, 297–333.

19

IRONIES OF THE HUMAN CONDITION: WELL-BEING AND HEALTH ON THE WAY TO MORTALITY

CAROL D. RYFF AND BURTON SINGER

Recently, we have witnessed a drumroll on behalf of positive psychology. Chastised for its preoccupation with human failings, the field of psychology has been admonished to attend to human strengths. This message is usefully juxtaposed with centuries of scholarly efforts to depict our more noble attributes (Coan, 1977). Socrates and Aristotle spoke of the triumphant human capacity for reason and rationality; St. Augustine elevated the virtue of achieving close contact with the divine; Michelangelo embodied the heights of creative self-expression defining the Renaissance; Wordsworth, Raphael, and Goethe captured the passionate sensitivities of the Romantic era; and closer to our own crossing of the human stage have been those finding greatness in the human struggle. Sartre and Camus, for

This research was supported by the John D. and Catherine T. MacArthur Foundation Research Networks on Successful Midlife Development and Socioeconomic Status and Health, as well as a National Institute on Aging grant (R01-AG13613), National Institute of Mental Health grant (P50-MH61083) and a grant to the General Clinical Research Center of the University of Wisconsin—Madison (M01-RR03186).

example, called for transcendence of suffering via the existential responsibility to find meaning amidst the chaos and absurdities of life. These Western varieties of redeeming features can be further contrasted with Eastern depictions that elevate the human capacities for enlightenment, selfless action, compassion, and oneness with nature (Coan, 1977).

This diverse legacy of human virtues heightens the challenge of determining what, if anything, can be usefully added to this topic. While appreciating what has gone before, we suggest there is a social scientific contribution to be made to understanding human strengths. The empirical era has led to efforts to operationally define and measure human virtues. As such, there is the weighty burden of having to decide whether social scientists are measuring the right things. That is, are social scientific microscopes focused on criteria that capture noble human qualities? We offer a provisional affirmative response to this question, summarizing our own work to date on the operationalization of psychological well-being. However, we also underscore the need to move beyond false dichotomies that separate positive and negative features of the human condition. Human strengths are inevitably a two-act play involving plummeting descents and soaring heights. This awareness requires that we penetrate more deeply the ironies, paradoxes, and contradictions that are essential features of how we are ennobled.

Those who have examined the human experience via novels, poetry, short stories, and plays, have a deep appreciation of these ironies. Bloom (2000) argued that a primary reason for reading the great works of literature is to "recover" our sense of the ironic so as to "clear the mind of cant" (p. 27). This insight has significance for how social science depicts core features of what it means to be well and positively functioning. The critical message is that life is a pursuit requiring effort. It is not, as Russell (1930/ 1958) noted metaphorically in *The Conquest of Happiness*, a journey of deliciously ripened fruit dropping effortlessly into one's mouth. Rather, good lives are about the zest that comes from effortful, frequently challenging and frustrating, engagement in living.

Beyond enriching conceptions of well-being with appreciation of irony and inevitable dialectics between positive and negative aspects of living, we will also argue that extant formulations of human health—what it is and how it is promoted—need refinement and reformulation. The major requirement is to broaden the meaning of health to encompass core features of well-being, as articulated and studied in the social sciences. This demands expansion of medical conceptions of "quality of life" to include psychological and social well-being, essential features of what it means to be healthy. We call for new research probing the connections between the health of the mind, broadly defined, and the health of the body. And, true to our concern for enriching the scientific understanding of how the indomitable powers of the human spirit creatively blend life's failures, pain, and disappointments with its successes and renewed beginnings, we also lobby for greater research on the successful negotiation of challenge. This is a call to bring the exigencies of life, as they are lived "alfresco," more fully into scientific laboratories to investigate the neurobiological mechanisms whereby psychosocial strengths are instantiated in neurons and cells and thereby help keep people biologically equipped for the journey of life.

WELL-BEING AS STRENGTH HONED BY CHALLENGE

Psychology's Persistent Interest in the Positive

Within psychology and its subfields, much has been written over the past century about human virtues, strengths, and the meaning of well-being. William James, father of American psychology, wrote about "healthy-mindedness" in *The Varieties of Religious Experience* (1902/1958). He observed that at every age there are those who passionately fling themselves onto the goodness of life, in spite of their own hardships. These individuals have souls of "a sky-blue tint" (p. 77); they are the ones who divert humanity's attention from disease, death, and the "slaughter-houses and indecencies" into what is "far handsomer and cleaner and better" in life (p. 85). For James, the poet Walt Whitman exemplified such an individual—"the only sentiments he allowed himself to express were of the expansive order" (p. 81); he possessed an optimism that was both "voluntary and defiant" (p. 82).

The philosophy of the "mind-cure movement," central to the Jamesian evaluation of the positive, was a blend of the four gospels of the Bible, Emersonian transcendentalism, Berkeleyan idealism, spiritism, evolutionism, and even Hinduism. Those of this faith, he said, have an "intuitive belief in the all-saving power of healthy-minded attitudes as such, in the conquering efficacy of courage, hope, and trust, and the correlative contempt for doubt, fear, worry, and all nervously precautionary states of mind" (p. 88). James, however, criticized this realm as being "so moonstruck with optimism and so vaguely expressed that an academically trained intellect finds it almost impossible to read" (p. 89). Despite these observations, his book was a bold tribute to the view that religion, in the shape of mind-cure, gives some "serenity, moral poise, and happiness, and prevents certain forms of disease as well as science does, or even better" (p. 107).

Likely reflecting his own struggles under darkened skies, James' summary of healthy-mindedness was followed with a chapter on the "sick soul." He described those "morbid-minded individuals" who "cannot so swiftly throw off the burden of consciousness of evil" (p. 116). They know that "all natural goods perish; riches take wings, fame is a breath; love is a cheat; youth and health and pleasure will vanish" (p. 120) and ultimately that "the skull will grin at the banquet" (p. 121). Thus, James depicted two strikingly disparate worlds:

> The sanguine and healthy-minded live habitually on the sunny side of their misery-line, the depressed and melancholy live beyond it, in darkness and apprehension. There are men who seem to have started in life with a bottle or two of champagne inscribed to their credit, whilst others seem to have been born close to the pain threshold, which the slightest irritants fatally send them over. (p. 117)

The happy souls seem "unspeakably blind and shallow" (p. 137) to those who live in darkness. Alternatively, to the healthy-minded, the way of the

> sick soul seems unmanly and diseased. With their grubbing in rat-holes instead of living in the light; with their manufacture of fears, and preoccupation with every unwholesome kind of misery, there is something almost obscene about these children of wrath. (p. 137)

We include this lengthy segment to remind present-day scholars of James's astonishing insights and unrivaled capacities for expressing them with eloquence and verve. In addition, his work is valuable because it poignantly illustrates the point–counterpoint between positive and negative features of the human condition. He was deeply aware of both the sunny and dark sides of life, although his own efforts to unify them were curiously limited. James knew that the mind-cure movement and its formulation of healthy-mindedness needed to accord a place for sorrow, pain, and death and to recognize that the normal process of life contains "moments in which radical evil gets its innings and takes its solid turn" (p. 138). Nonetheless, James left the darkness and the light surprisingly distant and distinct, not appreciating the deeper dialectic between them. This, we argue, is part of the needed stride forward in the present era.

We would also draw attention to others in the formative years of psychology who took it upon themselves to depict human strengths. Many of these individuals were reacting to Freud's dramatically negative view of the human psyche as tangled in emotional turmoil and conflict and driven instinctively by propensities toward sexual gratification and aggression. Jung's formulation of individuation (1933; Von Franz, 1964) challenged Freud's grim account and emphasized the harmonious integration of the person's good and bad features, masculine and feminine qualities, and rich capacities for self-expression and acceptance of the unknown. Erikson's bold vision of ego development carried the idea of continuing growth, the advancing to ever-higher life tasks across the entire life course. Bühler (1935; Bühler & Massarik, 1968) articulated the basic life tendencies through which human fulfillment occurs. Allport (1961) offered a conception of maturity that encompassed such qualities as self-extension, warm relating to others, emotional security, and realistic self-perception. Maslow (1968) detailed extensive characteristics of those who are self-actualized, and Rogers (1961) formulated the qualities of the fully functioning person. Jahoda (1958), recognizing that mental health is more than the absence of mental illness, drew on many of these formulations to enumerate positive features of mental health.

Detailed reviews of how these scholars depicted human well-being are available elsewhere (see Ryff, 1985, 1989a, 1989b). Taken together, the works speak powerfully to psychology's long and abiding interest in articulating adaptive, healthy, optimal human functioning. Thus, notwithstanding the recent fanfare, positive psychology has been an enduring tradition, continually providing a counterpoint to those elaborating negative, dysfunctional features of human emotions and behavior.

Nonetheless, it is the case that empirical research on the negative has persistently overshadowed investigations of the positive. This imbalance has been due, in part, to the absence of credible assessment tools to measure positive functioning. Lacking reliable and valid instruments, it is impossible to advance knowledge of the human strengths psychologists have identified. A further contributing factor has been the structure of the incentive system. Simply put, studies of ill-being are more likely to receive funding than studies of well-being. The latter are dismissed as fanciful frosting on the cake, a low-priority luxury vis-à-vis the need to address the real problems and suffering of our era. Such thinking is deeply flawed and is increasingly recognized as such. Scientific agendas built on principles of prevention and health promotion now legitimize the funding of research to advance knowledge of human strengths (Raczynski & DiClemente, 1999; Ryff & Singer, 2000a).

Operationalizing Strengths and the Dialectic Between Positive and Negative Experience

Given the new legitimacy to study human strengths (Seligman & Csikszentmihalyi, 2000), it is all the more imperative to focus on the quality of scientific tools to measure positive features of the human condition. Over a decade ago, the previously described formulations were drawn on to delineate a multidimensional model (see Figure 19.1) of well-being (Ryff, 1985, 1989a). Six dimensions, emerging from points of convergence in these depictions of positive functioning, provided the conceptual starting points to develop assessment tools (Ryff, 1989b). Numerous empirical studies have subsequently been conducted with these instruments—some to evaluate how well-being varies by age, gender, or socioeconomic standing (Clarke, Marshall, Ryff, & Rosenthal, 2000; Marmot, Ryff, Bumpass, Shipley, & Marks, 1997; Ryff, 1989b; Ryff & Keyes, 1995; Ryff, Magee, Kling, & Wing, 1999); others to examine well-being as an outcome of various life experiences or life transitions (e.g., Kling, Ryff, & Essex, 1997; Kling, Seltzer, & Ryff, 1997; Ryff, Lee, Essex, & Schmutte, 1994); and still

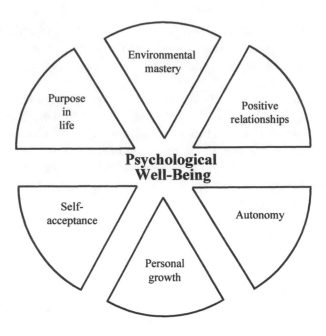

Figure 19.1. Dimensions of psychological well-being.

others to elaborate the role of psychological well-being in understanding resilience in the face of adversity (Ryff, Singer, Love, & Essex, 1998; Singer & Ryff, 1997, 1999; Singer, Ryff, Carr, & Magee, 1998). The well-being instruments have also been used extensively by other investigators, both within psychology (e.g., McGregor & Little, 1998; McKinley, 1999; Staudinger, Fleeson, & Baltes, 1999) and beyond (e.g., Carr, 1997; Fava, Rafanelli, Grandi, Conti, & Belluardo, 1998; Li, Seltzer, & Greenberg, 1999; Marks & Lambert, 1998). Speaking to their international presence, the instruments have been translated into 18 different languages and are being used across behavioral, social, and health sciences to understand the positive sides of human experience.

What, after more than a decade of use, is the hindsight judgment of these instruments? What have they accomplished or failed to accomplish? For those who would embark on empirical operationalization of the positive, it is important to underscore the time and effort required to establish psychometric credentials (Ryff, 1989b; Ryff & Keyes, 1995). Lacking evidence of scale validity and reliability, subsequent work is pointless. As substantive research tools, the well-being scales have proved useful in documenting the psychological strengths (e.g., autonomy, mastery) and vulnerabilities (e.g., purpose in life, personal growth) that accompany human aging, in identifying the unique psychological strengths of women (e.g., positive relations with others, personal growth), and in showing how social disparities in education and income reduce the likelihood of experiencing well-being. The instruments have been informative as tools for assessing how typical life experiences (e.g., parenting, marriage and divorce, later life relocation) and atypical challenges (e.g., growing up with an alcoholic parent, having a mentally retarded child, caregiving for an ill spouse or parent) influence well-being. Our recent life history studies of well-being in the face of cumulative adversity have also offered compelling empirical evidence of human resilience (Ryff, Singer, Wing, & Love, 2001; Singer & Ryff, 1999; Singer, Ryff, Carr, & Magee, 1998).

At the same time, qualitative inquiries have clarified that certain aspects of the positive, such as the capacity to accept change (particularly in old age) or sheer joy in living (e.g., humor), are not strongly evident in the current formulation (Ryff, 1989c). The instruments may also fall short of the differentiation required to adequately capture interpersonal well being. That is, the Positive Relations With Others scale may not go far enough in detailing the diverse dimensions along which individuals experience the positive in life via their connections with others (Markus, Ryff, & Barnett, in press; Ryff & Singer, 2000b; Ryff, Singer, Wing, & Love, 2001). Thus, there could doubtlessly be refinements in these research tools. For present purposes, however, we draw attention to a particular feature of the six dimensions: namely, the ways in which they blend positive and negative features of the human condition. We do so to underscore the ironies of well-being—the paradox that human strengths are frequently born in encounters with life difficulties. Strength is often fired in the crucible of adversity.

For example, self-acceptance, a key feature of well-being, is about having positive regard for one's self. This is not narcissistic self-love or superficial self-esteem, but a deep form of self-regard built on awareness of one's positive and negative attributes. Jung (1933; Von Franz, 1964) emphasized that the shadow lurks within everyone and suggested that coming to accept one's failings is an important feature of being fully individuated. Erikson's (1959) ego integrity also involves coming to peace with the triumphs and disappointments of one's past life. This resonant acceptance of self is thus built on honest self-evaluation, awareness of personal failings and limitations, and compassionate love for and embracing of one's self, warts and all.

Purpose in life, the capacity to find meaning and direction in one's experiences, as well as to create and pursue goals in living, is profoundly grounded in confrontations with adversity. The first and most eloquent articulation of purpose in life came from Frankl (1992), whose own challenge to meaning was honed during his 3-year ordeal in a Nazi concentration camp. So deep was his insight about the life-enhancing, indeed, life-saving features of purpose and meaning, particularly when confronted with unimaginable horror, that Frankl devoted his subsequent professional life to developing a form of psychotherapy (logotherapy) designed to help individuals find meaning that can sustain and empower them as they struggle with life's trials and tribulations.

Similarly, *personal growth*, or the capacity to continually realize one's talent and potential, as well as to develop new resources and strengths, frequently involves encounters with adversity that require one to dig deeply to find one's inner strength. When are people most likely to discover these strengths? Ironically, paradoxically, it is when they are most down and out that inner resources are frequently found and exert their powers of renewal. This phenomenon of growth through trauma and adversity has gained notable attention of late (e.g., Emmons, Colby, & Kaiser, 1998; Ickovics & Park, 1998; Tedeschi, Park, & Calhoun, 1998), as it well should. Self-expansion through challenge quintessentially illustrates the human spirit's remarkable capacity to survive loss, recover from adversity, and thrive in the face of overwhelming obstacles.

Environmental mastery, another key dimension of well-being, involves the challenge of managing one's surrounding world. This ability requires capacities to create and sustain environments suited to one's personal needs. Such mastery is achieved through personal effort and action. That is, it is a proactive, not passive, version of person–environment fit. Played out in contexts of work, family, and community life, environmental mastery is for most individuals a lifelong challenge. This aspect of well-being thus underscores the enduring personal initiative required to build and nurture work and family environments that bring out the best in one's self and one's significant others. When optimally experienced, such mastery is a powerful human strength.

Autonomy addresses the capacity to march to one's own drummer, to follow personal convictions and beliefs even if they go against accepted dogma and conventional wisdom. Jung (1933; Von Franz, 1964), in fact, asserted that the fully individuated person experiences a "deliverance from convention." This aspect of well-being appears to be a quite Western conception of virtue, in that the quest for autonomy may well involve isolation, or even opprobrium, from others for carrying out life choices consistent with one's own inner vision. It is thus about the capacity to stand alone, if need be; living autonomously, however, may involve both courage and loneliness.

The last dimension of psychological well-being, *positive relations with others*, involves the human strengths, pleasures, and delights that come from close contact with others, deep intimacy, and abiding love. We have written extensively elsewhere about the ups and downs, the elevating and debasing features of our social connections (Ryff et al., 2001). That is, relational well-being is a story of both "elective affinities," Goethe's term for the enormous power of romantic love, and "uninvited agonies," our term for the pain and problems that may accompany one's most significant social ties. Deeper analysis of human intimacy or, more broadly, what we refer to as "interpersonal flourishing" is profoundly about the mix of positive and negative emotions that characterize our deepest and most significant human ties (Ryff & Singer, 2000b). How negative and positive emotions intermingle is, we argue, central to understanding optimal human functioning (Ryff & Singer, in press).

In sum, it is not the absence of negative experience or negative emotion that defines the good, well-lived, richly experienced life, but how challenges and difficulties are managed, responded to, dealt with, and transformed. Returning to the theme of irony, we note that the deepest levels of human meaning and connection are frequently found when individuals come face to face with their vulnerabilities, insecurities, or pain. Gottman, Katz, and Hooven (1996) observed that one of the most valuable contributions parents make to the development of their children is to "coach" them to recognize, name, and communicate their fears, frustrations, anger, and pain. Thus, quality human relations and quality living are not achieved via escape, avoidance, or evasion of what is negative in life, but by effective negotiation of adversity—that is, through profiles of action and reaction that deepen self-knowledge and meaning, enrich social bonds, and expand personal effectiveness.

To summarize, the six key components of well-being that have been the focus of empirical study for the past decade reveal an important and abiding insight: Wellness comes from active encounters with life's challenges, setbacks, and demands, not from blissful, conflict-free, smooth sailing. Those who would advance a social scientific understanding of human strengths must recognize this dialectic between pain and pleasure, between what is high-minded and inspiring and what is painful, debasing, and cause for despair. Human well-being is fundamentally about the joining of these two realms.

HUMAN HEALTH AS THE BIOLOGICAL EMBODIMENT OF WELL-BEING

We have previously argued (Ryff & Singer, 1998a, 1998b) that extant formulations of human health, defined largely in terms of illness, disease, and physical symptomatology, do not address what it means to be truly healthy. To fill in the positive side of human health requires bringing social science into basic formulations of health. Why are the social sciences needed? Because they provide conceptualizations of, and measurement tools for, evaluating what it means to thrive and flourish in life. If health is to be defined as more than the absence of illness, psychological and social well-being must be included as essential features.

These observations come close to medical interest in quality of life, a valuable and much-needed construct in the health arena. Current quality of life approaches tend to emphasize basic mobility and self-care capacities, along with effective management of treatment side effects. Primary emphasis is given to health limitations, such as the restriction of physical and role activities due to physical or emotional problems (see, e.g., the SF-36 Health Survey, Ware & Sherbourne, 1992). Missing are more salubrious aspects of functioning, such as positive self-regard, a sense of mastery, quality ties to others, and purpose in life. Adding these elements of well-being offers a richer, more enlightened view of health. More importantly, however, psychosocial strengths appear to be critical ingredients for understanding who stays well and why (Ryff & Singer, 2000a). Put in epidemiological terms, psychological and social well-being may be prominent factors contributing to delayed onset of morbidity and mortality.

Much needed in the science of positive health is research on the physiological substrates of flourishing. The central questions are twofold: First, what are the neurological, endocrinological, immunological, cardiovascular, metabolic, and other profiles of those with lives of high purpose, mastery, and quality ties to others? Social integration has been repeatedly linked to better health and longer length of life (Berkman, 1995). With regard to the power of purpose in life, Frankl (1992), himself a physician, was among the first to observe that those who gave up hope and meaning were less likely to survive. Scientifically, what we lack is an understanding of the mechanisms that account for these effects.

We have previously suggested three promising venues for studying the neurobiology of flourishing: allostatic load, cerebral activation asymmetry, and immune competence (Ryff & Singer, 1998a). The first of these links psychosocial strengths with a measure of cumulative wear and tear on numerous physiological systems (cardiovascular, metabolic, hypothalamic-pituitary-adrenal axis, sympathetic nervous system; Seeman, Singer, Rowe, Horwitz, & McEwen, 1997). The key question is whether psychosocial strengths decrease the likelihood of high wear and tear (i.e., high allostatic load)—that is, do they serve a protective function? The second venue, cerebral activation asymmetry, builds connections to affective neuroscience, with its interest in the neural circuitry of emotion (Davidson, 1995; Sutton & Davidson, 1997). Those showing greater left prefrontal activation in response to emotional stimuli show greater positive affect and reduced vulnerability to depression compared to those showing greater right prefrontal activation. Is psychological well-being neurally instantiated in such a profile? The third venue, immune competence, builds on the growing literature in psychoneuroimmunology showing links between psychosocial factors and immune function (Maier, Watkins, & Fleshner, 1994). The positive health question is whether immune competence is fostered by the presence of psychological and social strengths.

To date, we have documented links between social and relational well-being and allostatic load; individuals on more positive relationship pathways (i.e., good quality relationships with parents in childhood; intimacy with spouse in adulthood) have lower allostatic load than those on more negative relational pathways (Ryff et al., 2001). We have also shown that positive relational strengths afford biological resilience in the face of cumulative economic adversity—that is, individuals with persistently low economic standing over the course of their lives, but who nonetheless have had good quality social ties, show reduced likelihood of high allostatic load compared to those lacking such relational strengths in the face of economic hardship (Singer & Ryff, 1999). Links between psychosocial strengths and cerebral activation asymmetry and immune function are currently under investigation in our newly funded Mind/Body Center at University of Wisconsin—Madison.

A particularly needed and promising avenue for future positive health research pertains to the use of challenge paradigms to probe the nexus between psychosocial and biomedical factors. Why challenge studies? As we have suggested earlier, challenge is a ubiquitous feature of the human experience. Moreover, it is during challenge that strengths (be they biological, psychological, or social) are most clearly evident. Thus, confrontations with difficult experiences help give a deeper understanding of how, across multiple levels of functioning, people are able to meet, withstand, and maybe even be strengthened by adversity.

For example, neuroendocrine response to a driving simulation challenge has been shown to be moderated by levels of self-esteem (Seeman et al., 1995). Studies of marital conflict conducted in the laboratory have also shown links to neuroendocrine and cardiovascular function (Broadwell & Light, 1999; Kiecolt-Glaser et al., 1997). Across these challenges, key outcome assessments pertain to recovery functions. The driving simulation revealed differences between those whose neuroendocrine markers (e.g., cortisol) went up, but then recovered, and those whose markers went up and stayed up (thereby contributing to high allostatic load). Similarly, in linking social support to levels of systolic and diastolic blood pressure, both high- and low-support groups showed increments in blood pressure during conflictual marital interaction and decrements during the recovery period. However, for those with better social support profiles (especially men), these temporal dynamics occurred at lower levels of blood pressure (diastolic and systolic) than those with more limited social support. In the emotion realm, diverse indicators constitute "affective chronometry" (Davidson, 1998), including threshold for reactivity, peak amplitude of response, rise time to peak, and recovery time. Thus, across multiple neurobiological systems the goal is to understand how challenge activates responses and how psychological, social, and emotional strengths facilitate recovery.

Future work needs to continue the development of studies that blend detailed assessment of what occurs mechanistically in the brain and downstream systems along with detailed, longitudinal assessments of psychosocial strengths. The latter provide insight into factors that account for individual differences in response to laboratory challenge. For example, couples engaged in interaction about conflict may vary in cardiovascular, endocrine, and immunological responses as a function of prior histories of settling differences constructively versus living with chronic conflict, ill will, or even abuse. To achieve an integration of information about psychosocial histories of well-being with mechanistic neurobiology will require creative combinations of longitudinal and laboratory studies. These, we believe, offer enormous promise for advancing the science of positive health as a biopsychosocial phenomenon.

CONCLUSION

For 19th-century poet Emily Dickinson, the sublime consisted of a "pleasurable difficulty" (Bloom, 2000). The capacity to find what is valuable, meaningful, and fulfilling in life by pursuit of the difficult has deep significance for the study of human strengths. Positive psychology will fulfill its promise not by simply marking what makes people feel good, hopeful, and contented, but by tracking deeper and more complex processes by which we come to know and accept ourselves, find meaning in life struggles, realize our talents, love and care for those dear to us, manage complex lives, and be true to our own inner convictions. We propose that these challenges of "engaged living" are the essence of what it means to be well. They are also core ingredients of life quality and as such constitute an important part of what it means to be healthy.

The scientific tasks ahead are many. Needed is a greater understanding of the dialectic between positive and negative experience (e.g., in events, emotions, well-being, and distress), which will require studying both side by side. How is the negative transformed into the positive? Is the negative necessary to achieve heightened well-being, or is the negative simply offset by the positive? Mapping the neurobiological signature of positive and negative experience is also essential for understanding the underlying mechanisms whereby human strengths contribute to health outcomes, including delayed onset of morbidity and mortality and recovery from stress and illness. Finally, as exemplified by the work of Fava (Fava, 1999; Fava et al., 1998), there is an enormous need to advance interventive strategies and programs designed to promote well-being, particularly among those who need it most (e.g., those who suffer from recurrent depression).

To those who resonate to the ironic in life, we conclude with an amusing, perhaps perverse, twist to these efforts to capture the meaning of and promote human health and well-being: The processes we so earnestly seek to understand culminate in death. Ours is thus, in the final analysis, a doomed enterprise. Despite our status as mere mortals, there is nonetheless much to be learned about differences in how we get to death, and this is ultimately what the positive health agenda is about.

Returning to literary insight, Bloom (2000) spoke of the powerful urge to go on in life even when death is approaching. He examined Tennyson's *Ulysses* to reveal these final depths of the human experience. Ulysses, "always roaming with a hungry heart," was a seeker after meaning who made a mad, final voyage in his later years on the brink of death that revealed his continual quest:

> Old age hath yet his honor and his toil;
> Death closes all: but something ere the end,
> Some work of noble note, may yet be done,
> Not unbecoming men that strove with Gods. (p. 77)

Tennyson ends the poem with a clash of antithetical voices that Bloom describes as universally human:

> Though much is taken, much abides; and though
> We are not now that strength which in old days
> Moved heaven and earth; that which we are, we are;
> One equal temper of heroic hearts,
> Made weak by time and fate, but strong in will
> To strive, to seek, to find, and not to yield. (p. 78)

The heroic heart, weakened by time and fate but continuing to strive, to seek, and to find, epitomizes the human strength we of the present era seek to understand.

REFERENCES

Allport, G. W. (1961). *Pattern and growth in personality.* New York: Holt, Rinehart, & Winston.

Berkman, L. F. (1995). The role of social relations in health promotion. *Psychosomatic Medicine, 57,* 245–254.

Bloom, H. (2000). *How to read and why.* New York: Scribner.

Broadwell, S. D., & Light, K. C. (1999). Family support and cardiovascular responses in married couples during conflict and other interactions. *International Journal of Behavioral Medicine, 6,* 40–63.

Bühler, C. (1935). The curve of life as studied in biographies. *Journal of Applied Psychology, 19,* 405–409.

Bühler, C., & Massarik, F. (Eds.). (1968). *The course of human life.* New York: Springer.

Carr, D. (1997). The fulfillment of career dreams at midlife: Does it matter for women's mental health? *Journal of Health and Social Behavior, 38,* 331–344.

Clarke, P. J., Marshall, V. W., Ryff, C. D., & Rosenthal, C. J. (2000). Well-being in Canadian seniors: Findings from the Canadian Study of Health and Aging. *Canadian Journal on Aging, 19,* 139–159.

Coan, R. W. (1977). *Hero, artist, sage, or saint? A survey of what is variously called mental health, normality, maturity, self-actualization, and human fulfillment.* New York: Columbia University Press.

Davidson, R. J. (1995). Cerebral asymmetry, emotion, and affective style. In R. J. Davidson & K. Hugdahl (Eds.), *Brain asymmetry* (pp. 361–387). Cambridge, MA: MIT Press.

Davidson, R. J. (1998). Affective style and affective disorders: Perspectives from affective neuroscience. *Cognition and Emotion, 12,* 307–330.

Emmons, R. A., Colby, P. M., & Kaiser, H. A. (1998). When losses lead to gains: Personal goals and the recovery of meaning. In P. T. P. Wong & P. S. Fry (Eds.), *The human quest for meaning* (pp. 163–178). Mahwah, NJ: Erlbaum.

Erikson, E. (1959). Identity and the life cycle. *Psychological Issues, 1,* 18–164.

Fava, G. A. (1999). Well-being therapy: Conceptual and technical issues. *Psychotherapy and Psychosomatics, 68,* 171–179.

Fava, G. A., Rafanelli, C., Grandi, S., Conti, S., & Belluardo, P. (1998). Prevention of recurrent depression with cognitive behavioral therapy. *Archives of General Psychiatry, 55,* 816–821.

Frankl, V. E. (1992). *Man's search for meaning* (4th ed.). Boston: Beacon.

Gottman, J. M., Katz, L. F., & Hooven, C. (1996). Parental meta-emotion philosophy and the emotional life of families: Theoretical models and preliminary data. *Journal of Family Psychology, 10,* 243–268.

Ickovics, J. R., & Park, C. L. (Eds.). (1998). Thriving: Broadening the paradigm beyond illness to health. *Journal of Social Issues, 54*(2), 237–244.

Jahoda, M. (1958). *Current concepts of positive mental health.* New York: Basic Books.

James, W. (1958). *The varieties of religious experience.* New York: New American Library. (Original work published 1902)

Jung, C. G. (1933). *Modern man in search of a soul.* New York: Harcourt, Brace, & World.

Keyes, C. L. M., Shmotkin, D., & Ryff, C. D. (2002). Optimizing well-being: The empirical encounter of two traditions. *Journal of Personality and Social Psychology, 82,* 1007–1022.

Kiecolt-Glaser, J. K., Glaser, R., Cacioppo, J. T., MacCallum, R. C., Snydersmith, M., Cheongtag, K., & Malarkey, W. B. (1997). Marital conflict in older adults: Endocrinological and immunological correlates. *Psychosomatic Medicine, 59,* 345–362.

Kling, K. C., Ryff, C. D., & Essex, M. J. (1997). Adaptive changes in the self-concept during a life transition. *Personality and Social Psychology Bulletin, 23,* 989–998.

Kling, K. C., Seltzer, M. M., & Ryff, C. D. (1997). Distinctive late-life challenges: Implications for coping and well-being. *Psychology and Aging, 12,* 288–295.

Li, L. W., Seltzer, M. M., & Greenberg, J. S. (1999). Change in depressive symptoms among daughter caregivers: An 18-month longitudinal study. *Psychology and Aging, 14*, 206–219.

Maier, S. F., Watkins, L. R., & Fleshner, M. (1994). Psychoneuroimmunology: The interface between behavior, brain, and immunity. *American Psychologist, 49*, 1004–1017.

Marks, N. F., & Lambert, J. D. (1998). Marital status continuity and change among young and midlife adults: Longitudinal effects on psychological well-being. *Journal of Family Issues, 19*, 652–686.

Markus, H. R., Ryff, C. D., & Barnett, K. (in press). In their own words: Well-being among high school and college-educated adults. In C. D. Ryff & R. C. Kessler (Eds.), *A portrait of midlife in the U.S.* Chicago: University of Chicago Press.

Marmot, M., Ryff, C. D., Bumpass, L. L., Shipley, M., & Marks, N. F. (1997). Social inequalities in health: Converging evidence and next questions. *Social Science and Medicine, 44*, 901–910.

Maslow, A. (1968). *Toward a psychology of being* (2nd ed.). New York: Van Nostrand.

McGregor, I., & Little, B. R. (1998). Personal projects, happiness, and meaning: On doing well and being yourself. *Journal of Personality and Social Psychology, 74*, 494–512.

McKinley, N. M. (1999). Women and objectified body consciousness: Mothers' and daughters' body experience in cultural, development, and familial context. *Developmental Psychology, 35*, 760–769.

Raczynski, J. M., & DiClemente, R. J. (Eds.). (1999). *Handbook of health promotion and disease prevention*. New York: Kluwer Academic/Plenum Publishers.

Rogers, C. R. (1961). *On becoming a person*. Boston: Houghton Mifflin.

Russell, B. (1958). *The conquest of happiness*. New York: Liveright. (Original work published 1930)

Ryff, C. D. (1985). Adult personality development and the motivation for personal growth. In D. Kleiber & M. Maehr (Eds.), *Advances in motivation and achievement: Motivation and adulthood* (Vol. 4, pp. 55–92). Greenwich, CT: JAI Press.

Ryff, C. D. (1989a). Beyond Ponce de Leon and successful aging: New directions in quest of successful aging. *International Journal of Behavioral Development, 12*, 35–55.

Ryff, C. D. (1989b). Happiness is everything, or is it? Explorations on the meaning of psychological well-being. *Journal of Personality and Social Psychology, 57*, 1069–1081.

Ryff, C. D. (1989c). In the eye of the beholder: Views of psychological well-being in middle-aged and older adults. *Psychology and Aging, 4*, 195–210.

Ryff, C. D., & Keyes, C. L. M. (1995). The structure of psychological well-being revisited. *Journal of Personality and Social Psychology, 69*, 719–727.

Ryff, C. D., Lee, Y. H., Essex, M. J., & Schmutte, P. S. (1994). My children and me: Mid-life evaluations of grown children and of self. *Psychology and Aging*, 9, 195–205.

Ryff, C. D., Magee, W. J., Kling, K. C., & Wing, E. H. (1999). Forging macro-micro linkages in the study of psychological well-being. In C. D. Ryff & V. W. Marshall (Eds.), *The self and society in aging processes* (pp. 247–278). New York: Springer.

Ryff, C. D., & Singer, B. (1998a). The contours of positive human health. *Psychological Inquiry*, 9, 1–28.

Ryff, C. D., & Singer, B. (1998b). Human health: New directions for the next millennium. *Psychological Inquiry*, 9, 69–85.

Ryff, C. D., & Singer, B. (2000a). Biopsychosocial challenges of the new millennium. *Psychotherapy and Psychosomatic Medicine*, 69, 170–177.

Ryff, C. D., & Singer, B. (2000b). Interpersonal flourishing: A positive health agenda for the new millennium. *Personality and Social Psychology Review, 4,* 30–44.

Ryff, C. D., & Singer, B. (in press). The role of emotion on pathways to positive health. In R. J. Davidson, H. H. Goldsmith, & K. Scherer (Eds.), *Handbook of affective science.* New York: Oxford University Press.

Ryff, C. D., Singer, B., Love, G. D., & Essex, M. J. (1998). Resilience in adulthood and later life. In J. Lomranz (Ed.), *Handbook of aging and mental health* (pp. 69–94). New York: Plenum.

Ryff, C. D., Singer, B., Wing, E., & Love, G. D. (2001). Elective affinities and uninvited agonies: Mapping emotion with significant others onto health. In C. D. Ryff & B. Singer (Eds.), *Emotion, social relationships, and health* (pp. 133–175). New York: Oxford University Press.

Seeman, T. E., Berkman, L., Gulanski, R., Robbins, R., Greenspan, S., & Rowe, J. (1995). Response to challenge as a mechanism of successful aging: Self-esteem as a predictor of neuroendocrine response. *Psychosomatic Research, 39,* 69–84.

Seeman, T. E., Singer, B. H., Rowe, J. W., Horwitz, R. I., & McEwen, B. S. (1997). The price of adaptation: Allostatic load and its health consequences: Mac-Arthur Studies of Successful Aging. *Archives of Internal Medicine, 157,* 2259–2268.

Seligman, M. E. P., & Csikszentmihalyi, M. (2000). Positive psychology: An introduction. *American Psychologist, 55,* 5–14.

Singer, B. H., & Ryff, C. D. (1997). Racial and ethnic inequalities in health: Environmental, psychosocial, and physiological pathways. In B. Devlin, S. E. Fienberg, D. Resnick, & K. Roeder (Eds.), *Intelligence, genes, and success: Scientists respond to the bell curve* (pp. 89–122). New York: Springer-Verlag.

Singer, B., & Ryff, C. D. (1999). Hierarchies of life histories and associated health risks. In N. E. Adler, B. S. McEwen, & M. Marmot (Eds.), *Socioeconomic status and health in industrialized countries. Annals of the New York Academy of Sciences, 896,* 96–115.

Singer, B., Ryff, C. D., Carr, D., & Magee, W. J. (1998). Life histories and mental health: A person-centered strategy. In A. Raftery (Ed.), *Sociological methodology, 1998* (pp. 1–51). Washington, DC: American Sociological Association.

Staudinger, U. M., Fleeson, W., & Baltes, P. B. (1999). Predictors of subjective physical health and global well-being: Similarities and differences between the United States and Germany. *Journal of Personality and Social Psychology, 76,* 305–319.

Sutton, S. K., & Davidson, R. J. (1997). Prefrontal brain asymmetry: A biological substrate of the behavioral approach and inhibitor systems. *Psychological Science, 8,* 204–210.

Tedeschi, R. G., Park, C. L., & Calhoun, L. G. (Eds.). (1998). *Posttraumatic growth: Positive changes in the aftermath of crisis.* Mahwah, NJ: Erlbaum.

Von Franz, M. L. (1964). The process of individuation. In C. G. Jung (Ed.), *Man and his symbols* (pp. 158–229). New York: Doubleday.

Ware, J. E., & Sherbourne, C. D. (1992). The MOS 36-item short-form health survey (SF-36): I. Conceptual framework and item selection. *Medical Care, 30,* 473–483.

20

POLITICAL SYMBOLS AND COLLECTIVE MORAL ACTION

DAVID O. SEARS

One of the most potent forces in human society is collective political action. This activity normally requires both leaders ("elites") and followers drawn from the mass public. In this chapter my main focus is on the behavior of mass publics, but the roles of both sets of actors must be taken into consideration. A second focus is on collective political actions that are carried out with an explicitly moral purpose. Examples include the civil rights legislation of the mid-1960s and the 1999 NATO actions in Yugoslavia to protect Kosovars of Albanian descent.[1] Of course, the moral purpose is rarely the sole motive, because economic and political interests are almost always also at stake.

In particular, the moral purpose often does not dominate elites' decision making but may be used primarily to justify the action rhetorically to a mass public whose support is critical for success but whose interests are not very obviously involved. Or a moral purpose may be used primarily to legitimate the action in the eyes of outsiders or opponents. Nevertheless, such qualifications are not crucial for the purposes of this chapter, as my

---

[1]My examples will be drawn primarily from the world of U.S. politics, because I can claim little expertise at any detailed level about other political systems.

primary focus is on the behavior of mass publics. Whatever elites' "true" motives, I would argue that mass publics often do evaluate collective political actions in principled or moral terms. Philosophers, social commentators, and religious and political leaders have often regarded this capacity for collective moral action as a major human strength and, sometimes, as the most important of all. So it stands as a prime case of the phenomena treated in this volume. However, it is easier to conclude that such a capacity is an unalloyed human strength than it is to decide whether it is generally a force for good or a force for evil.

THE PSYCHOLOGY OF POLITICAL MOTIVATION

One starting point in thinking about whether collective political action is a force for good or for evil is to consider motivation. Broadly speaking, political psychologists have approached the issue of motivation in two different ways. One is to assess whether political action comes from elites who are, crudely speaking, psychologically healthy or pathological. The mainstream view on this point has undergone quite a swing over time. In 1930, Lasswell published his pioneering *Psychopathology and Politics*, a study of political elites from the perspective of psychoanalytic theory. Its core thesis was that the political actions of individual activists were often motivated by quite personal and idiosyncratic psychodynamic needs and then rationalized as being in the general good. Even if such a psychological process had beneficial results, which it surely would on occasion, it plainly would be driven by irrational processes—that is, by elites' intrapsychic conflicts rather than by their objective assessments of the public good. In 1941 Fromm published *Escape From Freedom*, an analysis in much the same genre though focusing more on mass publics. Then *The Authoritarian Personality* (Adorno, Frenkel-Brunswik, Levinson, & Sanford, 1950) focused primarily on mass publics but still highlighted the role of idiosyncratic intrapsychic conflicts. The emphasis on the irrational was surely, in these last two cases, much influenced by the phenomenon they sought to explain —the rise of fascism.

By the late 1950s, however, the pendulum had started to swing. In 1959, Lane published a contrasting account in *Political Life*, whose equally psychological theme was that political activists are ordinarily relatively healthy, happy, effective, and well-adjusted human beings. And recently a most popular vein of political analysis has used the theory of rational choice drawn from neoclassical economics (Mansbridge, 1990). This analysis begins with the assumption that individuals tend to act rationally and in their own interests within the constraints of limited information. Although the definition of interests is nominally quite broad (indeed, the omnibus term "preferences" is often used, and they are often treated as a given rather than being analyzed in their own right), in the end most attention is given to economic goods or political power. In this theory, then, the psychopathology and irrationality of people struggling with their unconscious intrapsychic conflicts have been replaced by alert, reality-testing, objective, and rationally acting individuals. This shift of psychological emphasis toward rational choice theories—a visible though not universal trend—would bring political psychology closer to theories of "positive psychology" that prefer the view of humans as self-organizing, self-directed, adaptive decision makers rather than as passive vessels blown about by powerful external and internal forces (Seligman & Csikszentmihalyi, 2000).

A second approach has been to develop comprehensive typologies of motives for political action. There are some striking parallels across disciplines. A number of authors have proposed typologies that contrast principled motives with self- or group-interested motives. For example, social psychologists have proposed functional theories of attitudes that distinguish the value-expressive and instrumental functions that an attitude might serve (e.g., Katz, 1960). Political scientists have distinguished purposive (principles) from material (self-interest) and solidary (group interest) motives (Wilson & Clark, 1961). The economist Amartya Sen (1977) distinguished "commitment" (concerned with morals and public goods) from egoistic (self-interest) or sympathetic (behavior that helps others with whom one identifies) motivation.

THE THEORY OF SYMBOLIC POLITICS

The role of principled or value-expressive motives in mass politics has been developed in the theory of "symbolic politics" (Sears, 1993). This theory involves several assumptions: that people acquire strong affective predispositions about particular attitude objects in their early years, that these predispositions can be quite stable across the life course, and that presenting appropriate political symbols activates those predispositions. For example, most Americans have acquired strongly negative, and quite stable, attitudes toward Nazism as they grew up. In adulthood, hate crimes attributed to neo-Nazis often will stimulate demand for punitive action and preventive legislation. According to this perspective, mass collective action should be triggered by political symbols that evoke strong predispositions in substantial numbers of people. It would therefore reflect principled action based on long-standing values or preferences, at least in part.

Everyone is familiar with the rallying power of evocative political symbols. Concord and Lexington, the Boston Tea Party, Bunker Hill, Valley Forge, and the storming of the Bastille all were used as moralized symbols to motivate support for revolution. The attack on Fort Sumter; the sinking of the battleship Maine and the passenger liner Lusitania; and the attacks on Pearl Harbor, Kuwait, and the World Trade Center and the Pentagon were all successfully used by American leaders as symbols to motivate engagement in wars. The New York firefighters and police who died in the World Trade Center were used as unifying symbols after the attacks of September 11, and American flags suddenly appeared everywhere. On the other hand, President Lyndon Johnson tried to use the supposed attacks on American ships in the Tonkin Gulf in similar fashion to justify expanded military activity in Vietnam, but as is well known that proved less effective.

Symbolic predispositions tied to evocative moralized symbols can be perpetuated and reproduced across many generations. Some Muslims, most recently Osama bin Laden and his followers, have recurrently fought to restore a medieval caliphate unifying all of Islam. The founding of Serbia in Kosovo and Serbs' aggrieved reaction to the battlefield loss to 14th-century Ottomans have remained strong emotional commitments for many Serbs. The same is true for the city of Jerusalem, holy to Jews, Muslims, and Christians alike. In his Gettysburg Address, President Abraham Lincoln was able to appeal to the symbols embedded in a document written "four score and seven years" earlier, long before most of his audience was born. Civil rights leader Martin Luther King, Jr., mesmerized his audience with those same symbols in the March on Washington a century later, and they continue to have the power to move today. French schoolchildren as late as the 1960s still were highly politically polarized over the symbols representing support or opposition to the French Revolution, an event that had occurred almost two centuries earlier (Roig & Billon-Grand, 1968). In the 1990s, White Georgians who most wanted to retain the Confederate battle emblem in their state flag were those who had been reared and steeped in the Jim Crow system of the Old South: those who had been born in the South, who were most fond of the old Confederacy, and who were most racially prejudiced (Reingold & Wike, 1998).

Highly salient political events become particularly evocative political symbols if they become the subject of collective memory. Both the understandings shared among large numbers of people and the strong affect associated with such symbols give them a particular potency. A number of examples of such collective memories have been documented in recent years by Schuman and his colleagues (Schuman, Belli, & Bischoping, 1997; Schuman & Scott, 1989). What is most striking is that political events seem to leave their strongest attitudinal residues in people just passing from adolescence into young adulthood. For example, World War II was most often cited as an especially important event by the cohort aged 20 in 1943, the Vietnam War by the cohort aged 20 in 1968, and President Franklin Delano Roosevelt's Works Progress Administration by the cohort aged 19 when it began in 1938.

What are the conditions for creating such evocative collective memories? There are probably many, but two are suggested by the theory of symbolic politics. First, highly salient political events attract strong information flows, in the sense that they stimulate much media coverage and interpersonal communication. Such events therefore provide especially good occasions for the youthful acquisition of highly crystallized predispositions. This process was illustrated in a study of the 1980 presidential campaign (Sears & Valentino, 1997). Adolescents' attitudes toward the candidates and parties, the focal points of the campaign, became considerably more crystallized from the beginning to the end of the campaign. However, not all attitudes were so affected: Their attitudes in domains more peripheral to the campaign did not become more crystallized; none of their political attitudes became more crystallized during the year following the campaign; and their parents' partisan attitudes, which were more fully crystallized at the outset, were not much affected. So the socializing effects of the campaign were specific to younger people and to attitude domains that generated the heaviest information flows.

A second condition for developing highly crystallized collective memories should, by the symbolic politics theory, be political controversy. Intense debate provides clarifying and simplifying social constructions of the events in question. It also adds affect, as competing perspectives line up on opposite sides and the good guys and bad guys are identified. One example is the "riot ideology" that developed in Los Angeles after the race riots there in 1965. Over time, some Black people developed an increasingly coherent view of those events as a collective racial protest that would draw sympathetic attention to the legitimate grievances of the Black population (Sears & McConahay, 1973). Most White people developed the equally coherent but opposite view that it was simply a random explosion of antisocial and criminal behavior and would only worsen the conditions of Black people. These two views mirrored the contrasting elite views of some outspoken Black leaders, on the one hand, and conservative White leaders on the other, who debated these issues at length. Likewise, in its early stages the Vietnam War was supported by most American elites and most of the mass public. Over time, however, the elites became increasingly split, and "hawks" and "doves" in the mass public began to diverge sharply (Zaller, 1992).

But not all salient political events leave such evocative collective memories among young people. The Korean War evidently left very little (Schuman & Scott, 1989). Why it did not is puzzling, in some ways, because the casualty rate and elite debate were both intense, and divisions in the mass public were substantial. A more understandable example, perhaps, concerns the internment of West Coast Japanese Americans in World War II. It was not widely debated at the time. Also, according to one analysis, young internees themselves were so surprised, confused, and humiliated by their fate that they were left with a desire not to think or talk about it for many years to come. As a result, few developed a coherent political ideology about it, quite unlike the civil rights and anti-Vietnam protestors of the 1960s, for example. Indeed, it took a later generation of Japanese American youths, inspired by the civil rights movement, to take up the cause and make it a centerpiece of their appeal to pride in their own ethnicity (Rhea, 1997).

A third example is the assassination of President John F. Kennedy in 1963. He was widely admired among young people; his death was widely experienced as a tragic loss and indeed, for many, a first experience of the death of a loved one. This left a powerful and poignant collective memory among young Americans (Schuman et al., 1997), but perhaps a particularly conflicted one. A strong socially constructed account of his life and the political meaning of his regime took hold, which seems to have influenced political liberals for many years. But there was no comparable account of his death; no clear enemy emerged, or even a consensual account of the event, so that the great distress experienced by so many seems not to have been converted into any possibly vengeful lasting predisposition (Sears, 2002).

GROUPS: IDENTITIES AND INTERESTS

The symbolic politics perspective centers on the role of past experience in promoting the acquisition of symbolic predispositions. It contrasts with theories that highlight the role of realistic material self-interest in mass political action; if strong predispositions are acquired early in life, they are not likely to be based on careful calculations of one's own economic interests. Indeed, considerable research shows that self-interest, defined in terms of short-term material benefits and costs to one's personal life, is not a major factor most of the time in the mass public's political attitudes (Sears & Funk, 1991). Much evidence also indicates that human happiness has less to do with accumulation of wealth and economic growth than with such noneconomic factors as close relationships, work satisfaction, and religious faith (Lane, 2000; Myers, 2000). Such findings dovetail nicely with the theme in positive psychology that some of the most important aspects of the human experience involve neither markets nor money (Schwartz, 2000).

However, theories of the motivating power of interests are not exhausted by reference to self-interest. Indeed, collective moral action by its nature ordinarily involves groups, identifiable categories of actors with shared values who are in combat with some reviled enemy. Theories of realistic group conflict or of a "sense of group position" suggest that political attitudes are motivated by what is perceived as in the interest of one's group (Bobo, 1999). The theory of social identity similarly views group identity as central to one's preferences, though without the focus on shared interests (e.g., Tajfel & Turner, 1986). These theories describe the pathologies that are introduced into politics by conflict between warring tribes, each blindly attached to its own in-group and hostile to some out-group or another. At times, such as in the Balkans recently, such intergroup conflicts seem so ingrained and so intractable that they appear to be essential and inevitable destructive aspects of ordinary human life. And at other times, as with the medieval Christian Crusaders or today's Islamic mujahideen, the mass commitment to destroy entire civilizations on behalf of a particular religious in-group seems far out of keeping with normal human motivations.

For the sake of parsimony, a symbolic politics theory does not privilege attitudes about in-groups and out-groups in this way. Instead, it treats groups like other political symbols. One might acquire positive attitudes toward them, or negative attitudes, or even perhaps indifference in the course of growing up. For example, one might indeed acquire strong in-group loyalties, as Israeli Jews have in the years since World War II. But another in-group might not be a matter of strong attachment; blue collar workers in America have historically had a relatively weak sense of class consciousness. One out-group might attract strong negative predispositions, as in the strong anti-Anglophone feelings of the French Quebecois, the anti-German prejudices of many Americans during World War I, or the desire of Islamic extremists to destroy the United States. But another out-group, or the same out-group in other times, might not; most Americans currently regard Americans of German ancestry with equanimity.

These contrasting perspectives raise a number of important issues that seem to me unresolved at this time. One set is empirical: How central are in-group identity and interests in the real world? The "minimal group experiments" pioneered by Tajfel and his colleagues (e.g., Tajfel & Turner, 1986) are important reminders that group loyalties can be readily established without much basis in experience or real tangible interests. But they do not tell us much about whether or not they will indeed be established in more complex real-world contexts. Bosnian Serbs had generations of interethnic experience, not a brief arbitrary experimental manipulation. But then so have American socioeconomic classes, despite the relatively mild class consciousness that has traditionally marked American politics. To test the centrality of group interests in the real world requires direct measurement of constructs such as in-group identity and perceived group interests. So far such measurement is in its infancy (Sears & Henry, 1999). At this point one can say with some confidence only that if strong senses of in-group identity and interest are sufficient for collective moral action, they are not necessary. For example, extensive research has turned up little positive evidence that either group identity or group interest is centrally involved in White Americans' resistance to liberal race-targeted policies (Sears & Funk, 1991; Sears & Jessor, 1996; but see Kinder & Sanders, 1996).

A second set of unresolved questions concerns matters of theoretical boundaries. The simple distinctions among concepts we began with do have considerable force, as indicated by the empirical research just cited. But at their boundaries they become clouded and other theoretical questions are raised. One example is the boundary between *interests* and *symbolic predispositions*. It is easy to distinguish an adult's realistic economic calculation about a personally damaging tax policy from a value acquired in adolescence. Critiques of economic sanctions against Iraq that result in the deaths of thousands of Iraqi children can be distinguished from a supposed religious duty to expand Islam by killing all Americans.

But where do threats to social status fit in? The "sense of group position" theory (Bobo, 1999) describes a minority group's threats to a dominant group's status as just as psychologically motivating as threats to its economic superiority. Again, the case of the Old South seems to fit that point well: Many areas of the South did not depend heavily on cheap Black labor, and many White Southerners were presumably not realistically threatened economically very much by such a poor and uneducated population, yet racism was virulent there. Issues of social status seem to have been central. It is unclear how those threats to status fit with a symbolic politics or realistic group conflict theory.

Finally, some forms of group consciousness are clearly based in a realistic sense of one's group interests. They involve actually being a member of a group, feeling politically close to it, and feeling a sense of common fate with other group members. But one also can imagine a more "symbolic" form of group consciousness, in which the real stakes are much less clear but the feelings just as passionate (Sears & Kinder, 1985). Some Jewish Americans feel quite attached to their religious identity and feel passionately about an undivided Jerusalem as a sovereign capital of the state of Israel. But what real interests are involved? A contemporary Serb might identify with those who lost a 14th-century war to the Ottomans without feeling any sense of common fate with those long-dead warriors. Are these similar psychological phenomena to those involved in a union member's support for union efforts to negotiate a pay raise?

ELITES AND MASS PUBLICS

What does a symbolic politics theory say about the relationship between elites and masses? To frame the question in terms of extreme alternatives, are mass publics like wind-up toys, to be energized and directed at the whims of elites? Or are political elites mere panderers seeking to ingratiate themselves with the public for the purpose of re-election?

It is easy to depict mass publics as quite vulnerable to elites' control. But that power can easily be overdrawn. Ordinary citizens often have strong political predispositions that make them active players themselves. A good example is the civil rights movement in the United States in the 1950s and 1960s. In explaining both the passage of civil rights legislation in the 1960s and the realignment of the Southern White population into the Republican party, Carmines and Stimson (1989) focused particular attention on elites. Northern liberal Democratic gains in the 1958 election had shifted the ideological centers of gravity of the two political parties in Congress, with the Democratic party becoming more liberal as conservative Southern Democrats lost influence and the Republican party becoming more conservative with the defeat of several Northern liberals. Both sides later responded predictably to the "exogenous shock" of the civil rights movement. Lee (2002), by contrast, showed convincingly that this change at the elite level was preceded by over a decade of intensive grassroots effort, first by White liberals and Black civil rights activists, and then by White conservatives in reaction to them. Passionate grassroots efforts in the service of powerful long-standing symbolic predispositions can also further ignoble causes, of course. Goldhagen (1996) argued that a widespread "eliminationist" anti-Semitism among ordinary Germans was responsible for many of the horrors of the Holocaust, whatever the orders issued from on high by Nazi elites.

A second point regarding the relationship between masses and elites concerns the power of community norms. Lincoln's prosecution of the Union side of the Civil War was constantly jeopardized by the widespread racism then existing among the Northern White population. He treated emancipation of the slaves as a principal goal of the war only late and then with much trepidation, fearing that it would cost him the 1864 election and that his opponents would then negotiate a settlement that preserved slavery. Similarly, historians seem to provide relatively few accounts of strenuous White resistance to mob lynchings of Black people in the Old South. That leads one to suspect that community norms often accepted lynching as a legitimate response to Black people's supposed offenses. And whatever one thinks of Goldhagen's (1996) controversial thesis, the Holocaust plainly could not have occurred had fully egalitarian and inclusive norms about Jews dominated in the German mass public.

Finally, crediting mass publics with the capacity to generate grassroots political change in the service of what they perceive to be moral causes should not be taken to claim that elites have little or no role. Much is written about the power of elites to use the mass media to influence public opinion. To be sure, relatively little empirical research has demonstrated any great ability of the media to change strongly held attitudes in the general public. Rather, the strong information flows reflected in extensive media coverage have typically been shown mainly to polarize people around their preexisting predispositions, as in the early "minimal effects model" literature on short-term media effects (Klapper, 1960; see also McGuire, 1986) and as symbolic politics theory would expect. Over longer periods of time, strong but conflicting flows of information to people with strong predispositions also tend to polarize them (Zaller, 1992, 1997).

Nevertheless, if elites have limited power to control what people think, their agenda-setting capabilities can influence what people think about, benefitting one side at the expense of the other by priming predispositions that work to the advantage of the former (Iyengar & Kinder, 1987). President George H. W. Bush benefited by using the Willie Horton case in the 1988 presidential campaign to get voters thinking about Democrats' reputation for being too permissive about violent crimes committed by Black people (Mendelberg, 2001). Similarly, the Bush administration was successful in placing the Gulf crisis high on the public's agenda in 1990, and evaluations of President Bush became increasingly tied to evaluations of that venture (Krosnick & Brannon, 1993). Elites can also influence which predispositions are evoked by influencing how issues are framed. Framing affirmative action as providing Black people with unfair advantages may evoke racial prejudice among White people; framing it as reverse discrimination against White people may instead evoke feelings of threat (Kinder & Sanders, 1996). Likewise, framing bilingual education as intended to maintain an alien culture rather than as a way to teach foreign-born children the English language may evoke nationalism and increase opposition to it (Sears & Huddy, 1992).

SYMBOLIC POLITICS AND POSITIVE PSYCHOLOGY

Are the processes described by a symbolic politics theory also examples of a psychology of human strengths? These two perspectives would seem to converge in appreciating the strong human capacity to become attached emotionally to abstract political symbols. Those attachments can readily be evoked by the ambient informational environment in adulthood and can form a strong basis for collective political action. This would seem to be a major human strength, of as much social consequence as any other human strength I can think of.

But these perspectives also diverge on an important point. Symbolic politics theory expects that the most politically important symbolic predispositions are likely to be acquired prior to mature adulthood, as part of a relatively passive social learning process by which individuals come to reflect the predominant norms of their social environments. They then remain largely stable throughout the life span. Some versions of the psychology of human strengths emphasize, instead, humans' self-determination and need for autonomy and their continuing absorption with challenges and the unfolding of individual strengths through the entire life span (see Myers, 2000; Ryan & Deci, 2000; Seligman & Csikszentmihalyi, 2000). To be sure, symbolic politics theory would agree that some political attitudes are under continual revision in adulthood, but primarily those that are simply not very strong and so unlikely to have much influence on major political decisions (Sears, 1983).

More wiggle room is provided by the general finding that symbolic predispositions seem to undergo a period of vulnerability to change during the "impressionable years" of late adolescence and early adulthood (Sears, 1990). An example would be students becoming more politically liberal when attending a predominantly liberal college (e.g., Alwin, Cohen, & Newcomb, 1991). Another example would be the use of madrasa schools by fundamental Islamic clerics in Pakistan to create a cadre of young Islamic extremists ready to engage in a suicidal holy war against the West. Symbolic politics theorists usually explain such conversion experiences as reflecting passive adjustments to a changed attitudinal environment (Miller & Sears, 1986). But the same data could be interpreted from a human strengths perspective as reflecting a process of more active deliberation and choice, though probably not with the same stage-specific limitation.

Are the processes described by a symbolic politics theory examples of a "positive psychology"? The moral purpose in collective political action is usually regarded as a supremely, perhaps even uniquely, positive feature of human nature. And some of people's strongest collective memories concern events whose effects are widely and consensually regarded as benefiting humanity in general. Americans almost universally regard the defeat of the Axis powers in World War II as their "good war." The civil rights movement and the accompanying legislation that eliminated the Jim Crow system is widely regarded as a major success story (even though many believe that "we have gone too far" in the direction of guaranteeing equality; see Sears, Henry, & Kosterman, 2000). By the same token, some powerful collective memories involve events now consensually regarded as having had horrendous effects. Few Americans today would restore slavery, and few Germans would restore the Nazi regime (although controversy still swirls about the scope of the Holocaust, and visible neo-Nazi and skinhead movements do exist).

But is this "human strength" generally used by ordinary citizens in the service of good, or is it also sometimes used in the service of evil? Symbolic politics theory would take the view that it does not work intrinsically for either good or evil. For one thing, whether collective moral action is positive or negative is in practice often in the eye of the beholder. The Crusades were justified as a way to promote the ideals of Christianity, but they were fiercely bloody and ethnocentric. The abolitionist movement today is often seen as a necessary force in overthrowing an evil system of chattel slavery, but at the time many viewed it as undercutting the foundations of a civilized society. Lynchings in the Old South were often condemned, but many were justified as punishing antisocial behavior by Black people. Even the Holocaust was justified by Hitler's Nazi movement as having the noble goal of purifying the Aryan race from degrading influences. Many applauded Martin Luther King, Jr.'s, relentless moral impulse, but others thought him badly misguided or even subversive. Most view the killing of doctors who perform abortions as unconscionable murder, but others see it as having the noble goal of protecting the rights of helpless unborn infants. Some view the terrorist actions of devout Muslim fundamentalists as part of a holy war, or jihad, that will carry suicide bombers directly to an eternal paradise, whereas President George W. Bush has described them as "evil" acts committed by "evildoers."

The very considerable human strength of collective political action does not necessarily translate into beneficent outcomes for all concerned, then, any more than does the strength reflected by a powerful army or a rapidly growing cell system. It might be appropriate therefore to be cautious about equating it too quickly with positive psychology. The ability of elites to mobilize strong public passions through effective use of political symbolism can have constructive effects, it can have destructive effects, or it can have mixed effects wherein some people are benefitted and others are harmed. It is intrinsically neither good nor bad. But it is a powerful ability indeed. Trying to understand which direction it will take will remain a central question for political psychologists.

In this process, as Key (1961) pointed out long ago, elites bear a considerable moral burden of responsibility, both because of their inherent political powers and also because they greatly influence the grounds on which the public's predispositions will play out. In the case of the civil rights revolution in the 1960s, it is clear that much of Carmines and Stimson's (1989) attention to elite leadership is well placed. The Southern racial conservatives in the Democratic party had prevented any serious consideration of racial issues by the federal government from the 1930s until the 1960s through their control of key roles in Congress. When the civil rights movement could no longer be ignored, the enhanced strength of racial liberals in the Democratic caucuses in Congress and the leadership of Presidents Kennedy and Johnson and much of the Republican leadership in Congress, however reluctant and belated, were central to providing an information flow both powerful in volume and acceptable in content to the great majority of the American public and assembling mass support for radical change. At the same time, the candidacies of the conservative Republican Barry Goldwater in 1964 and of George C. Wallace in 1968 were centered on opposition to civil rights legislation and contributed greatly to "White backlash."

If a positive psychology holds that people make choices, and symbolic politics theory holds that political choices often reflect long-standing moral commitments, then one must remember that elites are human, too, and must reflect the same process, however much their choices are influenced also by desire for political and economic power. President Johnson, in 1964, chose to throw his lot in with the civil rights revolution, even though he accurately predicted that it would sacrifice the White South to the Republican party and so cost the Democratic party the substantial national majority it then held. It is perhaps ironic that Key's (1961) injunction was followed so quickly by elite actions that would fulfill just the responsibilities he called for.

REFERENCES

Adorno, T. W., Frenkel-Brunswik, E., Levinson, D. J., & Sanford, R. N. (1950). *The authoritarian personality.* New York: Harper & Row.

Alwin, D. F., Cohen, R. L., & Newcomb, T. M. (1991). *Aging, personality and social change: Attitude persistence and change over the life-span.* Madison, WI: University of Wisconsin Press.

Bobo, L. (1999). Prejudice as group position: Micro-foundations of a sociological approach to racism and race relations. *Journal of Social Issues, 55,* 445–472.

Carmines, E. G., & Stimson, J. A. (1989). *Issue evolution: Race and the transformation of American politics.* Princeton, NJ: Princeton University Press.

Fromm, E. (1941). *Escape from freedom.* New York: Holt.

Goldhagen, D. J. (1996). *Hitler's willing executioners: Ordinary Germans and the Holocaust.* New York: Knopf.

Iyengar, S., & Kinder, D. R. (1987). *News that matters: Television and American opinion.* Chicago: University of Chicago Press.

Katz, D. (1960). The functional approach to the study of attitudes. *Public Opinion Quarterly, 24,* 163–204.

Key, V. O., Jr. (1961). *Public opinion and American democracy.* New York: Knopf.

Kinder, D. R., & Sanders, L. M. (1996). *Divided by color: Racial politics and democratic ideals.* Chicago: University of Chicago Press.

Klapper, J. T. (1960). *The effects of mass communications.* Glencoe, IL: Free Press.

Krosnick, J. A., & Brannon, L. A. (1993). The media and the foundations of presidential support: George Bush and the Persian Gulf conflict. *Journal of Social Issues, 49*(4), 167–182.

Lane, R. E. (1959). *Political life.* Glencoe, IL: Free Press.

Lane, R. E. (2000). *The loss of happiness in market democracies.* New Haven, CT: Yale University Press.

Lasswell, H. D. (1930). *Psychopathology and politics.* New York: Viking.

Lee, T. (2002). *Mobilizing public opinion: Black insurgency and racial attitudes in the civil rights era.* Chicago: University of Chicago Press.

Mansbridge, J. J. (Ed.). (1990). *Beyond self-interest.* Chicago: University of Chicago Press.

McGuire, W. J. (1986). The myth of massive media impact: Savagings and salvagings. In G. Comstock (Ed.), *Public communication and behavior* (Vol. 1, pp. 173–257). Orlando, FL: Academic Press.

Mendelberg, T. (2001). *The race card: Campaign strategy, implicit messages, and the norm of equality.* Princeton, NJ: Princeton University Press.

Miller, S., & Sears, D. O. (1986, February). Stability and change in social tolerance: A test of the persistence hypothesis. *American Journal of Political Science, 30,* 214–236.

Myers, D. G. (2000). The funds, friends, and faith of happy people. *American Psychologist, 55,* 56–67.

Reingold, B., & Wike, R. S. (1998). Changing the Georgia state flag: The impact of racial attitudes and southern identity. *Social Science Quarterly, 79,* 568–580.

Rhea, J. T. (1997). *Race pride and the American identity.* Cambridge, MA: Harvard University Press.

Roig, C., & Billon-Grand, F. (1968). La socialisation politique des enfants [The political socialization of children]. *Cahiers de la Fondation Nationale des Sciences Politique, No. 163.*

Ryan, R. M., & Deci, E. L. (2000). Self-determination theory and the facilitation of intrinsic motivation, social development, and well-being. *American Psychologist, 55,* 68–78.

Schuman, H., Belli, R. F., & Bischoping, K. (1997). The generational basis of historical knowledge. In J. W. Pennebaker, D. Paez, & B. Rime (Eds.), *Collective memory of political events: Social psychological perspectives* (pp. 47–77). Mahwah, NJ: Erlbaum.

Schuman, H., & Scott, J. (1989). Generations and collective memories. *American Sociological Review, 54,* 359–381.

Schwartz, B. (2000). Self-determination: The tyranny of freedom. *American Psychologist, 55,* 79–88.

Sears, D. O. (1983). The persistence of early political predispositions: The roles of attitude object and life stage. In L. Wheeler & P. Shaver (Eds.), *Review of personality and social psychology* (Vol. 4, pp. 79–116). Beverly Hills, CA: Sage.

Sears, D. O. (1990). Whither political socialization research? The question of persistence. In O. Ichilov (Ed.), *Political socialization, citizenship education, and democracy* (pp. 69–97). New York: Teachers College Press.

Sears, D. O. (1993). Symbolic politics: A socio-psychological theory. In S. Iyengar & W. J. McGuire (Eds.), *Explorations in political psychology* (pp. 113–149). Durham, NC: Duke University Press.

Sears, D. O. (2002). Long-term psychological consequences of political events. In K. Monroe (Ed.), *Political psychology* (pp. 249–269). Mahwah, NJ: Erlbaum.

Sears, D. O., & Funk, C. L. (1991). The role of self-interest in social and political attitudes. In M. Zanna (Ed.), *Advances in experimental social psychology* (Vol. 24, pp. 1–91). Orlando, FL: Academic Press.

Sears, D. O., & Henry, P. J. (1999). Ethnic identity and group threat in American politics. *Political Psychologist, 4,* 12–17.

Sears, D. O., Henry, P. J., & Kosterman, R. (2000). Egalitarian values and contemporary racial politics. In D. O. Sears, J. Sidanius, & L. Bobo (Eds.), *Racialized politics: The debate about racism in America* (pp. 75–117). Chicago: University of Chicago Press.

Sears, D. O., & Huddy, L. (1992). The symbolic politics of opposition to bilingual education. In J. Simpson & S. Worchel (Eds.), *Conflict between people and peoples* (pp. 145–169). Chicago: Nelson-Hall.

Sears, D. O., & Jessor, T. (1996). Whites' racial policy attitudes: The role of White racism. *Social Science Quarterly, 77,* 751–759.

Sears, D. O., & Kinder, D. R. (1985). Whites' opposition to busing: On conceptualizing and operationalizing group conflict. *Journal of Personality and Social Psychology, 48,* 1141–1147.

Sears, D. O., & McConahay, J. B. (1973). *The politics of violence: The new urban blacks and the Watts riot.* Boston: Houghton Mifflin. [Reprinted by University Press of America, 1981.]

Sears, D. O., & Valentino, N. A. (1997). Politics matters: Political events as catalysts for preadult socialization. *American Political Science Review, 91,* 45–65.

Seligman, M. E. P., & Csikszentmihalyi, M. (2000). Positive psychology: An introduction. *American Psychologist, 55,* 5–14.

Sen, A. (1977). Rationality and morality: A reply. *Erkenntnis, 11,* 225–232.

Tajfel, H., & Turner, J. C. (1986). The social identity theory of intergroup behavior. In S. Worchel & W. G. Austin (Eds.), *Psychology of intergroup relations* (2nd ed., pp. 7–24). Chicago: Nelson-Hall.

Wilson, J. Q., & Clark, P. B. (1961). Incentive systems: A theory of organization. *Administrative Science Quarterly, 6,* 129–166.

Zaller, J. (1992). *The nature and origins of mass opinion.* New York: Cambridge University Press.

Zaller, J. (1997). The myth of massive media impact revisited: New support for a discredited idea. In D. Mutz (Ed.), *Political persuasion and attitude change* (pp. 17–78). Ann Arbor, MI: University of Michigan Press.

21

POSITIVE CLINICAL PSYCHOLOGY

MARTIN E. P. SELIGMAN AND CHRISTOPHER PETERSON

"My good sir," said the professor in remonstrance, "don't you believe
that criminology is science?"
"I'm not sure," replied Father Brown. "Do you believe that hagiology
is a science?"
"What's that?" asked the specialist sharply.
"No; it's not the study of hags, and has nothing to do with burning
witches," said the priest, smiling. "It's the study of holy things, saints
and so on. You see, the Dark Ages tried to make a science about good
people. But our own humane and enlightened age is only interested
in a science about bad ones."
                        —G. K. Chesterton, "The Man with Two Beards"

The science of positive psychology, as we see it, has three constituent
parts: the study of positive subjective experience, the study of positive
individual traits, and the study of institutions that enable the first two
(Seligman & Csikszentmihalyi, 2000). In this chapter we shall discuss the
possible changes that a science of positive psychology, if successful in becoming a discrete approach within the social sciences, would likely wreak
on the field of clinical psychology.

SETTING THE STAGE: POSITIVE PSYCHOLOGY YESTERDAY, TODAY, AND TOMORROW

Because positive psychology first took form in 1998, during a time of
peace and prosperity for the United States, our initial view was that pos-

This research was supported by grants MH19604 and MH52270 from the National Institute of
Mental Health. We also acknowledge the encouragement and support of the Manuel D. and
Rhoda Mayerson Foundation in creating the Values in Action (VIA) Institute, a nonprofit
organization dedicated to the development of a scientific knowledge base of human strengths.
The content of the prevention and therapy sections uses material from Seligman (2002), from
the Positive Psychology Network, and from the VIA Institute.

itive psychology would most flourish under benign social conditions. If the good times stopped rolling, the world would rightly turn its scientific resources back to defense and damage and its sentiments back to victimology. Negative emotions would generally trump positive emotions. So we thought.

In the wake of the terrorist attacks on the World Trade Center on September 11, 2001, our thinking has changed. Positive psychology is showing no sign of withering away. Indeed, positive psychology is now more relevant than ever. In times of trouble, like the present, the understanding of the positive emotions does not go by the boards: Confidence, optimism, hope, and trust, for example, serve us best not when life is easy, but when life is difficult. In times of trouble, understanding and building such strengths and virtues as valor, perspective, integrity, fairness, and loyalty may become more urgent than in good times. And in times of trouble, shoring up and enabling the positive institutions like democracy, strong family, and a free press take on added and immediate importance.

Because of its explicit focus on the positive, we now think that positive psychology provides one of the best ways to help people in trouble. It should have been obvious all along that persons who are impoverished, depressed, or suicidal care about much more than the relief of their suffering. These persons care—sometimes desperately—about strength and virtue, about authenticity, about purpose, and about integrity. Furthermore, the relief of suffering very often depends on the fostering of happiness and the building of character. Positive emotion undoes negative emotion. In the laboratory, movies that induce positive emotion cause negative emotion to dissipate rapidly (Fredrickson, 1998). The strengths and virtues buffer against misfortune and against the psychological disorders, and they may be the key to building resilience (Scales, Benson, Leffert, & Blyth, 2000). As we discuss later in this chapter, the best therapists do not merely heal damage; they help people identify and build their strengths and their virtues.

In discussing the future impact of positive psychology, we need to emphasize the qualification "if successful." Ten years from now, what criteria might we use to judge whether this fledgling movement, begun in 1998, succeeded? The first criterion is surely serious scientific discovery. Neither the present science nor the mere addition of well-intentioned armchair tracts (e.g., this one) about the importance of positivity will be sufficient to generate a field we would count as successful. A second criterion is the development of a well-accepted classification of aspects of human excellence and reliable and valid means of measuring its entries. A third criterion is useful and widespread applications of the scientific discoveries and the classification entries—in industry, parenting, education, communications, and the clinic. Because we are optimistic about the flourishing of the science, we will turn now specifically to the influences that positive psychology would have on clinical psychology, discussing in turn our thoughts about classification, measurement, etiology, therapy, and prevention.

A CLASSIFICATION OF HUMAN STRENGTHS

The starting place for positive psychology is the creation of an authoritative classification, or a set of categories reflecting areas of human excellence. Positive clinical psychology cannot make much progress as long as it uses the language of disease and deficiency. The positive classification we envision can be thought of as the un-DSM-I, and by the time this volume is printed, there will be a full-blown infrastructure devoted to just this project. In February of 1999, a group of senior figures met to begin this daunting endeavor. The participants were Don Clifton, Mike Csikszentmihalyi, Ed Diener, Kathleen Hall Jamieson, Robert Nozick, Dan Robinson, Martin E. P. Seligman, and George Vaillant, with Derek Isaacowitz as recording secretary.

The goal of this meeting was the enumeration of potential components of a good life, which would form the basis of a classification and research agenda for positive psychology and positive social science. After discussing concerns about the culture specificity of such an endeavor and how this project would relate to classical notions of the good life, the group devised a list of characteristics as a first approximation of such entries. We called these romantically "mansions," then more neutrally "wellsprings," and now simply "strengths." Occasionally, we use "virtues," intending the connotations of excellence that adhere to Aristotle's term *arête*.

In July of 2000, the Values in Action (VIA) Classification project began, funded by the Mayerson Foundation and the Positive Psychology Network and led by Christopher Peterson and George Vaillant. Following is a preliminary report of this work, just one year into the three-year project. Using the start forged at the 1999 meeting, we asked, "What qualifies a human characteristic as a strength in our nosology?" We came up with seven criteria:

1. A strength should be trait-like in the sense of having some *generality across situations and stability across time.* In keeping with the broad premise of positive psychology, strengths entail more than the mere absence of distress and disorder. They "break through the zero point" of psychology's traditional concern with disease and deficit and draw attention to the quality of life.
2. A strength is *celebrated when present and mourned when absent.* A strength is valued in its own right, even in the absence of obvious benefits.

3. *Parents try to inculcate strengths within their children.* We found useful a thought experiment: What does a parent wish for his or her newborn? Most parents would say, "I want my child to be kind, to be honest, to be prudent." Most would not say that they want their child to avoid psychopathology. They would not say that they want their child to work in middle management.

4. The larger society *provides institutions and associated rituals for cultivating strengths.* These can be thought of as simulations: trial runs that allow children and adolescents to display and develop a strength in a safe (as-if) context in which guidance is explicit. High school student councils presumably foster citizenship; Little League teams are thought to contribute to the development of teamwork; catechism classes attempt to lay the foundation for spirituality.

5. Cultures provide *role models and parables* that illustrate a strength in compelling fashion. These models may be real (Cal Ripken and perseverance), apocryphal (George Washington and honesty), or explicitly mythic (Luke Skywalker and flow).

6. *There exist prodigies* with respect to a strength—for example, children who show a strength at a much earlier age than typical or at a much more sophisticated level than typical. Conversely, there might exist other children who are completely and strikingly devoid of a given strength. These criteria imply that the strength in question is discrete and lends itself to biopsychological explanation.

7. To include a strength in our classification, it *must be recognized and valued in almost every major subculture.* Whether these will apply in Germany in 2005 or applied in mainland China in 1966 is an empirical matter, but at minimum if the VIA Classification exercise is useful for the present, parallel endeavors should be useful at other times. One could try for a universal classification of strengths to apply at all times and in all cultures. Such an ambitious project, if possible, is well beyond our first aim. The strengths on which we focus are also intended to be noncontroversial and apolitical, hence the requirement that all subcultures value each strength. We do not intend a list of strengths adumbrated by a bunch of middle-aged white academics sitting in armchairs in Philadelphia—otherwise there would be no reason to take our classification more seriously than the heavenly virtues of Thomas Aquinas or the Boy Scout oath to be "trustworthy, loyal, helpful." This premise is an attempt to make the

project descriptive and to free it from political, racial, ethnic, gender, and socioeconomic bias.

How can we distinguish "strengths" from "talents" and "abilities?" The line is fuzzy, and its placement depends on distinctions that are debatable. Nonetheless, we want to distinguish strengths and virtues (like honesty and hope) from talents and abilities (like fast-twitch muscles, facial symmetry, perfect pitch, verbal IQ, and immunocompetence). Some of the contrasts we are considering include the following: First, talents and abilities on the face of it seem more innate, more immutable, and less voluntary than strengths and virtues. Second, talents and abilities seem valued more for their tangible consequences (acclaim, wealth) than in their own right. Indeed, someone who "does nothing" with a talent like a high IQ courts eventual disdain. In contrast, we never hear the criticism that a person did nothing with his or her kindness or authenticity.

This chapter is not the right forum for a discussion of free will and determinism, so we will just note in passing our strong suspicion that positive psychology, as the field evolves, will necessarily lead social scientists to grapple anew with the crucial role in human activity that is played by choice. If we cannot speak of ostensibly virtuous activity as voluntarily chosen, then it is only masquerading as virtue. And so we have a third possible distinction: The identification of talents and abilities does not need the qualification of "freely chosen."

How can we distinguish strengths from fulfillments, or the outcomes that result from activity in accordance with the strengths? Fulfillments that are likely consequences of the strengths include positive emotions (happiness, joy, contentment); rewarding intimate relationships (love, friendship); approval by self and others; mental health and quality of life; vocational satisfaction and success; satisfying leisure and recreational activities; supportive and consistent families; and safe and responsive communities.

Table 21.1 provides a very tentative enumeration of the strengths and virtues. This list is not intended to be exclusive or exhaustive, just a useful beginning. The list will undoubtedly change several times over the course of the classification project. For the sake of convenience, we began with six superordinate categories of strengths that emerged from our literature reviews, subdividing each into subgroups phrased in more psychological language.

Such a classification, of course, bears on DSM-IV. How does a patient rank on each of the strengths? How do these strengths buffer against or feed into pathological categories? How does treatment change these strengths, and how does building the strengths change the disorders? The fields of psychology and psychiatry have come to accept the notion that the "real" mental disorders are those entities enumerated in DSM: unipolar

TABLE 21.1
Tentative List of Strengths

Wisdom and knowledge	Curiosity, interest Love of learning Judgment, critical thinking, open-mindedness Practical intelligence, creativity, originality, ingenuity Perspective
Courage	Valor Industry, perseverance Integrity, honesty, authenticity Zest, enthusiasm
Love	Intimacy, reciprocal attachment Kindness, generosity, nurturance Social intelligence, personal intelligence, emotional intelligence
Justice	Citizenship, duty, loyalty, teamwork Equity, fairness Leadership
Temperance	Forgiveness, mercy Modesty, humility Prudence, caution Self-control, self-regulation
Transcendence	Awe, wonder, appreciation of beauty and excel- lence Gratitude Hope, optimism, future-mindedness Playfulness, humor Spirituality, sense of purpose, faith, religiousness

depression, caffeine intoxication, dissociative identity disorder, and the like. Perhaps the VIA Classification will provide a better alternative: What, after all, is the absence of a character strength? Consider a person without a shred of honesty, with no hope, or devoid of kindness. We want to venture the possibility that these absences may be the true disorders, the natural classes, and that the entities listed in DSM may be mere congeries, clumsily overlapping collections of these more elementary deficits.

Measurement

There is a large variety of measurement strategies for these strengths: behavioral, spouses' reports, biological substrates, and so on. For the DSM entries, the two most common measurement strategies are structured interviews and questionnaires; these two strategies are also being used for strengths. Wolin and Wolin (1996) have pioneered the first attempt at an interview strategy, which can be converted into a structured interview to parallel the Schedule for Affective Disorders and Schizophrenia (SADS) and Structured Clinical Interview for DSM (SCID). The VIA group will also try to create structured interviews for youths and for adults that map onto the classification entries. There are numerous questionnaires that measure the putative strengths identified in Table 21.1, and part of the task of the VIA group will be to evaluate and make recommendations about the most useful questionnaires.

One attempt at a new questionnaire should be mentioned, however. The Gallup Corporation, along with Edward Diener, Derek Isaacowitz, and Martin Seligman, has developed and tested a global questionnaire, the Wellsprings,[1] to measure many of the putative strengths across time, place, and political system. The existence of valid, stable, and reliable tools of measurement is crucial to asking the etiological questions of the strengths and to asking about the etiological interactions of the strengths with the clinical disorders.

Etiology

The central hypothesis about the strengths and the causes of clinical disorders is that certain strengths buffer against the development of certain disorders. Optimism, for example, might buffer against depression, flow in sports against substance abuse, and work ethic and social skills against schizophrenia. Testing these hypotheses requires measurement of the strengths and of the disorders across time and the use of longitudinal and experimental strategies. In general, the perspective of positive psychology suggests that the notion of buffering by protective factors, most particularly the VIA character strengths, will illuminate the heretofore largely elusive etiology of the major disorders.

Therapy

We are going to venture a radical proposition about why psychotherapy works as well as it does. We suggest that positive psychology, albeit intuitive and inchoate, is a major active ingredient in therapy as it is now done and, if recognized and honed, will become an even more effective approach to psychotherapy (Saleebey, 1992). But before doing so, it is necessary to say what we believe about specific ingredients in therapy. We believe there are some clear specifics in psychotherapy, such as Applied Tension for Blood and Injury Phobia, Cognitive Therapy for Panic, and Exposure for Obsessive–Compulsive Disorder (see Seligman, 1994, for a review). But specificity of technique to disorder is far from the whole story.

There are three serious anomalies on which specificity theories of the effectiveness of psychotherapy stub their toes. First, effectiveness studies (field studies of real-world psychotherapy), as opposed to laboratory efficacy studies of psychotherapy, show a substantially larger benefit of psychother-

---

[1]Information about Wellsprings can be obtained from ediener@s.psych.uiuc.edu.

apy. *The Consumer Reports* study, for example, showed that over 90% of the respondents reported substantial benefits, as opposed to about 65% in efficacy studies of specific psychotherapies (Seligman, 1995, 1996). Second, when one active treatment is compared to another active treatment, specificity tends to disappear or becomes quite a small effect (Elkin et al., 1989; Luborsky, Singer, & Luborsky, 1975; Smith & Glass, 1977). The lack of robust specificity is also apparent in much of the drug literature.

Methodologists argue endlessly over flaws in such outcome studies, but they cannot hatchet the general lack of specificity away. The fact is that almost no psychotherapy technique of which we can think (with the exceptions mentioned earlier) shows large, specific effects when compared to another form of psychotherapy or drug, adequately administered. Finally, consider the seriously large placebo effect found in almost all studies of psychotherapy and of drugs. In the depression literature, a typical example, around 50% of patients respond well to placebo drugs or therapies. Effective specific drugs or therapies usually add another 15% to this, and 75% of the effects of antidepressant drugs may be accounted for by their placebo nature (Kirsch & Sapirstein, 1998).

Why is psychotherapy so robustly effective? Why is there so little specificity of psychotherapy techniques or specific drugs? Why is there such a huge placebo effect? Let us speculate on this pattern. Many of the relevant ideas have been put forward under the derogatory misnomer "nonspecifics." We are going to rename two classes of nonspecifics as *tactics* and *deep strategies*. Among the tactics of good therapy are paying attention, being an authority figure, building rapport, deploying a grab bag of tricks of the trade (e.g., saying "Let's pause here" rather than "Let's stop here"), requiring that the patient pay for services, building trust, encouraging the patient to open up, naming the problem, and much more.

The deep strategies are not mysteries. Good therapists almost always use them (cf. Frank, 1974), but they are seldom named and infrequently studied. So locked into the disease model are we that we do not train our students to learn them. However, we believe that these deep strategies are for the most part techniques suggested by positive psychology. For example, one of the important deep strategies is the instilling of hope (Seligman, 1991; Snyder, Ilardi, Michael, & Cheavens, 2000). We believe that these deep strategies can be the subject of large-scale science, and we believe that new techniques will be invented that will maximize the strengths. But we are not going to discuss this issue now, as it is often discussed elsewhere in the literature on placebo, on explanatory style and hopelessness, and on demoralization (Seligman, 1994).

Another strategy is the building of buffering strengths. We believe that it is a common strategy among almost all competent psychotherapists first to identify and then to help their patients build a variety of strengths, rather than just to deliver specific damage-healing techniques. Among the strengths built in psychotherapy are courage, interpersonal skill, rationality, insight, optimism, authenticity, perseverance, realism, capacity for pleasure, future-mindedness, personal responsibility, and purpose. Assume for a moment that the building of such strengths has a larger therapeutic effect than the specific healing ingredients that have been discovered. If this is true, the relatively small specificity found when different active therapies and different drugs are compared and the massive placebo effects both follow.

Another illustrative deep strategy is narration. We believe that telling the stories of one's life, making sense of what otherwise seems chaotic, distilling and discovering a trajectory in one's life, and viewing one's life with a sense of agency rather than victimhood are all powerfully positive (Csikszentmihalyi, 1993; Pennebaker, 1990). We believe that all competent psychotherapy forces such narration, which buffers against mental disorder in just the same way hope does. Notice, however, that narration is not a primary subject of research on the therapy process, that we do not have categories of narration, that we do not train our students to facilitate narration, and that we do not reimburse practitioners for it.

The consideration of positive psychology in psychotherapy exposes a fundamental blind spot in outcome research: The search for EVTs (empirically validated therapies) has in its present form handcuffed the field by focusing only on validating the specific techniques that repair damage and that map uniquely into DSM-IV categories. The parallel emphasis in managed care organizations on delivering only brief treatments directed solely at healing damage may rob patients of the very best weapons in the arsenal of therapy—making patients stronger human beings. By working in the medical model and looking solely for the salves to heal the wounds, we psychologists have misplaced much of our science and much of our training. By embracing the disease model of psychotherapy, we have lost our birthright as psychologists—a birthright that embraces both healing what is weak and nurturing what is strong.

Prevention

How can problems like depression or substance abuse or schizophrenia be prevented in young people who are genetically vulnerable or who live in worlds that nurture these problems? How can murderous schoolyard violence be prevented in children who have access to weapons, poor parental supervision, and a mean streak? What we have learned over 50 years is that the disease model does not move us closer to the prevention of these serious problems. Indeed, the major strides in prevention have come largely from a perspective focused on systematically building competency, not correcting weakness (see Greenberg, Domitrovich, & Bumbarger, 1999, for a review of all documented effective prevention programs for youths).

Psychologists have discovered that there are human strengths that act as buffers against mental illness: courage, future-mindedness, optimism, interpersonal skill, faith, work ethic, hope, honesty, perseverance, the capacity for flow, and insight, to name several. Much of the task of prevention in this new century will be to create a science of strength whose mission will be to understand and learn how to foster these virtues in young people. Building the buffering wellsprings is likely to be the key element of prevention of the clinical disorders.

Our own work in prevention takes this approach and amplifies a skill that all individuals possess but usually deploy in the wrong place. The skill is called disputing (Beck, Rush, Shaw, & Emery, 1979), and its use is at the heart of learned optimism. If a rival for your job accuses you falsely of failing and not deserving your position, you will dispute him. You will marshal all the evidence that you do your job very well. You will grind the accusations into dust. But if you accuse yourself falsely of not deserving your job—which is just the content of the automatic thoughts of pessimists—you will not dispute it. If it issues from inside, we tend to believe it. So, in learned optimism training programs, we teach both children and adults to recognize their own catastrophic thinking and to become skilled disputers (Peterson, 2000; Seligman, 1991; Seligman, Reivich, Jaycox, & Gillham, 1995; Seligman, Schulman, DeRubeis, & Hollon, 1999).

This training works, and once learned, it is self-reinforcing. We have shown that learning optimism prevents depression and anxiety in children and adults, roughly halving the incidence of these disorders over the next two years. We mention this work only in passing, however, to show that building a strength—optimism—and teaching people when to use it, rather than repairing damage, effectively prevents depression and anxiety. Similarly, we believe that in the case of drug abuse among teenagers who grow up in a neighborhood that puts them at risk, effective prevention is not remedial. Rather, it consists in identifying and amplifying the strengths that these teens already have. A teenager who is future-minded, who is interpersonally skilled, or who derives flow from sports is at reduced risk for substance abuse. If schizophrenia is to be prevented in a young person at genetic risk, we propose that the repairing of damage is not going to work. Rather, we suggest that a young person who learns effective interpersonal skills, who has a strong work ethic, and who has learned persistence under adversity is at lessened risk for schizophrenia.

This, then, is the general stance of positive psychology toward prevention. It claims that there is a set of buffers against psychopathology: the positive human traits, the entries of the VIA classification. By identifying, amplifying, and concentrating on these strengths in people at risk, psychologists will do effective prevention. Working exclusively on personal weakness and on damaged brains, in contrast, has left science poorly equipped to do effective prevention. Psychologists need now to call for massive research on human strengths and virtues. The classification of human strengths and their reliable and valid measurement will be the central scientific pillars of such prevention. Researchers need to do the appropriate longitudinal studies and experiments to understand how these strengths grow (or are stunted; Vaillant, 2000). Psychologists need to develop and test interventions to build these strengths. Practitioners must recognize that much of the best work they already do in the consulting room is to amplify strengths rather than repair the weaknesses of their clients. Psychologists working with families, schools, religious communities, and corporations must develop climates that foster these strengths.

CONCLUSION

The major psychological theories now undergird a new science of strength and resilience. No longer do the dominant theories view the individual as a passive vessel "responding" to "stimuli." Rather, individuals are now seen as decision makers, with choices, preferences, and the possibility of becoming masterful and efficacious or, in malignant circumstances, helpless and hopeless. Science and practice that rely on the positive psychology approach may have the direct effect of preventing much of the major emotional disorders. It may also have two side effects: making the lives of clients physically healthier, given evidence about the effects of mental well-being on the body, and reorienting psychology back to its two neglected missions—making normal people stronger and more productive and maximizing human potential.

The practice of positive psychology transcends the health care system as it presently exists. Intervention to enhance a client's life may take place within a health care context—for example, by building courage to buffer against social phobia. The growth of the positive traits and of subjective well-being, however, is also a matter of child development, of education, of work, and of play. Improving the lives of people across all the realms of life is psychology's birthright, and our time has come to reclaim it.

REFERENCES

Beck, A., Rush, J., Shaw, B., & Emery, G. (1979). *Cognitive therapy*. New York: Guilford Press.

Csikszentmihalyi, M. (1993). *The evolving self*. New York: HarperCollins.

Elkin, I., Shea, T., Watkins, J. T., Imber, S. D., Sotsky, S. M., Collins, J. F., et al. (1989). National Institute of Mental Health treatment of depression collaborative research program. *Archives of General Psychiatry, 46,* 971–982.

Frank, J. D. (1974). *Persuasion and healing* (rev. ed.). New York: Schocken Books.

Fredrickson, B. (1998). What good are positive emotions? *Review of General Psychology, 2,* 300–319.

Greenberg, M., Domitrovich, C., & Bumbarger, B. (1999). *Preventing mental disorders in school-age children.* Washington, DC: Center for Mental Health Services, U.S. Department of Health and Human Services.

Kirsch, I., & Sapirstein, G. (1998). Listening to Prozac but hearing Placebo: A meta-analysis of antidepressant medication. *Prevention and Treatment, 1.* Retrieved July 2, 2002 from http://journals.apa.org/prevention/volume1/pre0010002a.html.

Luborsky, L., Singer, B., & Luborsky, L. (1975). Comparative studies of psychotherapies: Is it true that "Everyone has won and all must have prizes"? *Archives of General Psychiatry, 32,* 995–1007.

Pennebaker, J. (1990). *Opening up.* New York: Morrow.

Peterson, C. (2000). The future of optimism. *American Psychologist, 55,* 44–55.

Saleebey, D. (Ed.). (1992). *The strengths perspective in social work practice.* New York: Longman.

Scales, P. C., Benson, P. L., Leffert, N., & Blyth, D. A. (2000). Contributions of developmental assets to the prediction of thriving among adolescents. *Applied Developmental Science, 4,* 27–46.

Seligman, M. E. P. (1991). *Learned optimism.* New York: Knopf.

Seligman, M. E. P. (1994). *What you can change and what you can't.* New York: Knopf.

Seligman, M. E. P. (1995). The effectiveness of psychotherapy: The *Consumer Reports* study. *American Psychologist, 50,* 965–974.

Seligman, M. E. P. (1996). Science as an ally of practice. *American Psychologist, 51,* 1072–1079.

Seligman, M. E. P. (2002). Positive psychology, positive prevention, and positive therapy. In C. R. Snyder & S. J. Lopez (Eds.), *Handbook of positive psychology* (pp. 3–9). New York: Oxford University Press.

Seligman, M. E. P., & Csikszentmihalyi, M. (2000). Positive psychology: An introduction. *American Psychologist, 55,* 5–14.

Seligman, M. E. P., Reivich, K., Jaycox, L., & Gillham, J. (1995). *The optimistic child.* New York: Houghton Mifflin.

Seligman, M. E. P., Schulman, P., DeRubeis, R. J., & Hollon, S. D. (1999). The prevention of depression and anxiety. *Prevention and Treatment, 2.* Retrieved July, 2, 2002 from http://journals.apa.org/prevention/volume2/pre0020008a.html.

Smith, M. L., & Glass, G. V. (1977). The meta-analysis of psychotherapy outcome studies. *American Psychologist, 32,* 752–760.

Snyder, C., Ilardi, S., Michael, S., & Cheavens, J. (2000). Hope theory: Updating a common process for psychological change. In C. Snyder & R. Ingram (Eds.),

Handbook of psychological change: Psychotherapy processes and practices for the 21st century (pp. 128–153). New York: Wiley.

Vaillant, G. E. (2000). Adaptive mental mechanisms: Their role in a positive psychology. *American Psychologist, 55,* 89–98.

Wolin, S., & Wolin, S. (1996). The challenge model. *Child and Adolescent Psychiatric Clinics of North America, 5,* 243–256.

22

DRIVEN TO DESPAIR: WHY WE NEED TO REDEFINE THE CONCEPT AND MEASUREMENT OF INTELLIGENCE

ROBERT J. STERNBERG

The conventional notion of intelligence-related skills and the ways in which they are measured drives many people to despair, especially those who lose educational or employment opportunities because their scores on tests are not high enough. From the perspective of positive psychology, however, intelligence may be capable of being seen in a more positive light. In particular, in this chapter we suggest three principles for positive psychology and then apply them to intelligence. First, people have their own idiosyncratic definitions of success, which may or may not correspond to societal ones. Second, people not only adapt to but also shape and select their environments. Third, people adapt, shape, and select most effectively when they capitalize on strengths and compensate for or correct weaknesses.

Most definitions of intelligence do not follow these principles, which

Preparation of this chapter was supported by grant REC-9979843 from the U.S. National Science Foundation and award R206R950001 from the U.S. Department of Education, Office of Educational Research and Improvement. The article does not necessarily reflect the positions of the sponsoring agencies.

is why people are often driven to despair. Of course, their being driven to despair is figurative. In other places, it is literal.

PLANETARY EXCURSIONS

On the Planet Arret, there is no public transportation, so everyone over the age of 16 years needs to drive to survive. Most of the residents are clustered around the capital, Despair, and so they drive themselves to Despair daily. Because the roads are awful, the people rude, the streets overcrowded, the road signs and speed limits nonexistent, and the need to drive omnipresent, driving is far more important than anywhere else in the galaxy. Those who do not acquire outstanding driving skills frequently are injured or even die in car accidents, bringing others with them to the eternal rest.

On Arret, students start learning about driving from early on during their lives. Whole courses are devoted to driving, starting in elementary school. All universities at all levels require driving tests for admission. People who do not do well in the courses and the tests feel shame. Many find the content boring or unimportant to their lives, but the society has decided that driving tests are important, so they are.

There is one other fact worth mentioning about instruction and assessment on Arret. For most students, all of the instruction and testing up to the age of 22 is written. Students do not actually drive until they finish their schooling. Some people have noticed that many individuals who do extremely well in the courses and on the tests do not drive well, and vice versa. Nevertheless, many authoritative volumes have been written showing that written tests of driving skill tend to correlate positively with each other and that results of the written driving tests predict not only actual driving skill but other aspects of adaptation as well. The tests account for only about 10% of the individual-difference variation in driving skill, but as learned scholars have pointed out, even tests that account for 10% of the variation can save enormous funds when insurance companies take them into account in assessing people's susceptibility to accidents.

This pathetic story about the Planet Arret (which is "Terra"—another name for our own planet—spelled backward) characterizes fairly well what many Earthly countries, including my own (the United States), do with regard to the identification, development, and assessment of intellectual talents and achievements. We recognize that the ability to adapt to the environment is important and define it as intelligence ("Intelligence and Its Measurement," 1921; Sternberg & Detterman, 1986). This definition is fine as far as it goes, but it does not go far enough.

First, social scientists measure intelligence-related skills and achievement via paper-and-pencil tests. The problems on such tests do not seem much on their face to measure skills fundamental to adaptation. Second, the tests predict about 25% of the variation in academic performance but only about 10–15% of the variation in various kinds of life performance, but social scientists have decided that 10–15% is good enough (see, e.g., Herrnstein & Murray, 1994). Third, society opens educational and employment doors for those who do well on these only partially relevant tests and closes the doors of opportunity to those who do not do well, thereby driving many of those whose opportunities are lost to despair. Fourth, the system is self-validating, but it is attributed nevertheless to an "invisible hand of nature" (Herrnstein & Murray, 1994). People who do well on the tests and in school are given opportunities that people who do not do well do not get. Societies then notice that the people who are given opportunities to succeed do in fact succeed more frequently and at higher levels than people who are not given opportunities. Unfortunately, what people succeed in, on Terra as on Arret, is only weakly relevant to what they later will have to do in life. Fifth, social scientists declare this system a success, despite the lack of any meaningful "control" group that would show how an alternative system would fare.

REDEFINING THE CONCEPT OF INTELLIGENCE: THE THEORY OF SUCCESSFUL INTELLIGENCE

In recent years, my colleagues and I at Yale and elsewhere have attempted to redefine both the concept of intelligence and the system in which it is embedded. This redefinition is taking the form of a theory of successful intelligence.

Definition

The core of our work is the theory of successful intelligence (Sternberg, 1997, 1999a, 1999b). The theory defines *successful intelligence* as the set of skills needed to achieve success in life, as defined by the individual within his or her sociocultural context, in order to adapt to, shape, and select environments by identifying and capitalizing on strengths and identifying and compensating for or correcting weaknesses through a balance of analytical, creative, and practical skills. The definition of intelligence in this theory is much more in keeping with the goals and notions of positive psychology than is the traditional definition of intelligence as the ability to adapt to the environment. Why? First, the definition emphasizes the importance of each person defining success for himself or herself. The definition is not societally imposed (e.g., school grades, income), but rather socially constructed by the individual to represent his or her own aspirations. Second, the definition emphasizes one's ability not only to adapt to the environment, as is emphasized in traditional definitions, but also to shape and select environments. The individual thus plays a more important and positive role in creating environments rather than just trying to mold himself or herself to them. Third, the definition emphasizes capitalization on strengths. Rather than intelligence being seen as a single thing, it is seen as creating the most positive interaction with the environment of which one is capable, given one's pattern of strengths and weaknesses.

One can see contemporary examples of the definition of successful intelligence in three candidates for the U.S. presidency in the year 2000: Al Gore, Bill Bradley, and George W. Bush. All had modest scores on the test used for college admissions in the United States, a test that is similar to verbal intelligence tests. On a 200 to 800 scale, where 500 is average, Gore's score was somewhat, but not much, above average (625); Bush's was high average (566); and Bradley's was slightly below average (485). Yet all three individuals have been successfully intelligent in any meaningful sense of the term. Gore and Bradley have had distinguished careers as U.S. senators, and Gore has also been U.S. Vice President. Bush has been governor of Texas. Each individual has made the most of his strengths and found ways of correcting or compensating for weaknesses.

The theory of successful intelligence emphasizes that high intelligence is not some linear or other obvious mathematical combination of a set of scores with respect to analytical, creative, and practical skills. More important, rather, is the balance among these skills and how individuals capitalize on and compensate for or correct their pattern of abilities to maximize their success, however they define it.

Structure

The theory of successful intelligence comprises three subtheories: componential, experiential, and contextual (Sternberg, 1984, 1985). The componential subtheory specifies a set of three information-processing components that are used to think intelligently. *Metacomponents* are used to plan and evaluate. For example, they are used in recognizing and identifying problems, monitoring problem solving, and evaluating problem solutions. *Performance components* are used to execute the instructions of the metacomponents. For example, they are used in inferring relations between things or applying these relations in new domains. *Knowledge-acquisition components* are used to acquire these other kinds of skills in the first place. For example, they are used in distinguishing information that is relevant from that which is irrelevant for one's purposes. When knowledge acquisition components are applied to fairly familiar but decontextualized problems, they contribute to analytical intelligence, which is used when one analyzes, judges, evaluates, compares and contrasts, and so forth.

The experiential subtheory specifies that two regions of experience are particularly relevant to intelligence. The first is experiences in which the tasks and situations one confronts are relatively novel. When the components of intelligence are applied in this region of experience, they contribute to creative intelligence. This kind of intelligence is used when one creates, designs, invents, discovers, and explores. Creative intelligence may be only weakly correlated with analytical intelligence, because people may be adept at solving relatively familiar problems but not at solving relatively novel ones, and vice versa. The components are also relevant to intelligence in the second region of experience—automatization. When automatized, the components are executed rapidly and without conscious thought.

The contextual subtheory specifies that the components of intelligence are applied to experience in order to adapt to, shape, and select environments. Adaptation involves modifying oneself to suit an environment. Shaping involves modifying the environment to suit oneself. Selection involves deciding to choose a new environment. These three functions of intelligence contribute to practical intelligence.

Validation of the Theory of Successful Intelligence

The Importance of Prediction

Good theories need to be predictively validated. The importance of predictive validation is that postdictive validations almost inevitably are selective with regard to the evidence they consider. For example, two major postdictive theoretical statements, those of Gardner (1983) and of Carroll (1993), claim to be comprehensive in their considerations of literature, and yet there is practically no overlap between the literatures reviewed in the respective works. Similarly, Gardner's review overlaps practically not at all with that of Jensen (1998). The various theories of intelligence, such as Gardner's and Carroll's, among many others, are not equal with respect to empirical work. There have been numerous empirical studies validating general intelligence (see Jensen, 1998) but none, to my knowledge, validating Gardner's theory of multiple intelligences. Certainly selective literature reviews do not adequately validate any theory of intelligence.

For positive psychology or any other new movement in the field of psychology to be taken seriously and to enter into the scientific as well as the popular mainstream, it needs to meet the rigorous standards of scientific psychology, which means measurement of constructs and successful predictive validation. It is not enough to show how a theory is plausible or can be applied loosely to account for existing data. Typically, other extant theories also can be applied postdictively to account for extant data. The theory must show itself able to predict future data that other theories cannot predict or cannot predict as well.

Internal Validity of the Theory of Successful Intelligence

If there are so many studies validating a concept of general intelligence, how can one argue with the results? My argument is that the studies have restricted the universe of item types and situations in which the item types are measured (Sternberg, 1985, 1999a, 1999b; Sternberg et al., 2000). Our studies of internal validity have been of three general types:

1. *Task modeling.* One type is to study specific tasks and to model performance on them (Sternberg, 1983, 1985; Sternberg & Gastel, 1989a, 1989b; Sternberg & Kalmar, 1997). (Because much of this work is older, I do not review it here.) The general outcome of the research was to show the viability of the componential structure of the theory.

2. *Studies of relations of analytical, creative, and practical tasks.* We sought to investigate creative and practical tasks and their relations to analytical tasks. In one set of studies (Sternberg & Lubart, 1995), we asked adult participants to write short stories, draw pictures, design advertisements, and solve quasi-scientific problems. We evaluated products for their novelty, technical quality, and task appropriateness. We found relatively high levels of domain specificity and relatively low correlations between creativity scores and scores on more conventional tests of intelligence. Correlations increased with the levels of novelty of the conventional tests. In another set of studies, carried out over a period of years with thousands of participants, we have found that tests of practical intelligence show average correlations with tests of analytical abilities that are typically about zero. Although on rare occasions the correlations are signficantly positive, on other rare occasions they are significantly negative (Sternberg et al., 2000).

3. *Factor-analytic studies.* In more recent work, we have done confirmatory factor analyses based on samples in the United States, Spain, and Finland (Sternberg, Castejón, Prieto, Hautamäki, & Grigorenko, 2001; Sternberg, Grigorenko, Ferrari, & Clinkenbeard, 1999). The bottom line is that we have found support for the triarchic model (distinct analytical, creative, and practical factors) over competing models when ability tests include the creative and practical domains as well as the analytical domain. From our point of view, therefore, the reason that factor analyses of conventional tests yield a general (g) factor is because they measure almost exclusively the analytical aspect of intelligence.

External Validity

The limitation of conventional tests to analytical abilities means also that external validity is not as high as it can or ought to be. By measuring creative and practical abilities, it is possible to increase prediction both of academic and of school performance (Sternberg et al., 2000; Sternberg & Lubart, 1995). Redefining intelligence tests to include these two aspects will serve more to open than to close doors.

REDEFINING THE SYSTEM IN WHICH INTELLIGENCE IS EMBEDDED

To illustrate how an entire system of identification of abilities, instruction, and assessment can be done, we chose to do a rather large-scale study that would look at education from a different slant (Sternberg & Clinkenbeard, 1995; Sternberg, Ferrari, Clinkenbeard, & Grigorenko, 1996; Sternberg et al., 1999). We devised a triarchic abilities test (Sternberg, 1993) that would measure not only the conventional analytical abilities, but also creative and practical abilities. These abilities were measured in four ways: with multiple-choice (a) verbal, (b) quantitative, and (c) figural content, and with (d) essays. (We have since added performance tests of creative and practical abilities.)

We selected for a summer program in university-level introductory psychology 199 high school students from all over the United States who were distinctive in one of five ways: high analytically, high creatively, high practically, high in all three skills, or low in all three skills. These students were then assigned to instructional conditions that emphasized memory, analytical, creative, or practical instruction. Students were assigned at random, so that some were in an instructional condition that was a better match to their pattern of abilities and others were in an instructional condition that was a worse match. Then all students were assessed for their memory, analytical, creative, and practical achievement. For example, a memory question might ask the student to remember Freud's theory of depression. An analytical question might ask the student to compare Freud's theory to Beck's. A creative question might ask the student to generate his or her own theory of depression. A practical question might ask the student how to use what he or she has learned to help a friend who is depressed.

There were many findings, but a few key ones are worthy of mention here. First, who is intelligent? The analytical section of the test identified as intelligent those students typically identified as intelligent in school. Most of the students had high grades in good schools, were of middle to upper-middle socioeconomic class, and were predominantly White. The creative and practical sections of the test, however, identified a broader cross-section of students as intelligent. Students identified in these areas were less likely to be excellent students in the traditional sense, were more mixed in their socioeconomic levels, and were more mixed in their ethnic-group identifications.

Second, who achieves highly in school? In our study, all three tests (analytical, creative, and practical) predicted success in our course. Thus, creative and practical ability tests will predict school achievement if the teaching and assessment of achievement emphasizes the use of creative and practical skills.

Finally, how important is capitalization on strengths and compensation for or correction of weaknesses? We further found that students who were better matched to instruction with respect to their ability profiles outperformed students who were more poorly matched. In other words, if at least some of the time the teacher's way of teaching matches the student's particular strengths, the student will achieve at higher levels. One does not want the teaching always to match, because it is important also to learn to compensate for or correct weaknesses.

In follow-up studies (Sternberg, Torff, & Grigorenko, 1998a, 1998b), we concerned ourselves not with interactions but with main effects. We hypothesized, quite simply, that students taught analytically, creatively, and practically would outperform students taught either only analytically or only for memory, regardless of the students' ability pattern. We did our study with 213 3rd-grade students studying social studies and 141 entering 8th-graders studying science. We found in both groups that students taught for successful intelligence outperformed students in the two (analytically based and memory-based) control groups, even on memory tests of achievement! In other words, teaching for successful intelligence was superior, regardless of how achievement was assessed. These results were replicated in teaching reading to a large sample of low-income students (Grigorenko, Jarvin, & Sternberg, 2002).

CONCLUSION

Many students who currently are achieving at low levels could be achieving at high levels. They are achieving at low levels because many nations in Terra, as in Arret, use tests and instruction that take into account only a partial range of abilities. When identification of abilities, instruction, and assessment of achievement are redefined to encompass creative and practical as well as memory and analytical abilities, student achievement increases, and so does the base number of students identified as "intelligent."

A narrow conception of intelligence and achievement is not just an academic matter. It closes doors to educational and societal opportunities on the basis of measures that are overly narrow and not well related to the skills needed to succeed in life or even, arguably, in schools the way they should be. Effectively, many of the people who potentially have the greatest contribution to make—the highly creative and practical ones—never even get the chance to make this contribution. Not only are the individuals robbed of opportunities, therefore; the societies in which the individuals live and, potentially, even the world are robbed of talent as well.

We cannot do anything about the systems of instruction and assessment used on Arret. We can do a lot about the systems used on Earth. The time to change them is now. Can we afford to do otherwise?

The study of intelligence has important implications for the study of positive psychology. Although these implications are drawn from the study of intelligence, much the same conclusions could be reached from the study of personality or even of human motivation.

First, a conception of intelligence is needed, such as the conception of successful intelligence, that meets the standards of positive psychology. Three principles were described in this chapter, but more generally, intelligence must be measured and taught in a way that helps and is perceived as helping people rather than as putting up blockades. Too often in the past, tests of intelligence served more as case studies in "negative psychology" than in "positive psychology," because the tests were used to serve institutional needs at the expense of individual ones. Second, the study of intelligence and of other constructs in positive psychology needs a rigorous scientific footing. If scientific psychologists perceive the field of positive psychology as "soft," the field will be dismissed before it ever has a chance to be integrated into psychology as a science. Third, scientific rigor and humanitarian advancement must be combined in a way that produces a new, constructive outlook, largely absent in the past. To the extent that positive psychology aids in the achievement of that goal, it has performed a valuable service for psychology as a whole.

REFERENCES

Carroll, J. B. (1993). *Human cognitive abilities: A survey of factor-analytic studies*. New York: Cambridge University Press.

Gardner, H. (1983). *Frames of mind: The theory of multiple intelligences*. New York: Basic Books.

Grigorenko, E. L., Jarvin, L., & Sternberg, R. J. (2002). School-based tests of the triarchic theory of intelligence: Three settings, three samples, three syllabi. *Contemporary Educational Psychology, 27*, 167–208.

Herrnstein, R. J., & Murray, C. (1994). *The bell curve*. New York: Free Press.

Intelligence and its measurement: A symposium. (1921). *Journal of Educational Psychology, 12,* 123–147, 195–216, 271–275.

Jensen, A. (1998). *The g factor: The science of mental ability.* Westport, CT: Praeger/Greenwood.

Sternberg, R. J. (1983). Components of human intelligence. *Cognition, 15,* 1–48.

Sternberg, R. J. (1984). Toward a triarchic theory of human intelligence. *Behavioral and Brain Sciences, 7,* 269–287.

Sternberg, R. J. (1985). *Beyond IQ: A triarchic theory of human intelligence.* New York: Cambridge University Press.

Sternberg, R. J. (1993). *Triarchic abilities test.* Unpublished test.

Sternberg, R. J. (1997). *Successful intelligence.* New York: Plume.

Sternberg, R. J. (1999a). Successful intelligence: Finding a balance. *Trends in Cognitive Sciences, 3,* 436–442.

Sternberg, R. J. (1999b). The theory of successful intelligence. *Review of General Psychology, 3,* 292–316.

Sternberg, R. J., Castejón, J., Prieto, M. D., Hautamäki, J., & Grigorenko, E. L. (2001). Confirmatory factor analysis of the Sternberg Triarchic Abilities Test in three international samples: An empirical test of the triarchic theory of intelligence. *European Journal of Psychological Assessment, 17,* 1–16.

Sternberg, R. J., & Clinkenbeard, P. (1995). A triarchic model of identifying, teaching, and assessing gifted children. *Roeper Review, 17,* 255–260.

Sternberg, R. J., & Detterman, D. K. (Eds.). (1986). *What is intelligence? Contemporary viewpoints on its nature and definition.* Norwood, NJ: Ablex.

Sternberg, R. J., Ferrari, M., Clinkenbeard, P. R., & Grigorenko, E. L. (1996). Identification, instruction, and assessment of gifted children: A construct validation of a triarchic model. *Gifted Child Quarterly, 40,* 129–137.

Sternberg, R. J., Forsythe, G. B., Hedlund, J., Horvath, J., Snook, S., Williams, W. M., Wagner, R. K., & Grigorenko, E. L. (2000). *Practical intelligence in everyday life.* New York: Cambridge University Press.

Sternberg, R. J., & Gastel, J. (1989a). Coping with novelty in human intelligence: An empirical investigation. *Intelligence, 13,* 187–197.

Sternberg, R. J., & Gastel, J. (1989b). If dancers ate their shoes: Inductive reasoning with factual and counterfactual premises. *Memory and Cognition, 17,* 1–10.

Sternberg, R. J., Grigorenko, E. L., Ferrari, M., & Clinkenbeard, P. (1999). A triarchic analysis of an aptitude-treatment interaction. *European Journal of Psychological Assessment, 15,* 1–11.

Sternberg, R. J., & Kalmar, D. A. (1997). When will the milk spoil? Everyday induction in human intelligence. *Intelligence, 25,* 185–203.

Sternberg, R. J., & Lubart, T. I. (1995). *Defying the crowd: Cultivating creativity in a culture of conformity*. New York: Free Press.

Sternberg, R. J., Torff, B., & Grigorenko, E. L. (1998a). Teaching for successful intelligence raises school achievement. *Phi Delta Kappan, 79,* 667–669.

Sternberg, R. J., Torff, B., & Grigorenko, E. L. (1998b). Teaching triarchically improves school achievement. *Journal of Educational Psychology, 90,* 374–384.

23

THE ECOLOGY OF HUMAN STRENGTHS

DANIEL STOKOLS

The field of positive psychology offers an exciting and provocative counterpoint to a psychology of deficits and debilitation (Csikszentmihalyi, 1990; Kahneman, Diener, & Schwarz, 1999; Seligman & Csikszentmihalyi, 2000; Sheldon & King, 2001). As the field has evolved to date, however, it reflects certain limitations that warrant further consideration. This chapter examines these conceptual concerns from the perspectives of environmental and ecological psychology in light of key constructs and findings from prior studies of environment and behavior (e.g., Barker, 1968; Craik, 1973; Proshansky, Ittelson, & Rivlin, 1976; Stokols, 1995). I will address three specific concerns: (a) the incomplete conceptualization of environmental contexts as they influence well-being, (b) the disproportionate emphasis on positive emotional states and underemphasis on the temporal links between individuals' positive and negative experiences, and (c) the incomplete assessment of the threshold levels at which exposure to environmental constraints either enhances or undermines the development of psychological strengths. These theoretical concerns present opportunities for developing an ecologically grounded analysis of human strengths. Finally, I suggest future research efforts to chart the ecology of human

331

strengths as a basis for expanding the conceptual and empirical scope of positive psychology.

In this chapter, the term *subjective well-being* refers broadly to a set of interrelated affective phenomena including specific, pleasurable emotional states (e.g., happiness, contentment, satisfaction, love) as well as more generalized positive affect (Diener, 2000; Fredrickson, 2001; Lyubomirsky, 2001). Subjective criteria of well-being and physiological indices of health (or wellness) are closely interrelated and can influence each other (e.g., Antonovsky, 1987; Cohen & Williamson, 1991; World Health Organization, 1984). Moreover, certain personal resources and psychological strengths, such as high socioeconomic status, wisdom, and resilience, can facilitate individuals' efforts to achieve higher levels of subjective and physiological well-being (e.g., Adler et al., 1994; Baltes & Staudinger, 2000; Masten, 2001). The terms *emotional* and *subjective well-being* are used interchangeably to differentiate these affective phenomena from physiological or somatic criteria of well-being.

ENVIRONMENTAL INFLUENCES ON WELL-BEING

Positive psychology, while highlighting personal strengths and resilience, has given less attention to identifying environmental conditions that either constrain individuals from realizing their full potential or, alternatively, enhance their capacity to achieve positive life goals and an enduring sense of well-being. Although many researchers in the field acknowledge the effects of contextual factors on emotional states and human strengths (e.g., Buss, 2000; Diener & Suh, 2002; Simonton, 2000; Staudinger & Baltes, 1996), positive psychology still lacks a systematic conceptualization of the ways in which environmental conditions influence the cultivation and expression of certain human strengths. Ecological perspectives on life-span development and health promotion, articulated earlier (e.g., Bronfenbrenner, 1979; Friedman & Wachs, 1999; Moos, 1979; Stokols, 1992b) have yet to be incorporated into analyses of human strengths such as optimism, hope, and self-determination (e.g., Peterson, 2000; Schwartz, 2000).

Ecological research on human–environment relations reflects certain conceptual principles that can serve as guidelines for identifying environmental antecedents of well-being. First, ecological theories posit that human environments comprise both physical and social features. In some instances, the physical and social dimensions of environments are closely interrelated and jointly influence behavior and well-being (e.g., Altman, 1975; Barker, 1968; Firey, 1945). Second, environmental conditions can be grouped according to whether they have a positive impact on well-being by enhancing the congruence or fit between a person's goals, activities, and surroundings or, alternatively, have a negative effect on well-being by reducing levels of person–environment fit (Michelson, 1970; Wicker, 1972).

Table 23.1 categorizes selected physical and social dimensions of environments that exert either a positive or negative influence on well-being. The table incorporates only a small subset of potentially relevant environmental variables, but it is useful for illustrating certain general principles of ecological analysis. Examples of benign environmental conditions include aesthetic qualities of places that evoke pleasurable experiences among occupants (e.g., Nasar, 1988) and the clarity or legibility of physical environments that enables visitors to navigate places effectively and avoid feelings of confusion and disorientation (e.g., Lynch, 1960). The interior features of homes, offices, and health care settings can have a positive effect on both subjective and physiological well-being to the extent that they are comfortably arranged and ergonomically designed (e.g., Reizenstein Carpman, Grant, & Simmons, 1986; Stokols, 1998; Sundstrom & Sundstrom, 1986). Also, restorative environments (e.g., wilderness settings that are both beautiful and tranquil) enable individuals to engage in spontaneous or nondirected attention and to experience a sense of "getting away" from their usual activity routines (e.g., R. Kaplan & Kaplan, 1989). Across several studies, restorative environments have been shown to promote relaxation and alleviate stress (e.g., S. Kaplan, 1995, Korpela & Hartig, 1996; Ulrich, 1984).

The social attributes of environments can have positive effects on emotional well-being (Table 23.1). For instance, certain objects and places are associated with symbolic meanings of personal or group identity (e.g., Cooper, 1974; Firey, 1945; Rochberg-Halton & Csikszentmihalyi, 1981). These shared meanings convey the continuity of people's attachments to

TABLE 23.1
Physical and Social Features of Environments That Have a Positive or
Negative Impact on Well-Being

Influence on Well-Being	Physical	Social
Positive	Aesthetic quality Environmental clarity and imageability Comfortable interior design of buildings Restorative qualities of natural settings	Shared social meanings of places Understaffing of behavior settings Social support Social capital
Negative	Noise Overcrowding Vehicle traffic in neighborhoods Natural and technological disasters	Social isolation Lack of privacy Conflict-prone organizations Environmental racism

particular places and reinforce their feelings of belonging to a community and of a sense of "place identity" (Proshansky, Fabian, & Kaminoff, 1983; Tuan, 1974). Another feature of social environments that encourages group members (of, e.g., athletic teams, church congregations, high school clubs, business organizations) to participate actively in leadership roles while acquiring self-confidence through their participation are the staffing levels of behavior settings (Barker, 1968). To the extent that social settings are understaffed (i.e., have a small number of applicants to fill the roles available in an organization), they are more welcoming and supportive of their members (e.g., Barker & Schoggen, 1973; Wicker, McGrath, & Armstrong, 1972). Similarly, other studies have demonstrated that the availability of friendship networks, social support, and high levels of social capital in a community (i.e., the extent to which people trust each other and participate in shared activities) are associated with higher levels of both emotional and physiological well-being (Berkman & Syme, 1979; Cohen, Underwood, & Gottlieb, 2000; Putnam, 2000).

The physical and social features of environments are often closely intertwined and can jointly affect individuals' well-being. Table 23.1 lists physical factors that not only have direct negative impacts on well-being (e.g., the emotional annoyance and discomfort prompted by high levels of noise and overcrowding), but also can provoke social problems (e.g., interpersonal conflict, inadequate levels of privacy, social isolation and loneliness) that exert their own negative influence on well-being (e.g., Altman, 1975; Evans & Lepore, 1993; Glass & Singer, 1972; Perlman & Peplau, 1998; Rook, 1984). High levels of vehicular traffic in residential neighborhoods not only evoke feelings of annoyance and anxiety (about pollution and safety hazards), but also curtail interpersonal contacts among neighbors, which in turn leads to greater social isolation and reduced social support (Appleyard, 1981). Also, the occurrence of natural and technological disasters (e.g., hurricanes, earthquakes, tornados, toxic spills) are physical events that cause extensive damage, injury, and stress, but because technological mishaps result from human error, they often provoke longer-term social problems—for example, greater tendencies among citizens toward blame, resentment, and distrust of government officials (Baum, Fleming, & Davidson, 1983).

The contextual factors listed in Table 23.1 suggest some additional aspects of environmental conditions that are often considered in ecological research. The first is the duration or chronicity of exposure to an environmental factor. For instance, individuals may be exposed to comfortable or restorative surroundings for brief or extended periods. The positive effects of those circumstances on well-being are likely to be greater to the extent that they are enduring rather than transitory. On the other hand, prolonged exposure to noisy and congested environments typically has a more negative impact on well-being than brief encounters with stressful situations (Evans, 1999).

Just as the duration of a person's exposure to an environmental condition can be abbreviated or prolonged, the impact of that condition on well-being can vary along a continuum ranging from minimal to extreme. The social structures of conflict-prone organizations, for example, provoke more frequent interpersonal hassles than those found in conflict-resistant settings (Stokols, 1992a). To the extent that an employee lacks alternative employment opportunities and must remain in a conflict-prone company for an extended period, the impact on his or her well-being is likely to be severe and manifested not only in negative mood states at work but also in chronic experiences of depression, anxiety, and fatigue. Similarly, the disproportionate exposure of low-income minority neighborhoods to environmental pollutants stemming from institutionalized environmental racism at community levels can have deleterious effects not only on individuals' emotional well-being but also on their physical health status and longevity (e.g., Bullard, 1990; Bullard & Johnson, 2000).

The example of environmental injustice highlights another core principle of ecological analysis: the assumption that environmental units of analysis vary in scale from micro-level stimuli, objects, and momentary situations to meso-level behavior settings (e.g., homes, workplaces, classrooms) and macro-scale environments such as neighborhoods and whole communities (e.g., Ittelson, 1973; Magnusson, 1981; Michelson, 1985). Thus, an individual's cumulative exposure to environmental circumstances that have a positive or negative impact on well-being depends on the quality of conditions that he or she encounters in proximal settings as well as at the macrosystem level (e.g., political, economic, and cultural factors; Bronfenbrenner, 1992; Diener & Suh, 2002).

The preceding discussion offers a rather brief summary of ecological influences on well-being, but it does call attention to certain physical and social features of people's everyday environments that have direct and sometimes substantial impacts on well-being. The development of a more complete conceptualization of contextual influences on subjective and physiological well-being, and on the cultivation and expression of psychological strengths, would be a useful direction for future theory development in the field of positive psychology.

TOWARD A MORE INTEGRATED CONCEPTUALIZATION OF POSITIVE AND NEGATIVE EMOTIONAL STATES

In an effort to clearly distinguish positive psychology from more traditional clinical research on psychological deficits and dysfunction, participants in this new field may give disproportionate emphasis to positive affective states, while neglecting the inherent interdependencies between positive and negative emotions. By focusing predominantly on positive subjective states, researchers also may overlook the pivotal role of negative life experiences in facilitating the development of coping skills and psychological strengths (e.g., Antonovsky, 1987; Masten, 2001; Schaefer & Moos, 1992).

The opponent-process theory of motivation posits a cyclical pattern of positive and negative emotions, in which individuals' pleasurable subjective states eventually give way to more negative experiences and vice versa (Solomon, 1980). One explanation for these sequential shifts between positive and negative emotions is the statistical principle of regression toward the mean (Campbell, 1969), which suggests that extreme emotional states have a probabilistic tendency to shift over time toward milder levels. Another explanation for the temporal interdependence of positive and negative emotions is based on Thibaut and Kelley's (1959) concept of comparison level—a subjective standard that individuals use to evaluate the quality of their environments and social relationships. Negative emotional states provide a psychological "benchmark" for evaluating one's situation and deciding whether or not to enact behaviors that might bring about improved circumstances. Moreover, negative experiences enable individuals to better recognize, appreciate, and strive toward more favorable emotional states (Aldwin & Stokols, 1988). For some individuals the cyclical shifts between positive and negative emotional states can be both frequent and dramatic, as observed in studies linking manic–depressive personality styles to high levels of creative achievement (Pickering, 1974).

Thus, another potentially useful direction for research in the field of positive psychology is the development of more integrated theoretical accounts of the interdependencies between pleasant and unpleasant emotional states. Fredrickson's (2001) "broaden-and-build" theory of emotions addresses the ways in which positive emotions undo (or neutralize) negative emotional states and expand individuals' thought-action repertoires, but this theory does not consider the influence of negative emotions on a person's subsequent development of positive affect and psychological strengths. Those issues warrant greater attention in future studies.

LEVELS OF EXPOSURE TO ENVIRONMENTAL CONSTRAINTS THAT ENHANCE OR UNDERMINE HUMAN STRENGTHS

In the short run, environmental variables such as the aesthetic qualities of a place can evoke highly positive subjective states. Similarly, excessive levels of noise and overcrowding can have an immediate and negative impact on individuals' emotions. Yet the influence of contextual factors on emotional well-being and health is considerably more complex than these examples suggest. Earlier research indicates that when individuals encounter environments that are too predictable and too controllable, they experience those settings as boring and unchallenging (S. Kaplan, 1983). Ideally, people prefer environments that offer opportunities for exploration and for acquiring new information and skills (S. Kaplan, 1995), although these exploratory tendencies and preferences for novel surroundings may diminish during later stages of the life course (Lawton, 1999).

Psychological strengths such as the capacity to persevere under difficult circumstances may develop gradually as individuals cope with challenging situations. Prior studies further suggest that exposure to negative events may be a prerequisite for cultivating personal strengths such as self-confidence, creativity, sense of coherence, and capacity for hard work, which are essential for maintaining longer term emotional stability and well-being (e.g., Antonovsky, 1987; Eisenstadt, 1978; Maddi, 1974; Maddi, Kahn, & Maddi, 1998; Masten, 2001). On the other hand, confinement to degraded and impoverished environments for extended periods may overwhelm individuals' best efforts to rise above these constraints, thereby fostering dispositions toward helplessness and despair (e.g., Sarbin, 1970; Seligman, 1992). Similarly, the ever-widening gap between information-rich and information-poor segments of society may foster greater psychological deficits and a spiral of increasing poverty among individuals who find themselves on the wrong side of the "digital divide" (e.g., Castells, 1998; National Telecommunications and Information Administration, 2000; Stokols & Montero, 2001).

These considerations suggest that it is important for researchers to identify critical threshold levels at which individuals' cumulative exposures to environmental constraints begin to impede rather than facilitate the cultivation and expression of personal strengths. Further, it may be useful for researchers in the field of positive psychology to give greater attention to previously drawn distinctions between temporary motivational states and more enduring dispositional traits (e.g., Cattell, 1966; Mischel, 1969; Rotter, 1966; Spielberger, 1972). Whereas positive and negative emotional states can be expected to vacillate in a cyclical pattern from one situation to another, the more telling criterion of human strengths may be the cultivation of personal dispositions toward self-confidence, sense of coherence, self-determination, wisdom, optimism, faith, and hope and the avoidance of enduring tendencies toward helplessness, subservience, and despair.

In those instances where an individual's cumulative exposure to environmental risks and deficits is so overwhelming that resilience is impossible to achieve and dispositional helplessness ensues, it may be possible to develop new psychosocial and community interventions aimed at transforming these negative circumstances into more positive ones (Maddi et al., 1998; Schneider, 2001). At the same time, it is crucial that disadvantaged persons not be stigmatized or derogated for their inability to cultivate resilience and optimism in the face of overwhelming odds (e.g., Becker, 1991; Lerner, 1980). Research in the field of positive psychology may yield new strategies for reversing the all-too-common tendencies toward stigmatizing and blaming the victims of misfortune.

CONCLUSION

This chapter has addressed certain conceptual issues that warrant greater attention in future research on human strengths. Drawing upon the constructs and findings of environmental and ecological psychology, three general topics for further investigation were proposed for development: (a) a more complete conceptualization of environmental contexts as they influence well-being; (b) a more integrated conceptualization of the interdependencies between positive and negative emotional states and experiences; and (c) a more fine-grained analysis of the threshold levels at which individuals' cumulative exposures to environmental constraints begin to impede, rather than facilitate, the cultivation and expression of psychological strengths. Future research on the ecology of human strengths is needed to broaden the conceptual and empirical scope of positive psychology.

REFERENCES

Adler, N. E., Boyce, T., Chesney, M. A., Cohen, S., Folkman, S., Kahn, R. L., & Syme, S. L. (1994). Socioeconomic status and health: The challenge of the gradient. *American Psychologist, 49,* 15–24.

Aldwin, C., & Stokols, D. (1988). The effects of environmental change on individuals and groups: Some neglected issues in stress research. *Journal of Environmental Psychology, 8,* 57–75.

Altman, I. (1975). *The environment and social behavior.* Monterey, CA: Brooks/Cole.

Antonovsky, A. (1987). *Unraveling the mystery of health: How people manage stress and stay well.* San Francisco: Jossey-Bass.

Appleyard, D. (1981). *Livable streets.* Berkeley, CA: University of California Press.

Baltes, P. B., & Staudinger, U. M. (2000). Wisdom: A metaheuristic (pragmatic) to orchestrate mind and virtue toward excellence. *American Psychologist, 55,* 122–136.

Barker, R. G. (1968). *Ecological psychology: Concepts and methods for studying the environment of human behavior.* Stanford, CA: Stanford University Press.

Barker, R. G., & Schoggen, P. (1973). *Qualities of community life.* San Francisco: Jossey-Bass.

Baum, A., Fleming, R., & Davidson, L. M. (1983). Natural disaster and technological catastrophe. *Environment and Behavior, 15,* 333–354.

Becker, M. H. (1991). In hot pursuit of health promotion: Some admonitions. In S. M. Weiss, J. E. Fielding, & A. Baum (Eds.), *Perspectives in behavioral medicine: Health at work* (pp. 178–188). Hillsdale, NJ: Erlbaum.

Berkman, L. F., & Syme, S. L. (1979). Social networks, host resistance, and mortality: A nine-year follow-up study of Alameda County residents. *American Journal of Epidemiology, 109*, 186–204.

Bronfenbrenner, U. (1979). *The ecology of human development: Experiments by nature and design.* Cambridge, MA: Harvard University Press.

Bronfenbrenner, U. (1992). Ecological systems theory. In R. Vasta (Ed.), *Six theories of child development: Revised formulations and current issues* (pp. 187–249). London: Jessica Kingsley.

Bullard, R. D. (1990). *Dumping in Dixie: Race, class, and environmental quality.* Boulder, CO: Westview Press.

Bullard, R. D., & Johnson, G. S. (2000). Environmental justice: Grassroots activism and its impact on public policy decision making. *Journal of Social Issues, 56*, 558–578.

Buss, D. M. (2000). The evolution of happiness. *American Psychologist, 55*, 15–23.

Campbell, D. T. (1969). Reforms as experiments. *American Psychologist, 24*, 409–429.

Castells, M. (1998). *End of millennium.* Malden, MA: Blackwell.

Cattell, R. B. (Ed.). (1966). *Handbook of multivariate experimental psychology.* Chicago: Rand McNally.

Cohen, S., Underwood, L., & Gottlieb, B. (Eds.). (2000). *Social support measurement and interventions: A guide for health and social scientists.* New York: Oxford University Press.

Cohen, S., & Williamson, G. M. (1991). Stress and infectious disease in humans. *Psychological Bulletin, 109*, 5–24.

Cooper, C. (1974). The house as symbol of the self. In J. Lang, C. Burnette, W. Moleski, & D. Vachon (Eds.), *Designing for human behavior* (pp. 130–146). Stroudsburg, PA: Dowden, Hutchinson, & Ross.

Craik, K. H. (1973). Environmental psychology. *Annual Review of Psychology, 24*, 403–422.

Csikszentmihalyi, M. (1990). *Flow: The psychology of optimal experience.* New York: Harper & Row.

Diener, E. (2000). Subjective well-being: The science of happiness and a proposal for a national index. *American Psychologist, 55*, 34–43.

Diener, E., & Suh, E. M. (Eds.). (2002). *Subjective well-being across cultures.* Cambridge, MA: MIT Press.

Eisenstadt, J. M. (1978). Parental loss and genius. *American Psychologist, 33*, 211–223.

Evans, G. W. (1999). Measurement of the physical environment as a stressor. In S. L. Friedman & T. D. Wachs (Eds.), *Measuring environment across the lifespan:*

Emerging methods and concepts (pp. 249–277). Washington, DC: American Psychological Association.

Evans, G. W., & Lepore, S. J. (1993). Household crowding and social support: A quasi-experimental analysis. *Journal of Personality and Social Psychology, 65,* 308–316.

Firey, W. (1945). Sentiment and symbolism as ecological variables. *American Sociological Review, 10,* 140–148.

Fredrickson, B. L. (2001). The role of positive emotions in positive psychology: The broaden-and-build theory of positive emotions. *American Psychologist, 56,* 218–226.

Friedman, S. L., & Wachs, T. D. (Eds.). (1999). *Measuring environment across the lifespan: Emerging methods and concepts.* Washington, DC: American Psychological Association.

Glass, D. C., & Singer, J. E. (1972). *Urban stress.* New York: Academic Press.

Ittelson, W. H. (1973). *Environment and cognition.* New York: Seminar Press.

Kahneman, D., Diener, E., & Schwarz, N. (Eds.). (1999). *Well-being: The foundations of hedonic psychology.* New York: Russell Sage Foundation.

Kaplan, R., & Kaplan, S. (1989). *The experience of nature: A psychological perspective.* New York: Cambridge University Press.

Kaplan, S. (1983). A model of person-environment compatibility. *Environment and Behavior, 15,* 311–322.

Kaplan, S. (1995). The restorative benefits of nature: Toward an integrative framework. *Journal of Environmental Psychology, 15,* 169–182.

Korpela, K., & Hartig, T. (1996). Restorative qualities of favorite places. *Journal of Environmental Psychology, 16,* 221–233.

Lawton, M. P. (1999). Environments for older people. In S. L. Friedman & T. D. Wachs (Eds.), *Measuring environment across the lifespan: Emerging methods and concepts* (pp. 91–124). Washington, DC: American Psychological Association.

Lerner, M. J. (1980). *The belief in a just world: A fundamental delusion.* New York: Plenum Press.

Lynch, K. (1960). *The image of the city.* Cambridge, MA: MIT Press.

Lyubomirsky, S. (2001). Why are some people happier than others? The role of cognitive and motivational processes in well-being. *American Psychologist, 56,* 239–249.

Maddi, S. (1974). The strenuousness of the creative life. In I. A. Taylor & J. W. Getzels (Eds.), *Perspectives in creativity* (pp. 173–190). Chicago: Aldine.

Maddi, S. R., Kahn, S., & Maddi, K. (1998). The effectiveness of hardiness training. *Consulting Psychology Journal: Practice and Research, 50,* 78–86.

Magnusson, D. (1981). Wanted: A psychology of situations. In D. Magnusson (Ed.), *Toward a psychology of situations: An interactional perspective* (pp. 9–32). Hillsdale, NJ: Erlbaum.

Masten, A. S. (2001). Ordinary magic: Resilience processes in development. *American Psychologist, 56,* 227–238.

Michelson, W. (1970). *Man and his urban environment: A sociological approach.* Reading, MA: Addison-Wesley.

Michelson, W. H. (1985). *From sun to sun: Daily obligations and community structure in the lives of employed women and their families.* Totowa, NJ: Rowman & Allenheld.

Mischel, W. (1969). Continuity and change in personality. *American Psychologist, 24,* 1012–1018.

Moos, R. H. (1979). Social ecological perspectives on health. In G. C. Stone, F. Cohen, & N. E. Adler (Eds.), *Health psychology: A handbook* (pp. 523–547). San Francisco: Jossey-Bass.

Nasar, J. L. (Ed.). (1988). *Environmental aesthetics: Theory, research, and applications.* Cambridge, England: Cambridge University Press.

National Telecommunications and Information Administration. (2000). Americans in the information age falling through the net. Retrieved March 26, 2001, from http://www.ntia.doc.gov/ntiahome/digitaldivide/

Perlman, D., & Peplau, L. A. (1998). Loneliness. In H. S. Friedman (Ed.), *Encyclopedia of mental health* (Vol. 2, pp. 571–581). San Diego: Academic Press.

Peterson, C. (2000). The future of optimism. *American Psychologist, 55,* 44–55.

Pickering, C. (1974). *Creative malady.* New York: Delta Books.

Proshansky, H. M., Fabian, A. K., & Kaminoff, R. (1983). Place identity: Physical world socialization of the self. *Journal of Environmental Psychology, 3,* 57–83.

Proshansky, H. M., Ittelson, W. H., & Rivlin, L. G. (Eds.). (1976). *Environmental psychology: People and their physical settings* (2nd ed.). New York: Holt, Rinehart, & Winston.

Putnam, R. D. (2000). *Bowling alone: The collapse and revival of American community.* New York: Simon & Schuster.

Reizenstein Carpman, J., Grant, M. A., & Simmons, D. A. (1986). *Design that cares.* Chicago: American Hospital Association.

Rochberg-Halton, E., & Csikszentmihalyi, M. (1981). *The meaning of things: Domestic symbols and the self.* New York: Cambridge University Press.

Rook, K. S. (1984). Promoting social bonding: Strategies for helping the lonely and socially isolated. *American Psychologist, 39,* 1389–1407.

Rotter, J. B. (1966). Generalized expectancies for internal vs. external control of reinforcement. *Psychological Monographs, 80*(Whole No. 609).

Sarbin, T. R. (1970). The culture of poverty, social identity, and cognitive outcomes. In V. L. Allen (Ed.), *Psychological factors in poverty* (pp. 29–47). Chicago: Markham.

Schaefer, J. A., & Moos, R. H. (1992). Life crises and personal growth. In B. N. Carpenter (Ed.), *Personal coping: Theory, research, and application* (pp. 149–170). Westport, CT: Praeger.

Schneider, S. L. (2001). In search of realistic optimism: Meaning, knowledge, and warm fuzziness. *American Psychologist, 56,* 250–263.

Schwartz, B. (2000). Self-determination. *American Psychologist, 55,* 79–88.

Seligman, M. E. P. (1992). *Helplessness: On depression, development, and death.* New York: Freeman.

Seligman, M. E. P., & Csikszentmihalyi, M. (2000). Positive psychology: An introduction. *American Psychologist, 55,* 5–14.

Sheldon, K. M., & King, L. (2001). Why positive psychology is necessary. *American Psychologist, 56,* 216–217.

Simonton, D. K. (2000). Creativity: Cognitive, personal, developmental, and social aspects. *American Psychologist, 55,* 151–158.

Solomon, R. L. (1980). The opponent process theory of acquired motivation: The costs of pleasure and the benefits of pain. *American Psychologist, 35,* 691–712.

Spielberger, C. D. (1972). Anxiety as an emotional state. In C. D. Spielberger (Ed.), *Anxiety: Current trends in theory and research* (Vol. 1, pp. 23–49). New York: Academic Press.

Staudinger, U. M., & Baltes, P. B. (1996). Interactive minds: A facilitative setting for wisdom-related performance? *Journal of Personality and Social Psychology, 71,* 746–762.

Stokols, D. (1992a). Conflict-prone and conflict-resistant organizations. In H. Friedman (Ed.), *Hostility, coping, and health* (pp. 65–76). Washington, DC: American Psychological Association.

Stokols, D. (1992b). Establishing and maintaining healthy environments: Toward a social ecology of health promotion. *American Psychologist, 47,* 6–22.

Stokols, D. (1995). The paradox of environmental psychology. *American Psychologist, 50,* 821–837.

Stokols, D. (1998). Environmental design and occupational health. In J. Stellman & C. Brabant (Eds.), *ILO encyclopedia of occupational health and safety* (Vol. 4, pp. 34.19–34.22). Geneva, Switzerland: International Labor Office.

Stokols, D., & Montero, M. (2001). Toward an environmental psychology of the Internet. In R. B. Bechtel & A. Churchman (Eds.), *New handbook of environmental psychology* (pp. 661–675). New York: Wiley.

Sundstrom, E., & Sundstrom, M. G. (1986). *Work places: The psychology of the physical environment in offices and factories.* New York: Cambridge University Press.

Thibaut, J. W., & Kelley, H. H. (1959). *The social psychology of groups.* New York: Wiley.

Tuan, Y. F. (1974). *Topophilia: A study of environmental perception, attitudes, and values.* Englewood Cliffs, NJ: Prentice Hall.

Ulrich, R. S. (1984). View through a window may influence recovery from surgery. *Science, 224,* 420–421.

Wicker, A. W. (1972). Processes which mediate behavior-environment congruence. *Behavioral Science, 17,* 265–277.

Wicker, A. W., McGrath, J. E., & Armstrong, G. E. (1972). Organization size and behavior setting capacity as determinants of member participation. *Behavioral Science, 17,* 499–513.

World Health Organization. (1984). Health promotion: A discussion document on the concept and principles. *Health Promotion, 1,* 73–76.

AUTHOR INDEX

Elder, G. H., Jr., 14, 20, 25, 34, 241, 242
Elkin, I., 312, 315
Emery, G., 314, 315
Emmons, R. A., 278, 284
Emrich, C. E., 109, 114
Epstein, S., 199, 208, 219, 220, 223
Erber, R., 219, 225
Erez, A., 185, 192
Ericsson, K. A., 14, 20, 28, 30, 34
Erikson, E. H., 9, 20, 25, 34, 266, 269, 277, 284
Ernst, J. M., 212, 225
Essex, M. J., 275, 276, 284–286
Estrada, C. A., 182, 185, 188, 192
Evans, G. W., 334, 335, 339, 340

Fabes, R. A., 110, 114, 118–120, 122, 123, 127
Fabian, A. K., 334, 341
Fahey, J. L., 220, 222
Fava, G. A., 276, 282, 284
Feather, N. T., 88, 99
Feldman, S., 64, 73, 247, 249, 254, 255
Fennema, E., 111, 114
Fernández-Ballesteros, R., 68, 72, 139, 142, 143, 145
Ferrari, M., 324, 325, 328
Feshbach, N. D., 118, 120, 127
Fiedler, K., 198, 208
Filipp, S. H., 18, 20
Firey, W., 332, 333, 340
Fisher, J. E., 77, 84
Fiske, A. P., 42, 46
Fiske, S. T., 52, 59, 199, 205, 208, 209
Fleeson, W., 276, 287
Fleming, R., 334, 338
Fleshner, M., 280, 285
Foa, E., 220, 223
Fogarty, S. J., 180, 182, 188, 194
Folkman, S., 55, 59, 212, 213, 215, 219–221, 223–225, 338
Foner, A., 82, 86
Forgas, J. P., 184, 192
Forsythe, G. B., 328
Francis, M. E., 214–216, 224
Frank, E., 154, 162
Frank, J. D., 312, 315
Frankl, V. E., 277, 280, 284
Frederick, S., 13, 20, 168, 173, 177
Fredrickson, B. L., 186, 192, 306, 316, 332, 336, 340

Freitas, A. L., 249, 254
Frenkel-Brunswik, E., 290, 301
Frese, M., 18, 20
Freud, K., 205, 210
Freund, A., 18, 21
Freund, A. M., 23, 24, 29–31, 34, 93, 99
Frey, D., 151–157, 162–164
Friedman, H. S., 212, 223
Friedman, S. L., 332, 340
Fries, J. F., 142, 145
Fromm, E., 290, 301
Fulcomer, M., 77, 86
Funk, C. L., 294, 296, 303

Gaertner, S. L., 183, 191
Gardner, H., 323, 327
Gardner, W. L., 211, 212, 222
Garraghty, P. E., 63, 72
Gastel, J., 324, 328
Gaunt, R., 199, 205, 210
Gazzaniga, M. S., 39, 46
George, J. M., 182, 192
Gest, S. D., 239, 242
Geva, N., 185, 186, 193
Gigerenzer, G., 168, 177, 197, 198, 200, 206, 207, 208
Gilbert, D. T., 105, 113
Gillham, J., 314, 316
Gilovich, T., 170, 177
Ginosar, Z., 201, 205, 209
Girgus, J. S., 169, 177
Glaser, R., 212, 214, 223, 224, 284
Glass, D. C., 334, 340
Glass, G. V., 312, 316
Glück, J., 28, 34
Gold, D. P., 79, 84, 85
Goldberg, L. R., 167, 177
Goldhagen, D. J., 297, 301
Goldman, R., 203, 210
Goldstein, D. G., 207, 208
Goleman, D., 247, 254
Golisano, V., 191
Gollwitzer, P. M., 13, 21, 34, 91, 101, 252, 254
Gonzalez, R., 167, 177
Gottheil, E., 214, 225
Gottlieb, B., 334, 339
Gottlieb, G., 63, 72
Gottman, J. M., 80, 85, 279, 284
Gould, O. N., 79, 85
Gould, R. L., 140, 146

Iyengar, S., 298, *301*

Jacobs, W. J., 247, *255*
Jahoda, M., 9, *20*, 275, *284*
James, L. E., 79, *85*
James, W., 252, *254*, 273, 274, *284*
Janis, I. L., 155, *163*
Janoff-Bulman, R., 96, *99*
Jarvin, L., 326, *327*
Jaycox, L., 314, *316*
Jencius, S., 64, *72*
Jensen, A., 323, *328*
Jensen, M. R., 218, *224*
Jepson, D., 172, *177*
Jessor, T., 296, *303*
Jiwani, N., 67, *72*
John, D., 105, *114*
John, O. P., 123, *128*
Johnson, B. T., 108, *114*
Johnson, E. J., 168, *178*
Johnson, G. S., 335, *339*
Johnson, M. K., 78, *85*
Johnson, M. M., 182, *193*
Johnson, S. D., 123, *127*
Jonas, E., 154, *163*, *164*
Jonas, H., 159, *164*
Jost, J. T., 106, *114*
Jung, C. G., 277, 278, *284*

Kagan, J., 65, *73*
Kahn, B., 182, 183, *193*
Kahn, R. L., 142, *146*, 338
Kahn, S., 337, *340*
Kahn, W. A., 110, *114*
Kahneman, D., 166, 168–173, *177*, *178*,
        198, 199, 201, 203, *209*, *210*,
        229, *242*, 331, *340*
Kaiser, H. A., 278, *284*
Kalmar, D. A., 324, *328*
Kaminoff, R., 334, *341*
Kannisto, V., 25, *34*
Kant, I., 159, *164*
Kanwisher, N., 39, *46*
Kaplan, R., 333, *340*
Kaplan, R. M., 41, *45*
Kaplan, S., 333, 337, *340*
Karau, S. J., 110, 112, *113*
Karp, L., 180, *193*
Katz, D., 291, *301*

Katz, L. D., 189, *193*
Katz, L. F., 279, *284*
Kauffeld, S., 154, *164*
Keith, B., 42, *45*
Kekes, J., 24, 27, *35*
Keller, M., 123, *127*
Kelley, H. H., 336, *342*
Kelly, G. A., 51, 57, 59, 96, 97, 99, 250,
        253, *255*
Kelso, J. A., 233, *242*
Kemeny, M. E., *21*, 140, *146*, *147*, 220,
        222
Kennedy, Q., 80, *84*
Kenrick, D. T., 39, *45*, 107, *113*
Kernis, M. H., 53, *59*
Kerr, N., 156, *163*
Kerschreiter, R., 156, *162*
Kessler, R. C., 77, *86*
Ketcham, A. S., *19*
Key, V. O., Jr., 300, 301, *301*
Keyes, C. L. M., 275, 276, *284*
Khouri, H., 249, *254*
Kibler, J., 212, *225*
Kiecolt-Glaser, J. K., 212, 214, *222–224*,
        281, *284*
Kiekman, A., *113*
Kihlstrom, J. F., 51, 54, 57, 58, 252, *254*
Kilbourn, K. M., *98*
Kim, M., 249, *254*
Kinder, D. R., 296, 298, *301*, *303*
King, L. A., 214, *224*, 267, 269, 331,
        342
Kirsch, I., 312, *316*
Kitayama, S., 42, *46*, 65, *73*, 121, *127*
Kite, M., 104, *114*
Kitzinger, C., 107, *114*
Klapper, J. T., 298, *301*
Kleban, M. H., 77, *86*
Klein, G., 261, *269*
Klein, W., 142, *146*
Kling, K. C., 275, *284*, 286
Klinger, E., 38, *46*, 88, 90, *99*
Knäuper, B., 77, *86*
Knight, G. P., 110, *114*
Kohut, H., 262, *269*
Kolb, B., 63, *73*
Konfuzius, 160, *164*
Konrad, A. M., 110, *114*
Kopp, C. B., 218, *224*
Korn, W. S., 110, *112*
Korpela, K., 333, *340*
Kosterman, R., 299, *303*

Mancuso, R. A., 186, *192*
Mandler, G., 43, *46*
Mangun, G. R., 39, *46*
Mansbridge, J. J., 290, *302*
Markides, K. S., 77, *86*
Marks, N. F., 275, 276, *285*
Markus, H. R., 42, *46*, 52, *59*, 65, *73*,
    121, *127*, 252, *255*, 277, *285*
Marmot, M., 275, *285*
Marshall, V. W., 275, *284*
Marsiske, M., 10, *21*, 24, 29, 31, *35*, 93,
    94, *100*
Martell, R. F., 109, *114*
Martignon, L., 198, *208*
Maslow, A. H., 37, *46*, 134, *146*, 274,
    285
Massarik, F., 274, *283*
Massimini, F., 140, *146*, 266, *269*
Masten, A. S., 118, *127*, 332, 336, 337,
    341
Mather, M., 80, *85*
Matsumoto, H., 121, *127*
Matthews, K. A., *224*
Mayne, T. J., 212, *224*
Mayr, E., 237, *243*
Mayr, U., 78, *85*
Mazzeo, J., 111, *113*
McAuley, E., 67, *73*
McCabe, M., 121, *129*
McClearn, G. E., 94, *100*, 246, *256*
McConahay, J. B., 293, *303*
McCrae, R. R., 54, *59*, 62, *72*, 143, *145*
McDermott, J., 39, *46*
McDonald, H. E., 182, *192*
McElroy, M., 67, *73*
McEwen, B. S., 280, *286*
McGrath, J. E., 334, *343*
McGraw, A. P., 212, *224*
McGregor, B. A., *98*
McGregor, I., 276, *285*
McGuire, W. J., 298, *302*
McKinley, N. M., 276, *285*
Meehl, P. E., 167, 168, 171, *177*
Meier, P., 219, 220, *223*
Melton, R. J., 182, 184, *192*, *194*
Mendelberg, T., 298, *302*
Mendoza-Denton, R., 251, *254*, *255*
Mertz, E., 182, *193*
Messé, L. A., 156, *163*
Metalsky, G. I., 251, *253*
Metcalfe, J., 246, 247, 250, *255*
Michael, S., 312, *316*

Michealis, B., 249, *254*
Michel, M. K., 122, *126*
Michelson, W. H., 333, 335, *341*
Miller, D. C., 110, *113*
Miller, J. G., 121, *127*
Miller, L. C., 56, *59*
Miller, N., 183, *195*
Miller, S., 299, *302*
Miner, K. N., 214, *224*
Miniard, P. W., 183, *191*
Mira y Lopez, E., *146*
Mischel, W., 12, *20*, 50, 51, 54, *59*, 60,
    64, 65, *73*, 246–252, *254–256*,
    337, *341*
Mitchell, V., 51, *59*
Moane, G., 51, *59*
Modell, J., 241, *242*
Moffat, F. L., Jr., *19*
Moffitt, T. E., 54, *59*, 123, *128*
Mojzisch, A., 156, *162*
Montero, M., 337, *342*
Moore, B., 248, *255*
Moos, R. H., 332, 336, *341*
Moreland, R. L., 155, 156, *164*
Moscovici, S., 156, *164*
Moskowitz, G. B., *34*
Moskowitz, J. T., 219, 220, *223*
Moss, M., 77, *86*
Mueller, C. M., 251, *256*
Murch, R. L., 95, *100*
Murphy, B. C., *127*
Murray, C., 321, *327*
Mussen, P., 118, *128*
Myers, D. G., 294, 299, *302*

Naderer, G., 198, *210*
Nasar, J. L., 333, *341*
National Collegiate Athletic Association,
    111, *114*
National Telecommunications and Infor-
    mation Administration, 337, *341*
Nesselroade, J. R., 78, *85*, 93, *98*
Neter, E., 182, 186, *194*
Neuberg, S. L., 199, 205, *208*, *209*
Newcomb, T. M., 299, *301*
Newman, D. L., 123, *128*
Nicholas, J. P., 188, *195*
Niedenthal, P., 183, *193*
Nisbett, R. E., 42, *46*, 172, *177*, 199,
    202, *208*, *209*
Noice, H., 182, *192*

SUBJECT INDEX

Evolutionary psychology, 39–41, 139

Face perception, 39, 169
Fame, 258–259, 265
Fascism, 290
Fitness, adaptive, 26–27
Flourishing, 280. *See also* Human Strengths
Flow, 131, 262, 264, 266, 311, 314
Frankenstein (Mary Shelley), 44
French Quebecois, 295
French Revolution, 292
Freud, Sigmund, 274
Fromm, Erich, 290

Gender. *See* Sex differences
Generations, research across, 240–241
Generosity, 183
Germans/Germany, 295, 297, 299
Giftedness, 134–136. *See also* Talent
Giving up, 89–95. *See also* Coping; Human strength(s)
　and lifespan development, 93–95
　perseverance vs., 95
　as self-regulation, 90–93
Globalization, 25, 26, 32–33, 69, 152, 160
Goal pursuit, 52–55, 57
　and affect, 184–186
　and aging, 78
　and collective efficacy, 69
　and creativity, 262
　and giving up, 90–95
　and optimism, 12
　and perseverance, 88–89, 95
　and self-efficacy, 67
　and SOC model, 31
　of teams, 155
　and willpower, 253
　in workplace, 152
Goethe, Johann, 271, 278
Gratification, delay of, 247–249. *See also* Self-regulation
Group identity
　and environment, 333–334
　and politics, 294–296
Groups
　collective efficacy of, 68–70
　collective memory of, 292–294
　and decision making, 15, 155–156

"Groupthink," 155–156
　human strengths of, 132, 137
　performance of, 154–156
　and positive affect, 188
Group therapy, 221
Growth. *See also* Development; Human Strengths; Personality
　adversity promoting, 14, 16, 95–96, 278
　with age, 76
　as human strength, 95–97
　technology promoting, 26
　in workplace, 153
Gulf crisis, 298

Happiness. *See also* Joy
　cultural considerations for, 121
　effect of relationships on, 38, 42
　effort required for, 272
　factors in, 294
　as fulfillment, 309
　literature discussing, 134–136
　in old age, 81
　as positive emotion, 137, 138
　and positive psychology, 131, 306
　and sadness, 221
　wisdom as basis for, 144
HB program. *See* Heuristics and biases program
Health, human, 279–282. *See also* Health psychology
　and aging, 75–76
　and coactivation of positive and negative emotions, 212
　effect of positive focus on, 81–83
　effect of relationships on, 41–42
　and life expectancy, 25, 75–76, 139–141
Health psychology, 211–225
　and accentuating the positive, 219–220
　and coactivation model, 216–218
　and effects of emotional reactions, 213–215
　and eliminating the negative, 218–219
　and evaluative space model, 212–213
　and taking the good with the bad, 220–221
Healthy-mindedness, 273

Helplessness, 90, 267, 337
Heuristics, 166–168, 173–175, 198–203.
    See also Judgment
Heuristics and biases (HB) program,
    166–178, 199. *See also* Judgment
    associative system of reasoning in,
        172–175
    and cognitive illusions, 168–171
    and costs of judgmental heuristics, 172
    and rationality, 175–176
    research strategy for, 168–175
    rule-based system in, 173–175
HIV, 220–221. *See also* AIDS
Hobbes, Thomas, 132–133
Holistic individual development, 231–
    232, 237–238
Holocaust, 297, 299, 300
Hope
    as buffer, 314
    as coping strategy, 306
    and creativity, 267
    and environment, 337
    and mind-cure movement, 273
    as positive emotion, 137
    and positive psychology, 131
    as survival element, 280
    as therapy technique, 312
    in workplace, 151
Hostility, 212, 249
Humanity, 43, 158–159
Human nature, 43–45
Human strength(s), 9–24, 131–141. *See
    also* Positive psychology
    challenge resulting in, 273–279, 281
    as characteristics or processes, 11–13
    classification of, 137–138, 307–310
    commitment, 88, 90, 155
    conscious and intentional, 13–14
    in context, 14–15, 23–24
    criteria for defining psychological,
        139–141
    difficulty of defining, 10–11
    dimensions in study of, 134, 137–141
    dispositional approach to, 12
    ethical characteristics of, 137
    factors that hide, 50–51
    on group level, 132, 137
    on individual level, 131–132, 137
    moral characteristics of, 137
    multidisciplinary/contextually dynamic/
        norm dependent, 23–24
    physical functioning, 16

positive and negative interaction in.
    See Emotion(s)
process approach to, 11–13, 50
psychological characteristics of, 137

Illness. *See* Disease
Illusion(s)
    cognitive, 168–171
    interview, 171
    positive, 219
    of validity, 171
    visual, 169
Immune system, 140, 212, 221, 280, 281.
    See also Neuroendocrine Function
Individual development, 230–238
    differences in, 232–235
    holistic, 231–232, 237–238
    research goals for, 235–236
    synchronized, 232
Infant mortality, 82. *See also* Life expec-
    tancy
Integration, professional and social, 153
Intelligence, 133, 319–329
    as category of human strength, 137–
        138
    componential subtheory of, 322
    contextual subtheory of, 323
    creative, 323
    emotional, 134–136
    and environment, 321–322
    experiential subtheory of, 322–323
    as element of human nature, 43
    knowledge-acquisition components of,
        322
    and life expectancy, 140
    metacomponents of, 322
    paper-and-pencil tests of, 320–321
    performance components of, 322
    redefining the system of, 325–326
    social, 55–57
    successful, 321–325
    validation of successful, 323–325
    and wisdom of aging, 144
Internet, 70, 75
Interviews, structured, 310–311
Iraq, 296
Islam, 292, 295, 299
Isolation (of the individual), 51, 334
Israeli Jews, *see* Jews

Japanese, internment of, 293–294

Meta-analysis, 108–110
Michelangelo, 258, 271
Mind-cure movement, 273–274
Mistakes, learning from, 157, 159, 160
Mood. *See* Affect
Morbidity, 41–42, 139–142. *See also* Disease
Mortality, 41–42, 82, 139, 140, 142, 221. *See also* Life expectancy
Motivation, 259–263
    as category of human strength, 137–138
    in center of excellence cultures, 158
    and constructive cognition, 52
    creative, 258–263
    deficit-based, 259–260, 262, 263
    Frey's principles of, 152–153
    and group decision making, 156
    intrinsic, 137
    and judgment, 203–206
    meaningful purpose as, 262–263
    of older adults, 80
    opponent-process theory of, 336
    passion for the work as, 260–262
    and politics, 290–291
    and positive affect, 184–185
    and self-regulation, 65
    strength-based, 260–263
    for volunteerism, 56

Naïve optimism, 219–220
Narcissism, 259, 260, 262, 263, 265, 266
"Nathan der Weise" (Gotthold Ephraim Lessing), 159
Natural disasters, 334
Nazis/Nazism, 119, 277, 291, 297, 299, 300
Negative affect, 186–187
    coactivation of positive and, 15–17, 216–221
    and evaluative space model, 212–213
    in older adults, 80
    and positive psychology, 306
    and self-regulation, 123
    and stress, 214
    suppression of, 218–219
Neuroendocrine function, 212, 281. *See also* Immune system
Neuroscience, 17
    and coactivation model of affect, 212
    in cross-disciplinary research, 240

evolutionary aspects of, 39, 40
and individual development, 232–233
and positive affect, 180, 189
and well-being, 280
Neuroticism, 212. *See also* Personality

Ohio Longitudinal Study of Aging and Adaptation, 143
Old South, 292, 296, 297, 300
Opponent-process theory of motivation, 336. *See also* Motivation
Opportunism, 52, 55
Optimism, 12–13, 89. *See also* Pessimism
    as buffer, 311, 314
    as coping strategy, 16, 182, 306
    and creativity, 267
    defensiveness reduced with, 182
    and disputing skill, 314
    and enviroment, 337, 338
    and life expectancy, 140
    literature discussing, 134–136
    and mind-cure movement, 273
    and persistence, 185
    as positive emotion, 137, 138
    and quality of life, 219–220
    as therapy technique, 313
    in workplace, 188
Optimization. *See* Selective optimization with compensation model
Organizational psychology, 15, 134
Organizations
    change management in. *See* Change management
    decision making in, 15
    efficacy in, 68–69
    identification with, 152
    and positive affect, 188
    and positive psychology, 149–150
    and responsibility, 159

Parametric unimodel of judgment, 199–206. *See also* Judgment; Heuristics
Parents, 308
Participation
    and life expectancy, 140
    patterns of social, 55
    in workplace, 152
Peace, 123–125, 155. *See also* Culture(s)

Perseverance, 88–89, 131
  as buffer, 314
  and environment, 337
  giving up vs., 95
  and positive affect, 185
  as therapy technique, 313
Personal agency. *See* Self-regulation;
    Willpower
Personality
  psychology, 61–74
  and collective efficacy, 68–69
  consistency, 50–51
  crystallization theory of, 234
  models of, 62–66
  in modern life, 69–71
  person-situation reciprocity model of,
    62–63
  potentials model of, 65–66
  and self-efficacy, 67–68
  and self-reflection, 66–69
  self-system and personal agency model
    of, 63–65
Pessimism, 18, 53–54, 89, 185, 314. *See*
    also Optimism
Philosophy, change management and,
    160
Placebo effect, 312, 313
Political Life (R. E. Lane), 290
Politics, 289–303
  controversy in, 293
  elites and mass publics in, 296–298
  and group identity, 294–296
  and motivation, 290–291
  and positive psychology, 298–301
  symbolic, 291–294
Popper, Sir Karl Raimund, 159
Positive affect, 132, 138. *See also* Nega-
    tive affect
  accentuating, 219–220
  coactivation of negative and, 15–17,
    216–221
  and disclosure studies, 215
  and evaluative space model, 212–
    213
  induced, 17, 182, 186–188, 306
  and memory, 180, 182
  and motivation, 184–186
  negative vs., 186–187
  and thinking, 182–184
Positive clinical psychology, 305–317
  and classification of human strengths,
    307–310
  etiology of, 311

measurement in, 310–311
  prevention in, 313–315
  therapy in, 311–313
Positive development research, 227–243
  basic propositions in, 229–230
  goal for, 235–236
  the individual in, 230–235
  integration of, 236–241
  methodological implications for, 238–
    240
  strategy implications for, 240–241
Positive psychogerontology, 141–144. *See*
    also Aging
Positive psychology, 117–129. *See also*
    Human strength(s)
  and aging, 81–82
  balanced view of, 82–84
  clinical. *See* Positive clinical psychol-
    ogy
  core of, 257
  at group level, 132, 137
  history of, 133–136
  and human strengths, 121–124
  at individual level, 131–132, 137
  and organizations, 149–150
  pitfalls studying, 118–121
  and politics, 298–301
  pros and cons of, 132
  and rationality, 175–176
  and self-regulation/coping, 122–123
  at subjective level, 131, 137
  and tolerance/understanding, 123–124
  tradition of, 49–51, 273–275
Post-traumatic stress syndrome, 14
Prediction of behavior, 97, 171, 172, 205,
    323
Premature death, 41, 42. *See also* Death
Prevention, 118, 140, 141, 313–315
Probability theory, 168, 197–198
Problem solving, 10, 12–15, 18
  and affect, 182
  and critical reasoning, 159
  culture of, 157
  optimism in, 182
  role of psychology in, 133
Prodigies, 308
Professional and social integration, 153
Prosocial behavior. *See also* Altruism
  and affect, 183
  and cognition, 52

ABOUT THE EDITORS

Lisa G. Aspinwall is associate professor of psychology at the University of Utah. She received her PhD from the University of California, Los Angeles in 1991. She was previously associate professor of psychology at the University of Maryland. Her research interests are in the areas of self-regulation, adaptation to adversity, and health and include such topics as positive emotions, optimism, and other aspects of future-oriented thinking, such as proactive coping, planning, and preventive health behavior. Dr. Aspinwall holds a grant from the National Science Foundation to study how positive emotions affect the processing of negative information and is the recipient of a Templeton Positive Psychology Prize as well as two teaching awards. She currently serves as associate editor of the journal *Motivation and Emotion*.

Ursula M. Staudinger is full professor of psychology at Dresden University. She received her PhD in 1988 from the Free University of Berlin. Until recently she was senior researcher at the Max Planck Institute for Human Development. She has coedited several books, such as an interdisciplinary volume on gerontology and a volume on interactive minds. She is an APA Fellow (Division 20) and has been a member of the committee "Aging and Social Development" of the Berlin-Brandenburg Academy of Science and of the MacArthur Network on "Successful Midlife Development." She serves on the editorial boards of the *Psychology and Aging*, the *Journal of Gerontology*, and the *International Journal of Behavioral Development*. Among her research interests are the study of plasticity and reserves in lifespan development; the social–interactive nature of human functioning; and the development of life experience, life insight, and wisdom across the life span.